A HISTORICAL GRE]

A Historical
Greek Reader

Mycenaean to the Koiné

STEPHEN COLVIN

OXFORD
UNIVERSITY PRESS

OXFORD
UNIVERSITY PRESS

Great Clarendon Street, Oxford OX2 6DP

Oxford University Press is a department of the University of Oxford.
It furthers the University's objective of excellence in research, scholarship,
and education by publishing worldwide in

Oxford New York

Auckland Cape Town Dar es Salaam Hong Kong Karachi
Kuala Lumpur Madrid Melbourne Mexico City Nairobi
New Delhi Shanghai Taipei Toronto

With offices in

Argentina Austria Brazil Chile Czech Republic France Greece
Guatemala Hungary Italy Japan Poland Portugal Singapore
South Korea Switzerland Thailand Turkey Ukraine Vietnam

Oxford is a registered trade mark of Oxford University Press
in the UK and in certain other countries

Published in the United States
by Oxford University Press Inc., New York

© Stephen Colvin 2007

The moral rights of the author have been asserted
Database right Oxford University Press (maker)

First published 2007

British Library Cataloguing in Publication Data
Data available

Library of Congress Cataloging in Publication Data
Data available

Typeset by RefineCatch Limited, Bungay, Suffolk
Printed in Great Britain
on acid-free paper by
Biddles Ltd., King's Lynn, Norfolk

ISBN 978–0–19–922659–7
ISBN 978–0–19–922660–3 (pbk.)

1 3 5 7 9 10 8 6 4 2

Preface

Archaeology of the book

This book was originally commissioned from James Hooker (1931–91), then Reader in Classics at University College London. A parallel *Reader* in Latin was commissioned from Patrick Considine and is in preparation. At the time of his death Hooker had prepared the first draft of a manuscript, which the distinguished linguist and phonetician Katrina Hayward (1951–2001) agreed to take forward to publication; Hayward was then in the Department of Linguistics at the School of Oriental and African Studies, London. Hooker's early death was by sad coincidence to be shared by Hayward. In the last months of her illness she spent time annotating the manuscript; when her friend and colleague Patrick Considine suggested that I take over the commission after her death in 2001 I was honoured to do so (Hayward, a student of Anna Morpurgo Davies, had been my doctoral examiner at Oxford in the early 1990s). I inherited Hooker's original draft, with Hayward's (always useful and perceptive) comments. After some hesitation I decided it would be impossible to bring it out in its original form, since it was well over a decade old, and its original author had not intended the draft for publication in the form in which it survived. Nor was it clear that, if I made the substantial additions that were necessary, either of the two earlier scholars would have wanted to take responsibility for my views. I therefore retained the structure of the book, but rewrote it almost from scratch within that framework. Some of the passages reflect Hooker's original selection, and in those instances I mostly retained his elegant translations. I referred constantly to his commentary, of course, in preparing my own, and made use of Hayward's remarks on the texts wherever possible. For the most part, however, I take full responsibility for the book, and any errors in judgement or execution are mine.

Notes on use

The book is intended as an introduction to the history of the ancient Greek language for university-level students. It includes a selection of epigraphic and literary texts from the Mycenaean period (roughly the fourteenth century BC) to the koiné (the latest text dates to the second century AD). In the epigraphic section I wanted to balance a selection of well-known epigraphic texts with recent discoveries which may not be easily available elsewhere. I have linked commentary to an outline reference grammar, and have tried to provide a basic amount of up-to-date bibliography so that advanced students and others can pursue linguistic issues at greater depth where necessary. The reference grammar is not a comprehensive historical grammar: it is an outline which is meant to provide a general historical context, and to explain features which occur in the texts in a more orderly way than is possible in the commentary. A general aim has been to provide an overview of recent linguistic thinking, especially in areas such as dialectology and the koiné, where excellent work by international scholars in the last couple of decades has not yet become easily accessible.

In the literary section the choice of passages was difficult to make, especially as the book is not intended as a chrestomathy of Greek literature. I chose passages which would illustrate the general lines of the linguistic development of Greek as economically as possible. I was not thinking primarily of the stylistic development of the language, though the two are often difficult to untangle. I ended the selection with the koiné in line with the original conception of the book: and indeed for obvious cultural and sociolinguistic reasons a detailed study of the development of Greek after the Hellenistic period would have to be a very different enterprise, given the diglossia which adds an extra level of complication to the analysis of written texts after the disappearance of the dialects.

The book may also serve as a practical introduction to historical linguistics and linguistic method as applied to a corpus language. No prior experience of Indo-European or theoretical linguistics is assumed, though in fact anyone who has mastered the ancient Greek language will have developed a range of practical linguistic skills that theoreticians might well envy. There is a glossary of linguistic terms at the back; beginners may have to do some basic homework such as familiarizing themselves with a small range of characters from the International Phonetic Alphabet.

Texts and transliterations

Since the book is linguistic in design, direct transliterations from Greek have in general been used rather than the Latinized version (thus *Sotairos* rather than *Sotaerus*). The usual cultural exceptions have been made in the case of familiar literary and historical names (*Thucydides, Lucian,* etc.); but thematic (second declension) names in *-os* are not changed to *-us.*

In epigraphic and papyrological texts dotted letters have been kept to a minimum, especially where there is a well-established modern text whose readings are widely accepted. The best or most recent edition available has served as the basis for the extracts, supplemented by any recent commentary or revision. The use of diacritics varies from editor to editor (for example, some use rough breathings in inscriptions from psilotic areas in line with the conventions of a modern printed text, and likewise iota subscript). In this book the notation of breathings in inscriptions reflects what is known of the local phonology (sometimes this is doubtful); iota subscript is not used; and makrons are printed on vowels in Greek texts as an aid to the reader (and in some cases they indicate an editorial judgement). Standard Attic accentuation is printed except in the case of eastern Aeolic (§23.10). In the case of literary texts with a continuous transmission I have indicated the edition used and noted significant departures. In the case of fragments (surviving in quotation, papyri, etc.) I have referred to a standard modern collection. The use of an apparatus has been kept to an absolute minimum.

Acknowledgements

My debts to scholars in the field will be obvious to anyone who has worked on the history of Greek. I have relied so heavily on the ideas of Albio Cassio, Anna Morpurgo Davies, and Cornelius Ruijgh that citation became an almost superfluous exercise. There are many others, in particular a generation of post-war Spanish and French scholars and their students, who shaped the discipline after the appearance of the great German handbooks of the early part of the twentieth century. I have tried to rein in the list of citations, given the intended readership, and I hope that the absence of a reference to an important piece of work will not be taken as a slight. Buck's *Greek Dialects* has been a near-constant companion for over two decades;

the nature of the present book and considerations of space ruled out any attempt at a grammar of the Greek dialects on the same scale.

It remains to thank friends and colleagues who have read versions of the present work. Patrick Considine read a draft of the epigraphic commentary and saved me from numerous mistakes and omissions. Philomen Probert and Eleanor Dickey read an entire draft with customary acumen and patience, and I am deeply indebted to their kind suggestions. Alan Griffiths and Donna Shalev also read sections of the literary commentary: the resulting text benefited greatly from their expert advice. The list of scholars who have endured importuning on specific issues, and made courteous and helpful suggestions, includes Victor Bers, Ann Hanson, Simon Hornblower, Stephen Instone, Bentley Layton, Herwig Maehler, Craig Melchert, Andrew Sihler, Elizabeth Tucker, Michael Weiss, and Jula Wildberger. Much of the work was completed while on research leave at Yale University, and completed at University College London. It is a pleasure to record thanks to both of these institutions.

SCC

London
September 2006

Dis manibus

James T. Hooker
Katrina Hayward

Contents

PART II. TEXTS WITH TRANSLATION
AND COMMENTARY

MYCENAEAN

DIALECT INSCRIPTIONS

LITERARY TEXTS

List of Figures

Abbreviations and Symbols

A Glossary of Linguistic Terms can be found at the back of the book.

Languages and dialects

Aeol.	Aeolic
Arc.	Arcadian
Att.	Attic
Boe.	Boeotian
Cyp.	Cypriot
Hom.	Homeric
IE	Indo-European
Ion.	Ionic
Lac.	Laconian
Lesb.	Lesbian
Myc.	Mycenaean
NW Gk.	North-west Greek
Skt.	Sanskrit
Thess.	Thessalian
WGk.	West Greek

Linguistic abbreviations and symbols

C	Consonant (e.g. C-stem: consonant stem)
V	Vowel
R	Resonant (r, l, m, n, w, y and the laryngeals): see Glossary
*	Reconstructed form, no longer extant
<	Develops out of, is derived from
>	Becomes, develops into
$i̯$	Consonantal i
$m̥$, $n̥$	Vocalic m, n (or any resonant)
[a:]	Colon indicates a long vowel
[a:]	Square brackets denote a sound in (broad) phonetic transcription
<A>	Angle brackets are occasionally used to make it clear that a letter of the alphabet is being discussed, as opposed to a sound (in general they are dispensed with for typographic economy)

them., athem.   thematic, athematic (see Glossary)

[ɛ:]   η   open mid front, as in Fr. *élève* (second syllable), Brit. Engl. *snared*
[e̞:]   ει   close mid front, as in Fr. *élève* (first syllable), Ger. *Beet*
[ɔ:]   ω   open mid back, as in Engl. *more*
[o̞:]   ου   close mid back, as in Fr. *beau*, Ger. *Kohl*

Editorial abbreviations and symbols

cj.	Conjecture
ed. pr.	*Editor prior*: first modern editor of an ancient text
[ ]	Square brackets in a text enclose restorations (typically where the stone or papyrus is damaged)
< >	Angle brackets in a text enclose additions suggested by editors (letters or words mistakenly omitted by the engraver or scribe)
{ }	Curly brackets in a text enclose letters which the editor believes were mistakenly added by the engraver (or scribe): e.g. repeated letters or words
(s)	Round brackets in a text are occasionally used to indicate single writing of a double consonant (normal in archaic inscriptions) across a word boundary: e.g. τὰ(ς) στήλας where the stone has ταστηλας.
ạ	A dot under a letter indicates that only part of the letter is visible (its reading may be in doubt)

Epigraphic publications and edited collections

Buck	C. D. Buck, *The Greek Dialects* (Chicago 1955)
Calame	C. Calame, *Alcman. Introduction, texte critique, témoignages, traduction et commentaire* (Rome 1983)
CEG	*Carmina epigraphica Graeca saeculorum VIII–V a.Chr.n.*, ed. P. A. Hansen (Berlin 1983)
CID	*Corpus des Inscriptions de Delphes*, vol. 1, ed. G. Rougemont (Paris 1977)
IEG	*Iambi et elegi Graeci ante Alexandrum cantati*[2], ed. M. L. West (Oxford 1992)
I. Erythrai	*Die Inschriften von Erythrai und Klazomenai* (*IGSK* 1–2), ed. H. Engelmann and R. Merkelbach (1972–3)
LSAG	L. H. Jeffery, *The Local Scripts of Archaic Greece*, 2nd edn. rev. A. W. Johnston (Oxford 1990)

LXX	Septuagint: J. W. Williams (ed.), *Septuaginta* (Göttingen 1974)
Meiggs–Lewis	R. Meiggs and D. Lewis (eds.), *A Selection of Greek Historical Inscriptions to the end of the 5th Century B.C.* (Oxford 1969)
NAGVI	R. Wachter, *Non-Attic Greek Vase Inscriptions* (Oxford 2001)
Nomima	*Nomima: recueil d'inscriptions politiques et juridiques de l'archaïsme grec*, ed. H. van Effenterre and F. Ruzé, 2 vols. (Rome 1994–5)
PCG	*Poetae Comici Graeci*, eds. C. Austin and R. Kassel (Berlin and New York 1983–)
PMG	*Poetae Melici Graeci*, ed. D. L. Page (Oxford 1962)
Schwyzer	E. Schwyzer, *Dialectorum Graecarum exempla epigraphica potiora* (Leipzig 1923)
SEG	*Supplementum Epigraphicum Graecum* (Leiden)
Sihler	A. Sihler, *New Comparative Grammar of Greek and Latin* (Oxford 1995)
Ventris–Chadwick	M. Ventris and J. Chadwick, *Documents in Mycenaean Greek*, 2nd edn. (Cambridge 1973)
Voigt	*Sappho et Alcaeus. Fragmenta edidit Eva-Maria Voigt* (Amsterdam 1971)

Journals and ancient authors

Unless self-evident, the abbreviations of journals follow *L'Année philologique*, and those of ancient authors follow Liddell–Scott–Jones, *Greek–English Lexicon* (9th edn.). General abbreviations, such as parts of speech, also follow Liddell–Scott–Jones.

I. Introduction

§1. GREEK AND INDO-EUROPEAN

1. Greek is one of a number of interrelated languages that spread over a vast area of Europe and Asia during the second and first millennia BC. These languages are now known as 'Indo-European', since at the time of the discovery of the relationship the languages were known to exist in Europe and the Indian subcontinent. Apart from Greek, the earliest attested Indo-European languages are Sanskrit (India); Avestan and Old Persian (Iran); the Anatolian languages (Hittite, Luwian, and others); and Latin and the Italic languages of central Italy. Celtic (continental) is attested in inscriptions starting in the VI cent. BC, but is not well documented until the seventh century AD (Old Irish). Indo-European languages (or language-groups) which are not attested until the common era include Albanian, Armenian, Baltic, Germanic, Slavic, and Tocharian (central Asia). The hypothesis that all these languages are derived from an original 'parent' language (never written down) was put forward by Sir William Jones (in a now-famous speech in Calcutta) in the eighteenth century, but the term 'Indo-European' to denote this language did not come into use until the nineteenth century. Jones argued that the correspondences between Sanskrit, Greek, and Latin were so many and so striking that they could not be ascribed to mere chance. We owe the comparative method for the systematic study of Indo-European to the nineteenth-century Indo-Europeanists, beginning with Franz Bopp, Rasmus Rask, and Jacob Grimm; Bopp's pioneering comparison of the verbal systems of Sanskrit, Avestan, Latin, Greek, and Germanic was published in 1816.

The nineteenth- and early twentieth-century linguists relied on the family tree as model for language history (i.e. a 'genetic' model which saw language history largely in terms of parent and daughter languages). This was influenced by the emergence of disciplines such as botany and natural history (Charles Darwin, *Origin of Species*, 1859). In the second half of the twentieth century the development of sociolinguistics led to a slightly modified view of language development. Although languages are constantly evolving (and an earlier stage of the language may in that sense be thought of as a parent language), it is recognized (*a*) that most languages are in fact agglomerations of dialects (social and regional) rather than unitary phenomena, and (*b*) that interaction with neighbouring languages, or other types of language contact (such as the arrival in the community of people speaking a different language), can have as much influence on what a language looks like as its historical roots.

Modern linguists do not recognize any important difference between a language and a dialect: the distinction is political and ideological, not linguistic.

2. The movements of peoples and the interaction of one language with another make it very difficult to plot the dispersion of Indo-European and the development of the individual languages. The processes by which the various language-groups were carried to their destinations from a hypothetical Indo-European homeland must have been complex. The location of this homeland has been the subject of much speculation. If there was indeed an Indo-European language (which is likely, like most languages, to have consisted of a group of dialects), then it must indeed have been spoken by specific people living in a specific area. But the methods employed to determine this region have not yet produced a solution that is universally accepted. Proposals for a centre of Indo-European dispersement stretch east from central Europe to Anatolia, the Black Sea and Caucasus region, and across the southern Russian steppes as far as the Ural mountains.

3. Speakers of an Indo-European dialect reached Greece at some point during the first half of the second millennium BC (estimates range from 2100 to 1600 BC). The nineteenth-century view that Greek-speakers entered Greece in three waves, each separated from the next by as much as 400 years, has now been abandoned. These waves were thought to correspond to early dialect groups (Ionic, Aeolic, and Doric), and it followed that the Greek language had

developed its salient characteristics outside of Greece proper. Research in the second half of the twentieth century led scholars to conclude that this cannot have been the case: Greek—including the historical dialects—developed within Greece, and dialect differences are due to normal processes of interaction and differentiation that arose as a function of Greek geography and human agency. By whatever means they arrived and were assimilated into the indigenous peoples, the newcomers borrowed many items of vocabulary that were eventually absorbed into the Greek language. This category includes nouns containing the non-Greek elements -νθος or -σ(σ)ος. The words in question are names of natural features (for instance Mount Παρνασσός, the river Κηφισός), plant-names (ὑάκινθος), towns (Κνωσός), and certain cultural artefacts (ἀσάμινθος, 'bathtub', πλίνθος, 'brick'). These non-Greek words may conceivably belong to an Indo-European language that was brought to Greece before the arrival of the Greek-speakers (either an unknown language, sometimes named Pelasgian, or a neighbouring language such as Luwian). But this 'substrate' language cannot be reconstructed from the meagre evidence at our disposal, and its affinities are probably beyond the reach of our research.

Arrival of the Greeks: Drews (1988), Garrett (1999). *Indo-European*: Mallory (1989), Baldi (1983). *Comparative method*: Meillet (1924). *Nineteenth-century scholarship*: Morpurgo Davies (1998).

§2. MYCENAEAN GREEK

At the beginning of our historical survey, *c*.1500 BC, we find two civilizations occupying a dominant position in the Aegean area. These have become known in modern times as the 'Minoan' civilization in Crete and the 'Mycenaean' in southern and central Greece. The non-Greek Minoan was the older of the two: the Mycenaeans were heavily influenced by Minoan culture, and Mycenaean civilization at its height was essentially a fusion of the Minoan and the native ('Helladic') culture of the Greek mainland. Between the sixteenth and the twelfth centuries BC, Mycenaean power and influence expanded at the expense of the Minoans, and the Mycenaeans seem to have taken control of Crete itself in the fifteenth century. Mycenaean power was at its height between 1400 and 1200, with the establishment of great palatial centres at Pylos, Mycenae, and Tiryns in the Peloponnese, and Thebes and Orchomenos in Boeotia. Mycenaean settlement is attested in the Cycladic Islands, the Dodecanese, and on the west coast of Asia Minor. There is also evidence for Mycenaean trading activity around the Mediterranean, with Cyprus and the Levant in particular, and with Sicily and southern Italy in the West.

The Mycenaean world went into decline during the twelfth century, at a time of unrest throughout the eastern Mediterranean world. Widespread destruction brought the life of many of the palatial centres to an end (including Pylos and Thebes), while others, such as Mycenae and Tiryns, survived for a time in spite of severe devastation.[1] The date of the final destruction of the palace at Knossos, which was inhabited by Mycenaeans in its final phase, is a matter of some controversy.[2] Most archaeologists (following Evans, the original excavator of the site) have argued that the material evidence points to a date around 1400–1375; others believe that a date closer to 1200 is more likely, as this would bring the events at Knossos into line with the destruction of the mainland sites. The dispute affects the dating of the Linear B tablets found at Knossos (the conventional dating of 1375–1350 is followed in this book).

---

[1] Murray (1993: 7–8).   [2] Palmer and Boardman (1963), MacGillivray (2000: 308–9).

§3. Linear B Script

Many of the 'palaces' (administrative centres) of Mycenaean Greece and Crete contained archives of clay tablets inscribed in the Linear B script. These tablets survived because they were baked in the fires which destroyed the palaces: substantial numbers of tablets have been found at Pylos, Mycenae, and Thebes on the mainland, and at Knossos on Crete. Linear B was so named by Arthur Evans because it is a linear (as opposed to pictographic) script that is clearly derived from an older script found at Knossos that he named Linear A. This script presumably records the language of the Minoans, which is unknown; too little survives to permit a verifiable decipherment.

Linear B conveys information partly by means of words spelled out in syllabic signs (*syllabograms*), and partly by means of ideograms. These ideograms (often stylized drawings of the object in question) are not used in the body of the text, but typically stand at the end of a line or clause in a totalling formula, and are followed by a numeral (almost all of the tablets are lists of one sort or another). Nearly a hundred syllabic signs are used in the Linear B documents, and sound-values can be assigned to about three-quarters of these (the most common) with reasonable certainty. The script is often ambiguous: it does not represent all the phonemic distinctions of Greek (see below), and is not suited to writing consonant clusters.

§4. *Syllabification*

Linear B signs denote a vowel (V) or consonant + vowel (CV). In a very few cases a sign denotes two consonants followed by a vowel (CCV), but in general consonant clusters have to be written either by inserting extra vowels, or by omitting consonants:

1 Most syllables of the pattern CCV have to be written either
   (*a*) with the aid of 'empty' vowels: e.g. *Ϝρινίω* 'leather' is spelled *wi-ri-ni-jo*;
   (*b*) by omitting consonants (this is normal with clusters *s* + obstruent): *pe-mo* = *σπέρμο*.
2 In the case of syllables of the shape VC or CVC (i.e. closed syllables)
   (*a*) the final consonant is not usually represented: e.g. *pa-we-a₂* = *φάρϜε(h)a*, *pe-mo* = *σπέρμο*;
   (*b*) but a final obstruent is spelled out: *τέκτονες* 'carpenters' *te-ko-to-ne*.
3 Word-final consonants (i.e. *-n*, *-r*, and *-s*) are ignored.

These 'rules' do not fully capture Linear B spelling, and the underlying principles have been much disputed.[1]

[1] Woodard (1997: 8–132).

*08 a	*38 e	*28 i	*61 o	*10 u	*25 a₂	*43 ai	*85 au	*18 .	*83 .
*01 da	*45 de	*07 di	*14 do	*51 du	*71 dwe	*90 dwo		*19 .	*86 .
*57 ja	*46 je		*36 jo					*22 .	*89 .
*77 ka	*44 ke	*67 ki	*70 ko	*81 ku				*34 .	
*80 ma	*13 me	*73 mi	*15 mo	*23 mu				*35 .	
*06 na	*24 ne	*30 ni	*52 no	*55 nu	*71 nwa			*47 .	
*03 pa	*72 pe	*39 pi	*11 po	*50 pu	*29 pu₂	*61 pte		*49 .	
*16 qa	*78 qe	*21 qi	*32 qo					*56 .	
*60 ra	*27 re	*53 ri	*02 ro	*26 ru	*76 ra₂	*33 ra₃	*68 ro₂	*63 .	
*31 sa	*09 se	*41 si	*12 so	*58 su				*64 .	
*59 ta	*04 te	*37 ti	*05 to	*69 tu	*66 ta₂	*87 twe	*91 two	*65 .	
*54 wa	*75 we	*40 wi	*42 wo					*79 .	
*17 za	*74 ze		*20 zo					*82 .	

There is some consensus that *82 may be *swa*. *34/*35 may be variants of the same sign, and may denote *lu*.

Figure 1 The Linear B syllabary

§5. *Vowels*

Vowel-length is not indicated, and *i*-diphthongs are generally represented by the simple vowel (*ko-wo*, κόρϜοι).

§6. *Liquids*

Only one series of signs is used for *l* and *r*: this series is by convention transcribed with *r* (*re-u-ko*=λευκός). The glide-sound *w* is usually inserted between two vowels when the first vowel is *u* (*ta-ra-nu-we*, θράνϝες), and *y* (written -*j*-) when the first vowel is *i* (*i-je-re-u*, ἱερεύς).

§7. *Stops*

1. PLAIN   There is just one series for the labial stops (π, β, and φ), conventionally written *p*-; one series for the velar stops (κ, γ, χ), written *k*-; while the signs for apical stops differentiate between voiced and voiceless series (*d*-/*t*-, §10.5).

2. LABIOVELAR   A single series (transcribed *q*-) shows that the IE labiovelars had not yet merged with the dental and labial stops, as in later Greek. Their phonetic value can only be guessed, though it is generally assumed to be κ^w, γ^w, χ^w (§10.6).

§8. Mycenaean Dialect

The Linear B archives are written in a standard form of Greek (sometimes called a chancellery language). This official language used by the scribes obscures the fact that a number of different dialects must already have existed within Greek. In the alphabetic period (first millennium BC) the Greek dialects can be divided into West Greek, comprising Doric and North-west Greek, and East Greek, comprising Attic-Ionic and Arcado-Cypriot (§15 below). The Aeolic dialects do not fit easily into this scheme (see §33 below).

We can see in Mycenaean Greek that in verbal endings the third person *ti* (inherited from IE) has already become *si* (thus *e-ko-si*=ἔχουσι); and we can also see from alphabetic inscriptions of the first millennium that while the eastern dialects have *si* in this position, the dialects of western Greece retain original *ti* (thus West Greek ἔχοντι = Attic-Ionic ἔχουσι < ἔχονσι). In this and other respects Mycenaean seems to be part of the eastern grouping: for example, Myc. *o-te* 'when' represents ὅτε, which is characteristic of eastern Greek (western Greek has ὅκα); and *i-je-re-u* 'priest' recalls eastern ἱερ- (rather than western ἱαρ-). This indicates that the divergence between western and eastern Greek had already taken place in Mycenaean times, and that dialects of the western type must have existed somewhere in the Greek-speaking world (this in turn raises the question of where the Dorians were in the Bronze Age, and whether the Greek belief that they did not enter the Peloponnese until after the Trojan War should be given any credence).

Greek dialects in the Bronze Age: García Ramón (1975), Horrocks (1997: 6–15).

§9. Vocabulary

The vocabulary of Mycenaean Greek is more or less the same mixture of Indo-European, substrate, and borrowed items that we find in later Greek. Myc. words with well-established IE origins include:

de-	δε-	'bind, tie'	*ne-wo*	νέϜος	'new'
di-we	ΔιϜεί	'Zeus' (dat.)	*pa-te*	πατήρ	'father'
do-	δο-/δω-	'give'	*pe-ma*	σπέρμα	'seed'
e-ke	ἔχει	'have'	*po-de*	ποδεί	'foot' (dat./instr.)
e-q-	ἐπ-	'follow'	*-qe*	τε	'and'
me-no	μηνός	'month'	*te-ke*	θῆκε	'put, place' (aor.)
me-ri	μέλι	'honey'	*wi-de*	Ϝίδε	'see' (aor.)

Other words apparently lack IE cognates:

a-to-ro-qo	ἄνθρωπος	'human'	*ke-se-nu-w-*	ξενϜ-	'foreign'
do-e-ro	δοῦλος	'slave'	*o-no*	ὄνος	'donkey'
e-ra₃-wo	ἔλαιϜον	'olive oil'	*ra-wo-*	λαϜός	'people'
ka-ko	χαλκός	'bronze'	*re-wo*	λεϜοντ-	'lion'
ke-ra-me-u	κεραμεύς	'potter'	*wa-na-ka*	Ϝάναξ	'lord'

Certain words ending in *-(i)nthos* and *-(s)sos* have traditionally been associated with the substrate language(s) of Greece, i.e. the language (which may or may not have been Indo-European) spoken by the inhabitants of Greece before the arrival of the 'Greeks' (§1.3 above). In addition, some words are clearly loans from Semitic or other neighbouring languages:[1]

e-re-pa	ἐλέφας	'ivory'	*ku-ru-so*	χρυσός	'gold'
ki-to	χιτών	'tunic'	*ku-wa-no*	κύϜανος	'blue enamel'
ku-mi-no	κύμινον	'cumin'	*sa-sa-ma*	σάσαμα	'sesame'

As one would expect, some changes in meaning are detectable between the Mycenaean period and Homeric Greek:

Mycenaean:			Homeric:		
a-mo-ta	ἅρμοτα	'wheels'	ἅρματα	'chariot'[2]	
qa-si-re-u	γʷασιλεύς	'supervisor'	βασιλεύς	'king'[3]	

[1] Szemerényi (1974), Burkert (1992: 33–40).   [2] Ruijgh (1976).
[3] Murray (1993: 38), Yamagata (1997).

§10. Phonology

Mycenaean has been well described as a milestone between Indo-European and Greek.[1] While certain sound-changes characteristic of Greek have already occurred (for example **s- > h-*), others have not (notably the development of labiovelars to labials and dentals); and in a third category the writing system does not allow us to be certain (loss of final obstruents and Grassmann's Law, §23.5). It is worth noticing that a number of characteristic Greek sound-changes have not yet happened in Mycenaean, and cannot therefore be ascribed to a stage of 'common' (i.e. undifferentiated) Greek. This implies that it was not only dialect differentiation that occurred on Greek soil (§1.3), but also processes of integration or coalescence by which the Greek language was formed.[2]

[1] Szemerényi (1968*b*).   [2] Morpurgo Davies (1985: 76), Garrett (1999).

1. Vowels

Although Greek vowels are conservative until the early classical period, the Myc. vowel system must nevertheless have been different from classical Gk. in important respects, owing to the post-Myc. creation of a new series of long vowels.

The inherited long vowels [ɛ:] (η) and [ɔ:] (ω) were low (or open). The 'new' long vowels [e̩:] and [o̩:] had a close quality: they developed from contraction and compensatory lengthening (they were written with the digraphs ει, ου from the late V cent., §23.1). It is unlikely that secondary long *e* and *o* had developed in Myc. Greek, since they were triggered by changes in the consonant system which are post-Mycenaean:

(*a*) loss of intervocalic *y* (τρεῖς < τρέyες), *h* (from *s*: γένους < γέν-εhος), and *w*;

(*b*) a tendency to open syllables by dropping (e.g.) *n* before *s* (this was accompanied by compensatory lengthening of the vowel to preserve the syllabic structure): λυθένς > λυθείς.

The Attic-Ionic change ā > η is to be dated to the early first millennium BC, and may have been triggered by the new long *a* produced by the developments outlined above: i.e. πάνς (from **pant-s*) > πᾶς (the new [a:] being lower than the inherited vowel, which moved towards [ä:] before merging finally with [ɛ:]).

2. Semi-vowels

*y • Intervocalic **y* is preserved: e.g. in the gen. sing. ending -*o-jo* (from **-osyo*).

• Initial **y-* develops into two separate sounds in Greek (viz. *h-* and *z-*): the reasons for this have never been properly understood. Myc. shows already the split treatment familiar from later Greek: cf. *ze-u-ke-si* versus the relative stem *o-/jo-* (indication that the change *y- > h-* was in progress).

*w • That *w* is preserved in Myc. is hardly surprising, given that it survives in many dialects into the alphabetic period: thus *wa-na-ka*, Ϝάναξ, *ko-wo*, κόρϝος.

3. Syllabic resonants

The syllabic resonants $*\underset{\circ}{m}$, $*\underset{\circ}{n}$, $*\underset{\circ}{r}$, $*\underset{\circ}{l}$ of Indo-European show the reflexes familiar from alphabetic Greek:

$*\underset{\circ}{m}$, $*\underset{\circ}{n}$ • Become *a* before a consonant and at word end (*a-ki-ti-to*, ἄκτιτος 'uncultivated' < $*\underset{\circ}{n}$*-kti-*); but also *o* when preceded by a labial consonant (cf. *pe-mo*, much more frequent than *pe-ma*, σπέρμα, 'seed' < $*sper$-$m\underset{\circ}{n}$).
• Are vocalized *am, an* before a vowel (*a-na-mo-to*, ἀνάρμοστος, 'unassembled').

$*\underset{\circ}{r}$, $*\underset{\circ}{l}$ • Are vocalized *or* ~ *ro* etc. as in later Aeolic and Arc.-Cyp. (*tu-ka-to-si* [tʰugatorsi], class. θυγατράσι, 'daughters' dat. plur.).

(They are vocalized *ar* ~ *ra* in Att.-Ion. and West Gk.)

4. Fricative: *s* (and aspirate *h*)

The sign transcribed a_2 is the only indicator of aspiration in Myc., and is used irregularly. The characteristic Gk. sound-change $*s > h$ (before a vowel, §23.10) is already evident in: *e-me* (instr.) < $*sem$-, 'one'.[1] Intervocalically there is every indication that the *-h-* was still present in Myc., as opposed to the hiatus of later Greek: *pa-we-a₂* [pʰarweʰa] < $*pʰarwes$-*a*.[2] The *s* has been analogically restored in some places (the sigmatic aorist and future: *do-se*, δώσει), but not yet in others (such as the 1st–2nd decl. dat. plur.): *e-pe-to-i* [ʰerpetoiʰi], 'serpents'. The irregular aspiration metathesis seen in alphabetic Greek (εὕω < $*ew^h\bar{o}$ < $*ews\bar{o}$) seems to be post-Mycenaean: e.g. *a-mo*, 'wheel' [arʰmo] (Pylos and Knossos) from $*ar$-*smn̥* is never spelled with a_2-. Contrast the initial aspirate in classical ἅρμα, 'chariot'.

[1] Palmer (1980: 235) for Gk. development of an aspirate from pre-vocalic σ-.   [2] Colvin (2006).

5. Stops: apical

The voiced apical δ is written with one series *da de di do du*, the unvoiced τ θ with a distinct series *ta te ti to tu* (§2.2 above). The presence of two separate series for the apical stops provides valuable evidence that the IE voiced aspirate stops were already devoiced in Mycenaean: cf. *tu-ka-te*, θυγάτηρ < IE $*d^hug^{(h)}H_2$ *ter-*.

6. Stops: labiovelar

Labialized velar stops seem to have been preserved in Mycenaean (§7.2 above), except that the voiced aspirates will have been devoiced in line with other obstruents: κ^w, γ^w, χ^w ($< {}^*g^{wh}$).

By the time of alphabetic Greek the labiovelars had fallen together with either labial or dental stops in most dialects (but cf. Arc.-Cyp. §27.2), depending on the phonetic environment:

$^*k^w > \pi$ before *a*, *o*, or consonant; τ before a front vowel (*e*, *i*).
Cf. *re-qo-me-no* [leik^{w}omenoi] 'leaving', class. λειπόμενοι.

$^*g^w > \beta$ before *a*, *o*, consonant (and *i*); δ before *e*.
Cf. *qo-u-ko-ro* [g^{w}ou-kolos], 'cow-herd', class. βουκόλος.

$^*g^{wh} > \varphi$ before *a*, *o*, consonant (and *i*); θ before *e*.
No clear examples from Myc., but see the following.

In addition, all labiovelars had lost their labial element by dissimilation when they were next to a *u*, and had ended up as plain velars. This is already evident in Mycenaean.

Cf. *e-u-ke-to* [euk^{h}etoi], 'declares' ($^*eug^{wh}$-), class. εὔχεται.

7. Consonant clusters: stop + *y*

The combination of a velar or apical stop and a consonantal *y* gave a new sound in Greek (the effect known as palatalization). This has already happened in Mycenaean:

me-zo-e < $^*meg\text{-}yohes$ (cf. class. μείζων), 'bigger';
to-pe-za < $^*tr̥ped\text{-}ya$ (cf. class. τράπεζα), 'table';
to-so < $^*totyos$ (cf. class. τόσος, τόσσος), 'so much';
pa-sa < $^*pant\text{-}ya$ (cf. class. πᾶσα), 'all'.

It is not at all clear, however, how the series transcribed *z*- was pronounced in these cases: most likely it represented some sort of voiced affricate, [dd^z] or [dž]. It is usually assumed that the -*s*- here represents a voiceless affricate or a geminate -*ss*-.

8. Combination: *t* + *i*

The change -*ti* > -*si* in verbal endings is an important indication of the dialectal affiliations of Mycenaean (§4 above).

pa-si < *pʰā-ti (cf. Doric φᾱτί, Attic φησί), 's/he says'.

9. Word-final position

All obstruents were lost in Greek at word end: thus *melit > μέλι, aor. *widet > Fίδε, etc. Most classical scholars assume the loss had happened in Myc., although it is impossible to be certain. A possible reason for thinking that it had in fact happened rather early in the history of Greek is that Homeric language does not make use of the final consonant as a metrical licence (but cf. on πτόλιν **8** 1).[1]

---

[1] See Garrett (2006:140–1) for arguments in favour of a post-Myc. date for loss of final obstruents.

Morphology

INFLECTION: NOUNS AND ADJECTIVES

§11. *Nominal inflection*

Inflectional patterns are relatively straightforward: the interpretation of archaic features is, however, often obscured by the writing system.

1 GEN. SING. Thematic *-o-jo* recalls Hom. *-οιο* (IE **-osyo*).
2 DAT.-INSTR. SING. Consonant-stem *-e* is ambiguous:
   (a) Dative function: to be read as [-ei] (e.g. *di-we*, and cf. later *ΔιFείφιλος*).
   (b) Instr. function: usually read as [-ei] (e.g. *e-me po-de* 'with one foot'), but perhaps more likely to represent [-e:], a dedicated instr. < **-eh*.[1]
3 DAT.-INSTR. PLUR. Thematic dat.-loc. *-o-i* [-oihi] versus instr. *-o* [-ois].
   The formal distinction seems guaranteed both by the spelling (§3.2) and by the evidence of the PY Ta tablets (cf. **5**), where adjs. in *-o* agree with nouns in *-pi* (cf. *e-re-pa-te-jo a-di-ri-ja-pi*, 'with ivory figures of men'). The older view that both endings represent [-ois][2] is now generally rejected.
4 INSTR. PLUR. Consonant-stem *-pi* and *a*-stem *-a-pi*.
   -φι continues an IE instr. marker **-bhi(s)*. In Myc. the instr. is formally distinct from the dative in the plural (cf. *a-ni-ja-pi*

[haːniaːphi], 'with reins'); with place-names it has a locatival function. This morphological clarity has to a large extent been lost in Homeric language: the ending -φι is extended to almost any substantive (including *o*-stems and sing. nouns), and is a general marker of loc., dat., abl. as well as instr. function.[3]

[1] Hajnal (1995: 242–6). [2] e.g. Ruijgh (1967: §54). [3] Hainsworth (1957), Thompson (1998).

ADJECTIVE FORMATION

§12. *Comparative adjective*

The comparative was formed by adding the suffix **-yos-* to the stem. Outside the nom. sing. this suffix was affected by the change **-s-* > *-h-* (§10.4).[1] Thus the neut. plur. **meg-yos-a* appears in Myc. as *me-zo-a₂* (§10.7): cf. Lat. *melius* → *meliōra*.

1. Later Greek used an *-n-* extension to prevent hiatus (so μείζονα, but also older μείζω < *μείζοα): there is no sign of this in Myc., so we assume that nom. *me-zo* ends in *-s* rather than *-n*.

2. The suffix *-teros* exists in Mycenaean in adj. formation (cf. *wa-na-ka-te-ro* **6** 1), but is not used as a comparative marker (its original significance appears to have been contrastive, as in Lat. *sinister* vs. *dexter*).

[1] Szemerényi (1968*a*).

§13. *Adjectives in* **-went-*

Greek inherited an adj. suffix **-ϝεντς* > *-(ϝ)εις* meaning '[endowed] with *x*' (IE **-went-*, Sihler §346): *pe-ne-we-ta* **1** (a) and χαρίϝετταν **12** 2. The fem. is built on **-wn̥t-ya*, but Myc. *-we-sa* and class. *-(ϝ)εσσα* show an ε analogical on the masc. (for **Cn̥C* in Gk. see §10.3). The suffix is added directly to the root in Myc. (in later Gk. a linking *-o-* vowel was generally inserted between root and suffix).

§14. *Verbs*

There are relatively few verbal forms in the Mycenaean tablets, owing to their inventory format.

1. Personal endings: 3 sing. (med.-pass.)
In alphabetic Greek the 3rd person endings -ται/-νται are found in all dialects except Arc.-Cyp., which has -τοι/-ντοι. Myc. *e-u-ke-to* [eukʰetoi], 'declares' indicates that Arc.-Cyp. has retained the inherited ending, while the other dialects have innovated (extending the *a*-vocalism from the 1st person).

2. Augment
The augment is mostly absent in Mycenaean (one reasonably certain case: *a-pe-do-ke*, which is also found in the unaugmented form *a-pu-do-ke*). This means that unaugmented forms in Homer cannot be regarded as a mere literary device: but the history and early function of the augment in Greek remain obscure.[1]

[1] Bakker (1999), Duhoux (1987).

§15. THE ALPHABETIC PERIOD

The passing of Mycenaean civilization was followed by a dramatic decline in population, disintegration of trading links, and in general a much poorer material culture.[1] This transformation has been connected with movements of population in Greece in the centuries following the Mycenaean collapse. There were also far-reaching migrations from Greece to the coast of Asia Minor and the offshore islands during this period, no doubt triggered to some extent by unsettled conditions in Greece. The Greek settlers who occupied Lesbos and the most northerly part of Asia Minor called the region they inhabited 'Aeolis': these Aeolians seem to have migrated from Thessaly. To the south of Aeolis lay Ionia, which was settled for the most part by migrants from Attica; most of the central Aegean islands between Attica and Ionia were also settled by Ionic-speakers. The Asiatic coast south of Ionia, and the southern Aegean islands (Crete, Carpathos, Rhodes, and Cos) were occupied by Dorians from southern Greece.

    The migrations within and beyond Greece were complex movements, which took centuries to run their course. But the major upheavals had taken place by about 800 BC, by which time the speakers of the major dialects occupied those parts of the Aegean world which they were to inhabit for centuries to come. In the eighth and seventh centuries more settled conditions and re-establishment of trading links with East and West led to an increase in prosperity and population levels. Prompted by trading possibilities, internal political struggle, and perhaps the strain on resources caused by rapidly expanding numbers, the new *poleis* (city-states) sent out colonies around the Mediterranean world.[2] This no longer took the form of the movement of entire populations: individual cities planted new settlements in France and Spain, north Africa, Syria, Sicily, Italy, and around the Black Sea. These adventures had linguistic repercussions, since normally the inhabitants of a given colony would continue to speak a dialect closely resembling that of their mother-city. There was clearly scope, however, for areal innovation: over time the idiom of the colonies must have started to reflect their new geographic context, including perhaps the arrival of colonists from different regions. Sicily, for example, is a region where there is clear evidence for areal convergence of a number of dialects from different 'genetic' groups.

[1] Murray (1993: 1–15), Drews (1988: 203–25), Whitley (2001: 77–80).
[2] Murray (1993: 64–5, 102–23), Boardman (1980).

§16. The Greek Alphabet

An important result of the commerce between Greece and the east was the adaptation of a north Semitic (probably Phoenician) alphabet to write Greek. It is not clear where this adaptation took place: it might have happened in Crete, Al Mina (a trading post in Syria), or Cyprus. Rhodes and Euboea have also been proposed as candidates.[1]

The date of the adaptation has long been disputed. Until recently the oldest alphabetic inscriptions known were the cup of Nestor (**25**) and the Dipylon vase (**28**), both dated to the second half of the VIII cent. BC. In the 1980s and 1990s discoveries in Egypt (a bronze tablet with an early version of the alphabet) and Italy (five letters found scratched onto a pot in a burial site in Gabii), both dated to the first half of the VIII cent. BC, led scholars to push the adaptation back to at least 800 or (perhaps a century) earlier.

The process of adaptation, and the diffusion of the resulting Greek alphabet, are obscure in many details. Some facts, however, seem clear. The Greeks borrowed both the letter names and order of the letters:

'aleph ~ ἄλφα
beth   ~ βῆτα
gimel   ~ γάμμα
daleth ~ δέλτα, etc.

The Phoenician alphabet ended with /t/, *taw* (Greek *tau*). The five letters of the Greek alphabet which follow *tau* are Greek additions, the so-called supplementals.

The direction of writing in the earliest Greek inscriptions is either from right to left, or *boustrophedon* ('as the ox ploughs'—alternately right to left and left to right). The left-to-right direction gradually became the norm in the seventh century.

[1] Coldstream (2003: 295–302).

§17. Adaptation of the Phoenician signs

The Greek adapter(s) made some practical changes: the Phoenician script (in common with most Semitic alphabets) had no vowel signs, and more signs for sibilants than Greek needed.

1. About half of the letters were used by the Greeks with approximately the same value as they had been given by the Phoenicians: such are *B, Γ, Δ, Ϝ, K, Λ, M, N, Π, P, T*.
2. Other letters were taken over with partial reassignment of values: the voiced affricate *Z* (a Phoen. sibilant); the voiceless aspirate *Θ* (Phoen. emphatic *t*); the back velar Ϙ or *qoppa*, used only before *O* and *Y* (Phoen. emphatic velar); and the voiceless fricative (sibilant) written either *Σ* (*sigma*) or, in a few cities, *M* (*san*). Greek *H* (aspirate or long *e*) derives from Phoen. /ħ/, emphatic *h*.
3. Letters with reassignment of value include the Greek vowel signs: *A* (Phoen. /ʔ/, glottal stop), *E* (Phoen. /h/, aspirate), *O* (Phoen. /ʕ/, pharyngeal).
   (*a*) The Greek vowels *I, Y* were written with the signs for the corresponding semi-vowels (glides) in Phoenician: *yod* /y/ and *waw* /w/.

(*b*) Both consonantal *F* and vocalic *Y* derive from Phoen. *waw* (*F* has the appropriate alphabetic position, *Y* joined the supplementals).

4. *Omega* was derived by the Greeks from *omicron* (and joined the supplementals).
5. Although the Greeks gradually introduced the special signs *H*, *Ω* for long *e* and *o* (§19), they did not develop any way to distinguish long and short vowels in the case of *a*, *i*, and *u*.

§18. *Blue and Red epichoric alphabets of Greece*[1]

Before the fourth century BC there were many local varieties of the Greek alphabet. These varieties can be broadly divided into two major groups (plus two small ones). The distinction rests on different uses of the letters *xi* and the supplementals *phi*, *chi*, and *psi*:

1. The original Greek alphabet (i.e. as adapted without the supplementals) oddly included one consonant cluster sign, namely *Ξ* (= [ks]), deriving from Phoen. /s/ (*samek*).
2. The three supplemental letters *Φ*, *X*, *Ψ* have a curious relationship with *Ξ*. The use and distribution of these four is as shown in the table.

	'Red'	**'Blue'**
	Euboea, Boeotia, Thessaly, Western Greece and western colonies, Rhodes	Attica, Megarid, Argolid, Corinth, Megara, Cyclades, Ionia, Aeolis
Φ	p^h	p^h
X	k + s	k^h
Ψ	k^h	p + s
Ξ		k + s
	(*ΦΣ* = p + s)	

(*a*) A subsection of the Blue alphabets did not use *Ψ* or *Ξ*, but wrote instead *ΦΣ* = [ps], *XΣ* = [ks]. These so-called 'light

Blue' alphabets were used in Athens, Aegina, and some
Ionic islands. The use of *Φ, X* in these clusters implies that
the *s* had an acoustic effect on a preceding stop which was
reminiscent of aspiration.

(*b*) The 'Green' group: Crete, Thera, and Melos lack the supplementals and have no letter with the value *ks*.

3. The Euboean alphabet (a Red alphabet) was exported to
Euboean colonies in Italy, where it was adapted by the Etruscans
and then passed on to the Romans.

[1] The colour terms derive from the first printed map of the distribution
of the Greek alphabets, by A. Kirchhoff in 1887.

§19. *Spread of Ionic script*

The local (or epichoric) alphabets were in use until the V cent., when
they were gradually usurped by the Ionic alphabet. Each had its
idiosyncrasies, both in the use of the letters and in the letter shapes:[1]
this may be partly due to accidents of transmission and selection,
and partly to a conscious desire on the part of each *polis* to have a
distinctive script.[2]

The Ionians, whose dialects were psilotic (§23.10), reused the
aspirate sign *H* for long *e* (*eta*): then they created a sign for
the corresponding long *o* by opening up *o* to make *Ω*. Neither *F* nor
Ϙ was used: *F* because the sound [w] disappeared early in Ionic, and
Ϙ because it was functionally irrelevant (the difference between front
and back velars in Greek is not phonemic). Ionia standardized the
alphabet (and an 'official' epigraphic dialect) at an early stage, and to
this extent was atypical. The Ionic alphabet seems to have enjoyed
great prestige in the Greek world, perhaps because of its association
with the archaic literature and culture of the region (including epic
and scientific prose). Most high literature in Athens seems to have
been written in the Ionic alphabet in the V cent., and an increasing
number of private inscriptions.[3] Official inscriptions (paid for by the
state) continued to be written in the Attic alphabet until the official
adoption of Ionic script in 403/2.

[1] Jeffery (1990).   [2] Luraghi (forthcoming).   [3] Colvin (1999: 92–103),
D'Angour (1999).

§20. *Cypriot syllabary*

While the rest of the Greek world without exception adopted some
form of the alphabet, the Cypriots continued to use a syllabic system
to write Greek until the III cent. BC. The earliest texts are dated to the
VIII cent. (one inscription is perhaps as early as the XI cent.). This
script was adapted from an earlier syllabary used in Cyprus known as
Cypro-Minoan, since it is clearly related to Cretan Linear A. Cypro-
Minoan is attested (in slightly different forms) from the XVI to the
XII centuries BC, and may have been used to record more than one
language (but probably not Greek).

The classical Cypriot syllabary was better suited to writing Greek
than Linear B had been, in that it differentiated *l* from *r* and represented final -*n* and -*s*. But it made no distinction between voiced
(*b*, *d*, *g*), voiceless (*p*, *t*, *k*), or aspirate (*p^h*, *t^h*, *k^h*) stops, and had no
means of indicating aspiration or vowel length. Unlike Linear B, the
Cypriot syllabary made no use of ideograms.

§21. DIALECT DIVERSITY: THE EIGHTH TO THE FOURTH CENTURIES BC

Mycenaean script disappeared with Mycenaean civilization, and the
Greek dialects flourished and diverged for two or three relatively
unsettled centuries, free (outside of Cyprus) from the checks that a
writing system imposes.

The end of the Dark Ages brought political stability and a new
alphabet, and a four-hundred year window in the history of Greek
when the regional diversity of the language was reflected (to a large
extent) in writing.

The political structure of the ancient Greek world meant that
there was no standard language corresponding to Latin in Roman
Italy, or a modern standard such as English, French, or Italian. It is
hard to think of a parallel, ancient or modern, for this situation:
a collection of small states speaking closely related dialects, with a
loose sense of political and ethnic affiliation, each state using its
own written standard (and indeed its own variety of the alphabet).

Even within the Greek world, however, there were exceptions to the principle of unchecked diversity: the larger Greek city-states such as Attica and Laconia must have contained numerous 'sub-dialects' (social and regional) for which there was no written form; and in Ionia the Ionian states adopted a written standard based on Miletos at such an early stage that there is very little evidence for the diversity which Herodotos (1. 142) records and general dialectology would in any case predict.

The Greek dialects of the first millennium BC clearly fall into several sub-groups, and the Greeks related these to 'tribal' subdivisions among the Greek themselves. They identified three kin groups: the Ionians, the Dorians, and the Aeolians (cf. §15 above). In a fragment of Hesiod[1] the three sons of Hellen ('Greek') are presented as the mythological ancestors of these subdivisions:

Ἕλληνος δ' ἐγένοντο φιλοπτολέμου βασιλῆος
Δῶρός τε Ξοῦθός τε καὶ Αἴολος ἱππιοχάρμης.

From Hellen the warrior king sprang Doros and Xouthos and Aeolos lover of horses.

The Greeks took this type of kinship seriously (cf. **65**): there were religious, cultural, and political ties within the groups, and anomalies (e.g. a Dorian ally of the Athenians) were commented on.[2] The Greeks, then, recognized three principal dialect groupings, though they also saw that contiguity could cause dialects to grow together.[3]

[1] Frag. 9 (Merkelbach–West 1967).   [2] See Thuc. 7. 57 for a classic account of dialect and ethnic loyalty in war.   [3] e.g. Thuc. 6. 5 (Himera).

§22. Dialects: Traditional Classification

Modern dialectology has added a fourth group to this trio, namely Arcado-Cypriot. These regions were politically and culturally marginal in the classical period, which may explain the Greeks' failure to integrate them properly into their ethnic and linguistic classification.

The traditional genetic classification of the dialects is as follows:

- Arcado-Cypriot
  Arcadian
  Cypriot
- Attic-Ionic
  Attic
  Ionic   (Euboean, central Ionic, eastern Ionic)
- Aeolic
  Lesbian
  Thessalian
  Boeotian
- West Greek
  Doric   (Saronic, Argolic, Laconia/Messenia,
                          Insular, Crete)
  North-west Greek   (Phokis, Lokris, Achaea, Elis)
- Unclassified: Pamphylian

The schema provides a useful reference point for describing the dialects, so long as two related features of the classification are taken into account:

(*a*) It is more or less inherited from the Greeks, and is therefore based on non-linguistic (cultural, political) as well as linguistic factors.

(*b*) The grouping of the dialects is to a large extent historical, meaning that it indicates as much about the evolution of the dialects between the mid-second millennium BC and the end of the Dark Ages as it does about synchronic relations in the archaic and classical periods (cf. §8 above).

Historical grammar: an overview of distinctive developments in Greek

§23. *Phonology (general characteristics)*

VOWELS

1. Spurious diphthongs

Inherited long *e* in Greek was an open mid vowel [ɛ:] (*η* in the Ionic alphabet). In the history of Greek a new long *e* emerged from contraction and compensatory lengthening: in many dialects this had a close quality, i.e. [ẹ:] distinct from inherited [ɛ:]/*η*. These dialects include Att.-Ion., WGk. dialects of the Saronic area, Phokis and Lokris (contrast §38.3).

The new long vowel was written *E* in Att. inscriptions until the VI cent. BC, when the inherited diphthong [ei] simplified its articulation and became [ẹ:]. As a result of this the digraph *EI* came into use for [ẹ:], even though in many cases the sound did not (historically) continue a diphthong (e.g. infin. ἔχειν [ekʰẹ:n] < ἔχε(h)εν). In these cases classical scholarship has traditionally, if inaccurately, referred to the digraph as a 'spurious diphthong'. The same applies to the digraph *OY*, which continues both lengthened omicron and the old diphthong [ou] > [ọ:].

The use of *EI* for lengthened [e] became common after *c*.450 BC, and standard by the early IV cent.; the use of *OY* for lengthened [o] spread a little more slowly, and was standard by around 350 BC.

Note: (a) εἰμί 'I am' < *esmi* is frequently written with <EI> from the earliest period. This must, then, be a real diphthong imported analogically from the 2nd sing. εἶ rather than the (expected) lengthened ε.[1]

(b) In Attic the new vowel [ọ:] very soon became [u:] (the slot was free, as original [u:] had moved to [ü:], §30.4): e.g. τοῦ [tu:] < [tọ:] < τό(ι)ο. This had happened by the IV cent. BC, but it is difficult to be precise.

2. Synizesis (loss of syllabicity)

(a) In many areas across the Greek-speaking world inscriptions show ι in place of ε before α, ο. A natural conclusion is that this spelling tries to capture a raised quality of ε before a back vowel: and it

probably also denotes synizesis (i.e. loss of syllabicity), by which the vowel became a glide $(i > y)$: $\pi\omega\lambda\acute{\iota}o\nu\tau\alpha\varsigma$ **15** 6, [pɔːlʸontas].[2] This is not a feature associated with Att.-Ion. (but cf. §30.2, quantitative metathesis).

(*b*) $\epsilon + o$: the maintaining of ϵo in writing is most likely a conservative spelling in all dialects where this occurs (exceptions are words like $\theta\epsilon\acute{o}\varsigma$, where the desire to retain two syllables may have inhibited sound-change). There is evidence for four treatments of this cluster: (*i*) $\epsilon > \iota$ (above). (*ii*) Assimilation of ϵ to o resulting in a lengthened o, either [ọː] (Att. $o\upsilon$, §23.1) or [ɔː] (Lac. ω, §38.3). (*iii*) Raising of o to υ, giving a diphthong $\epsilon\upsilon$ in many West Greek and Ionic dialects (§30.7). (*iv*) Syncope $\epsilon o > o$ in certain conditions (**37** 10): this is rare.

When the spelling ϵo occurs the actual realization is likely to have been (*i*) or (*iii*).

3. Osthoff's Law
A long vowel was shortened (in pre-alphabetic Greek) before resonant + consonant:[3]

$*\acute{\epsilon}\theta\eta\nu\tau > *\acute{\epsilon}\theta\epsilon\nu\tau > \acute{\epsilon}\theta\epsilon\nu$ (3 plur. aor., §32.1).

$*\mu\acute{\eta}\nu\varsigma$ 'month' $> *\mu\acute{\epsilon}\nu\varsigma >$ Ion. $\mu\epsilon\acute{\iota}\varsigma$: since gen. $*\mu\eta\nu\sigma\text{-}o\varsigma > \mu\eta\nu\acute{o}\varsigma$ (Lesb. $\mu\hat{\eta}\nu\nu o\varsigma$) without shortening, the law must have operated after the ancient deletion of s after n and before a vowel (§23.6). Attic nom. $\mu\acute{\eta}\nu$ must be analogical.

CONSONANTS

4. Assimilation
When two consonants are next to each other one of them will often influence the articulation of the other, with the result that they become more similar (or identical). This process is common to all languages: in Greek literary texts assimilation is generally observed in writing within a word, but not across word boundaries. Inscriptions often represent assimilation across words (this is known by the Sanskrit term *sandhi*): e.g. in $\pi\acute{o}\sigma o\delta o\mu$ $\pi o\acute{\epsilon}\nu\tau\omega$ **7** 9 final -ν has assimilated to the labial articulation of the following π-.

5. Dissimilation: Grassmann's Law
A process of dissimilation which occurred in all dialects before alphabetic literacy: an aspirate or aspirated stop at the beginning

of a word was de-aspirated if there was another aspirate following (separated by at least one vowel); e.g. $\theta\rho\acute{\iota}\xi$ (nom.) but $\tau\rho\iota\chi\acute{o}s < *\theta\rho\iota\chi\acute{o}s$ (gen.).

6. Intervocalic clusters: resonant and *s*

(*a*) Nasal clusters (with original *$*s$): $\nu\sigma$ $\sigma\nu$ $\mu\sigma$ $\sigma\mu$
When *s* disappeared from forms such as aor. $*\acute{\epsilon}\kappa\rho\iota\nu\text{-}\sigma\alpha$ (syllabified *e.krin.sa*) re-syllabification took place:[4]

- in most dialects by compensatory lengthening (Att.-Ion. and WGk. $\acute{\epsilon}\kappa\rho\bar{\iota}\nu\alpha$)
- in the Aeolic area (sporadically elsewhere) gemination is attested (Lesb. $\acute{\epsilon}\kappa\rho\iota\nu\nu\alpha$); except that Boeotian went with West Greek in adopting compensatory lengthening.

(*b*) Liquid clusters (with original *$*s$): $\sigma\lambda$ $\sigma\rho$ $\lambda\sigma$ $\rho\sigma$
- development similar to (*a*) above: $*\acute{\epsilon}\sigma\tau\epsilon\lambda\sigma\alpha >$ Att.-Ion. $\acute{\epsilon}\sigma\tau\epsilon\iota\lambda\alpha$, Lesb. $\acute{\epsilon}\sigma\tau\epsilon\lambda\lambda\alpha$
- but in isolated cases $\lambda\sigma$ $\rho\sigma$ remain: e.g. $\theta\acute{\alpha}\rho\sigma\sigma$ (> Att. $\theta\acute{\alpha}\rho\rho\sigma$) §31.5).

(*c*) Later development: the cluster *n* with secondary *s*
- In most dialects the *n* is lost, with lengthening: $*\pi\acute{\alpha}\nu\tau\gamma\alpha > \pi\acute{\alpha}\nu\sigma\alpha > \pi\hat{\alpha}\sigma\alpha$
- In Lesb. the 'lengthening' takes the form of a diphthong: $\pi\alpha\hat{\iota}\sigma\alpha$
- In a few dialects (Crete, Thess., Arc.) the *n* is retained: $\pi\acute{\alpha}\nu\sigma\alpha$.

7. Inherited clusters of resonant + *y* (intervocalic)
The treatment is similar to that of resonant + *$*s$: in most dialects the result is compensatory length ($\kappa\rho\bar{\iota}\nu\omega < *\kappa\rho\acute{\iota}\nu\text{-}\gamma\omega$), while Lesb. and Thess. show gemination ($\kappa\rho\acute{\iota}\nu\nu\omega$).
But:
- (*a*) when the cluster -R*y*- is preceded by *a*, *o* all dialects show metathesis of the *y*: $*\mu\acute{\epsilon}\lambda\alpha\nu\text{-}\gamma\alpha > \mu\acute{\epsilon}\lambda\alpha\iota\nu\alpha$, $*(\sigma)\mu\sigma\rho\text{-}\gamma\alpha > \mu\sigma\hat{\iota}\rho\alpha$. Except that—
- (*b*) almost all dialects have a geminate from *l* + *y* ($\acute{\alpha}\lambda\lambda\sigma < *alyos$, but Cypriot §26.8).

It is widely assumed that between *[krin-yo:] and attested [kri:no:] ~ [krinno:] was an intermediate stage of palatalized geminates, *[kriñño:] (and so for all -Ry- clusters).

8. Dialect difference in the treatment of obstruent + _y_
The prehistory of these clusters is complex and much disputed. Assuming a stage of palatalized geminates in early Greek, a simplified account of the development might be as follows:[5]

*_ty_ > *[ttʸ]	• either depalatalized (> ττ): Attica, Boeotia, Crete (ἐρέττω);
	• or became assibilated (e.g. *[tš] > *[šš] > σσ): all other areas (ἐρέσσω);
*_ky_ > *[kkʸ]	• then merged with *[ttʸ]: φυλάττω (Attica, etc.), φυλάσσω (other areas);
*_dy_ > [ddʸ]	• either depalatalized (> δδ): Laconia, Crete, Elis, Thessaly, Boeotia;
	• or became an affricate ζ: all other areas;
*_gy_	• merged with *_dy_.

(_a_) Att.-Ion. (and Arc.) ὅσος (*_yotyo-_), τόσος, μέσος form a special category (the phonological difference is explained by the fact that in these words *_ty_ does not occur at the boundary of a morphologically productive suffix: i.e. the sequence *_yotyos_ was not obviously analysable as a combination root + suffix, unlike *ἐρετ-_yω_).
(_b_) Note also that *_tw_ gives the same result as *_ty_.

9. Dialect difference in the treatment of final -_ns_
The acc. plur. article τόνς, τάνς formed a close accentual unit with the following noun. At an early date the sequence τόνς + C- gave τός (since the cluster -_ns_C- lost the _n_ in pre-alphabetic Greek); while τόνς + V- was not affected.
(_a_) Most dialects generalized either τός or τόνς (the latter usually in the form τούς or τώς).
(_b_) On Crete the distinction τόνς ~ τός was maintained.
(_c_) In Lesb. τόνς > τοίς by regular sound change (§34.11).
Compare the development of εἰς ~ ἐς < ἐν-ς (§§28.8, 32.10). In the acc. plur. of nouns most dialects generalized -ονς (the prevocalic

form): Thessaly, Cyprus, and Insular Doric have -*os*, but it may have been heard more widely than the epigraphic record suggests.

10. The aspirate [h]

(*a*) The aspirate in Greek comes from IE *s- (and *sw-, for which see *hικάδι* **50** 2). There are also words in which it is a secondary analogical feature (see on *ἵππος* **2**); and conversely, some words lost it for analogical reasons. In Laconian the *s* which developed within Greek (secondary *s*) also started to be written *h* from the V cent. BC (probably also in Cypriot: §27.5).

(*b*) By the beginning of alphabetic literacy Ionian and Lesbian had lost the aspirate (this is known as psilosis, and the dialects as psilotic). The Ionians therefore felt free to reuse *H* for the long open vowel [ε:] (§19). Other regions continued to use it for [h] until adoption of the Ionic alphabet: by convention the transcription uses a Roman *h* for this. Other regions which were psilotic at an early date are Elis and Crete (at least the central region, which includes Gortyn). In many dialects outside of Asia Minor the aspirate seems to have been weakly articulated. This is true for some of the dialects of the north-western area, including western Lokris. Loss of *h*- does not in Greek imply de-aspiration of the aspirated consonants *θ*, *φ*, *χ*.

(*c*) Ancient inscriptions signal the presence of the aspirate in two ways: by the use of the letter *H*, and by the use of aspirated consonants *Θ*, *Φ*, *X* at word junctions: *ἐφ' ἱερέως*, etc.). The *spiritus asper* ʻ and *spiritus lenis* ʼ familiar from modern printed texts were brought into use for literary texts in the Alexandrian period. They should be regarded with caution in the transcription of ancient epigraphic texts: the presence of an aspirate must have been a function of region, sociolect, date, and even lexeme. After the adoption of the Ionic alphabet it is impossible to see what is going on (the phoneme [h] probably disappeared from Attica during the Hellenistic period: the breathings on most koiné texts must therefore be conventional). Ionian literary texts have generally been transmitted and are printed with rough breathings on the Attic model (see *ὡς* **66** 93 and *χὡς* **72** 82), while Lesbian texts have conventionally been left psilotic.

NON-SEGMENTAL PHONOLOGY

11. Greek accentuation

With the exception of Lesbian we have little information about the details of accentuation of Greek dialects other than Attic-Ionic.[6] The accentuation of dialect texts (on the Attic system) is nothing more than a typographic convention, and the linguistic reality may have been quite different in some cases. The phonological interpretation offered by the commentary is occasionally at odds with the accent of the standard editions (cf. §26.5 on Arc. ἐργωνήσας **7** 12).

[1] Threatte (1980: 176), Wachter *NAGVI* p. 244. [2] Méndez Dosuna (1993*b*).
[3] Collinge (1985: 127–31). [4] Steriade (1982: 146–53). [5] Allen (1958), Diver (1958), Nagy (1970: 102–30). [6] Colvin (1999: 180–3), Probert (2006: 70–82).

§24. *Morphology (general characteristics)*

1. Thematic and athematic inflection of vowel-stem verbs

Vowel-stem (contract) verbs in Greek come from disparate sources but form a synchronically coherent pattern in the present, which is thematic in most dialects. Lesb., Thess. and Arc.-Cyp. show a long-vowel athematic pattern: the history of these competing types is disputed.

Attic-Ionic and West Greek:

> e-stems   οἰκέω (οἶκος);
> a-stems   τιμάω (τιμή): cf. Lat. *cūrō* < *cūrāō (*cūra*);
> o-stems   δουλόω, ἐλευθερόω (these are most often factitive in meaning).

(*a*) The o-stems are a purely Greek development.

(*b*) The e- and a-stems have IE cognates, but have undergone such extensive remodelling that it makes little sense to argue whether thematic or athematic conjugation is 'original'. They contain two inherited ingredients:[1]

(*i*) A suffix *-*ye/yo*- (also *-*éye/éyo*-), particularly associated with denominative verbs:

τροπέω (~ Lat. *torqueō*), οἰκέω etc. Cf. C-stems such as ἀγγέλλω < ἀγγέλ-*yω*, φυλάσσω < φυλάκ-*yω* (Lat. *custōdiō*).

(*ii*) A 'stative' marker $*-\bar{e} < *-eH_1-$ (cf. Lat. *tacēre, sedēre*), which appears clearly in the aorist: $\dot{a}\nu\theta\dot{\eta}\sigma a\varsigma$ 'in flower', $\theta a\rho\sigma\dot{\eta}\sigma a\varsigma$ 'summoning courage'.

In many cases the *e*-stem present may have been built with this suffix:

$\theta a\rho\sigma\dot{\epsilon}\omega < *\theta a\rho\sigma\eta\omega < *-eH_1-ye/yo-$ } Att.-Ion., WGk.
$\theta\dot{a}\rho\sigma\eta\mu\iota < *-eH_1-mi$ } Lesb. Thess., Arc.-Cyp.

(*c*) Isolated forms in -$\eta\omega$ are found in the Aeolic dialects, Arcadian, and West Greek; the ancient grammatical tradition ascribed $\kappa a\lambda\dot{\eta}\omega$ to 'Aeolians'.[2] They may represent back-formations from the aor. and fut. in -$\eta\sigma a$ etc., or thematization of -$\eta\mu\iota$.

2. The Future
There was no regular IE future: the IE dialects formed it (or not) from their own resources, which accounts for the competing patterns that can be seen in ancient Greek. The future was discarded in Byzantine Greek (partly owing to its messiness, and partly because sound-change had made it difficult to distinguish from the aor. subj.) and replaced with the periphrastic form $\theta\dot{a}$ (from $\theta\dot{\epsilon}\lambda\omega$) + present or perfective indic. An analogous development can be seen in classical $\mu\dot{\epsilon}\lambda\lambda\omega$ + infin.

(*a*) Contracted futures
Verbs such as $\beta\dot{a}\lambda\lambda\omega$ have a future $\beta a\lambda\dot{\epsilon}\omega < *\beta a\lambda\dot{\epsilon}\sigma\omega$, a normal sigmatic future built to the stem $\beta a\lambda\epsilon$- (disyllabic root $*g^wlH_1-$), with regular loss of intervocalic -s-. So also $\kappa a\lambda\dot{\epsilon}\omega < *\kappa a\lambda\dot{\epsilon}\sigma\omega$ (root $*klH_1-$), etc. These futures in -$\dot{\epsilon}\omega$ spread analogically to verbs ending in a resonant (μ, ν, λ, ρ) and a new type was born. Hence $\kappa\tau\epsilon\dot{\iota}\nu\omega$ forms a future $\kappa\tau\epsilon\nu$-$\hat{\omega}$, $\dot{a}\gamma\gamma\dot{\epsilon}\lambda\lambda\omega \rightarrow \dot{a}\gamma\gamma\epsilon\lambda\hat{\omega}$, etc.

Derived presents in -$\dot{\iota}\zeta\omega$ form a similar fut. in Attic ($\kappa o\mu\dot{\iota}\zeta\omega \rightarrow \kappa o\mu\iota\hat{\omega}$): this is clearly influenced by the resonant stems, but details are disputed: possibly an original pres. $*\kappa o\mu\dot{\iota}\omega \rightarrow$ fut. $\kappa o\mu\iota\hat{\omega}$ by adding the new future ending -$\dot{\epsilon}\omega$ to stem $\kappa o\mu\iota$- (the old pres. was later replaced by $\kappa o\mu$-$\dot{\iota}\zeta\omega$, which led to a competing fut. $\kappa o\mu\dot{\iota}\sigma\omega$).[3]

(*b*) Middle futures
A group of verbs in Greek have a future with middle endings and
e-vocalism of the stem: e.g. πάσχω → πείσομαι (*πένθ-σομαι),
λαμβάνω → λήψομαι (*sleH₁gʷ- ?). These have been connected to an
old IE desiderative (see Palmer 1980: 311): middle endings would be
appropriate to the 'inward deixis' of a desiderative.[4]

3. Masculine *a*-stem nouns
Early in Greek attempts were made to distinguish the inflection of
masc. from fem. *a*-stems. In the nom. an -*s* was added (analogy:
λόγος, etc.). In the gen. sing. original -ᾱς was replaced: Att. added -ου
(< *-oo) from the *o*-stems. Other dialects added -*o* (from the same
source) to the stem, giving -ᾱο. In Ionic this gave -ηο > -εω (§30.2),
in WGk. and Aeolic -ᾱ or -αυ.

4. Inherited archaisms: nominal inflection

(*a*) Collective nouns
There are faint traces in Greek of an old collective formation
inherited from Indo-European: the ending was *-a/-ā. It was taken
over by neut. nouns as a plural (so also Latin): in classical Gk. the
neut. plur. still takes a singular verb. The relationship with the fem.
a-stem nouns is difficult to unravel, but there are nouns which are
clearly built on an old collective: e.g. ἡνία, 'reins' (neut. plur. in
Homer, but a fem. *a*-stem in Myc. and later Greek).

(*b*) Archaic neuter stems in -*r/-n*
Many IE languages show traces of an old pattern in the inflection of
a class of neut. nouns: the nom.-acc. sing. had a stem in *-*r*, while
the rest of the paradigm had a stem in *-*n*: Lat. *femur, feminis*. This
gives the Gk. type ἧπαρ, ἥπατος (~ Lat. *iecur*), where the old stem in
-*n*- has been replaced by -*ατ*- (of uncertain origin, but common in
Gk. *n*-stems: cf. ὄνομα, -τος vs. Lat. *nōmen, -inis*).

5. Prepositions: apocope
Most dialects apart from Att.-Ion. use shortened forms of at least
some of the prepositions: this may depend on which consonant
follows the preposition. Thus ἀνά, παρά, κατά, ποτί appear as ἄν,
πάρ, κάτ, πότ, etc. Assimilation to a following consonant is frequent:
e.g. κάββαλλε < κάτ-βαλλε 75(*a*) 5 (Alkaios).

6. Tmesis

In Homeric Greek the first (prepositional) element of a compound verb is often separated from its stem (e.g. ἀπὸ ... δύω **66** 125). This was long assumed to be an archaic feature of epic language (borrowed as a poetic licence by late Greek poetry). It is, however, absent from Mycenaean Greek: the reasons for this may be stylistic[5] or chronological (epic preserves a feature of Greek which was already lost in XIV–XIII centuries BC).[6]

[1] Cf. Watkins (1971), Tucker (1990), Jasanoff (2003). [2] Blümel (1982: 175). [3] Ruijgh (1975). [4] Palmer (1980: 311), Rijksbaron (1994: 153–4). [5] Hajnal (2004). [6] Horrocks (1980).

The Greek dialects: an overview

§25. Arcado-Cypriot

This dialect group is the most closely related to the language of the Mycenaean tablets. The similarities which link these dialects appear relatively straightforward. Arcadian is the relic of a dialect spoken in the Peloponnese in the Mycenaean Age. At some period (before 1000 BC) Greeks emigrated from the Peloponnese to Cyprus. When the Dorians became dominant in coastal regions of the Peloponnese (Messenia, Laconia, Argolis, Corinthia) they did not penetrate the mountainous interior, with the result that Arcadia formed an isolated linguistic community, surrounded by states speaking a different dialect from its own. The Bronze Age dialect of the Peloponnese and its historical survivors are sometimes called 'Achaean'. The group has commonalities with Att.-Ion. which look inherited (assibilation -τι > -σι, and the athematic infin. -ναι): in addition Arc. has certain isoglosses with Att.-Ion. which may reflect a period of contact after the Mycenaean collapse (and the departure of Cypriot), but before Arc. was isolated by the surrounding Doric dialects (εἰ 'if', and the particle ἄν).

Cypriot syllabic script (§20) is often ambiguous, especially with regard to vowels. Arc. is of limited help, since there is no particular reason to assume that the two dialects would show similar reflexes in developments which postdate the eleventh century. After this period Cyp. will have been in interaction with its nearest Greek neighbours in Pamphylia, Rhodes (which had colonies on the Anatolian coast), and Ionia. Reconstructing the phonetic properties of the Cypriot vowel system remains conjectural, however.

§26. Vowels

1. The raising of ϵ to ι before a nasal: $\dot{\iota}\nu$ **7** 2.
2. The raising of o to υ before a nasal and at word end: $\epsilon\dot{\upsilon}F\rho\eta\tau\acute{a}\sigma\alpha\tau\upsilon$ **8** 4.
3. Vocalic resonants are generally vocalized with o (§10.3): but $\tau\rho\iota\alpha\kappa\acute{a}\sigma\iota\sigma\iota$ **7** 8 < *$-k\underset{\circ}{m}tioi$ (contrast Attic, §32.9*a*). The perf. $\dot{\epsilon}\varphi\theta\sigma\rho\kappa\acute{\omega}s$ **7** 10 (assuming $\ddot{\epsilon}\varphi\theta\sigma\rho\kappa\alpha$ was formed analogically on a mid. $\ddot{\epsilon}\varphi\theta\sigma\rho\mu\alpha\iota$) shows $o\rho <$ *$\underset{\circ}{r}$.

ARCADIAN ONLY:

4. Long vowels η and ω (inherited and from contraction etc.): cf. the 'severe' WGk. vocalism of the southern Peloponnese (§38.3).
5. In the acc. plur. the sequence *$-o\nu s > -os$ with a short vowel (§23.9): therefore the *a*-stem acc. plur. is probably also short ($\delta\alpha\rho\chi\mu\acute{a}s$ **7** 23), and so also the aor. ptcpl. $\dot{\epsilon}\rho\gamma\omega\nu\acute{\eta}\sigma\alpha s$ **7** 12 (§23.11 for the accent).

CYPRIOT ONLY:

6. ϵ is written ι before α and o ($\dot{\epsilon}\pi\iota\acute{o}\nu\tau\alpha < \dot{\epsilon}\pi\epsilon\acute{o}\nu\tau\alpha$ **8** 9): §23.2.
7. *$al\underset{\wedge}{i}os > \alpha\ddot{\iota}\lambda os$ (cf. Lat. *alius*), **8** 14: §23.7.
8. Vowel plus n : nasalized vowels are the most plausible interpretation of the graphic data.[1]
   (*a*) From vowel + n before a consonant: *panta* > [pāta] (written *pa-ta*): cf. parallels from Asia Minor (§42.5). The new nasalized vowel was probably long.
   (*b*) If the following consonant starts a new word the final -n is generally written unless it belongs to a 'prepositive' word (i.e. the article, or a preposition). However, nouns occasionally have a final -n elided: thus $\rho\acute{o}Fo(\nu)$ $\tau\grave{o}(\nu)$ $\varDelta\rho\acute{\upsilon}\mu\iota\sigma\nu$ **8** 19.
   (*c*) From vowel + n before s : *kāpons* > [ka:pōs] (written *ka-po-se*), *hexonsi* > [heksōsi] (written *e-ke-so-si*). For the article (§23.9)

we assume that when a consonant followed the result was a short vowel (as on Crete): τὸς κάπο(ν)ς **8** 30.

9. In common with most dialects, Cypriot probably maintained a distinction between inherited [ε:]/η and [ẹ:] from contraction (§23.1): on this view *e-ke-ne* (**8** 10) represents ἔχēν (Att. ἔχειν) rather than ἔχην (severe Doric) or ἔχεν (a WGk. morphological innovation). So also between inherited [ɔ:]/ω and [ọ:]: τô (Att. τοῦ) < *τό(ι)ο.

¹ So Ruijgh (1988).

§27. Consonants

1. Inherited *w* is maintained: starts to disappear in Arc. in the IV cent. (absent from **7** Tegea: cf. ἐργώναις < Fεργ-).

2. A labiovelar followed by *e* or *i* produced a sound written ζ/τζ or with a special letter Ϻ in Arcadia until the V cent. BC; and with the *s*-series in Cypriot (*si-se* ~ σις **8** 10, cf. Arc. ὄζις 'whoever' Buck 16, but IV cent. τις **7** 15). This probably represents an affricate such as [tˢ].

3. The change *-ti* > *-si* in verbal endings occurs in Arc.-Cyp. as in Myc. (§10.8): so also in a few other categories such as numerals (τριακάσιοι **7** 8).

4. The sequence *-νσ-* is retained in Arc. in the 3 plur. of thematic verbs: κρίνωνσι **7** 5. For Cyp. we posit a nasalized vowel (§26.8) to explain the general failure to write *n* in this position.

5. The lack of an *h*-series in the syllabary does not prove that Cypriot was psilotic. The dialect seems to have had a tendency (mostly ignored in inscriptions, but Hesych. preserves some words which show it) to make initial and intervocalic *s* into an aspirate:¹ thus κὰ(ς) ἀ(ν)τὶ τᾶ(ς) **8 5** is written *ka-a-ti ta*. Cf. §23.10.

¹ Woodard (1997: 90).

§28. Morphology/Syntax

CHARACTERISTIC FEATURES OF ARCADO-CYPRIOT

1. Third person med.-pass. ending in -(ν)τοι (§14.1).

2. Present infin. ending (thematic): Myc. *e-ke-e* [ekehen] suggests that Arc. -εν is the result of common development with neighbouring

WGk. dialects (e.g. Argolic). Cyp. *e-ke-ne* is ambiguous: for the reading ἔχεν see §26.9.

3. Athematic inflection of vowel-stem verbs: ἀδικήμενος **7** 3 (§24.1).

4. *a*-stem masc. gen. sing. in -αυ < -αο (§§24.3, 26.2): cf. Myc. gen. sing. *su-qo-ta-o*, 'swineherd' (Hom. συβώτης). In Arc. this was extended to fem. stems: ζαμίαυ **7** 21.

5. The prepositions meaning 'from' (ἀπύ and ἐξ) are constructed with a dat.-loc. rather than a gen. (so also Pamph.). This loss of ability to govern a genitive is probably the result of a tendency to reduce the number of cases governed by three-case prepositions such as παρά, which merged the gen. with the dat. This then spread to ablatival one-case prepositions.[1]

6. ἀπύ is found in Arc.-Cyp., Myc., Lesb. and (some) Thess., and often coexists with ἀπό in these dialects. Both forms appear to have been inherited from Indo-European (i.e. ἀπύ is not a phonological variant of ἀπό within Greek).[2]

7. Arc.-Cyp. πός < ποσί (the Myc. form) < ποτί (Att. πρός is a different stem, for which cf. Skt. *prati*). ποί (NW Gk. and eastern Argolic) must also come from ποτί (perhaps by dissimilation before the article). Arc.-Cyp. κάς 'and' has often been compared: for πός, ποσί, ποί cf. κάς, κασι- (κασίγνητος), καί.[3]

8. ἐν with the acc. ('into', as in Latin) is preserved in Arc.-Cyp. (also NW Gk., Thess., and Boe.): Att.-Ion. and Doric innovate ἐν-ς (variously εἰς, ἐς, ἐνς, §23.9).

9. ὀν (Att. ἀνά): both ὀν (Pelasgiotis, Lesb., Arc.-Cyp.) and ἀνά may derive from *ἀνο by vowel assimilation.[4]

---

[1] Morpurgo Davies (1966), Brixhe (1976: 126–7), Thompson (2001). [2] Dubois (1986: I, 137), Hodot (1990: 148). [3] Ruijgh (1966), (1981a): disputed by Willi (2003b). [4] Ruijgh (1970: 309).

ARCADIAN ONLY:

10. Dat. sing. ending -οι: ἔργοι **7** 2. This is also found in Euboea, Boeotia, Elis, and across the NW Greek area. It is the result of shortening of the long diphthong -ωι, and appears to be relatively late (the data can be ambiguous as the distinction depends on use of Ionic ω). It is not the old loc. ending.[1]

CYPRIOT ONLY:

11. Thematic gen. sing. in -ōν (syllabic -*o-ne*). This is unlikely to represent -ων, since it would be strange for the gen. sing. and gen. plur. to be identical. It can be connected with the loss of -*n* in Cypriot (§26.8): e.g. gen. plur. τῶν will have had two variants (final -*n* before vowels, lost before consonants), giving a proportional analogy τῶ : τῶν :: τō : *x* (*x* → τōν).[2]

12. The C-stem acc. sing. has -*n* added: τὸν ἰατῆραν **8** 3. There is some evidence that the C-stem acc. plur. had also added a nasal, on the analogy of the thematic decl. (hence the transcription τὸς παῖδα(ν)ς **8** 11, 24). So also in Crete (Gortyn): **53** 42 θυγατέρανς.

13. *i*-stem nouns are inflected with an intrusive -F- (presumably imported from *u*-stems): πτόλιFι **8** 6.

[1] Méndez Dosuna (1985: 413–25), Ruijgh (1989: 157).   [2] Ruijgh (1988: 137–8).

§29. *Attic-Ionic*

Attic-Ionic shares a range of 'East Greek' features with Mycenaean and Arcado-Cypriot (§8, §25): there are also, however, a number of isoglosses with West Greek, which may indicate a period of contact in the post-Mycenaean era. These include a common innovation in middle endings (-ται for -τοι, etc.), thematic conjugation of vowel-stem verbs (§24.1), and a general vocalization in *a* of the vocalic resonants (§10.3, 26.3). Differences between Attic and Ionic are relatively small: the separation must have started in the XI cent. with migrations across the Aegean from the Greek mainland (§15).

Eastern Ionic inscriptions appear to have been written in a standardized epigraphic koiné from the earliest period, and give little insight into regional variation (which Herodotos records at 1. 142 and which we would in any case expect). At least one variety of Ionic used κ rather than π in pronominal forms (§31.6). This appears in Ionic prose: its appearance in Hipponax, and imitation in Attic comedy, guarantees that it was widely heard. The π forms of the epigraphic language were perhaps based on older or prestige varieties (including epic).

Euboean has traditionally been subsumed under Ionic, though the group could as well be called Attic-Euboean-Ionic. The cities of Euboea spoke a dialect which shared many characteristic Attic innovations: lack of vowel lengthening after loss of digamma (ξένος), the assimilation of ρσ to ρρ, and the development of ττ from palatalized stops.

Phonology

§30. Vowels

1. Raising of [aː] to [εː] (*η*): universal in eastern Ionic and Euboea, partial in Attic (§30.3). In central Ionic (Cyclades) *E* was used for inherited [εː], and *H* only for the new vowel that had emerged from [aː], until the end of the V cent. This indicates that a complete merger did not take place till late (*H* presumably denoted a more open vowel than [εː], such as [äː]), and raises the interesting possibility that a difference might have been heard in Attica and Ionia as well for longer than is commonly assumed. Cf. §10.1.

2. Quantitative metathesis (or synizesis), *ηο* > *εω* and *ηα* > *εᾱ*. Caused in particular by the disappearance of intervocalic *w* and *y* (*βασιλῆϜος, *πόληγος). On the older view the two vowels simply swapped quantity,[1] but it is more likely that the first vowel became a glide (i.e. lost its syllabicity) and the second underwent compensatory lengthening: [eːo] > [ĕoː].[2] Thus the development of *ᾱ* + *o/ω* (e.g. in the gen. plur. of *a*-stems) gives *εω* > *ω* in Att.-Ion., but *ᾱ* in all other dialects.

ATTIC ONLY:

3. Raising of [aː] to [εː] was reversed after [e, i, r] and does not, synchronically, apply.

4. Inherited [u(ː)] was raised to [ü(ː)] (and *ου* became [uː], §23.1).

5. Widespread contraction of vowels (e.g. *s*-stem gen. sing. γένους < γένε(h)ος, where other dialects have γένεος, §23.2*b*).

IONIC ONLY:

6. Compensatory lengthening in ξεῖνος, κοῦρος, etc. after the loss of [w]. This also happened in some West Greek dialects (Argolic and insular Doric): ξῆνος, κῶρος (§38.3).

7. In contrast to Attic (§30.5), the vowels *εο* were often maintained uncontracted in spelling, but in pronunciation probably diphthong-

ized to εν at an early date (§23.2*b*). The same may be true in certain circumstances for εω.³

¹ Ruijgh (1968). ² So Méndez Dosuna (1993*a*), but see Probert (2006: 85, n.5). ³ Szemerényi (1956).

§31. Consonants

1. Disappearance of [w] (digamma) from the time of the earliest inscriptions.

2. In μέσος, ὅσος etc. *-ty-* > -σ-, as in Arcadia (§23.8*a*).

3. The change *-ti* > *-si* in verbal endings occurs in Att.-Ion. as in Myc. (§10.8): so also in a few other categories such as numerals (εἴκοσι §32.9). This gives the characteristic 3 plur. ending -ουσι [-o̧:si] < *-ονσι (WGk. -οντι): §23.6*c*.

ATTIC ONLY:

4. In ἐρέττω, ἥττων, etc. *-ty-* and *-ky-* > -ττ-, as in Boeotia and Eretria (§23.8), and very occasionally in Thessaly.

5. Assimilation of ρσ to ρρ (ἄρρην, θάρρος, etc.).

IONIC ONLY:

6. Psilosis (§23.10): loss of the aspirate, an areal development which affected eastern Aeolic (Lesbian) as well as eastern Ionic. Central Ionic and Euboea for the most part retained the aspirate.

7. Some pronominal forms have κ (rather than π) < *kʷ. The κ is generally assumed to be the result of labial dissimilation in *okʷo- (> ὅκοτε, ὅκως, etc.), from where it spread to *kʷo- forms. It is not found in epic poetry or in inscriptions (with the exception of ὁκοῖα, Erythrai, IV cent. BC): in literary Ionic it occurs in the texts of Herakleitos, Semonides, Kallinos, Anakreon, Hipponax, Herodotos, the Hippokratic corpus, and Herodas. Mimicked also by Aristophanes.¹

¹ Aristoph. *Triphales* 556 PCG.

§32. Morphology/Syntax

CHARACTERISTIC FEATURES OF ATTIC-IONIC

1. The athematic 3 plur. imperf. and aor. was originally ἔθεν, ἔδον, etc. < *ἔθε-ντ, ἔδο-ντ, and this is retained in some dialects. Att.-Ion.

ἔθεσαν, etc. has been recharacterized with -σαν from the sigmatic aor. (so also the aor. pass. *ἐλύθηντ → ἐλύθησαν); other dialects abstracted an ending -αν from the sigmatic aor., giving ἔθεαν, etc.

2. In line with the preceding, ἦν (< ἦεν < *ἦσεντ) 'they were' was replaced by ἦσαν, but was reused as the 3 sing. in place of ἦς < *ἦστ. (ἦεν was perhaps analysed as *ἦε + -ν, by analogy with the old 1 sing. ἦα.)

3. Imperative, 3 plur. active ending -ντων (-ντω + ν): so also at Delphi (Att.-Ion. influence?) and some insular Doric (Crete, Thera): cf. Lesb. -ντον. Most dialects have -ντω.

4. The most common *i*-stem inflection in Att.-Ion. (that of πόλις) is peculiar: it is marked by ablaut of the *i*-suffix (thus nom. plur. *polei̯-es > πόλεις), followed by extensive reorganization. The attested paradigm was built by reinterpreting (or refashioning) the old endingless loc. πόληι (lengthened stem and zero ending) as πόλη-ϊ (stem plus ending -ι): cf. Hom. πόληος **66** 110. Elsewhere *i*-stems were organized in a relatively simple pattern without ablaut, whereby endings were added to a stem in -*i* (πολι-). The inflection of *u*-stems is more or less parallel.

5. (*a*) Sing. pronouns: the *s*-/*t*- alternation of the 2 sing. σύ σέ σοί (WGk. τύ τέ τοί) was ironed out by extensive analogical levelling in the dialects. The *s*- got a foothold in the paradigm through the acc. sing. σέ < *τϝέ.

(*b*) Plur. pronouns (1 and 2 plur.): inherited *n̥sme was recharacterized with -ες in the nom. and -ας in the acc., giving ἡμεῖς, ἡμᾶς, etc. Most other dialects simply added -ς in the nom. (WGk. ἁμές) and left the acc. unchanged (ἁμέ). So also *us-me (for *us cf. Lat. uōs) > WGk. ὑμέ (Att. ὑμεῖς).

6. οἱ, αἱ (extended from the sing. ὁ, ἡ) replace inherited τοί, ταί (from a pronominal stem *to-). So also Arc.-Cyp., Lesb., and eastern Thess. (τοί found once in western Thess.).

7. Moveable -ν (νῦ ἐφελκυστικόν). This probably spread earlier in Ionia than in Attica, and must be due to a complex series of analogies.[1] In V cent. Attic prose inscriptions moveable *nu* is quite rare (most common in the dat. plur., no doubt on the analogy of ἡμῖν, ὑμῖν), but becomes increasingly common from the mid IV cent. (formulaic ἔδοξεν always occurs with -ν, even in early Attic texts). By the time of the koiné it is the norm not only before vowels and pauses, but also before consonants.

8. εἰ, 'if', and particle ἄν, with Arc. (Cypr. has ἦ and κε, other dialects have αἰ and κε/κα). Also ἐάν, in which ā suggests: *ei* + *an* > *ân*, subsequently recharacterized with *ei* (giving *ei-ân* > *e-ân*). The final contraction to *ân* is found in Thuc., perhaps under Ionic influence, but is rare in inscriptions until the Hellenistic period.

9. Numerals

(*a*) the -*o*- in εἴκοσι and the hundreds (διακόσιοι, etc.) is extended analogically from the decads in -κοντα < *-*komta* (WGk. dialects preserve, -*a*-, as in Ϝίκατι < IE *wikṃti*, Lat. *uīgintī*).

(*b*) Initial ε- in εἴκοσι is an apparently un-etymological vowel of a type found in Greek before some words beginning with a resonant (cf. ὄνομα vs. Lat. *nōmen*): such 'prothetic vowels' can sometimes be derived from IE laryngeals.

10. Att.-Ion. and Doric innovate ἐν-*s* (§23.9): Att. generalized εἰς, Ion. mostly has ἐς but in some areas maintained the distinction ἐς + C, εἰς + V.

ATTIC ONLY:

11. The present ptcpl. of εἰμί, 'be', is in most dialects ἐών ἐοῦσα ἐόν (*H_1s-on*-). Attic ὤν, οὖσα, ὄν is unexpected: loss of ἐ- is presumably the result of hypheresis[2] or contraction (§30.5): if contraction there must have been some analogical remodelling to account for neut. ὄν. Fem. οὖσα/ἐοῦσα must in any case have been remodelled on the masc./neut., since *H_1s-ṇt-ya* would give ἐάσσα (Myc. *a-pe-a-sa*), a form found in other dialects. So also subj. ἔω versus Att. ὦ.

12. Athem. verbs, 3 plur. present ending -ᾶσι (τιθέᾱσι, διδόᾱσι): an innovation associated with Attic (but Att.-Ion. ἴᾱσι and epic ἔᾱσι **61** 7 show the same ending). Homer, Herod., and other Ion. sources have τιθεῖσι (WGk. τίθεντι): cf. **77** 208 for the accent. -ᾶσι < *-*ανσι* may be a recharacterized version of -ἄσι < *-*ṇti*: but the details are difficult and disputed.[3]

13. Att. assigns relativizing function to the the pronoun ὅς < *yos*. Other dialects also use the 'article' pronoun ὁ, ἡ, τό < *so*, *sā*, *tod* as a relative (esp. Ionic, Aeolic, Arc.-Cyp.): this became a feature of the Hellenistic koiné.[4]

IONIC ONLY:

14. Ionic (with Lesb. and Pamph.) has the long dat. plur. in -οισι

(the original loc. ending), with *a*-stem -ησι (the result of *o*-stem influence on inherited -ησι < *-ᾱσι). Most dialects have -οις (the old instr. ending) in dat. function, and *a*-stem -αις (formed analogically). Att. dropped -οισι in the mid V cent. in favour of -οις; and *a*-stem -αις replaced -ησι/-αισι. The retention of the long form in V cent. Attic comedy is merely a metrical convenience. Cf. Myc. (§11.3).

[1] Kurylowicz (1972), Ruijgh (1989: 161).   [2] Cowgill (1965: 167–8), López Eire (1986).   [3] Rix (1976: 252, 256–7), Ruijgh (1992: 464–6). [4] Humbert (1960: 42), Horrocks (1997: 127).

§33. Aeolic

The Aeolic dialects bear witness to a relatively brief period of common development followed by a much longer process of areal convergence (Boeotian and Thessalian have features in common with West Greek, Lesbian with East Greek). Whether proto-Aeolic was in the Bronze Age a north-western or south-eastern idiom (§8) is a vexed question, and perhaps misconceived (it implies a strongly genetic rather than an areal model of how dialects develop). Aeolic was clearly a conservative dialect (and therefore resembled the conservative north-western dialects in many respects), and probably did not develop distinctively Aeolic features (innovations) until the post-Mycenaean period.[1] In the late second millennium the proto-Aeolians seem to have occupied the regions between Epirus and Thessaly, and to have migrated as far as the northern Peloponnese.

At the end of the Dark Ages the speakers of dialects traditionally classified as Aeolic were separated geographically and isolated: Boeotian is surrounded to the east by Attic-Ionic, and in all other directions by West Greek. Thessalian is surrounded by North-west Greek, and eastern Aeolic (Lesbian) by Ionic. Boeotian is often described as a mixed dialect (West Greek and Aeolic), and in fact all three are in varying degrees fusions of disparate elements. The group—even more than the other traditional dialect 'families'—is united by a series of overlapping similarities rather than a large number of diagnostic common features.[2]

An extra problem with the term *Aeolic* is that it was used by ancient grammarians and commentators to denote Lesbian (owing to the ancient and famous literary tradition associated with the dialect, including aspects of Homeric language), and this is reflected to a certain extent in modern usage.

[1] García Ramón (1975), Brixhe (2006: 49–55). [2] Vottéro (2006: 137–42).

Phonology

§34. Vowels

1. There is evidence that vocalic resonants (§10.3) were in some contexts vocalized with *o*, as in Arc.-Cyp. (§§26.3, 10.3): Boe. στροτειιάων **14** 9, Sapph. βροχέ(α) **74** b7.

2. In Lesb. and Thess. clusters of resonant and **s* (§23.6) or **y* (§23.7) characteristically result in the gemination of the resonant, rather than compensatory lengthening of the vowel: ἀμμέ (<*ņsme) **11** 13 (Thess.), Sapph. ἰμέρρει (-ρρ- < *-ry-) **74** a27.

THESSALIAN ONLY:

3. (*a*) Secondary long *e* and *o* merged with the inherited long vowels [ε:] (η) and [ɔ:] (ω). By the IV cent. long *e* and long *o* had a closed quality and were written ει, ου (with a spelling borrowed from Att.-Ion., §23.1): συνθείκα **10** 1. (*b*) There is a possible related sound-change at Larisa, by which αι came to be written ει (i.e. [ai] > [ε:] > [e̝:]), for which cf. §34.6 below. But the evidence is late and the spelling only attested in verbal endings.[1]

BOEOTIAN ONLY:

Boeotian vowels changed rapidly from the V cent., in most cases anticipating the developments that characterize modern Greek. The Boeotians attempted to keep track of sound-changes in the spelling, especially after the introduction of the Ionic alphabet at the beginning of the IV cent.

4. In the V cent. the diphthong ει [ey] began to be written ι, indicating transition to a monophthong [i:] (probably via [e̝:]). As in Attica (Threatte 1980: 205), it seems likely that this change was retarded before a vowel (cf. στροτειιάων **14** 9).

5. Secondary long *e* and *o* had merged with the inherited long vowels [ε:] (η) and [ɔ:] (ω); but at the beginning of the IV cent.

inherited long *e* (η) started to be written ει, indicating a closer pronunciation [e̞:].

6. From the end of the VI cent. the diphthong αι began to be
written αε, and by the mid IV cent. was written η. These changes
indicate transition to a monophthong [ε:].

7. In a parallel development to (6), the diphthong οι began to be
written οε and then (in the mid IV cent.) υ. This indicates a change to
the monophthong [ü:] (for the spelling cf. §30.4).

8. Inherited υ remained a true [u], unlike in Attic, and from the
early IV cent. was generally written ου to indicate this.

9. ε written ει (from the VI cent.) or ι (IV cent.) before another
vowel indicates synizesis (§23.2).

LESBIAN ONLY:

10. Ancient grammatical sources, and the accentuation of some
manuscripts, indicate that the accent in Lesbian was recessive (as
close to the beginning of the word as possible, as in the Att. verb). By
convention this is observed in the printing of modern accents.[2]

11. By way of compensatory lengthening, the sequence *V*ns > V*is*
(λύοισι < *λύονσι, etc.): word-final (§23.9) or with secondary *s*
(§23.6c).

12. Secondary long *e* and *o* merged with the inherited open vowels
[ε:] (η) and [ɔ:] (ω).

[1] Blümel (1982: 159–61).   [2] Probert (2003: 159–60), West (1970b).

§35. Consonants

1. Labiovelar *k^w (*g^w, *g^wh) > labial π (β, φ) even before *e, i*
(§10.6): Boe. πετράταν, 'fourth' **14** 19. (But note τίς < *$k^w$is even in
Aeolic.)

2. [w] (digamma) was lost early in Lesb. (cf. Ionic). Its appearance
in Sapph. and Alk. appears to be purely 'literary': it had already
disappeared from the spoken language in the VI cent.[1] Initial Ϝ- is
maintained in Boe. and Thess. until the koiné (sometimes written
internally in archaic Boe. inscriptions).

3. For Boe. (and probably also Thess., though evidence is scanty)
ττ in common with Attica and Eretria (§23.8).

[1] Bowie (1981: 69–74).

§36. Morphology/Syntax

OVERLAPPING FEATURES OF LESBIAN, THESSALIAN, BOEOTIAN

1. Athematic inflection of vowel-stem verbs (§24.1): but Boeotian inscriptions show thematic inflection with West Greek and Attic.

2. Perfect ptcpl.: the inherited suffix *-wos- was replaced with -ont- imported from the present (*-wos- had to be remodelled in all dialects after the disappearance of intervocalic *-s-): ἐπεστάκοντα **9** 8, 'in office' (ἐφ-ίσταμαι).

3. Infinitives: (a) the athematic infin. (active) is -μεν in Thess. Boe., extended to thematic verbs also. (b) Lesb. has athematic -μεναι (apparently a blend of -μεν and -ναι), but only in the case of short-vowel monosyllabic stems (ἔμ-μεναι, δό-μεναι, θέ-μεναι): other athematic stems share the thematic ending, viz. long vowel + -ν. (c) Sigmatic -σαι and med.-pass. -σθαι are common to all three, with the exception of Larisa in Thessaly where -σειν, -σθειν are found (cf. §34.3).

4. The athematic (C-stem) dat. plur. is -εσσι (the result of an analogical 'proportion' λύκοι : λύκοισι : : πάντες : x → πάντεσσι): it must have been created after the sound-change -ss- > -s- had ceased to be effective (cf. στήθεσιν **74** b6). Hom. s-stem forms such as ἔπεσσι are creations of the epic *Kunstsprache* (the doublet -εσσι/-εσι is metrically convenient).[1]

5. First sing. pronoun ἐγών (rare in epigraphic texts): associated with Aeolic and West Greek. For the final -ν cf. Indo-Iranian -m (Skt. *ahám*).

6. Patronymic adj. in -ios (also Myc.): other dialects use gen. of the father's name.[2]

7. αἰ, 'if', and particle κε (κεν in Homer and lyric poetry): κα in Boe. from West Greek.

THESSALIAN ONLY:

8. Thematic gen. sing. in -οιο (rarely), mostly -οι < -οιο (cf. Myc. *o-jo*): the form familiar from Homer.

LESBIAN ONLY:

9. Imperative, 3 plur. active/medio-pass.
Lesb. forms a 3 plur. imper. in -ντον (act.) and -σθον (medio-pass.), with an unusual short vowel. Greek generally builds these forms on

3 sing. -τω and -σθω (§32.3), but in this case the development is hard to trace.[3]

[1] Morpurgo Davies (1976).   [2] Morpurgo Davies (1968), Hodot (2006: 174–8).   [3] García Ramón (1978).

§37. West Greek

West Greek includes the group of dialects known traditionally to classicists as Doric, a term (and a concept) inherited from the Greeks. The Dorians had a distinct political and cultural identity: their dialect was particularly associated with choral poetry, which suggests that the form developed somewhere in the Doric world. For linguistic purposes it is useful, however, to distinguish a sub-grouping of north-western dialects which share a range of overlapping features. With the notable exceptions of Delphi and Elis, much of the north-western area was both geographically and culturally isolated in the classical period.[1]

Although West Greek is characterized by some striking isoglosses which mark it off from the eastern group, the individual dialects nevertheless developed in different linguistic contexts across a wide area of mainland and insular Greece. Since it seems likely that speakers of West Greek were involved in migrations across the Greek world in the sub-Mycenaean period (starting roughly in the XII cent.), the dialects as they appear in the archaic period can be expected to show the effects of interaction with the language of speakers who were absorbed or subdued by the new arrivals ('substrate' influence), as well as that of neighbouring population groups (Arcadia, Boeotia, Attica, and Thessaly). This is difficult to quantify, but for both North-west Greek and Doric there are features which appear anomalous, as well as sporadic irregularities which are difficult to account for; and in a couple of cases (Achaea and Elis) the written standards admit these features so freely that doubt has been cast on their classification as West Greek. This is not a particularly useful step: if we are to use the traditional groupings at all, we should recognize that for West Greek, and particularly for North-west Greek, the evidence is often both scanty and late; and it is therefore not unlikely that in many cases we are dealing with a koinéized written form which did not closely represent local vernacular. Better evidence would no doubt give us a whole new set of criteria for classifying the western dialects.

The literary dialect known as Doric cannot on the whole be located in a specific region: it seems to be a supra-regional creation (compare literary Ionic), and may in any case have borrowed features from other literary idioms such as epic or Aeolic. The choral 'Doric' of Attic tragedy is particularly feeble, and comprises little more than the occasional ā for η (as well as a number of epic features).

[1] Bile (2006).

Phonology

§38. Vowels

1. ἰαρός (eastern Gk. ἱερός): root *isH_1- and suffix in *-er/r̥-os (cf. §10.3 for *r̥ > ar in WGk. and Att.-Ion.).[1]

2. πρᾶτος (Att. πρῶτος) < *pr̥̄-tos with the long vowels from long vocalic r (root *prH-), but there may have been analogical interference.[2] So also Boe.

3. In Arc., Aeol., and some WGk. dialects secondary long e and o (§23.1) fell together with inherited [ɛ:] (η) and [ɔ:] (ω). WGk. dialects in which this occurs (traditionally labelled *severior*) are (a) Peloponnesian dialects outside of the Saronic area: viz. Elis, the western Argolid, Laconia, and their colonies (Taras, Heraklea, etc.); and (b) Crete, and some of the smaller islands.

4. The contraction of α + ε gives η (Att.-Ion. ā); for ā < ā + o/ω cf. §30.2.

[1] Ruijgh (1981b: 59).   [2] Lejeune (1972: §203), Sihler §106.

NORTH-WEST GREEK:

5. ε is lowered to α before ρ (as in Brit. Engl. *clerk*): φάρεν (Att. φέρειν) **54** 1. At Elis η > ā in most contexts.

§39. Consonants

1. [w] (digamma) is retained until the koiné period, especially in word-initial position. Exceptions: [w] is lost early in insular Doric (but retained in Crete), and the Saronic dialects (but post-consonantal Ϝ is found in early inscriptions from Corinth).

2. **ty* and **ky* give σσ (φυλάσσω < φυλάκ-γω etc.): but -ττ- is found on Crete (§23.8).

3. **dy* and **gy* give ζ in most dialects: but in Laconia, Crete, and Elis the result is δδ (initial δ-): §23.8.

4. Retention of inherited -τι in verbal endings and numerals: δίδωτι **42** 8, Ϝίκατι **41** 2.

NORTH-WEST GREEK:

5. στ for σθ (ἱλαξάστō **54** 2): best accounted for by assuming an early development of [kʰ], [tʰ] to fricatives [x], [θ] (as in Laconia). The writing στ would indicate that θ/[tʰ] had failed to become a fricative [θ] after [s]. Cf. also on πάσκοι **58** 8. Occasional examples are also found in Boe. and Thess. (it was clearly a feature of north-central Greece).

LACONIAN:

6. There is a regular change of intervocalic -*s*- > -*h*- in Laconian from the V cent. (and sporadically in other dialects, though not attested till the IV cent.): both epigraphic, and captured in Aristoph. *Lysistrata*. e.g. aor. ptcpl. νικάhας **33** 3.

7. The spelling <σ> for <θ> in sources (epigraphic, and Aristoph. *Lysistrata*) dating to the late V or early IV cent. indicates that [tʰ] had moved early to the fricative [θ] in Lac., as in Modern Gk. ([s] was the only fricative of classical Gk., which explains the choice of sign). It is difficult to know how early this change had occurred: but however Alkman pronounced the sound, it is unlikely that he would have used the spelling <σ> (which must be a later addition to the text).

§40. Morphology/Syntax

CHARACTERISTIC FEATURES OF WEST GREEK

1. Personal endings: 1 plur. -μες (cf. Lat. -*mus*). Athematic 3 plur. imperf. and aor. forms such as ἔθεν, ἔδον < *ἔθε-ντ, ἔδο-ντ are retained in most WGk. dialects (cf. §32.1).

2. Contracted future in -σῶ (-σέω). Built with a suffix -*se*-: ἐσσεῖσθαι < ἐσ-σέ-εσθαι **45** 12 (cf. §24.2*a*).

3. (*a*) Athematic infin. -μεν (cf. §36.3). Crete (ἤμην **53** 25) and insular Doric (Rhod. -μειν **49** 5) have a lengthened vowel.[1]

(*b*) Thematic infin. -ην (by §38.3), -ειν in 'mild' Doric (§23.1): also -εν (a morphological innovation) in insular Doric (not Rhodes), Heraklea, and eastern Argolic.[2]

4. Verbs in -ζω were built originally on velar or dental stems. These gave an aor. (and fut.) stem in -ξ- and -σ- respectively; WGk., Thess. and Arc.-Cyp. generalized -ξ- (Att.-Ion. preserved the difference): παρετάξωνσι 7 28 (aor. subj.).

5. Inherited τοί, ταί (article, nom. plur.) retained (but Crete shares οἱ, αἱ with Att.-Ion. and Arc.-Cyp., §32.6).

6. αἰ, 'if', and particle κα. The normal ordering αἰ τίς κα is different from Att.-Ion. ἐάν τις.

7. Conjunctions and temporal adverbs: WGk. dialects (and Boe.) typically have -κα in place of -τε in ὅτε, τότε, πότε.

8. ποτί (προτί at Argos) corresponding to Att.-Ion. πρός (§28.7): so also Thess., Boe.

NORTH-WEST GREEK:

9. The mediopass. ptcpl. of *e*-stem verbs ends in -ημενοι (or -ειμενοι, §38.3): the *e*-vowel has been extended from the infin. -ησθαι (-εισθαι) < *-ε-εσθαι. (It is not evidence of athematic inflection.)[3]

10. A shortened form of the thematic dat. sing. in -οι is found as a variant (with -ωι) across the NW Gk. area (cf. §28.10), but identifiable only after adoption of the Ionic alphabet. There is evidence that this variant reflects a less formal variety of the language.[4]

[1] Ruijgh (1988: 139).   [2] Ruijgh (1988: 139, n. 43).   [3] Méndez Dosuna (1985: 502 f.).   [4] Méndez Dosuna (1985: 453–6).

§41. *Pamphylian*

The history of the Greek dialect spoken in Pamphylia is obscure; inscriptions are poorly preserved and difficult to understand. It seems to have affinities with Arc.-Cyp., West Greek, and (to a lesser extent) Aeolic. There may have been an Achaean presence in Pamphylia in the Mycenaean or sub-Mycenaean period: but the preservation of -τι (§10.8) points to a fundamental West Greek stratum in the language (Aspendos was said to have been settled from Argos, and Rhodian colonies stretched up the western side of Lycia). Whatever the prehistory, contacts with Crete and Cyprus may also explain certain features shared with these dialects. The Greek-speakers of Pamphylia were surrounded by Luwian languages (Lycian, Sidetic, Cilician), and some degree of influence is to be expected from these.

Phonology

§42. Vowels

1. The raising of ϵ to ι before a nasal (§26.1, Arc.-Cyp.).
2. The raising of o to υ at word end (§26.2, Arc.-Cyp.).
3. ϵ is lowered to α before ρ (§38.4, NW Gk.).
4. ϵ is written ι (plus a glide) before α and o (§26.6, Cyp.).
5. Evidence for nasalized vowels from the sequence -V*n*C-, §43.3 (§26.8, Cyp.).

§43. Consonants

1. Inherited $^{*}w$ is retained in most positions: perhaps as a fricative (it seems to have merged with $^{*}b$). See on $\Sigma\epsilon\lambda\acute{\upsilon}\text{W}\iota\iota\upsilon\varsigma$ **63** 1.
2. Retention of inherited -$\tau\iota$ (verbal endings and numerals), as in WGk.
3. ν is not written before consonants (as in Cyp.), which points to nasalized vowels: e.g. $\pi\epsilon\delta\epsilon$ [pēde] **63** 5. Also absent at word end in many cases.

§44. Morphology/Syntax

CHARACTERISTIC FEATURES OF PAMPHYLIAN

1. Dat. plur. in -$o\iota\sigma\iota$/-$\alpha\iota\sigma\iota$ (as in Ionic, Lesb., early Att. and early Argolic): §32.14.
2. Prepositions meaning 'from' are constructed with the dat.-loc., as in Arc.-Cyp. (§28.5).
3. Imper. 3 plur. in -$o\delta\upsilon$ < -$o\nu\tau o\nu$ (cf. §32.3), similar to the Lesb. form (§36.8).
4. The sigmatic aor. has thematic endings (i.e. those of the imperfect): $\acute{\epsilon}\beta\bar{o}\lambda\acute{\alpha}\sigma\epsilon\tau\upsilon$ **63** 8. There are also examples in Homer ($\delta\acute{\upsilon}\sigma\epsilon\tau o$, etc.).

§45. LITERARY LANGUAGES

Greek literary language forces us to recognize that no society uses the same linguistic variety in oral literary texts, in written texts (whether literary or not), and in verbal interaction (the normal spoken language). A strict division between poetry and prose, fundamental in modern western thinking, has had an unhelpful effect on the appreciation of the literary languages of Greece (including the koiné). The various genres of ancient literature were all written in *koinai*: there is no a priori reason to expect that a historian would attempt to write his prose in the local vernacular any more than a poet would do so. It has long been recognized that poets wrote in a dialect associated with the genre they were working in, rather than their native idiom: the prose genres too were marked by a characteristic (and 'artificial') mixture of dialect forms. This implies not that all writers working within a tradition use an identical idiom, but that they refer back to a common idiom which their own production both represents and expands.

§46. Epic

Of all the literary dialects, the language of epic (Homer and Hesiod) offers the most perplexing mixture of real and invented elements. It seems likely that *Iliad* and *Odyssey* took a form close to the one we are familiar with between the late VIII and early VII cent., though there is some dispute as to whether they were committed to writing contemporaneously or later (following a period of oral transmission). They represent the climax of many centuries of oral epic composition, and this is reflected in the peculiar language of the poetry. It is a literary dialect (*Kunstsprache*) which contains elements from different dialects and different periods, and some which were never spoken at all but created by the bards within the tradition.[1]

It has generally been assumed that the two Homeric poems took more or less their final form in the eastern Ionic dialect area, since the prevailing dialectal affiliation (and hence the last phase of composition) reflects an Ionian context. This does not exclude the possibility that the tradition moved from Ionia to Euboea at the end of this phase, which might explain a few late features that seem to have entered from a mainland (Boeotian or West Greek) dialect.[2] Underlying the Ionic cast of the language there is also a significant component of Aeolic forms: analysis of these forms has convinced most scholars that the epic tradition was taken over by Ionian bards from neighbouring Aeolis, and that there was, therefore, an Aeolic period or phase of composition immediately prior to the Ionic phase within which the Homeric *Iliad* and *Odyssey* took shape.[3] However, a number of forms (e.g. nom. plur. of the article τοί besides οἱ) could just as well be archaisms as Aeolic forms, and this has given rise to an alternative theory that all Aeolic forms could actually be archaic forms in disguise,[4] rather than remnants of a phase when the whole tradition was in Aeolic. Finally, a small number of 'Achaean' elements (i.e. items shared with Arc.-Cyp. or Myc., §25) points to the earliest phase of epic poetry in the Mycenaean Bronze Age; this would be a continuation of the tradition of heroic song that the Greeks shared with most other Indo-European peoples. Much of the reconstructed history of the Homeric text is educated guesswork, and almost every detail is disputed, but the broad outline of a long tradition of oral formulaic hexameter poetry on Greek soil is necessary to account for its peculiarities.

Hesiod represents a slightly different epic tradition (didactic and wisdom literature), but the language of *Theogony* and *Works and Days* is the same Ionic literary dialect as the Homeric texts, even though the poet tells us he is Boeotian. Most scholars believe that the Hesiodic poems are a little later than the *Iliad* and *Odyssey*.[5]

The language of epic was enormously influential on all subsequent Greek literature, including 'sub-literary' production (epitaphs, etc.). It is not necessarily the case that the text was known in all regions in the same form as the vulgate which has come down to us: there may have been local variation in the surface phonology.

1. Epic diction: repetition and variation

Since the fieldwork on the oral poetry of the Balkans by Milman Parry in the 1930s it has been recognized that the structural and linguistic peculiarities of Greek epic poetry are indicators of oral composition.[6] The archaisms in the text derive from the use of traditional formulae by the bards: the tradition retains metrically useful formulae, but modernizes where it can (i.e. when it can do so without upsetting the metre). Most of the language reflects the most recent phases of composition (the Greek 'Dark Ages'); an increasingly small proportion goes back to the earlier periods.[7] The structural units which are generally identified can be set out in ascending order as follows (the categories are not necessarily distinct, or even complete):

(*a*) The traditional epithet: one epithet per person (or object) per metrical position: ξανθὸς Μενέλαος **67** 147.

(*b*) The formula: fills a slot in the line: εἶπε πρὸς ὃν μεγαλήτορα θυμόν **66** 98, τὴν [τὸν] δ᾿ ἀπαμειβόμενος προσέφη **67** 147.

(*c*) The line: **66** 98 (over ten times in *Il.* and *Od.*).

(*d*) The 'type' scene (arrival, deliberation, libation, meal, reception of visitor, etc.).

2. Homeric dialect: phonology
On the whole, in line with Ionic features outlined in §§30–1.

(*a*) Inherited [w]. Digamma is not written in the extant manuscripts of Homer. By the end of the VIII cent. the consonant [w] had disappeared from the spoken language of Ionia, but its original presence in Homeric formulae can be demonstrated by hundreds of examples (over 80% of cases where [w] would be reconstructed).[8] In most of these the loss of [w] produces apparent hiatus (I) between two vowels:

Il. 7. 296: αὐτὰρ ἐγὼ κατὰ I ἄστυ μέγα Πριάμοιο I ἄνακτος (earlier Ϝάστυ . . . Ϝάνακτος).

See also on τις (Ϝ)εἴπῃσι **66** 106 (original [w] has lengthened the preceding syllable).

(*b*) Some Aeolic features: πίσυρες beside Ion. τέσσαρες (initial labiovelar: §35.1), ἐρεβεννός, 'dark' < *ἐρεβεσ-νός (§23.6).

3. Homeric dialect: morphology
On the whole in line with Ionic features outlined in §32.

(*a*) Archaic features: gen. sing. -οιο and -οο (the latter spelled -ου in the vulgate), a 'dat.-loc.' ending -φι (§11.4), ὁ ἡ τό with demonstrative and relative force, optional augment (cf. §14.2), athem.

3 plur. ἔσταν etc. besides ἔστησαν (§32.1), short-vowel subjunctive ἴομεν, etc. (εἶμι, *ibo*), tmesis (§24.6).

(*b*) Some Aeolic features: dat. plur. in -εσσι (§36.4), plur. pronouns ἄμμε, etc. (§§32.5b, 34.2), athem. infin. δόμεν, δόμεναι, etc. (§36.2), vowel-stem verbs καλήμεναι etc. (§36.1).

(*c*) Some late mainland (Att./Boe./WGk.) features: κεῖντο (an analogical rebuilding of κέατο), τε(ϝ)ίν (both the stem *τεϝ- and the dat. -ιν are WGk./Boe.), and others.[9]

4. Homeric dialect: lexicon

(*a*) Archaic words, some of which may represent the oldest strata (perhaps 'Achaean', §46 above) in the poetry: αἶσα, δῶμα, ἦμαρ, ἰδέ, πτόλις (**8** 1), φάσγανον.

(*b*) The dialect mixture gave rise to convenient doublets: ἄν/κε(ν), πόλις/πτόλις, etc.

5. Homeric dialect: 'artificial' forms

This merely refers to forms which were produced analogically by the tradition over centuries of composition, and which were never heard in any dialect. Thus, for example, the extension of the ending (suffix) -φι (§11.4), or the diektasis of εὐχετόωνται **67** 139 (note ad loc.).

6. Hesiodic dialect

The language of Hesiod is very similar to that of Homer, and was composed in the same Ionic-based oral tradition.

The most striking feature in which Hes. differs from Hom. is the presence of around eight instances of an *a*-stem acc. plur. with a short vowel (cf. τροπάς **68** 663, δεινάς **68** 675): a roughly equal number have a long vowel.[10] If this is an 'artificial' feature of the diction, poetic innovation may have favoured the retention of a short *a*-stem acc. plur. (*a*) as an extension of Hom. formulae such as τροπαὶ ἠελίοιο (nom. τροπαί is ⏑⏑ before a vowel), and (*b*) on the analogy of the C-stem. acc. plur. in -ᾰς. But it has been plausibly argued that the feature has its roots in the language of 'mainland' Greek epic (it is found in Thess., Arc., and several WGk. dialects); in this case the absence of short-vowel *o*-stem acc. plur. forms could be explained by supposing that the imbalance arose in dialects which generalized -ᾰνς, -ονς (§23.9) and then extended -ᾰνς to the athem.

declension (cf. θυγατέραυς **53** 42). In poetry, however, the replacement of athem. -ᾰς by -ᾰνς before a vowel would have been blocked by the metre: thus -ᾰς became the prevocalic poetic variant, and spread to the *a*-stems as a handy doublet for new compositional contexts.[11]

[1] Palmer (1980: 83–101), Fowler (2004). [2] West (1988): cf. §46.3*c*
[3] See Janko (1994), West (1988). [4] So Horrocks (1987), Wyatt (1992).
[5] Janko (1982). [6] See Lord (1960: 3–12). [7] *Oral composition*: Lord
(1960), with rival interpretions by Nagy (1995) and Janko (1998). *History*:
Dickinson (1986). [8] Janko (1982: 46–7). [9] Cf. the list of West (1988:
167–8). [10] See Edwards (1971: 141-65). [11] Cassio (2006).

§47. Lyric Poetry: The Archaic Period (VII–early V cent. BC)

The term 'lyric' often subsumes all the poetry which survives from the centuries following the introduction of alphabetic writing to Greece down to Pindar (518–*c*.445 BC). This classificatory imprecision is partly due to ancient vagueness on the subject, and partly to modern difficulties with the term lyric, and, in general, with ancient notions of genre. By way of shorthand lyric has been described as the poetry which follows epic, a characterization which needs to be treated with caution since it is not clear when Homeric and Hesiodic epic took their final form, and since other epic poetry (including the 'Homeric Hymns') continued to be composed. Moreover, many of the disparate genres which constitute 'lyric' poetry must have been sung for centuries before the alphabetic period and the masters familiar to us from then. Lyric poetry was eclipsed (in Athens at any rate) by drama: if more non-dramatic poetry had survived from the V and IV cent. we would doubtless be able to see continuities between archaic and Hellenistic forms.

The poems can be grouped by metre, by dialect, and by the circumstances of performance, where these are known (musical accompaniment, the performers, and the context of performance). A grouping by dialect illustrates the diverse nature of the poetry:

Ionic: (a) poems in elegiac metre (Archilochos, Kallinos, Tyrtaios, Solon)

(b) poems in iambic and trochaic metre (Archilochos, Semonides, Hipponax)
(c) poems in non-stichic sung metres (Anakreon)
(d) poems in hexameters (Hipponax, Xenophanes)

Doric: (a) poems in non-stichic sung metres (Alkman, Stesichoros, Ibykos, Simonides, Bacchylides, Pindar)
(b) poems in hexameters (Alkman)

Lesbian: poems in non-stichic sung metres (Sappho and Alkaios)

In most cases the choice of dialect is determined by the genre (roughly defined as a mixture of metre, theme, and performance context). However, the notion of 'dialect' in this formulation is far from straightforward: exceptions such as Alkman's Doric hexameters (26 *PMG*), or the mixed metre of Archilochos **69**, make a schematic approach impossible. Literary dialect (and its interaction with metre) was clearly a fluid category, and one which developed over time in the hands of individual poets: in this respect Hellenistic poets were heirs to a long tradition of innovation.

1. Ionic: Elegy and Iambos[1]
Writers of elegiac couplets (which allow easy deployment of epic formulae) use a fairly standard epic diction, even when their native dialect is West Greek (Tyrtaios) or Attic (Solon). In their poetry, as in Hesiod's, the dialect of the genre overrode the local dialect. There are some small variations: Kallinos (an Ionian) uses Ionic κῶς, κότε where Tyrtaios and Solon have standard Homeric πῶς.[2] Writers of *iambos*, a colourful Ionian tradition independent of epic, used a literary dialect which was distinctly Ionic, and which more obviously suggested the vernacular; but they borrowed epic items freely when theme or metre suggested this (*iambos* denotes a genre rather than a metre: Archilochos and Semonides wrote poems in both elegiac and iambic/trochaic metre).

2. Doric: choral poetry
There is significant diversity in the Doric diction of surviving poetry, partly owing to the pervasive influence of epic, and also of an Aeolic poetic tradition (the early Lesbian poet Terpander was said to have

worked in Sparta).³ It is difficult to arrive at a satisfactory evaluation of Alkman's dialect owing to the uncertainties in the textual tradition, and the small amount which survives. On the whole it represents Doric with a number of Aeolic and epic elements, to which some later Laconian features have been added.⁴ We do not know enough about either Laconian in the VII cent. or Alkman's autograph to judge how close his literary dialect was to the spoken language. It may have been roughly as close to Laconian vernacular as were Sappho's poems to contemporary Lesbian (that is to say, not particularly close: probably both poets were working within a poetic koiné with an oblique rather than a direct relationship to the vernacular). Stesichoros, a speaker of West Greek, also uses a fairly thorough West Greek diction, but with epic features which reflect the dactylic quality of his metre and his Homeric flavour.

Pindar's language is heavily influenced by epic (much of the vocabulary is Homeric), with a surface phonology that reflects (so far as one can judge by the spelling) the Doric choral tradition. In line with this tradition he includes a number of Lesbian features (in particular Μοῖσα, the pres. ptcpl. in -οισα, the aor. ptcpl. -αις/-αισα, and 3 plur. -οισι): although there are important overlaps between his native Boeotian and WGk. (retention of inherited [a:], etc.), he avoids features associated narrowly with Boe. Following the example of epic, and no doubt of Alkman too, he selects dialect features for his poetic convenience, and this poetic freedom within a basic West Greek phonological frame is what came to be understood as 'literary Doric'. It was further developed (with a continuing diminution of the Doric elements) by the Ionian poets Simonides and Bacchylides.

3. Lesbian: Sappho and Alkaios

Sappho and Alkaios were clearly working within a tradition of Aeolic poetry, one which must have had a long history of interaction with the neighbouring Ionian traditions. As with Alkman, the earliness of these poets, combined with the difficulty of their dialect, makes it very hard to unravel the relationship between the received text and what they might actually have written. Hellenistic scholars put the texts into a form resembling the one that has come down to us (a process which included rewriting the texts in the Ionic alphabet); presumably hyper-Aeolic features go back to this period. The dialect is recognizably Lesbian, but, like the Ionic and Doric literary languages, contains forms from a poetic tradition which do not reflect contemporary vernacular.[5]

[1] Palmer (1980: 105–13); details of phonological and morphological variation are collected at West (1974: 77–111).   [2] Cf. §48.3   [3] Cassio (2005).   [4] Cassio (in press).   [5] A. Bowie (1981: 47–137).

§48. The Classical World: 480–320 BC

The Persian occupation of the Ionian Greek states in the mid VI cent. BC led to a shift in the intellectual centre of gravity in the Greek world, as Ionian thinkers moved west to mainland Greece and Ionia ceased to be the dominant force in Greek thought. Athens had been an important cultural centre in the VI cent. (the Peisistratid tyrants were patrons of the arts), but was distracted by political and constitutional upheaval for much of the period. After the Persian wars (490–79), however, a new-found self-confidence, stable democratic government, and a rapid increase in wealth and political influence through the Delian league led to undisputed Athenian leadership in the artistic and intellectual life of the Greek world.

The Peisistratid appropriation of the Homeric text in the VI cent.[1] reflected the Athenian desire to position themselves as the intellectual heirs to the Ionian tradition—a claim which was, of course, bolstered by ethnic and dialectal affiliations. Ionic had traditionally been the language of literary prose (scientific and artistic, to the extent that the distinction is valid); the Ionian alphabet was prestigious for this reason, and also perhaps because of an association with the Homeric text. Over the course of the V cent. it is clear that Athenian writers switched increasingly to the Ionian alphabet for literary production.[2] More importantly, they forged a new set of literary languages for themselves: in particular, a prose medium which retained the lexical and syntactic influence of Ionic, but which was to be the new literary standard of Attica (and, therefore, the Greek-speaking world), rather than the old language of Ionia.

In the following notes the term 'poetic' is occasionally used to describe vocabulary (less often syntax). Poetic diction is defined in two ways: negatively, the term covers vocabulary and syntax which are excluded from the IV cent. Attic orators, from comedy, and from documentary inscriptions. Aristotle (*Poetics* 22) noted that diction alien to the vernacular is appropriate for literary language (this reflects the different function of poetic language, which 'consists in the maximum foregrounding of the utterance').[3] Descriptively the language is alien because it is archaic, or is at home in a different dialect, or is the creation of a productive *Kunstsprache* (these categories often intersect).

[1] Fowler (2004). [2] Colvin (1999: 92–100), D'Angour (1999). [3] Mukařovský (1932 = 1964: 19).

1. Attic tragedy

The language of tragedy is tied closely to the metre. Passages of dialogue in iambic (occasionally trochaic) metre have a mostly Attic phonology: much of the lexicon and syntax is poetic, i.e. characteristic of Ionic, or Homeric *Kunstsprache*, rather than normal Attic. Phonological features of vernacular Attic which are avoided even in dialogue are -ττ-, and Att. -ρρ- for -ρσ-. It may be that these were avoided in the new high Attic (at least initially) because they are characteristics of Attic which are not shared with eastern Ionic: -ττ- in particular is a feature that Attic shared with Boeotian, and there are reasons for suspecting that the Athenians were keen to dissociate themselves from this particular dialect, even though they were connected by several striking isoglosses.[1] Choral passages are written in lyric metre, and in an idiom which makes a bow to the tradition of the Doric choral tradition (§47.2). In practice much of the Doric flavour of these choral sections, as with Bacchylides, comes from the substitution of ā for Att.-Ion. η, and the contraction of ā + o/ω to ā (§30.2).[2] The proportion of poetic words increases in lyric sections, though many of these reflect epic/Ionic poetry rather than (necessarily) West Greek usage: this of course begs the question of how much of the lexicon of Doric choral poetry was borrowed from, or in common with, epic poetry. Aeschylos uses lexical items associated with Doric (ἀγρέω, καίνω, μείων, μολεῖν, νιν, etc.): he also uses ποτί, but this is found in epic too (so also μείων, μολεῖν). Choral passages are also remarkable for an increase in the syntactic complexity, and for syntactic usages alien to the vernacular (this probably represents a mixture of archaism, dialectal syntax, and poetic licence).[3] The language of tragic lyric, however, does *not* include the substitution of ω/η for ου/ει (the spurious diphthongs), third plur. -ντι, or Aeolic-looking participles of the -οισα type (seen in Alkman and Pindar). In the field of morphology the most obvious categories are missing, such as the potential particle κα, the 1 plur. -μες, the athem. infin. -μεν, and the vowel-stem 'Doric' future. Apocope occurs, mostly in compounds and mostly with ἀνά, but this is more likely to reflect epic usage.

The last plays of Euripides were written around half a century after the death of Aeschylos, and it is unsurprising that there should have been some developments in the language of tragedy during this period. From a linguistic perspective the developments are not wildly significant: a slight relaxing of the strictness of the metrical scheme, and a greater willingness to admit colloquial idioms into the poetry accompany a general movement towards a blurring of the boundaries between tragedy and comedy. Euripidean language is in general less markedly poetic: the syntax is less dense, and the lexicon is often (not always) less rarified. There is a parodic comparison of the style and diction of Aeschylos and Euripides in Aristophanes, *Frogs* 795–1478.

[1] Colvin (2004).   [2] Björck (1950).   [3] Bers (1984).

2. Aristophanes

The language and structure of Old Comedy are largely parasitic on tragedy. Spoken passages are written in iambic (or trochaic) metre, and choral passages (which become increasingly rare) are written in a comic approximation of tragic lyric; however, once allowance is made for the constraints of the metre, the ordinary conversational language is Attic. Of course, Aristophanic language has to be treated with some caution since the playwright is constantly engaged in word-play and parody of other language registers (literary genres and individual or group speech styles); at the same time, the skill with which he evokes a range of linguistic repertoires makes comedy an unmatched source of information on social varieties of Attic.[1] The freedom with which he invents new compounds is both an example of the liveliness of comic language, and also parodies the compounds of serious poetry.

The extant Aristophanic plays were preserved (through the Byzantine school curriculum), in spite of their content, because of their usefulness as a source of 'pure' (i.e. unpoetic) Attic. It is generally assumed that the appearance of a lexeme in comedy or in the IV cent. orators guarantees that it existed in a least one variety of contemporary Attic (though not necessarily or even probably the lowest vernacular levels).

[1] Dover (1987), Willi (2003a).

3. Herodotos

The language of Herodotos (born c.485 BC) has received much attention from a stylistic perspective, and in recent years has been the subject of useful pragmatic analysis. Nevertheless, on a purely linguistic level (features of dialect and poetry) his text remains peculiar to look at owing to the large number of apparently epic forms, some of which seem to be 'eye dialect' (an orthographic device intended to give a dialectal character to the text without necessarily being intended to affect the oral performance), and some of which do not (lexicon, morphology, phrasing). A large part of the problem stems from uncertainties in the transmission of the text: the suspicion that we do not have what Herodotos wrote, but the result of embellishment by later (Hellenistic) editors. To give a rough hierarchy of examples:

(a) οὔνομα in the Hom. text denotes a purely metrical lengthening. Its appearance in Hdt. begs the question: was the digraph OY (§23.1) in regular use in late V cent. Ionia to denote [o:] ? On the balance of epigraphic evidence this seems unlikely, though not impossible. If in fact Hdt. was responsible for the spelling, is it conceivable that he intended [o:] to be pronounced in reading the text? This also seems very unlikely.

(b) βασιλέες could be a legitimate spelling for βασιλεῖς (assuming the digraph EI was not yet in use for [e:]), and it is easy to imagine a contracted pronunciation. But it is less easy to see what lies behind εὐδοκιμέειν (83 37. 2), unless it is a later editorial 'correction' of εὐδοκιμέεν, where -έεν (on the same principle) was an early spelling of -$\epsilon\hat{\iota}\nu$. Compare the spelling $\kappa\acute{\epsilon}\epsilon\tau\alpha\iota$ (2. 164. 1) of a historical diphthong (spelled $\kappa\epsilon\hat{\iota}\tau\alpha\iota$ at 7. 198. 2).

(c) Forms such as $\delta\alpha\iota\tau\upsilon\mu\acute{o}\nu\epsilon\sigma\sigma\iota$ are different from the above: both the word and the morphology are Homeric. It can hardly have been introduced by later editors, though it is conceivable (perhaps unlikely) that the dative ending was Homerized.

There are also pseudo-Ionic forms in the text such as $\alpha\dot{\upsilon}\tau\acute{\epsilon}\omega\nu$ (masc.), i.e. artificial forms which do not occur in the Homeric text. Historically, of course, they are neither more nor less pseudo-Ionic than $o\check{\upsilon}\nu o\mu\alpha$.

Halikarnassos was a Doric city, recently absorbed into the orbit of the Ionian world, and it is perfectly possible that Herodotos' native idiom was West Greek rather than Ionic. This is impossible to know, but in any case his historiographic *Kunstsprache* cannot closely reflect his vernacular. Nor is there any reason to expect that it would, since vernacular was no more suited to artistic prose than to epic or lyric poetry. Herodotos needed an appropriate linguistic frame for his 'epic' history: in addition to the tradition of historical, ethnographic, and scientific prose in Ionia, epic language, as the earliest Greek koiné, must have been a tempting reservoir for a universal prose language.[1] It is difficult to be sure whether his decision to use κ- rather than π-forms ($\kappa\hat{\omega}s$, $\kappa\acute{o}\tau\epsilon$, etc.) marks a break with epic, since it is possible that the Homeric texts that he was familiar with (at least in his youth) contained these forms. The epic heritage of Herodotos may go some way in explaining the character of the text: as he says in his proem (1. 1), his history is an *apodeixis* of deeds which require *kleos*: the emphasis is on performance, and 'saying and writing are treated as parallel speech-acts'[2] (while Thucydides, by contrast, is writing a $\kappa\tau\hat{\eta}\mu\alpha$ ... $\dot{\epsilon}s$ $\alpha\dot{\iota}\epsilon\acute{\iota}$ (1. 22. 4), a written text oriented on the absent reader).

[1] Leumann (1950: 303–15), Cassio (1996b: 147–50). [2] Nagy (1990: 219, and in general 213–49), Griffiths (2006: 135–6).

4. Hippokratic corpus

The Hippokratic corpus consists of around sixty works, most of which were written between the late V and late IV centuries BC.

Although *Airs, Waters, Places* has traditionally been ascribed to Hippokrates himself, it is difficult to identify 'genuine' works within the large corpus of medical literature associated with the name. Hippokrates was born on Kos around 460 BC: all of the material under his name is written in Ionic, however. This doubtless reflects the tradition of scientific prose in Ionia, especially in ethnography, but also to some extent in medicine (the ouput of the famous medical school at Dorian Knidos, near to Kos on the mainland, was also in Ionic). There does not appear to have been a tradition of literary Doric prose in the eastern Greek world: and since Hippokrates spent most of his working life in and around Thessaly, he will in any case have been writing for an international rather than a local audience.

5. Thucydides

The language of Thucydides (*c*.460–400 BC) is notoriously challenging to read. This is due to a combination of factors, including: long and structurally complex sentences; innovative uses of Greek syntax; and a striving after brevity or compression of phrasing. In dialect terms Thucydides is writing 'international' or expanded Attic: i.e. a form of Attic much influenced by the lexicon and innovative morphology of Ionic prose. He clearly made a decision to position his history in the Ionian tradition of technical or scientific prose: in this respect his language is an important precursor of the koiné. Part of the reason his language is difficult is that he is trying, perhaps in deliberate opposition to Herodotos, to create an appropriate idiom for his vision of scientific historiography. Not all of his innovations survived in Attic; nevertheless, his influence on the history of prose can be clearly seen in the work of the IV cent. masters Plato and Demosthenes. Logical antithesis is a characteristic of both the narrative and the speeches, but, in spite of a debt to the rhetorician Gorgias (*c*.485–380 BC), he goes to some pains to avoid the obvious symmetries and musical tricks associated with that name.

6. Xenophon

The prose of Xenophon (*c*.427–354 BC) marks a divergence from the line which leads to the Attic masters of the IV cent., but in the history of the Greek language it occupies a significant place. Although a native of Athens, Xenophon spent most of his life in an international or panhellenic milieu. He led a mixed army of Greek mercenaries (the 'ten thousand') back from Mesopotamia to the Aegean in 401–399 BC; after his return he worked with the Spartan king Agesilaos and was banished by Athens until 365. During his exile he lived in the Peloponnese near Elis, and at Corinth. As a historiographer he saw himself as inheriting the mantle of Thucydides, and his language partly reflects this: he writes in the expanded literary Attic which Thucydides had pioneered. We see in his writings the emergence of a pedestrian but lucid 'all-purpose' style, inadequate for the needs of a Plato but a competent medium of everyday communication. In other words, Xenophon is a forerunner of the literary koiné. His language is unusual by the standards of 'classical' Attic prose: he admits words and constructions which are not found elsewhere before the Hellenistic period, and his long association with Doric speakers seems to have led to a degree of dialect mixing which is evident in his writing.

§49. Hellenistic Poetry: Theokritos and Kallimachos

The language of passages **87** and **88** is a playful mixture of Homeric and poetic language with more informal or colloquial diction. Theokritos was a native of Syracuse, a Doric-speaking city in Sicily. The idylls (εἰδύλλια, 'vignettes') deal with many themes other than the purely bucolic, as **87** shows. Of the surviving hexameter poems, most are written in a predominantly Doric version of epic language, and a handful are in epic language; there are in addition four poems written in (archaic literary) Lesbian dialect and metre. The nature of the Doric dialect that he uses has been much disputed, a debate not helped by the usual textual problems which apply to dialect texts.[1] We have almost no dialect texts from Syracuse, which makes it difficult to judge how much Syracusan there is in the mixture: there was, however, a literary tradition at Syracuse in genres close to Theokritos (Epicharmos and Sophron), and this may have played a role. There was also a Doric vernacular in Ptolemaic Alexandria: there were many immigrants from Cyrene in the city, and from elsewhere in the Doric-speaking world (as **87** shows), but since we have little evidence for this variety it is again difficult to judge to what extent Theokritos based his poetic idiom on it. The most easily identifiable elements in his language are epic, and choral/lyric Doric poetry (Alkman, Stesichoros, epinician, etc.).

Kallimachos was a native of Cyrene, a West Greek-speaking colony of Thera, but spent his working life in the cosmopolitan city of Alexandria. His *Hymns* represent a reworking of the Homeric form, and are saturated in Homeric diction. He claims that his blurring of poetic and linguistic boundaries (πολυείδεια or ποικιλία) attracted criticism: in the fragmentary remains of *Iambos* 13 (lines 17–18) an imaginary critic specifically attacks his unconventional mixing of dialect. It is difficult to judge how unusual this was in Hellenistic literature (Theokritos' language is equally innovative). Another feature associated with Hellenistic poetry in general and Kallimachos in particular is the use of arcane (and regional) words. Most of his large output is lost or fragmentary: apart from the *Hymns* only a selection of his epigrams survives.

¹ Ruijgh (1984), Molinos Tejada (1990).

§50. POST-CLASSICAL PROSE: THE KOINÉ

The Greek-speaking world after Alexander the Great is more or less diglossic. For the first time in Greek history there is a common Greek language, which remains the standard for the next several centuries while becoming increasingly distant from the everyday spoken language. This is the era of the koiné (ἡ κοινὴ διάλεκτος), a term which probably dates to the beginnings of Alexandrian textual and grammatical activity in the III/II cent. BC. This common language was contrasted (*a*) with foreign languages, and (*b*) with the classical dialects Attic, Ionic, Aeolic, and Doric. It has proved difficult, however, to specify exactly which variety of the language should be called 'koiné'. One variety can be immediately excluded, and that is the spoken vernacular: the language spoken by most people most of the time. This may seem surprising: there are two reasons for it. First, the ancient writers ignored the vernacular in discussing language, and probably thought of it (if at all) as a decayed, corrupt, and impoverished version of the true Greek language. Secondly, the Greek world stretched over Greece, Asia Minor, the Near East, and beyond: there must have been many vernaculars over such a large region and extended time period, and it would be odd to refer to them as a single common variety (at the lowest social level they are not likely to have been all mutually intelligible).

Accordingly, two contenders for the title of koiné are commonly proposed: the dialect employed by prose writers of the Hellenistic/ Roman periods, such as Polybios and Plutarch,[1] and the highest 'code' spoken by the urban elite in formal situations.[2] These are both *koinai* in the sense that they are supra-regional standards which allowed communication between an educated elite. A problem with the first definition is that it is narrow, excluding prose which should historically be described as koiné (the Septuagint, documentary inscriptions, letters, etc.). The second is difficult for the simple reason that we have no access to the spoken language.

We shall therefore treat the koiné as an abstract quantity: an ideal which united the Greek-speaking world in the literary and educational heritage of Greece, rather than defining it as something that emerged from the mouth (or pen) of a particular speaker on a particular occasion. The concrete manifestations of koiné (written or spoken) might be 'higher' or 'lower' on a scale of formality, proximity to the classical language, etc. The reality of the koiné lay in the social psychology of the community: the sense that the Greek world was united by a common language which all educated people aspired to (with varying degrees of success). In the Hellenistic period there is no sense that koiné was inferior to Attic, Ionic, etc., although this attitude does emerge in the Roman (Imperial) period. A good modern analogy for this situation is modern standard Arabic:[3] this, like the koiné, is based on a classical corpus (the *Qur'ân* and early poetry) and reinforces a perception of common ethnicity and culture. It is the language of literature and formal written communication; and it can provide a medium of spoken communication between speakers from different areas of the Arabic-speaking world (there is of course a continuum between the standard and the vernaculars, and speakers may modify their language just far enough to allow efficient communication, rather than switching to the 'highest' form).[4]

The written language in the koiné period does of course give some insight into the contemporary development of the Greek language: but for the most part the orthography is fossilized and the grammar (morphology and syntax) is based on the classical language. It is extremely difficult to trace the details of the evolution of spoken Greek in the various regions of the Hellenistic world.

[1] Meillet (1929: 253), Brixhe–Hodot (1993: 20).   [2] Brixhe (1987: 22). [3] Versteegh (2002).   [4] Cf. Mitchell (1980).

§51. The Beginning and the End of the Koiné

The koiné is essentially an expanded, international variety of Attic, heavily influenced by Ionic.[1] Its roots go back to Athens in the period following the Persian wars (§48), as the city became the dominant cultural and political force in the Aegean. Both the 'high' (literary) and the 'low' (vernacular) strands of Hellenistic Greek (§50) can be traced to this period. On the one hand, high literature and culture in Athens came under increasing Ionian influence: literary prose and poetry used Ionic words and inflections, and the educated elite started to adopt some Ionic idioms in speech. On the other, the Athenian empire made Athens a hub of trade and military activity, with a high degree of interaction between Athenians and their Ionian allies; there is no doubt that the cosmopolitan character of the city (which the 'Old Oligarch' complains about in a famous passage)[2] left its mark on the language of the working urban population (many of whom will have been θῆτες, the lowest naval class).

The new international Attic was apparently adopted as the official language of the Macedonian court in the IV cent., as the expansionist Macedonian kingdom sought to position itself for a leading role in Greek affairs. Since it had become the language of education and literary prose, it was a natural choice as a panhellenic medium of administration and lingua franca.

It is difficult to say when the koiné ends. The linguistic culture of Greek-speakers underwent a significant shift in the I–II cent. AD, when the elite made an effort to emulate classical Attic, and koiné became, by comparison, a disfavoured term. This movement is known as Atticism, and the cultural context as the Second Sophistic. Nevertheless, at less exalted literary levels the koiné persisted as the general language of communication until the end of late antiquity.

[1] Browning (1969: 27–58), Palmer (1980: 174–98), Horrocks (1997: 32–70). [2] A writer of *c*.425 BC: ps.-Xenophon, *Ath. Pol*. 2. 7–8.

Phonology

The selection of variants from Attic and Ionic:

1. In most lexical items, and in most authors, -σσ- is preferred to Att. -ττ- (§31.4).
2. Att. retention of [aː] after [e, i, r] is the norm (§30.3). This combined with the preceding led to the hybrid form (Doric- or Aeolic-looking) πράσσω.
3. -ρσ- is retained in most words (§31.5): but θαρρῶ.

§52. Greek Phonology in the Hellenistic Period

Since the orthography is frozen it is difficult to trace precisely the phonological changes that were undoubtedly taking place in the vernacular. We may speculate whether in the *recital* of formal literary texts an archaizing pronunciation was adopted. There are spelling errors in less formal documents (inscriptions and papyri) which give an indication of the phonology of the writer. The development is usually (but not always) in the direction of modern Greek: since the modern Greek language is a continuation of just one of the many varieties which constituted the vernacular koiné, it is to be expected that some regional features are not continued in any known variety of the modern language.

In general the phonetic and phonological developments of the Attic-based vernacular were as follows. It is commonly assumed that many of the vowel changes were under way in Attic by the early IV cent.[1]

§53. Vowels

1. The pitch accent moves towards a stress accent, and distinctive vowel length is lost.
2. The front vowels ῑ [i:] and ει [e̩:] merge as [i], and are later (II cent. AD) joined by η [ɛ:].
3. ου [o̩:] > [u].
4. The diphthongs [ai] > [ɛ], [oi] > [ü].
5. The second element of the diphthongs [au], [eu] becomes a fricative: [af], [ef].
6. The second element of the long diphthongs [a:i], [e:i], [o:i] disappears.

§54. Consonants

1. Voiced stops β, δ, γ become fricatives [v], [ð], [ɣ].
2. Aspirated stops φ, θ, χ, become fricatives [f], [θ], [x].
3. The affricate/cluster ζ becomes a simple voiced fricative [z].
4. The aspirate disappears (psilosis): §23.10.
5. Final -*n* becomes weak or non-existent.

[1] Teodorsson (1974), Brixhe–Hodot (1993: 15 f.), Horrocks (1997: 102–7): against this Threatte (1980).

§55. Morphology/Syntax

Some characteristic features of Greek in the Hellenistic period:
1. Anomalous verbs such as οἶδα are regularized (3 plur. οἴδασι): cf. **21** 10. The gradual elimination of athematic verbs continues; εἰμί (*sum*) is transferred to the middle: εἶμαι (past ἤμην, ἦτο).
2. The middle starts to fade as a separate category; so too the optative.
3. In the aor., thematic endings are replaced by athematic ones: εἶπον → εἶπα. The characteristic -σα- marker of the aor. spreads; in the 3 plur. a mixing of the competing forms -ον and -σαν produced -οσαν.
4. The -σαν ending of the 3 plur. spreads to the 3 plur. imper.: ἔστωσαν.
5. The distinction between aor. and perf. starts to break down.

6. Nouns with an awkward morphology are replaced: e.g. ὗς (χοῖρος, and cf. **97** 3), ναῦς (πλοῖον). In some cases an easier (dialect) form was selected: λεώς → λαός.

§56. *Lexicon*

The lexicon of Hellenistic Greek is in many ways the area in which the differences from classical Attic are most striking; however, none of the developments below is new to the koiné.

1. A large proportion of the words were originally at home in Ionic: there are a number of reasons for this. The literary koiné (e.g. of historiography) aligned itself with the tradition of scientific prose, where, as we have seen, Ionic was always extremely influential. Secondly, the importance of Ionians in the hellenization of Asia Minor explains why a large number of Ionicisms entered the common language on a spoken level.

2. Some literary prose authors (notably Polybios) use words which seem oddly poetic from an Attic perspective. No doubt this is partly due to the presence of dialect words (mostly Ionic) in the constitution of the koiné, words which were confined to poetry in Attic (but vernacular elsewhere). Another reason is the artificial nature of the literary koiné: writers drew on the lexical resources of the classical past, and this sometimes included the poets (especially epic).

3. The language is enriched by borrowings: particularly from Latin, but also from other languages in the case of regional standards (such as Egypt).

4. New forms were created by derivation:
(a) Prepositional compounds in the case of verbs (often with multiple preverbs: e.g. προσαπελογίζοντο **65** 22).
(b) New verbs by means of derivational suffixes: e.g. -άζω, -ίζω, -εύω.
(c) New substantives by means of derivational suffixes: e.g. fem. -ισσα, abstracts in -μα, -ία, and adjs. in -ικός. Diminutive forms, which play a huge role in later Gk. morphology, start to appear in the written language in significant numbers.

5. Semantic shift
This is normal in all languages: thus, for example, φθάνω, 'I antici-

pate' → 'I arrive', δόξα, 'reputation' → 'glory'. Religious sects are particularly prone to investing words with a specific new significance, and this is of course to be found in Septuagint and New Testament Greek.

§57. Post-Classical Literary Prose

The distinction between literary prose of the Hellenistic period and formal inscriptions (such as **65**) is to a large extent artificial. The koiné takes many forms, and although the Atticizing movement of the I cent. AD is presented as a marked shift in attitude, there was always a continuum between 'low' koiné (the letters in **64**) and the 'high' variety which closely emulated classical prose, and which required a high level of education. The move to Atticism could be compared to the return to classicizing Latin in medieval Europe after the reforms of Charlemagne.

1. The Septuagint

A translation of the Pentateuch (*torah*, or first five books of the Hebrew Bible) was made in Alexandria in the III cent. BC. Translation of the rest of the Hebrew Bible was probably complete by the end of the I cent. BC. To refer to the Septuagint (LXX) as though it constitutes a unitary work is misleading, since it is likely that there were competing translations of much of it. According to tradition (documented in the so-called *Letter of Aristeas*), Ptolemy II wrote to the high priest of Jerusalem requesting six elders from each of the twelve tribes to make a translation: he hosted them in Alexandria, where it took them seventy or seventy-two days (hence the name *Septuagint*).[1] In fact the translation was probably undertaken by and for the hellenized Jewish community of Alexandria for whom Hebrew and Aramaic were becoming inaccessible. For obvious religious reasons the Greek text remains close to the Hebrew original: the result is a rather peculiar form of the koiné which has been described as 'translation Greek'. This is an exaggeration if it implies that the morphology and syntax are artificially tied to the Hebrew.[2] It is real Greek of its period, serving a very specific purpose; it is, of course, a far cry stylistically from the Greek of Jewish writers like

Philo or Josephus. The LXX is close but not identical to the Hebrew Bible (the Masoretic text): the Greek version reflects an earlier and slightly different Hebrew textual tradition.

[1] Jobes-Silva (2000: 29–38, 105–17), Fernández Marcos (2000: 3–31, 35–51).   [2] Evans (2001).

2. Polybios

Polybios was born in Arcadia around 210 BC and spent much of his working life in Rome under the patronage of the philhellene Scipio family. He has been called the first authentic representative of the literary koiné.[1] He writes clear and business-like Greek, though his style is dull and wordy; his prose has been compared to Hellenistic documentary inscriptions. His lexicon is innovative (with many previously unattested compounds), with a large Ionic component. Some of his words look poetic from an Attic perspective (§56.2). His morphology is essentially classical: unlike the LXX, for example, there are no 3 plur. forms in -οσαν (§55.3), although he uses εἶπα(ν) besides εἶπον.

[1] Foucault (1972: 5).

3. The New Testament

The NT was written in Greek by people who for the most part had neither the desire nor the *paideia* to write 'high' literary koiné: for evangelical reasons they valued clarity of language and accessibility above elegance. Quotations and allusions to the LXX show that the writers were familiar with a Greek translation of the Hebrew Bible. Although the mother tongue of the gospel writers and Paul was Aramaic, they were perfectly at home in Greek; and when the Greek phrasing recalls Semitic idiom this seems mostly to be in imitation of LXX usage (rather than influence of Aramaic substrate). In other words, we are dealing with the normal bilingualism of educated inhabitants of the Hellenistic world.[1] The Greek is by no means uniform: the four gospels show varying degrees of literary competence and attention to style: the narrative of Luke is generally considered to be the most polished, and that of Mark the least. The letters of Paul are on the whole written rather carefully: he pays

attention to balance, anaphora, and antithesis, and often attains
stylistic elegance or striking rhetorical effect.

¹ Voelz (1984), Wilcox (1984).

4. Atticizing texts

Both Lucian and Galen lived in the II cent. AD, the height of the
return to Atticism.[1] This was an era when public declamation was an
art form admired almost beyond all others. Lucian had an enormous
satirical output: in passage **92** he targets pretentious Atticizers: nevertheless, his own Greek is pure and elegant Attic, and it is noticeable
in this passage that the satire is directed at frauds: those who aim
to make a name as sophisticated speakers while lacking the true
educational preparation. The passage reflects the anxieties that a
diglossic society engenders. Presumably even the most determined
Atticist orator would not have used a form such as λεώς in informal
conversation. Galen also writes good (if inelegant) Atticizing Greek,
but (like Lucian) attacks excesses: elsewhere (*De aliment. facult.* 57.
633) he mocks the ἐπίτριπτον ψευδοπαιδείαν (pestilential pseudo-
erudition) of those who use the old Attic term ῥάφανος for cabbage,
'as though we were in conversation with Athenians of 600 years ago'.
In **93** he insists on the need for good 'common' Greek in scientific
discourse: the presence or absence of Attic seems not to be an issue.

For a sense of the diversity of 'common Greek' it is instructive to
compare these two texts to the Greek of the New Testament, much of
which was written at about the same time.

¹ Swain (1996).

II. Texts with Translation and Commentary

MYCENAEAN

1. Clay tablet from Knossos (KN Ld 571), recording quantities of textiles. *c*.1375 BC. Ventris–Chadwick 214. ▶▶ Melena (1975: 43–4), Chadwick (1976: 150–2), Killen (1979).

.a	*pe-ne-we-ta a-ro₂-a*	**158* 1
.b	*pa-we-a* / *e-qe-si-ja re-u-ko-nu-ka*	TELA³ 25
.a	— $Ϝεντα$ ἀρίοhα	**158* 1
.b	φάρϜεhα / ἐκʷέσια λευκώνυχα	TELA³ 25
.a	{........, of superior quality	**158* 1 *unit*
.b	Cloths	{ 'Follower'-type (?), with white-hook decoration (?) CLOTH 25 *units*

pa-we-a [pʰarweha]: nom. plur. of the neut. noun φάρϜος 'cloth', indicating the subject-matter of the inscription (usually written in larger characters, and conventionally signalled in transcription by the following oblique stroke). Inherited *w* is retained in all positions. At Pylos this word is spelled *pa-we-a₂*, but the sign *a₂* (= *ha*) seems not to have been in widespread use at Knossos. The intervocalic -*h*- comes from -*s*- (stem φάρϜεσ- + ending -α): in later Greek the -*h*- disappeared and the vowels contracted. The other four words are neut. plur. adjectives describing *pa-we-a*.

  (a) **pe-ne-we-ta** contains an unknown root *pe-ne*, but the suffix represents -Ϝεντα (§13): in later Gk. a linking -*o*- vowel was generally inserted between root and suffix.   **a-ro₂-a** is a comp. adj. with stem **ar-yos-* (root *ar* as in later ἀρείων, ἄριστος plus comparative suffix -*yos*, §12).

  (b) **e-qe-si-ja** is an adj. built to the noun *e-qe-ta* [hekʷetaːs], lit.

'follower', which became ἐπέτᾱς in classical Gk. (with development of *kʷ to p on analogy of ἕπομαι, §10.6). Formed from ἐκʷέτ- plus the adj. suffix -ιος (the change -τι- > -σι- has already taken place: §§8, 10.8). In the Linear B tablets from Pylos *e-qe-ta* seems to denote a person of high social status, and it is possible *e-qe-si-ja* here means 'destined for use by an *e-qe-ta*'; but in the Knossos textile tablets it alternates with the adj. *ke-se-nu-wi-ja* (ξένϝια, 'foreign') which suggests the interpretation *e-qe-si-ja*, 'for domestic use' versus 'for export' (in this case we should assume that the *e-qe-ta* 'had something to do with the control, keeping and distribution of domestic cloths', Melena 1975: 45). **re-u-ko-nu-ka** is interpreted as a compound of two Greek stems, λευκ- 'white' and ὀνυχ- 'nail, claw'. The compound seems to refer to a decoration on the textiles, perhaps of white claws or hooks; the adj. *po-ki-ro-nu-ka* (ποικιλο-) is found on other tablets of the same series. (The meaning of the ideogram conventionally numbered 158 is unknown; since it is always followed by the numeral 1, it perhaps signifies a container for the cloths.)

Compare *Odyssey* 24. 277 for textiles as 'gifts' among the Homeric elite.

2. Clay tablet from Knossos (KN Sd 4401) describing a pair of chariots. *c.*1375 BC. Ventris–Chadwick 266. ▶▶ Lejeune (1968), Ruijgh (1976: 15–24), Chadwick (1976: 164–70).

.b   *i-qi-jo / a-ja-me-no e-re-pa-te a-ra-ro-mo-te-me-no po-ni-ki[-jo*

.a   *a-ra-ru-ja a-ni-ja-pi wi-ri-ni-jo o-po-qo ke-ra-ja-pi o-pi-i-ja-pi* CUR [2

.b   ἱκκʷίω / [αἰαι?-]μένω ἐλεφάντει [ἀραρμοτ?-]μένω φοινῑκί[ω

.a   ἀραρυῖα(ι) ἀνίᾱφι ϝρῑνίοις ὀπώκʷοις κεραίᾱφι ὀπιhίᾱφι CUR [2

.b   A pair of chariots decorated with ivory, assembled (?), red,

.a   fitted with reins; with leather blinkers and horn bits: CHARIOT 2 *units*

(On the tablet line .b is under line .a but was written first.)
The subject of the inscription is the opening word *i-qi-jo*, i.e. [ikkʷio:] 'two chariots'. The fem. sing. *i-qi-ja* is used for 'chariot' in

Figure 2 KN Sd 4401 (CMIK)

Mycenaean; it is a collective noun (§24.4) formed from the adj. [ikkʷios], class. ἵππιος. The initial aspirate in class. ἵππος is plausibly explained as the result of the influence of ἅρμα, 'chariot' (Ruijgh 1979): the two were often coordinated in expressions, as in Homer. Note the use of the *q*-series to denote the development of a cluster [*k* + *w*]: elsewhere it is used for the reflexes of the unitary labiovelar phonemes (**kʷ* etc., §10.6). If they sounded similar there was nevertheless a difference in prosodic weight.

(b) **a-ja-me-no**: is a dual pres. ptcpl. pass. agreeing with *i-qi-jo*; stem is unclear, but the context requires some such meaning as 'decorated'. **e-re-pa-te**: instr. sing. of ἐλέφας. The transcription -ει of the ending implies that it was formally identical with the dat., but see §11.2. **a-ra-ro-mo-te-me-no**: medio-pass. participle, containing the stem of ἁρμόττω, 'put together, fit out' (class. ἡρμοσμένος): the reduplication is due to the analogy of *a-ra-ru-ja* (and the unusual spelling also: §4). A pointer to the meaning is the chariot ideogram *241, a fully assembled chariot (without wheels), which always accompanies it (as opposed to ideogram *242, a bare chariot frame). **po-ni-ki-jo**: φοινῑκίω, an adj. formed from φοῖνιξ (i.e. φοῖνικ-ς).

(a) **a-ra-ru-ja**: probably fem. sing. [araruʰya] under the influence of the other tablets of the Sd set which describe only *one* chariot. From **arar-us-ya* (with perf. ptcpl. suffix **-wos/us-*, §36.2): the neut. plur. *a-ra-ru-wo-ha* [ara:rwoha] is also attested in Myc. Notice the intransitive sense of the perfect, verging on a pass., continued in Homeric ἀρηρώς, ἀραρυῖα. **a-ni-ja-pi**: instr. plur. (ἡνία is neut.

plur. in Homer, but a fem. *a*-stem here and in later Greek: perhaps an old collective, §24.4). The aspiration is doubtful: if the word derives from **ansia* then the Linear B form may represent [aːnʰiai] (§10.4); -*φι* continues an IE instr. ending **-bhi(s)*, §11.4   ***o-po-qo*** (instr. plur.): a compound of ὀπί 'upon, at', an alternative form of ἐπί (see Morpurgo Davies 1983), and the stem **okʷ-* (as in Hom. acc. ὦπα, 'eye'); therefore 'things at the eye, blinkers'. *wi-ri-ni-jo* is an adj. of material formed from the stem Ϝρῑν- 'leather'.   ***o-pi-i-ja-pi*** (instr. plur.): a compound of ὀπί and (probably) ἴαφι; if the stem of the latter word is that of ἱμάς, 'thong' (from **si-*), then *o-pi-i-ja-pi* might mean 'with things on the bridle', namely 'bits'. *ke-ra-ja-pi* is instr. plur. (fem.) of κεραιός 'made of horn (κέρας)', §11.4.

3. Clay tablet from Pylos (PY Ad 666), recording a number of young men and boys. *c*.1200 BC. ▶ Chadwick (1988: 45–6, 67).

> *pu-ro a-ke-ti-ra₂-o ko-wo*   VIR 20   *ko-wo* 7
> Πύλος· ἀσκητριάhων κόρϜοι   VIR 20   κόρϜοι 7
> Pylos: sons of the (female) decorators   MAN 20   boys 7

The Aa, Ab, and Ad tablets at Pylos record groups of women and their children. Some of the women are designated as working at specific tasks: one group comprises the *a-ke-ti-ri-ja*=ἀσκητρίαι, '[textile] decorators, finishers' (Killen 1979: 165–7). The Ab series lists rations for the women and children mentioned in the Aa tablets; the Ad series specifies the women by profession and lists their sons.

The first word *pu-ro* gives the location of the group: either a nom. of 'rubric' (unconnected syntactically with the other words) or a loc. [Puloi].   ***a-ke-ti-ra₂-o***: [askeːtriaːhoːn], *a*-stem gen. plur. (the sign *ra₂* [rya] is a variant spelling of *ri-ja*).   ***ko-wo***: Att. κόροι 'sons', but also 'boys'. The Ad tablets are careful to distinguish adults and boys, which may be connected the issue of rations by the palace.

4. Clay tablet from Pylos (PY Ae 303), referring to a group of women. *c*.1200 BC. Ventris–Chadwick 27.

> *pu-ro i-je-re-ja do-e-ra e-ne-ka ku-ru-so-jo i-je-ro-jo*   MUL 14[
> Πύλος· ἱερείας δόhελαι ἕνεκα χρυσοῖο ἱεροῖο   MUL 14[
> Pylos: slaves of the priestess on account of the sacred gold WOMAN 14[

The expression 'slaves of the priestess' occurs several times in the Pylos tablets; it may allude to temple-servants or cult-officials of high standing who had the duty of attending the sacred treasure.
pu-ro: cf. **3** above.   ***i-je-re-ja*** (the regular Myc. form) is interesting: if the word comes from $*ἱερηϝ+$ ya (cf. ἱερεύς $<$ ἱερηϝ-ς) then we might expect to find the spelling $*i$-*je-re-wi-ja* (but see Ruijgh 1967, §212; Ruipérez 1966). On the aspirate see below.   ***do-e-ra***: [dohelai], class. δοῦλαι with loss of -*h*- and contraction.   ***e-ne-ka***: the spelling without -*w*- shows that ἕνεκα cannot be derived from $*ἐνϝεκα$, as formerly supposed (Hom. εἵνεκα must be the result of metrical lengthening).   ***ku-ru-so-jo***: cf. the Homeric gen. sing. ending -οιο ($<$ IE $*$-*osyo*). An early Semitic (prob. Phoenician) loan-word in Greek, Myc. *ku-ru-so* functions as both noun (here) and adj.   ***i-je-ro-jo***: class. ἱερός $< *iheros$ (from inherited $*iseros$, cf. Skt. *isirá-*). The forward-flip of -*h*- to the beginning of the word may not yet have happened in Myc. (§10.4): in this case the spelling would represent [iy^{h}eros].

5.   Clay tablet from Pylos (PY Ta 641), giving a list of vessels. *c.*1200 BC. Ventris–Chadwick 236. This is the famous 'tripod tablet' which confirmed Ventris' decipherment in 1953 (Chadwick 1958: 81–4).

.1   *ti-ri-po-de* / *ai-ke-u ke-re-si-jo we-ke* $*201^{VAS}$ 2
        ti-ri-po e-me po-de o-wo-we $*201^{VAS}$ 1
        ti-ri-po ke-re-si-jo we-ke a-pu ke-ka-u-me-no ke-re-a$_2$
        $*201^{VAS}$ [1
.2   *qe-to* $*203^{VAS}$ 3   *di-pa me-zo-e qe-to-ro-we* $*202^{VAS}$ 1
        di-pa-e me-zo-e ti-ri-o-we-e $*202^{VAS}$ 2
        di-pa me-wi-jo qe-to-ro-we $*202^{VAS}$ 1
.3   *di-pa me-wi-jo ti-ri-jo-we* $*202^{VAS}$ 1   *di-pa me-wi-jo a-no-we*
        $*202^{VAS}$ 1

.1   (a) τρίποδε   Αἰγεὺς(?) Κρησιοϝεργής $*201^{VAS}$ 2
        (b) τρίπως ἐμεὶ ποδεὶ οἰϝώϝης $*201^{VAS}$ 1
        (c) τρίπως Κρησιοϝεργὴς ἀπὺ κεκαυμένος σκέλεha $*201^{VAS}$ [1
.2   (d) —— $*203^{VAS}$ 3
        (e) δίπας μέζοhε κ^{w}ετρῶϝες $*202^{VAS}$ 1
        (f) δίπαhε μέζοhε τριώϝεhε $*202^{VAS}$ 2

(g) δίπας μείϜιος κʷετρῶϜες *202ᵛᴬˢ 1
.3 (h) δίπας μείϜιος τριῶϜες *202ᵛᴬˢ 1
(i) δίπας μείϜιος ἀνῶϜες *202ᵛᴬˢ 1

(a) a pair of tripods   'Aigeus' (?); of Cretan workmanship
     TRIPOD 2
(b) tripod on one foot, with one (?) handle   TRIPOD 1
(c) tripod of Cretan workmanship, burnt off at the legs
     TRIPOD [1
(d) *qe-to* PITHOS 3
(e) jar of larger size, four-handled   FOUR-HANDLED JAR 1
(f) a pair of jars of larger size, three-handled   THREE-HANDLED
     JAR 2
(g) jar of smaller size, four-handled   FOUR-HANDLED JAR 1
(h) jar of smaller size, three-handled   THREE-HANDLED JAR 1
(i) jar of smaller size, handleless   HANDLELESS JAR 1

(a) **ai-ke-u**: presents a considerable problem. If it represents a
personal name such as Αἰγεύς, it might refer to the maker of the
tripod (or a type? On the analogy of e.g. 'Wedgwood'); the word
seems grammatically unconnected with τρίποδε. **ke-re-si-jo
we-ke**: the translation is generally accepted and would be acceptable
from a historical point of view, since a long tradition in Crete of
manufacturing fine artefacts would have lent value and prestige to
vessels made by Cretan craftsmen; note that the word does not
cohere syntactically with dual τρίποδε. Writing compounds as two
words is not uncommon in Linear B (cf. *a-pu ke-ka-u-me-no* below).

(b) **ti-ri-po**: lengthened *o* (i.e. ω/[ɔ:], from *tri-pōd-s*) is assumed,
but Hom. τριπός is also possible (in Att. πούς the [ɔ:] has been
replaced by [o:], but the analogy is not clear: χείρ?). **e-me**: the
stem is ἐμ- < *σεμ- (cf. Lat. *sem-el*, and §10.4). In later Greek the
influence of neut. ἕν provoked the replacement of -μ- by -ν-
throughout the declension; hence classical dat. ἑνί. For the instr. ending -*e* see §11.2: it was replaced in later Greek by the loc. -ι. In item
(b), and in each of the items (e) to (i), we find an adj. derived from
uncontracted *owos 'ear', the ancestor of classical οὖς: either in -ώϜης
(as in Theokr. 1. 28, κισσύβιον ἀμφῶες) with lengthening of the first
vowel in composition, or in -όϜης (see Szemerényi 1967 for details).

These compounds refer to the number of 'ears' or 'handles' attached to the vessel in question, and the number is confirmed by the respective ideogram. This depicts a four-handled jar (corresponding to $\kappa^w\epsilon\tau\rho$-$\hat{\omega}\digamma\epsilon s$) in items (e) and (g), a three-handled jar (corresponding to $\tau\rho\iota$-$\acute{\omega}\digamma\epsilon h\epsilon$ or $\tau\rho\iota$-$\hat{\omega}\digamma\epsilon s$) in items (f) and (h), and a jar without handles (corresponding to $\dot{\alpha}\nu$-$\hat{\omega}\digamma\epsilon s$, with alpha privative) in item (i). In item (b) the tripod seems to be damaged, with only one foot and one handle (assuming *o-wo-we* contains the stem of $o\hat{\imath}\digamma os$ 'sole, single')—the ideogram does not reflect the damage.

(c) **a-pu**: §28.6. $\kappa\epsilon\kappa\alpha\upsilon\mu\acute{\epsilon}\nu os$ is perf. pass. ptcpl. of $\kappa\alpha\acute{\iota}\omega$, used just as in classical Greek.   **ke-re-a$_2$** : class. neut. plur. $\sigma\kappa\acute{\epsilon}\lambda\eta$ with loss of *-h-* and contraction; the acc. of respect, familiar in later Greek, here makes an early appearance.

(d) It is unclear what Greek term is represented by **qe-to**; it may be a loanword, in which case $\pi\acute{\iota}\theta os$ would be a possibility (with the fluctuation $e \sim i$ which is not uncommon in loanwords in Linear B).

(e) **di-pa** is probably a spelling of $\delta\acute{\epsilon}\pi as$, with the $e \sim i$ fluctuation noted above.   **me-zo-e**: the scribe has erroneously written the dual ending *-e* (perhaps anticipating the following entry). *me-zo* ($< *\mu\acute{\epsilon}\gamma$-$yos$) is nom. sing. neut. of the comp. of $\mu\acute{\epsilon}\gamma as$ 'large' (§10.7). **qe-to-ro-we**: [k^{w}etro:wes] contains the combining form of the word for 'four', with original labiovelar ($*k^w et\underset{\circ}{r}$-, which gave Attic $\tau\epsilon\tau\rho\alpha$-, §§10.3, 29).

(f) All words in the dual (with intervocalic *-s- > -h-*).

(g) **me-wi-jo**: also spelled *me-u-jo*. The alternation *me-wi-jo* ~ *me-u-jo* points to [meiwi^{y}os]. Class. $\mu\epsilon\hat{\imath}o\nu$ (see *a-ro$_2$-a* **1**a above). For the stem **mei(w)-* cf. (with nasal affix) $\mu\iota\nu\acute{\upsilon}\theta\omega$, Lat. *mīnus*.

6. Clay tablet from Pylos (PY Er 312), detailing plots of land. *c.*1200 BC. Ventris–Chadwick 152. ▶▶ Lejeune (1973), Chadwick (1976: 70–7), Dickinson (1994: 84–5).

.1 *wa-na-ka-te-ro te-me-no*
.2 *to-so-jo pe-ma*   GRANUM 30
.3 *ra-wa-ke-si-jo te-me-no*   GRANUM 10
        vacat
.5 *te-re-ta-o to-so pe-ma*   GRANUM 30
.6 *to-so-de te-re-ta*   VIR 3

.7   *wo-ro-ki-jo-ne-jo e-re-mo*

.8   *to-so-jo pe-ma*   GRANUM 6

(a)   Ϝανάκτερον τέμενος τόσ(σ)οιο σπέρμα   GRANUM 30

(b)   λᾱϝᾱγέσιον τέμενος   GRANUM 10

(c)   τελεστᾱ́hων(?) τόσ(σ)ον σπέρμα   GRANUM 30

(d)   τοσ(σ)οίδε τελεσταί(?)   VIR 3

(e)   Ϝ[—]ον ἐρῆμον, τόσ(σ)οιο σπέρμα   GRANUM 6

(a)   precinct of the lord: seed-corn in such an amount: WHEAT
       30 *measures*

(b)   precinct of the leader of the people: WHEAT 10 *measures*

(c)   so much seed-corn of the *telestai* (?):   WHEAT 30 *measures*

(d)   and so many *telestai* (?):   MAN 3

(e)   *w[—]on* unoccupied, seed-corn in such an amount: WHEAT
       6 *measures*

(a) **wa-na-ka-te-ro**: an adj. formed from Ϝάναξ, 'lord' (§12). Here
it agrees with neut. τέμενος, that which is 'cut off' (τεμ-) for the use
and enjoyment of god or human (cf. *Il.* 6. 194–5). In the extant Myc.
documents, only the Ϝάναξ and the λᾱϝᾱγέτᾱς are said to possess a
precinct; like all plots of land in the Linear B tablets, the area of the
precinct is measured by the amount of seed-corn (σπέρμα) needed to
sow it. The gen. τόσ(σ)οιο expresses value, as in Homer and classical
Gk.

(b) **ra-wa-ke-si-jo**: adj. built to λᾱϝᾱγέτᾱς (*λᾱϝᾱγέτ- plus the
adj. suffix -ιος: cf. *e-qe-si-ja* 1b), a compound of the stems of λᾱϝός
'people' and ἄγω 'lead' (Pindaric λᾱγέτᾱς by contraction). The translation expresses the formal elements of its composition, without
enlightening us about the precise function of the λᾱϝᾱγέτᾱς in Myc.
times. His importance as a participant in cult is suggested in other
texts, which speak of him as both a giver and a recipient of offerings.

(c–d) **te-re-ta-o** is the gen. plur. of *te-re-ta*, a masc. noun in -τᾱς
usually identified with class. τελεστᾱ́ς. The meaning of the word in the
Mycenaean context is much disputed (the derivation from τέλος is
not very helpful, as this word has the widest possible range of meanings); in **59** 8 (Elis) it means 'official' or 'magistrate', but the only
identifiable feature of the Myc. *te-re-ta* is the usufruct or possession
of a particular type of land (*ki-ti-me-na*, apparently 'cultivated' or
'private' land).

(e) The form and meaning of the first word in the entry are obscure; but the entry as a whole apparently refers to land which is, or which has been up to the present, 'deserted' or 'uncultivated'.

DIALECT INSCRIPTIONS

ARCADIAN
(Arcado-Cypriot)

7. Inscription on stone from Tegea concerning the awarding of building-contracts: only the first part is given here. Mid IV cent. BC. *IG* V 2. 6. Buck 19. Schwyzer 656. Thür–Taeuber (1994: no. 3). Rhodes–Osborne (2003, no. 60). ▶ Dubois (1986: II, 39–61).

[.........] | εἰκ ἄν τι γίνητοι τοῖς ἐργώναις τοῖς ἰν τοῖ αὐτοῖ | ἔργοι, ὅσα περὶ τὸ ἔργον. ἀπυέσθω δὲ ὁ ἀδικήμενος | τὸν ἀδικέντα ἰν ἀμέραις τρισὶ ἀπὺ ταῖ ἂν τὸ ἀδί ||⁵ κημα γένητοι, ὕστερον δὲ μή· καὶ ὅτι ἂγ κ[ρ]ίνωνσι | οἱ ἐσδοτῆρες, κύριον ἔστω. εἰ δὲ πόλεμος δια|κωλύσει τι τῶν ἔργων τῶν ἐσδοθέντων ἢ τῶν | ἠργασμένων τι φθέραι, οἱ τριακάσιοι διαγνόντω | τί δεῖ γίνεσθαι· οἱ δὲ στραταγοὶ πόσοδομ ποέντω, ||¹⁰ εἰκ ἂν δέατοί σφεις πόλεμος ἦναι ὁ κωλύων ἢ ἐ|φθορκὼς τὰ ἔργα, λαφυροπωλίου ἐόντος κατὺ τᾶς | πόλιος. εἰ δέ τι ἐργωνήσας μὴ ἰγκεχηρήκοι τοῖς | ἔργοις, ὁ δὲ πόλεμος διακωλύοι, ἀπυδόας [τ]ὸ ἀργύριον, | τὸ ἂν λελαβηκὼς τυγχάνη, ἀφεώσθω τῶ ἔργω, ||¹⁵ εἰκ ἂν κελεύωνσι οἱ ἐσδοτῆρες. εἰ δ' ἄ[ν] τις ἐπι|συνίστατοι ταῖς ἐσδόσεσι τῶν ἔργων ἢ λυμαίνη|τοι κατ' εἰ δέ τινα τρόπον φθήρων, ζαμιόντω | οἱ ἐσδοτῆρες ὅσαι ἂν δέατοί σφεις ζαμίαι, καὶ | ἀγκαρυσ[σόν]τω ἰν ἐπίκρισιν καὶ ἰναγόντω ||²⁰ ἰν δικαστήριον τὸ γινόμενον τοῖ πλήθι τᾶς | ζαμίαν. μὴ ἐξέστω δὲ μηδὲ κοινᾶνας γενέσθαι | πλέον ἢ δύο ἐπὶ μηδενὶ τῶν ἔργων· εἰ δὲ μή, ὀφλέτω | ἕκαστος πεντήκοντα δαρχμάς· ἐπελασάσθων | δὲ οἱ ἀλιασταί, ἰμφαίνεν δὲ τὸμ βολόμενον ἐπὶ τοῖ ||²⁵ ἡμίσσοι τᾶς ζαμίαν. κὰ τὰ αὐτὰ δὲ καὶ εἰκ ἂν [τ]ις | πλέον ἢ δύο ἔργα ἔχη τῶν ἱερῶν ἢ τῶν δαμ[ο]σίων | κατ' εἰ δέ τινα τρόπον, ὅτινι ἂμ μὴ οἱ ἀλιαστα[ὶ] | παρετάξωνσι ὁμοθυμαδὸν πάντες, ζαμιώ[σ]θω | καθ' ἕκαστον τῶν πλεόνων ἔργων κατὺ μῆνα ||³⁰ πεντήκοντα δαρχ|μαῖς, μέστ' ἂν ἐπισ[χῆ πάντα] | τὰ ἔργα τὰ πλέονα.

. . . if any (dispute) arises among the contractors (employed) on the same work, so far as it concerns the work; let the wronged party summon the wrongdoer within three days from the time at which the injury (5) arose, but not later; and whatever the contract-awarders decide, that is to be valid. Now if war hinders any of the works which have been contracted out or destroys any of those completed, let the Three Hundred decide what should be done; let the Generals provide revenue (10) if it seems to them that it is war which hinders or has destroyed the works, with a sale of booty at the city's expense. Now if anyone, having entered into a contract, has not taken the works in hand, but war hinders him, let him return whatever money he has received, and let him be excused the work, (15) if the contract-awarders so order. Now if anyone interferes with the letting-out of the works or damages them, doing harm in any way whatever, let the contract-awarders fine him in whatever sum seems good to them, and let them summon him to judgment and bring him (20) into a court competent to impose the penalty incurred (?). It shall not be permitted for more than two partners to be employed upon any one of the works; but if there are, let each be fined fifty drachmas, and let the heliasts enforce the fine, and whoever wishes may lay information for half the fine. And, in exactly the same manner, if anyone wishes to hold more than two works, sacred or civic, in any way whatever, unless the heliasts have allowed it to him by unanimous vote, let him be fined for each of the excess works (30) fifty drachmas per month, until all the excess works have ceased.

2. **εἰκ ἄν**: this form of εἰ probably arose (like οὐ ~ οὐκ) to prevent hiatus. The inscription of course has *EIKAN*, which could be read εἰ καν on the assumption of a modal particle καν (so Forbes 1958b, Palmer 1980: 67–8); but the presence of εἰ δ' ἄν at line 15, and εἰκ ἐπί in another inscription, argues against this. The apodosis appears to be in the missing lines earlier.   **γίνητοι**: 3 sing. pres. subj. (§28.1). The ι is probably long: [gi:n-] < [giŋn-] < [gign-] by assimilation and compensatory lengthening (this occurred at different dates in the dialects: not until the late IV cent. in Attic).   **ἐργώναις**: initial ϝ- has now disappeared in Arc. (§27.1).   **ἰν** (Att. ἐν): §26.1. **τοῖ αὐτοῖ ἔργοι**: dat. sing. (§28.10).
3. **ὅσα**: rough breathings are printed without much confidence,

since erratic notation of the aspirate in earlier Arc. inscriptions (which use *h*) indicates that it was disappearing from the spoken language (cf. §23.10). **ἀπυέσθω**: 3 sing. mid. imper. 'summon to justice' (cf. Hom. *ἠπύω* 'call, shout'). **ἀδικήμενος**: pres. ptcpl. (med.-pass.): for the athem. ending see §24.1.

4. **ἀδικέντα**: pres. ptcpl., athematic inflection (§24.1). **ἀπύ**: cf. *a-pu* 5 1 (§28.5–6). **ταῖ**: relative use of the article stem (fem. sing., understand *ἀμέραι*). **ἀμέραις**: for the breathing see on *ἀμέραν* 76 38.

5. **ἄγ** = ἄν, with assimilation of -*ν* to the following (velar) consonant. **κρίνωνσι**: 3 plur. pres. subj. (§27.3–4).

6. **ἐσδοτῆρες** (Att. *ἐκ-*): 'givers-out of contracts'; Arc. has *ἐξ* before a vowel and *ἐς* (< *ἐσς* < *ἐκς*) before a consonant (Attic drops the final -*s*). **εἰ δὲ πόλεμος**: *δέ* in this inscription is connective rather than disjunctive, and this may reflect koiné influence (Morpurgo Davies 1997). **διακωλύσει**: we expect an optative: but the evidence for an aor. opt. in -*ει* is weak (it would presumably be related to the common *παύσειε* type in Homer and Attic). It could be fut. indic. in a 'mixed' condition, in which the possibility of destruction (opt.) is conceived as more remote than mere impediment (vivid fut.): cf. Hdt. 1. 71 (fut. *εἰ νικήσεις* juxtaposed with subj. *ἢν νικηθῇς*). See also Forbes (1958*a*), Dubois (1986: I, 159–60).

8. **φθέραι**: 3 sing. aor. opt. of *φθείρω*. -*ρ*- is either graphic for -*ρρ*- (*φθέρραι* < **φθέρ-σαι*), or is a real phonetic reduction of -*ρρ*-. **τριακάσιοι**: a regular development from **-kn̥tioi* (for Att. -*κόσιοι* see §32.9). **διαγνόντω**: 3 plur. aor. imper. (§32.3).

9. **πόσοδομ** (Arc. *πός* = Att. *πρός*, §28.7): final -*ν* has assimilated to the labial articulation of the following *π*- (Dubois 1986: II, 43–4 takes the word to mean 'tribunal'). **ποέντω**: imper. (§32.3), athematic inflection (*ἀδικήμενος* 3 and §24.1).

10. **δέᾱτοι**: 3 sing. pres. subj. of a verb found also in Homer (*δέατο*, *Od.* 6. 242): equivalent in meaning to Attic *δοκεῖ* 'it seems (good)'. The *α* is marked as long by editors on the analogy of the long-vowel subj. of thematic verbs (*παύηται*); for the ending see §28.1. **σφεις**: Attic *σφισι*, dat. plur. of the enclitic 3 sing. pron. The form *σφέσι*, also attested in Arc. (*SEG* 37 340, 1987), shows that there was hesitation between inflectional patterns which followed the 2

and 3 declensions (as in ταῖς ἐσδόσεσι 16 below). Cf. Myc. *pe-i* [spʰehi] < *[spʰe-si]. **ἦναι**: 'to be', morphologically parallel to Att. εἶναι, from *ἔσ-ναι or *ἔσ-εναι. **ἐφθορκώς** (Att. ἐφθαρκώς): perf. ptcpl. of φθείρω, with ορ < *ŗ̥ (§26.3).

11. **λαφυρο-πωλίου**: 'sale of booty' (the verb λαφυροπωλέω is found in Att.); -ου is the koiné gen. sing. ending (vs. Arc. -ω, e.g. τῶ ἔργω 14). **ἐόντος**: §32.11. **κατύ**: probably analogical on ἀπύ.

12. **πόλιος**: gen. sg. (§32.4). **ἰγκεχηρήκοι** (Att. ἐγκεχειρήκοι): 3 sing. perf. opt. (ἰν §26.1, cf. ἄγ 3). χηρ- < *χεσρ-, but see Lejeune (1972: §120).

13. **ἀπυδόας**: aor. ptcpl. of ἀπυδίδωμι. An analogical rebuilding: the weak aor. ptcpl. ending (§26.5) has been attached to the stem δο- (cf. Att. δούς < *δο-ντ-s).

14. **λελαβηκώς**: perf. ptcpl. of λαμβάνω, formed by analogy with (e.g.) μεμαθηκώς from μανθάνω. Att. εἴληφα was probably formed to mid. εἴλημμαι < *se-slāgʷ-mai (Slings 1986). **τὸ**: cf. ταῖ 4. **τυγχάνη**: Arc. preserves the 2/3 sing. pres. subj. without -ι. Most dialects have -ηις, -ηι on the influence of indic. -εις, -ει (Palmer 1980: 309). **ἀφεώσθω**: 3 sing. imperat. of perf. pass. ἀφεῶσθαι 'be dismissed from' (ἀφίημι): Arc. and WGk. form a perf. act. ἀφέωκα, from which -ω- spread to the medio-pass.

15. **κελεύωνσι**: cf. κρίνωνσι 5. **ἐπισυνίστᾱτοι**: 3 sing. subj. mid. of ἐπι-συν-ίσταμι, 'conspire against' (for the ending see §28.1).

16. **ἐσδόσεσι**: the Attic ending reflects koiné influence (§32.4: contrast πόλιος 12).

17. **εἰ δέ τινα τρόπον**: the δέ is redundant in an ossified phrase (originally εἰ δέ τις with a verb) meaning 'any'. **ζᾱμιόντω**: 3 plur. imper. §32.3 (athematic, §24.1).

18. **ὅσαι ... ζᾱμίαι**: dat. sing. (instrument).

19. **ἀγκᾱρυσσόντω** (Att. ἀνακηρυττόντων): 3 plur. imper. (§32.3): ἀν- rather than ὀν- due to koiné influence, §28.9). **ἰν**: for ἐν with the acc. cf. **8** 27 (§§26.1, 28.8).

19–21. **ἰναγόντω ... τᾶς ζᾱμίαν**: the translation suggested is substantially that of Buck, in which πλήθι means 'amount'. Dubois takes γινόμενον closely with πλήθι and understands the latter word in the sense of δάμωι, hence: 'let them deposit with the court that part of the fine which belongs to the people'; but this interpretation suits the word-order less well.

20. **πλήθῑ**: early *πληθεσ-ι > Att. πλήθει. The Arc. form perhaps < πλήθυι (with raising of ε in hiatus after loss of -σ-), or (accented πλῆθι) could be an analogical extension of the replacement of -*ei* by -*i* in the masc. obstruent-stems (cf. on Myc. *po-de* 5 1b): Dubois (1978).

21. **ζᾱμίαν** (Att. ζημίας): gen. sing. in -ᾱο of masc. *a*-stems was extended to fem. nouns only at Tegea (§28.4 and Lillo 1987). **κοινᾶνας**: acc. plur. (κοινᾱ-ϝον- 'partner' > κοινᾱον- 'partner' > κοινᾱν- in most dialects except Att., where the contraction gave κοινών).

22. **πλέον**: advb., koiné form (Arcadian πλός).

23. **δαρχμᾱ́ς**: a noun in -*smâ-* formed from a verbal stem meaning 'to grab a handful' (the alternation δαρχ-/δραχ- among the dialects points to original vocalic *ŗ). **ἐπελασάσθων**: 3 plur. aor. mid. imper. of ἐπελάω (a form of ἐπελαύνω).

24. **ἰμφαίνεν** (Att. ἐμφαίνειν): a thematic infin. -εν is also found in some WGk. dialects (§28.2). **βολόμενον**: the dialect forms of this verb (Att. βουλ-, Thess. βελλ-, WGk. δηλ-, etc.) reflect an ablauting stem *gʷels- (present) ~ *gʷols- (perfect, with shift of the o-grade to the present in eastern dialects). For **τὸμ** cf. πόσοδομ 9.

25. **ἡμίσσοι**: dat. sing. of Arc./WGk. ἥμισσον (< *ἥμιτϝ-): cf. Att. ἥμισυ < *ἥμιτυ. **κά**: has lost a syllable (contrast κατύ 11), either by haplology before τὰ αὐτά, or apocope with simplification of the double consonant (κὰτ τὰ).

26. **ἔχη**: 3 sing. pres. subj. (cf. τυγχάνη 14).

27. **ὅτινι**: indefinite pron. 'whoever', with only the second element declined. **ἄμ**: see πόσοδομ 9.

28. **παρετάξωνσι**: 3 plur. aor. subj. παρετάζω 'approve' (§40.4). For the ending cf. κρίνωνσι 5.

30. **μέστ(ε)**: 'until' (cf. Thess. μέσποδι 11 13). **ἐπισχῆ** (if correctly restored): 3 sing. aor. subj. (for the ending cf. τυγχάνη 9). The sense is either intransitive 'cease' (with τὰ ἔργα as subject) or transitive 'abandon, desist from' (with τις 25 understood as subject). Restored ἐπιτ[ελέση] in Thür–Taeuber (1994), 'until he completes (the supernumerary contracts)'.

CYPRIOT
(Arcado-Cypriot)

8. Bronze tablet, inscribed on both sides in the Cypriot syllabary (§18), from Idalion, *c.*18 km south of Nicosia. The inscription records an agreement made between the Idalians on the one hand and the physician Onasilos and his brothers on the other, for free treatment of the wounded. *c.*475 BC. Here a transliteration of the first ten lines of the syllabic text is given (the 'word-divider' is marked with a dot), followed by a version in the Greek alphabet with the addition of Ϝ and the letter *j* (representing the glide-sound). Masson (1961), no. 217. Schwyzer 679. Buck 23. *Nomima*, i. 31. ▶▶ Chadwick (1987) for the relationship between the Cypriot and Linear B syllabaries. Powell (1991: 91–9).

o te · ta po to li ne e ta li o ne · ka te wo ro ko ne ma to i · ka se ke ti
e we se · i to i · pi lo ku po ro ne we te i to o na sa ko [2] ra u · pa si
le u se · sa ta si ku po ro se · ka se a po to li se · e ta li e we se · a no
ko ne o na si lo ne · to no na si ku po [3] ro ne to ni ja te ra ne · ka
se · to se · ka si ke ne to se · i ja sa ta i · to se · a to ro po se · to se · i ta
· i · ma ka i · i ki [4] ma me no se · a ne u · mi si to ne · ka sa pa i · e
u we re ta sa tu · pa si le u se · ka se · a po to li se · o na si [5] lo i · ka
se · to i se · ka si ke ne to i se · a ti to mi si to ne · ka a ti · ta u ke ro
ne · to we na i · e xe to i · [6] wo i ko i · to i pa si le wo se · ka se · e xe
ta i po to li wi · a ra ku ro · ta · **I** · ta · e tu wa no i nu · a ti to [7] a ra
ku ro ne · to te · to ta la to ne · pa si le u se · ka se · a po to li se · o na
si lo i · ka se · to i se · ka si [8] ke ne to i se · a pu ta i · ga i · ta i pa si
le wo se · ta i to i ro ni · to i · a la pi ri ja ta i · to ko ro ne · [9] to ni
to i · e le i · to ka ra u o me no ne · o ka to se · a la wo · ka se · ta te re
ki ni ja · ta e pi o ta [10] pa ta · e ke ne · pa no ni o ne · u wa i se · ga
ne · a te le ne . . .

ᴬ ὅτε τὰ(ν) πτόλιν Ἐδάλιον κατέϜοργον Μᾶδοι κὰς ΚετιῆϜες ἰ(ν) τῶι Φιλοκύπρōν Ϝέτει τō Ὀνασαγό|ραυ, βασιλεὺς Στασίκυπρος κὰς ἁ πτόλις ἘδαλιῆϜες ἄνωγον Ὀνάσιλον τὸν Ὀνασικύπ|ρōν τὸν ἰjατῆραν κὰς τὸς κασιγνήτο(ν)ς ἰjᾶσθαι τὸ(ν)ς ἀ(ν)θρώπο(ν)ς τὸ(ν)ς ἰ(ν) τᾶι μάχαι ἰκ|μαμένο(ν)ς ἄνευ μισθὸν· κάς παι εὐϜρητάσατυ βασιλεὺς κὰς ἁ πτόλις Ὀνασίⁱ|⁵λωι κὰς τοῖς κασιγνήτοις ἀ(ν)τὶ τō μισθὸν

κὰ(ς) ἀ(ν)τὶ τᾶ(ς) ὑχήρōν δοϜέναι ἐξ τῶι Ϝοίκωι τῶι βασιλῆϜος
κὰς ἐξ τᾶι πτόλιϜι ἀργύρō(ν) τά(λαντον) Ι τά(λαντον)· ἔδυϜαν οἶνυ
ἀ(ν)τὶ τô Ι ἀργύρōν τόδε τô ταλά(ν)τōν βασιλεὺς κὰς ἁ πτόλις Ὀνα-
σίλωι κὰς τοῖς κασι|γνήτοις ἀπὺ τᾶι γᾶι τᾶι βασιλῆϜος τᾶ(ι) ἰ(ν)
τ(ῶι) οἰρῶνι τῶι Ἀλα(μ)πριjάται τὸ(ν) χῶρον Ι τὸν ἰ(ν) τῶι ἔλει
τὸ(ν) χραυόμενον Ὄ(γ)κα(ν)τος ἄλϜō(ν) κὰς τὰ τέρχνιjα τὰ
ἐπιό(ν)τα ||[10] πά(ν)τα ἔχε̄ν πανώνιον ὐϜαῖς γᾶν(?) ἀτελήν· ἤ κέ σις
Ὀνάσιλον ἤ τὸς Ι κασιγνήτο(ν)ς ἤ τὸς παῖδα(ν)ς τῶ(ν) παίδων τῶν
Ὀνασικύπρōν ἐξ τῶι χώρωι τῶιδε Ι ἐξορύξῃ, ἰδέ παι ὃ ἐξορύξῃ πείσει
Ὀνασίλωι κὰς τοῖς κασιγνήτοι|ς ἤ τοῖς παισὶ τὸν ἄργυρον τό(ν)δε·
ἀργύρō(ν) τά(λαντον) Ι τά(λαντον)· Ι κὰς Ὀνασίλωι οἴϜωι, ἄνευ τῶ(ν)
κασιγνήτων τῶν αἴλων, ἐϜρητάσατυ βασιλεὺ||[15]ς κὰς ἁ πτόλις
δοϜέναι ἀ(ν)τὶ τᾶ(ς) ὑχήρōν τô μισθὸν ἀργύρō(ν) πε(λέκεϜας) ΙΙΙΙ
πε(λέκεϜας) Ι ΙΙ δί(δραχμα) Ε(δάλια)· ἔδωκ᾿ οἶνυ βασιλεὺς κὰς ἁ
πτόλις Ὀνασί||ᴮ||λωι ἀ(ν)τὶ τô ἀργύρō(ν) τόδε ἀπὺ τᾶι γᾶι τᾶι
βασιλῆϜος τᾶ(ι) ἰ(ν) Μαλανίjα|ι τᾶι πεδίjαι τὸ(ν) χῶρον τὸ(ν)
χραυζόμενον Ἀμενίjα ἄλϜō(ν), κὰς τὰ τέρ|χνιjα τὰ ἐπιό(ν)τα
πά(ν)τα, τὸ(ν) ποεχόμενον πὸς τὸ(ν) ῥόϜο(ν) τὸ(ν) Δρύμιον κὰς
πὸ||[20]ς τὰν ἱερηϜίjαν τᾶς Ἀθάνας, κὰς τὸ(ν) κᾶπον τὸν ἰ(ν) Σίμιδος
ἀρούρα|ι, τὸ(ν) ΔιϜείθεμις ὁ Ἀρμάνευς ἦχε ἄλϜο(ν), τὸ(ν) ποεχόμ-
ενον πὸς Πασαγόρα|ν τὸν Ὀνασαγόραυ, κὰς τὰ τέρχνιjα τὰ ἐπιό(ν)τα
πά(ν)τα, ἔχε̄ν πανώνιο(ν)ς ὐ|Ϝαῖς γᾶν(?), ἀτελίjα ἰό(ν)τα· ἤ κέ σις
Ὀνάσιλον ἤ τὸς παῖδα(ν)ς τὸ(ν)ς Ὀ|νασίλōν ἐξ τᾶι γᾶι τᾶιδε ἴ ἐξ τῶι
κάπωι τῶιδε ἐξορύξῃ, ἰ||[25]δέ ὁ ἐξορύξῃ πείσει Ὀνασίλωι ἤ τοῖς παισὶ
τὸν ἄργυρον τό(ν)δε· ἀργύρο|ν πε(λέκεϜας) ΙΙΙΙ πε(λέκεϜας) ΙΙ
δί(δραχμα) Ε(δάλια)· ἰδέ τὰ(ν) δάλτον τά(ν)δε, τὰ Ϝέπιjα τάδε
ἰναλαλισμένα, Ι βασιλεὺς κὰς ἁ πτόλις κατέθιjαν ἰ(ν) τὰ(ν) θιὸν τὰν
Ἀθάναν τὰν περ Ἐ|δάλιον, σὺν ὅρκοις μὴ λῦσαι τὰς Ϝρήτα(ν)ς τάσδε
ὐϜαῖς γᾶν(?). Ι ὄπι σίς κε τὰς Ϝρήτα(ν)ς τάσδε λύσῃ, ἀνοσίjα Ϝοι
γένοιτυ· τάς κε ||[30] γᾶ(ν)ς τάσδε κὰς τὸς κάπο(ν)ς τόσδε οἱ Ὀνα-
σικύπρōν παῖδες κὰς τῶ(ν) παίδων οἱ πα|ῖδες ἔξο(ν)σι αἰϜεί, ὁ(ΐ) ἰ(ν)
τ(ῶι) οἰρῶνι τῶι ἘδαλιῆϜι ἴωσι.

When the Medes and Ketians were laying siege to the city of
Edalion in the year of Philokypros the son of Onasagoras, King
Stasikypros and the city of the Edalians instructed Onasilos
the son of Onasikypros, the physician, and his brothers to treat the
men wounded in battle, without payment. And the king and the

city promised (5) to give Onasilos and his brothers, by way of
compensation and gratuity, from the king's household and from
the city a talent of silver: one *t*. Now instead of this silver, the
talent, the king and the city gave to Onasilos and his brothers,
from the estate of the king which is in the district of Alampria: the
land in the marshland bordering the vineyard of Onkas and all
the young plants upon it, to hold with all saleable products (10)
for ever, free of tax. If anyone expels Onasilos or his brothers or the
sons of the sons of Onasikypros from this land, then the expeller
shall pay to Onasilos and to his brothers or to his sons this
sum: one talent of silver. And to Onasilos alone, apart from the
other men his brothers, the king (15) and the city undertook to
give, by way of gratuity and compensation, four axes of silver and
two Edalian didrachms. Now the king and the city gave (B) to
Onasilos, instead of this money, from the estate of the king that
is in the plain at Malanea: the land adjoining the vineyard of
Amenea, and all the young plants upon it—the land bordering the
stream Drymios and (20) the shrine of Athena—and the garden
in the land of Simmis which Diweithemis the son of Armanes
held as his vineyard, bordering the land of Pasagoras the son of
Onasagoras, and all the young plants upon it, to hold with all
saleable products for ever, free of tax. If anyone expels Onasilos or
the sons of Onasilos from this land or from this garden, (25) then
the expeller shall pay to Onasilos or to his sons this money: four
axes of silver and two Edalian didrachms. Behold, the king and the
city have set up this tablet, with these words inscribed upon it, to
the goddess Athena, who protects Edalion, with oaths not to break
these undertakings for ever. Whoever does break these undertakings, may a curse befall him! These (30) lands and these gardens
the sons of Onasikypros and the sons of their sons shall hold for
ever, those who shall be in the land of Edalion.

Note: in the alphabetic transcription (*v*) indicates that the preceding
vowel is nasalized, [ã] etc. (it is not in the syllabic text: §26.8).

1. **ὅτε**: it is not clear whether Cyp. had [h], §27.5.   **τὰ(ν)**: for
the final -*n* see §26.8*b*.   **πτόλιν**: πτόλις is a doublet of πόλις found
in Arc.-Cyp., Myc., and (with ττ- for ππ) Thessalian. Common
in Homer, whence occasional use in Attic tragedy. The reason for

ππ-/π- doublets in Greek is unclear (Szemerényi 1979 suggested that false division of an early Greek syntagm, e.g. *ἤλυθετ πόλιν*, gave *ἤλυθε τπόλιν > ἤλυθε πτόλιν*, for which cf. Engl. *a newt < an ewt*).

Ἐδάλιον: spelled Ἰδάλιον in literary texts (the toponym *Κίτιον* is usually spelt with -ι-, but in this text the corresponding ethnic is *Κετιεύς*); the ε/ι alternation points to a close pronunciation of ε. **κατέϜοργον**: 3 plur. strong aor. of a verb *καταϜέργω* 'press hard' (*Ϝοργ-* from aor. stem **wr̥g-*, §26.3).   **κάς**: 'and', §28.7.   **ἰ(ν)**: Att. ἐν (§26.1).   **Φιλοκύπρōν**: gen. sing. (§28.11).   **Ϝέτει**: inherited *Ϝ*- maintained in all positions (§27.1).   **τô Ὀνασαγόραυ**: gen. (§§26.2, 28.4).

2. **ἘδαλιῆϜες**: nom. plur. of ethnic Ἐδαλιεύς, formed from Ἐδάλιον as *ΚετιῆϜες* 1 is formed from *Κέτιον*. The scribe writes 'the city Edalians'; for this formulation cf. ἁ πόλις οἱ Γορτύνιοι in a Cretan inscription (Schwyzer 184).   **ἄνωγον**: past tense formed to the perf. ἄνωγα, with ending borrowed from the imperf. (cf. on ἄνωγα **68** 687: poetic only in Attic).   **Ὀνασικύπρōν**: gen. sing. (§28.11). **ἰjατῆραν** (Hom. ἰητήρ, Att. ἰατρός): acc. sing. (§28.12) with glide between ι and the following vowel.

3. **τὸς κασιγνήτο(ν)ς ... τὸ(ν)ς ἀ(ν)θρώπο(ν)ς**: acc. plur. (§26.8).   **ἰjᾶσθαι**: infin. of ἰάομαι.   **ἰκμαμένο(ν)ς**: acc. plur. perf. pass. ptcpl. of a verb not otherwise attested; the context suggests the meaning 'wounded' (perhaps cognate with Lat. *īcō* 'strike').

4. **κάς παι**: the particle παι in a function that seems peculiar to Cyp.: the ensemble seems to have the force of Attic καὶ μήν ('progressive', in the terminology of Denniston 1954), but cf. also the use of καί κως in Hdt. (e.g. 3.40). See in general Morpurgo Davies (1997).   **εὐϜρητάσατυ**: 3 sing. aor. mid. of **Ϝρητάω* 'promise' (a denominative from *Ϝρήτα* 30: root **werH₁*, cf. Attic ἐρῶ, ῥήτωρ). The -υ- before -Ϝ- is merely a glide; it is omitted in the same word in 14. For the ending, see §26.2.

5. **κὰ(ς) ἀ(ν)τὶ τᾶ(ς)**: perhaps κὰh ἀ(ν)τὶ τᾶh (cf. ποεχόμενον 19 and §27.5).   **ὐχήρōν**: 'bonus, gratuity' (gen. sing.); cf. Att. ἐπίχειρα (n. pl.). Cyp. ὐ(ν) seems functionally equivalent to ἐπί, though perhaps formally cognate with Att. ἀνά (Strunk 1986): §28.9.   **δοϜέναι**: aor. inf. of δίδωμι. The -Ϝ- is unexpected, and may have originated as a glide (cf. on ἔδυϜαν 6, and Cowgill 1964: 354).

ἐξ + dat.: cf. ἀπὺ ταῖ 7 4 (§28.5). Other dialects (except Pamph.) simplify to ἐκ or ἐς before a cons. (cf. Woodard 1997: 118).

6. **πτόλιϝι**: dat. sing. (§28.13) **ἔδυϝαν οἰνυ**: this phrase needs to be considered together with ἔδωκ' οἰνυ 16. An earlier interpretation of the syllabic phrases *e-tu-wa-no-i-nu* and *e-to-ko-i-nu* was ἦ δυϝάνοι νυ and ἦ δώκοι νυ, with an imperatival opt. 'let . . . give', but serious problems are raised: (i) by the form *δυϝάνοι, pres. opt. of an unknown verb δυ-άνω, (ii) by the form *δώκοι, unparalleled aor. opt. based on the stem δωκ-, (iii) by the alternation between the two stems, and between pres. and aor. in what are apparently parallel formulae, (iv) by the fact that the tablet, which otherwise records decisions taken in the past by king and city, is here made to record a prescription for the future. Cowgill (1964) proposed a more attractive interpretation (here adopted): the verbs are aor. ind. expressing what actually took place, ἔδυϝαν being plur., ἔδωκε being sing. (as if 'king' and 'city' formed a single entity). ἔδυϝαν < *ἔδοαν, with raising of *o* to *u* and ϝ as a glide; *ἔ-δο-αν (the existence of which is implied by Arc. ἀπυδόας 7 8) is an athematic aor., parallel to κατέθιjαν 29 (§32.1). οἰνυ (not found elsewhere) is on this view a particle cognate with Att. οὖν + νυ. **τὸ ἀργύρον τόδε τὸ ταλά(ν)τον**: gen. sing. (§§26.8, 28.11).

8. **ἀπὺ τᾶι γᾶι**: the sign here represented *ga* was originally thought to represent *za*; but if, as seems likely, this means 'from the land', then γᾶι rather than ζᾶι must be read (Lejeune 1954). Cf. also ὐϝαῖς γᾶν [ζᾶν] 12. For the case after ἀπύ cf. ἐξ 5 (§28.5). **οἰρῶνι**: dat. sing. of οἰρών 'limit', so 'district'. **Ἀλαμπριjάται**: dat. sing. of adj. in -ατᾱς formed from the place-name Ἀλαμπρία.

9. **χρανόμενον**: synonym of χραυζόμενον 18, 'grazing', so 'adjoining'. **ἀλϝō(ν)**: gen. (of the object reached), 'vineyard, orchard': cf. Hom. ἀλω(ϝ)ή. **τέρχνιja**: neut. plur. of τέρχνος (< τέρχνεα): §26.6. **ἐπιό(ν)τα**: from ἐπεόντα (§§26.6, 32.11).

10. **ἔχεν**: ~ Att. ἔχειν < -ε(h)εν (§26.9). **παν-ώνιον**: root as in ὀνίνημι 'benefit'. **ὐϝαῖς γᾶν**: not fully understood. The context suggests a formula of emphasis ('for ever', 'completely'); ὐϝαῖς may be related to αἰϝεί 31, 'always', with initial ὐ- either as part of this root (Weiss 1994: 151–4), or a prefix equivalent to ἐπί (cf. ὐχήρων 5). γᾶν has been taken as an infin. 'to enjoy [forever]' (Lejeune 1954: 77, comparing Hom. γαίω 'rejoice') or an acc. of respect 'on earth'

(Calvert Watkins, at Weiss 1994: 152). ζᾶν (see γᾶι-ζᾶι 8) was interpreted as a noun related to ζάω 'live'.   **ἀτελήν**: acc. sing. of ἀτελής formed by analogy with the declension of o-stems; the meaning 'exempt from tax (τέλος)' is found also in literary Greek (e.g. Hdt. and Lys.).   **ἤ κέ σις**: corresponds to Att. ἐάν τις (ἡ is the Cyp. word for 'if'). **σις**: *kwi- (§§27.2, 10.6).

11. **παῖδα(ν)ς**: §28.11.

12. **ἐξορύξῃ**: 3 sing. aor. subj. of a verb which cannot be identified precisely. Perhaps ἐξορύσσω, 'dig out', so 'expel', or a denominative from ὄρϝος, 'boundary' (cf. Attic ἐξορίζω) meaning 'banish'. For the ending cf. τυγχάνη 7 9.   **ἰδέ παι**: 'then indeed', used to emphasize the apodosis (see κάς παι 4).   **ὅ**: 'whoever' (Att. ὅστις).   **πείσει** (Att. τείσει): 'shall pay', π- by analogy with ποινή 'fine'; both ποινή and τείσει derive from the root *kʷei-/kʷoi- (§10.6).

14. **οἴϝωι**: dat. sing. of οἶϝος 'sole, only'.   **αἴλων** (Att. ἄλλων): §26.7.

15. **τᾶ(ς)**: cf. 5 above.   **πε**: abbreviation for πελέκεϝας, acc. plur. of πέλεκυς, 'axe'. The term denotes a sum of money on Cyprus, perhaps ten *minae*.

16. **ἔδωκ' οἶνυ**: cf. ἔδυϝαν οἶνυ 6.

18. **πεδίjαι**: a fem. noun (only here) with the meaning of πεδίον, 'level ground, plain'.   **Ἀμενίja**: gen. sing. in -ā < -ao (more often -αυ, §28.4). For -ι- from -ε-: τέρχνιja 9.

19. **ποεχόμενον**: perhaps ποηεχόμενον (ποσεχόμενον, 'adjoining'), §27.5. πός < ποσί (Myc. form): §28.7.   **ῥόϝο(ν)**: 'stream', with o-grade of the stem found in ῥέϝω, 'flow' (Att. ῥοῦς, with loss of -ϝ- and contraction).

20. **ἱερηϝίjαν**: interpreted here as 'sanctuary' (with adj. suffix -ιᾱ), which fits the context, but the word could in theory mean 'priestess' (with fem. suffix -yᾰ).   **ἀρούρᾱι**: 'arable land' (Myc. and Homer, but poetic in Attic).

21. **ΔιϝείΑθεμις**: compound name containing Διϝει-, the original dat. of Ζεύς found also in Myc. di-we 'for Zeus' (§11.2). **Ἀρμάνευς**: probably patronymic, '(son) of Ἀρμάνης', with -ευς from -εος (for the loss of syllabicity cf. the gen. sing. -αυ < -αο).

23. **ἀτελίja ἰό(ν)τα**: < *ἀτελέα ἐόντα (§26.6): for the s-stem acc. plur. contrast ἀτελήν 10.

24. **ἴ**: apparently a form of ἤ 'or'. The simplest way to relate them

is to assume that ἤ was shortened in hiatus to ἔ before vowels, which in turn became ἴ before back vowels (§26.6). Here a front vowel follows, however, so it must have become generalized as the standard antevocalic form.   26. **δάλτον** (Att. δελτ-): 'tablet'. The variation reflects the origin of the word as a loan from Phoenician *dlt* (E. Masson 1967: 61–5). **Ϝέπιja**: cf. Hom. (Ϝ)έπεα (§26.6). **ἰναλαλισμένα**: perf. pass. ptcpl. of ἰναλίνω, 'engrave, inscribe'. ἀλίνω (= ἀλείφω, 'anoint, smear') seems to have been the standard Cypriot term for 'write': Hesychius gives διφθεράλοιφος ('skin-anointer') as the Cypriot for 'scribe'.   27. **κατ-έθιjαν**: 3 plur. aor. (κατ-έ-θε-αν, §32.1) from κατατίθημι.   **ἰ(ν)**: for ἐν with the acc. cf. 7 19 (§28.8).   **περ(ί)**: 'round about', so 'protecting'.   **Ϝρήτα(ν)ς**: from Ϝρή-τρᾱ, 'contract' (cf. 61 1) with dissimilation of ρ.   29. **ὄπι σίς κε**: corresponds in meaning to Att. ὅστις ἄν. The morphology of ὄπι is mysterious. If related to ὅπη in Crete ('where') and Thessaly ('when'), it could mean 'in the case that (somebody does *x* . . .)'.   **λύση**: 3 sing. aor. subj. (cf. ἐξορύξη 13).   **ἀνοσίjα**: what is not ὅσιος (established by the gods for human well-being): a curse formula.   **Ϝοι**: dat. sing. 3 personal pron., with original *w* (§27.1).   **γένοιτυ**: 3 sing. aor. opt. (§26.2).   30. **ἔξο(ν)σι**: 3 plur. fut. (§26.8).   **αἰϜεί**: see on ὐϜαις γᾶν 10.   **ἴωσι**: *ἔωνσι (§§32.11, 26.6), 3 plur. pres. subj. of the verb 'be'. The transcription ἴωσι rather than ἴω(ν)σι assumes that a long vowel plus nasal simply lost the nasal element (Ruijgh 1988: 137).

THESSALIAN
(Aeolic)

The dialects of western Thessaly (Thessaliotis, Hestiaeotis) show some WGk. influence: eastern Thessaly (Pelasgiotis) retains a greater number of Aeolic features.

9.   Bronze tablet from a site near Kierion recording the privileges conferred by the people of Thetonion upon Sotairos, a citizen of Corinth. The tablet has a line at the top, separated by a horizontal stroke, which is probably the last line of the text (the engraver ran out of space). Thessaliotis (western

Thessaly), V cent. bc. *IG* IX 2. 257. Buck 35. Schwyzer 557.
Nomima, i. 33.

A number of features anomalous in Thessalian may point
to an attempt to write the text in Ionic-influenced 'chancellery'
diction (perhaps by an Ionian secretary).

ε<ο>ς hυλōρέοντος Φιλονίκō hυιός

Θ͞ετόνιοι ἔδōκαν Σōταίρōι τōι Κλορινθίōι καὐτōι καὶ γένει καὶ
Ϝλοικιάταις καὶ χρέμασιν ἀσυλίαι|⁵ν κἀτέλειαν κεὐϜεργέταν
ἐ|ποίεσαν κἒν ταγᾶ κἒν ἀταγ|ίāι. αἴ τις ταῦτα παρβαίνοι, τὸ|ν ταγὸν
ἐπεστάκοντα ἐ|ξξανακάδ͞εν. τὰ χρυσία καὶ τὰ ‖¹⁰ ἀργύρια τὲς
Βελφαίō ἀπολ|όμενα ἔσōσε Ὀρέσταο Φερεκράτ-

(2) The Thetonians gave to Sotairos the Corinthian, to him and to
his family and to his household, both immunity for his property
(5) and freedom from taxation, and made him their benefactor
both in wartime and in peacetime. If anyone contravenes these
provisions, let the *tagos* in office enforce them. He saved the gold
and (10) silver objects lost from Delphi when Orestes (?) son of
Pherecrates son of Philonicos was *hyloros*.

3. **καὐτōι**: crasis (καὶ αὐτōι); cf. κἀτέλειαν 2 (καὶ ἀτέλειαν), etc.
Ϝλοικιάταις: Att. οἰκέτης is derived from οἶκος; some of the dialects
(including Ion.) derive the word from οἰκία.

4. **χρέμασιν**: the dat. plur. of consonant stems in Thess. (as in the
other Aeolic dialects) is normally -εσσι. Since the -ν at the end of the
word is a trait of Attic-Ionic, it looks like the legalistic formulae
of this inscription were simply borrowed *in toto*.   **ἀσυλίαν**: 'exemption of property from seizure (σῦλαι)'.   **ἀτέλειαν**: < *ἀτελεσ-ια
cf. adj. ἀτελής 8 10.   **εὐϜεργέτᾱν**: 'internal' -Ϝ- retained in the
transparent element Ϝεργ-, 'work' (§34.4): and there is a glide after
the υ.

6–7. **κἒν ταγᾶ κἒν ἀταγίᾱι**: equivalent in sense to καὶ ἐν πολέμωι
καὶ ἐν εἰρήνηι (a common epigraphic formula), probably 'when there
is a *tagos* in office and when there is not' (Hooker 1980). For ταγᾶ
(rather than ταγία) cf. δίκη ~ ἀδικία (see also Chadwick 1969 and
1992).

7. **αἰ**: §36.1.   **τις**: κις in eastern Thessaly (cf. κί **11** 11).
ταῦτα: the normal demonst. in Thess. is built with -νε (neut. plur.

τάνε). **παρβαίνοι** (Att. παραβαίνοι): short prepositional forms (§24.5) are the norm in Thess.
8. **τᾱγόν**: Thessalian magistrate. **ἐπεστάκοντα**: perf. ptcpl. (Att. ἐφεστηκότα): §36.2. The lack of aspiration (typical of Ion.) is unexpected in Thess. **ἐξξανακάδεν** (Att. ἐξαναγκάζειν): infin. expressing command (for the normal Thess. infin. see §36.3). For double ξ see ἐσστροτευμένας **14** 25. The κ is a simplex writing of κκ, assuming the original γ [ŋ] assimilated to the following obstruent. So also δ is a simplified writing of -δδ- < *-δγ- (§23.8).
10. **τές** (τὰ ἐς) + gen.: in Thess. and Boe. (and sporadically elsewhere) ἐξ + cons. > ἐς (7 6). **Βελφαῖο**: gen. of a sing. form (Att. Δελφῶν); the initial labial shows Aeolic treatment of labiovelar *gʷ (§34.3).
11 f. **Ὀρέστᾱο** ... **hυλōρέοντος**: gen. absolute on this intepretation. Φερεκράτε<ο>ς, if correctly restored, is gen. of the father's name: elsewhere in Thessaly patronymic adjectives are found (but the reading is disputed: see Morpurgo Davies 1968: 88). hυλōρέοντος, 'being *hyloros*', lit. 'keeper of the woodland' (cf. ὕλη + ὁράω), but the word presumably has a wider application here. In Thess. vowel-stem verbs are generally athematic (§24.1): this is either a western isogloss with WGk., or an Ionic form. **hυιός**: < *sujwos, gen. of an archaic nom. υἱύς (as in Homer, **67** 143).

10. Stone from Metropolis in Hestiaeotis (western Thessaly), confirming the privileges of the Basaidai clan. Second half of III cent. BC. *SEG* 36. 548. [▶] Helly (1970), García Ramón (1987).

θιός· τύχαν ἀγαθάν· | Συνθείκα Βασαίδουν τεῖς εἴντεσσι τοῦν
πειττάρουν γενίουν καὶ τᾶς ταγᾶς κοινανείντ|ουν τὲν πάντα χρόνεν,
καὶ αὐτεῖς καὶ τᾶι γελⁿ5νιᾶι τᾶι ἐς τύτουν γινυμέναι. μὰ ἔστου
πολδέξαστα πὸτ τὰν ἰσοτιμίαν μαδέμινα μαλδὲ ταγὰν δοῖν ἔξου τᾶς
συγγενείας. αἰ μά | κά τις ἐν τύτεις μὰ ἐμ[μ]έναι, ἀπόλαος ἔστου |
[ἄ]τ τᾶς συγγενεί[ας] καὶ τάλαντεν ἀργύρ||¹⁰[ρου] ὀφλέτου [τ]εῖς
συγγενέσσι· ὀνύματα τοῦν | [συγγ]ενίουν· Κλίανδρες Ἐπι|κρατίδαις
· · ·

· · · · · ·

. . . ξενδόκοι τύτο[υν πὰρ τὲν ||²⁰ Ἄπλουνα] Ἑκατόμβιεν· ὁ λείτορας
ὁ ἐν [Ματρο|πόλει, ὁ λείτ]ορας ὁ ἐπὶ Ττυλίχνας.

God. Good fortune. Compact for those of the Basaidai who belong to the four tribes and who participate in the *taga* in perpetuity, both for themselves and for the (5) progeny issuing from them. Let it not be lawful for them to receive anyone into an equality of privilege, nor to bestow the *taga* outside the clan. But if anyone does not abide by these provisions, let him be expelled from the clan and pay a talent of silver (10) to the clansmen. Names of the clansmen: Kleandros son of Epikratidas . . .
[*13 further names*]
Witnesses of these provisions in the presence of (20) Apollo Hekatombios: the priest at Metropolis, the priest for Polichnai.

In addition to regular Thess. vowel changes (§34.3), the Matropolis inscription shows further peculiarities:

(*a*) *v* is sometimes used where *ov* would be expected (as in τύτουν 3): this may be the result of a change [ow] > [uː], as in Attic and Boeotian (Blümel 1982: 64).

(*b*) ε: in word-final syllables ε is found in place of *o* (unparalleled in Greek): this probably denotes a loss of vowel colour in unstressed position, as in Engl. *talon* [tælən] (cf. Chadwick 1992). If this is true, the implication is that—as the accent moved from a pitch to a stress accent—vowel length ceased to be distinctive. This should be borne in mind as a possible factor in peculiar vowel spellings below: for example, there seems to be a neutralization of distinction between α, αι (perhaps now [ä], as in Boe.) and various *e*-vowels in final (or unstressed?) position.

2. **Βασαίδουν**: has the form of a patronymic (cf. **55** 19). **τεῖς εἴντεσσι** (Att. τοῖς οὖσι): for τεῖς cf. αὐτεῖς 4. εἰν- instead of expected ἐν- in the pres. ptcpl. of εἰμί may be analogical: φίλειμι (§24.1) exports its long vowel to the ptcpl. (φιλέντες → φιλεῖντες), from where it spreads to the ptcpl. of 'be' (ἔντες → εῖντες). See Morpurgo Davies (1978). **πεττάρουν** (Att. τεττάρων): initial π- < *k^w (§35.1). For -ττ- (< *-tw-) in common with Att., Boe. see §35.3.

3. **γενίουν**: < γενέων (Att. γενῶν), §23.2. **τᾶς ταγᾶς**: i.e. the chief Thess. magistracy. **κοινᾱνείντουν**: Att. κοινωνούντων (for the stem cf. κοινᾶνας 7 21), §24.1. For the long *e* in -είντουν cf. on εἴντεσσι 2.

4. **τὲν . . . χρόνεν**: <ε> is probably [ə] in an unaccented syllable: (*b*) above. **αὐτεῖς**: the spelling <ει> suggests monophthongiz-ation of [oi] > [ü] > [i] (as in Boeotian, and later in the koiné).

5. **ἐς**: < ἐκ-ς (**9** 10). **γινυμέναι**: for υ < o in this context cf. ὀνύματα 10. **μά** (Att. μή): elsewhere the usual Thess. form is μεί by (*a*) above. **ποδέξαστα** (Att. προσδέξασθαι): aor. mid. inf. The preposition ποτ (§24.5) assimilates to the following δ (> -δδ-, here written with a single). For -στ- see §39.5. For the odd ending -α (instead of -αι or -ει) cf. (*b*) above.

6. **μαδέμινα** (Att. μηδένα): unique form. Perhaps created by con-tamination of μήτινα with a part of μηδείς (cf. the fem. μᾱδεμίαν); or μηδάμα with μηδένα (cf. Alk. fr. 129. 16). Hesych. gives a form μηδαμινός (stem as in μηδάμα plus suffix -ινος).

7. **δοῖν**: 3 plur. aor. opt. of δίδωμι, expressing prohibition. Probably derives from δοῖεν, by syncope of unaccented [e]. **μά** (ᾰ): Thess. particle corresponding in function to Att. δέ (not to be confused with μά = μή). It occurs in Att. oaths, μὰ Δία, etc. (Mod. Gk. μά, 'but', is borrowed from It. *ma* < Lat. *magis*).

8. **κα**: usually κε in Thess. (§36.7) **τις**: κις in north-eastern Thessaly (cf. κί **11** 11). But the word order αἰ κά τις is the normal Thess. pattern (cf. §40.6). **ἐμμέναι**: apparently the 3 sing. aor. opt. of ἐμμένω. The use of the opt. rather than the subj. is striking, and García Ramón (1987: 117–19) may be right to see an anomalous spelling of the pres. sub. ἐμμένη(ι). **ἀπόλαος**: *hapax*, '[banished] away from the community (λᾱός)'.

9. **[ἂ]τ**: ἀπό (apocope and assimilation: cf. ἔπ **11** 10). **ἀργύρ[ρου]**: restored thus because Thess. has a tendency to palatalize and double a resonant before *i* (indicating that the *i* is consonantal: -Rʸ- > -RRʸ-): a secondary development analogous to §23.7.

10. **ὀφλέτου** (Att. ὀφλείτω): 3 sing. aor. imper. of ὀφλισκάνω. **ὀνύματα**: o > υ between resonant and labial may be an early sound-change common to all dialects (Cowgill 1965: 113), in which case Att. ὄνομα would be the result of assimilation (cf. Sihler §44).

11. **Ἐπικρατίδαις** (< -αιος): patronymic adj., nom. The final syllable is syncopated, helped perhaps by the phonetic similarity of <αι> = [ä(:)] and <o> = [ə] (cf. χρόνεν 4).

19. **ξεν-δόκοι**: syncopated form of ξενο-δόκοι, 'witnesses'.

20. **[Ἄπλουνα]**: acc. The dialects present various forms of the

god's name (Ἀπόλλων, Ἀπέλλων, Ἀπείλων, etc.): Thess. Ἄπλουν is syncopated (Fraenkel 1956: 82–6, and Plato *Crat.* 405c). **Ἑκατόμβιεν**: epithet of Apollo, 'to whom hecatombs are dedicated'. **λείτορας**: elsewhere in Thess. the expected form λείτ-ουρ is found. The agent-noun ending in -ορας is standard in Mod. Gk. (replacing -ωρ): this seems to be a uniquely early example (Helly 1970: 179). 21. **Ττυλίχνας** (Att. Πολίχνας): Ττ- by assimilation from Πτ- (cf. **8** 1 and §23.4).

11. Stone from Larisa in Pelasgiotis, recording letters in koiné from Philip V of Macedon which 'recommend' that the city enroll new citizens, and the decrees by the city in Thessalian enacting Philip's instructions (the decrees follow Philip's letters almost verbatim). Only the part containing the first decree is given here. 214 BC. *IG* IX 2. 517. Buck 32. Schwyzer 590.

ψαφιξαμένας τᾶς πόλιος ψάφισμα ‖¹⁰ τὸ ὑπογεγραμμένον· «Πανάμμοι τᾶ ἔκτα ἐπ ἰκάδι συνκλεῖτος γενομένας, ἀγορανομέντουν τοῦν
ταγοῦν πάν|τουν· Φιλίπποι τοῖ βασιλεῖος γράμματα πέμψαντος πὸτ
τὸς ταγὸς καὶ τὰν πόλιν διὲ κί Πετραῖος καὶ Ἀνάγκιππος καὶ |¹²
Ἀριστόνοος, οὺς ἆτ τᾶς πρεισβείας ἐγένονθο, ἐνεφανίσσοεν αὐτοῦ
ποκκὶ καὶ ἁ ἀμμέουν πόλις διὲ τὸς πολέμος πο|τεδέετο πλειόνουν
τοῦν κατοικεισόντουν· μέσποδί κε οὖν καὶ ἑτέρος ἐπινοείσουμεν
ἀξίος τοῖ πὰρ ἀμμὲ |¹⁴ πολιτεύματος, ἒτ τοῖ παρεόντος κρεννέμεν
ψαφίξασθειν ἀμμὲ ο<ὔ>ς κε τοῖς κατοικέντεσσι πὰρ ἀμμὲ
Πετθ[α]‖λοῦν καὶ τοῦν ἄλλουν Ἑλλάνουν δοθεῖ ἁ πολιτεία· τοίνεος
γὰρ συντελεσθέντος καὶ συμμεννάντουν πάν|¹⁶τουν διὲ τὰ
φιλάνθρουπα πεπείστειν ἄλλα τε πολλὰ τοῦν χρεισίμουν ἔσσεσθειν
καὶ εὐτοῦ καὶ τᾶι πόλι καὶ | τὰν χούραν μᾶλλον ἐξεργασθείσεσθειν·
ἐψάφιστει τᾶ πολιτεία πρασσέμεν πὲρ τούννεουν κὰτ τὰ ὁ
βα|¹⁸σιλεὺς ἔγραψε, καὶ τοῖς κατοικέντεσσι πὰρ ἀμμὲ Πετθαλοῦν
καὶ τοῦν ἄλλουν Ἑλλάνουν δεδόσθειν τὰν πολι|τείαν καὶ αὐτοῖς καὶ
ἐσγόνοις καὶ τὰ λοιπὰ τίμια ὑπαρχέμεν αὐτοῖς πάντα ὅσσαπερ
Λασαίοις, φυλᾶς ἑλομέ‖²⁰νοις ἑκάστου ποίας κε βέλλειτει· τὸ μὰ
ψάφισμα τόνε κῦρρον ἔμμεν κὰπ παντὸς χρόνοι καὶ τὸς ταμίας
ἐσδόλ|μεν ὀνγράψειν αὐτὸ ἐν στάλλας λιθίας δύας καὶ τὰ ὀνύματα
τοῦν πολιτογραφειθέντουν καὶ κατθέμεν |²² τὰμ μὲν ἴαν ἐν τὸ ἱερὸν

τοῖ Ἄπλουνος τοῖ Κερδοίοι, τὰμ μὰ ἄλλαν ἐν τὰν ἀκρόπολιν καὶ τὰν ὀνάλαν, κίς κε γιλνύειτει ἐν τάνε, δόμεν.»

The city passed the following decree: on the twenty-sixth of Panammos an assembly was held, with all the *tagoi* acting as *agoranomoi*; Philip the king having sent a letter to the *tagoi* and the city—because Petraios and Anankippos and Aristonoos, when they came on the embassy, declared to him that our city too on account of the wars was in need of more inhabitants—[saying that] until therefore we can think of others worthy of our citizenship, for the present he judges that we should decree that the citizenship be granted to those of the Thessalians (15) and the other Greeks who are resident among us; for if this is done and all stand together in friendship, he is convinced that many other benefits will accrue both to him and to the city and that the land will be cultivated more widely.—It was decreed, in respect of the citizenship, to act concerning these matters as the king had written, and that the citizenship should be conferred upon those of the Thessalians and the other Greeks living with us, both to them and to their descendants, and that all the other privileges should be available to them that are available to the Larisaians, each choosing (20) whichever tribe he wishes to belong to; and this decree is to be valid for all time, and the treasurers are to disburse money to inscribe it on two stone blocks along with the names of the enrolled citizens, and to set up one in the shrine of Apollo Kerdoios and the other on the acropolis and to pay the expenses which are incurred for this purpose.

9–10. The text starts with a series of genitive absolutes: ψαφιξ-αμένας τᾶς πόλιος, συνκλείτος γενομένας, ἀγορανομέντουν πάντουν.

9. **ψᾱφιξαμένᾱς**: aor. mid. ptcpl. of ψᾱφίζομαι, 'vote' (for aor. in -ξα §40.4). **πόλιος**: §32.4.

10. **Πανάμμοι**: gen. sing., shortened -οιο (§36.8), 'of (the month) Panammos'. *Πάναμμος* < *Πάνασμος (Doric *Πάνᾱμος*). **τᾶ ἕκτᾱ**: dat. sing. (the long diphthong has already disappeared); ἰκάδι from ἰκάς (< *Fικάς): 'on the sixth (day) after the twentieth' (Attic μετ' εἰκάδα, **41** 2). **ἔπ**: apocope (§24.5); so also πότ 11, ἄτ 12, πόκ 12, πάρ 13, ἔτ 14, πέρ and κάτ 17.

10. **συνκλείτος**: gen. sing. of a consonant-stem συνκλείς,

'assembly', for which cf. Attic ἡ σύγκλητος (βουλή). ει denotes close [ẹ:] < open η (§34.3). **ἀγορᾱ-νομέντουν**: pres. ptcpl. (Att. ἀγορᾱνομέω): in eastern Thess. 'contracted' (vowel-stem) verbs are athematic (§24.1). Here a technical term, perhaps 'presiding over the assembly'. ου denotes close [ọ:] < open ω (§34.3).

11–17. The syntax wanders hopelessly, since the composer starts with a gen. absolute (Φιλίπποι πέμψαντος), and then tries to reproduce the entire contents of Philip's letter before resuming with the main verb ἐψάφιστει at 17.

11. **πότ**: §24.5. **τὸς τᾱγός**: acc. plur. (cf. §23.9). **διὲ κί** (cf. Att. διότι 'because'): διέ, of uncertain origin, is used for διά in inscriptions at Larisa and Phalanna; these two places are unique also in producing κ- from labio-velar *kʷ before i (§10.6 and Dunnett 1970).

12. **οὖς ἆτ τᾶς πρεισβείᾱς** (Att. ὡς ἀπὸ τῆς πρεσβείᾱς): ἄτ < ἄπ (assimilation). πρέσβυς and related forms in the dialects are difficult to explain neatly; there seems to have been a variant containing the digraph ει in Boe., Thess., and WGk. **ἐγένονθο**: 3 plur. forms (act. and pass.) in Thess. and Boe. often have <νθ> instead of <ντ>. This probably represents aspiration extended from the mid. endings -μεθα, -σθε. **ἐνεφανίσσοεν** (Att. ἐνεφάνιζον): 3 plur. imperf. The stem in -σσ- is a back-formation from the aor. ἐνεφάνιξα (present stems in -σσ- and -ζ- are sometimes confused because they both have -ξ- in the aor. and fut., §40.4). The imperf. and aor. in Thess. end in -οεν/-αεν in the 3 plur. This unusual ending could have developed on the analogy of the opt., which it resembles (Morpurgo Davies 1965); or may be a digraph representing a weak unstressed vowel (so Chadwick 1992). **αὐτοῦ** (Att. αὐτῶι): dat. **ποκκί**: < *ποδ-κι (functionally equivalent to Att. ὅτι < *yod-kʷid, but with first element *kʷod). **ἀμμέουν**: the gen. plur. ending is added to the acc. ἀμμέ (§32.5) in Thess., just as in Att.-Ion. ἡμῶν < ἡμέων < *ἡμέ + ων (the acc. was later recharacterized in Att.-Ion. by the addition of -ας): §38a. **ποτεδέετο** (Att. προσεδεῖτο): in reported speech, Att. syntax would normally require opt. or pres. indic., but here the verb has been assimilated to the imperf. ἐνεφανίσσοεν (helped perhaps by the unusual closeness of opt. and imperf. in Thess.).

13. **κατοικεισόντουν** (Att. κατοικησόντων): fut. ptcpl. 'settle'. **μέσποδι**: Thess. conj. meaning 'until' (García Ramón 1993: 137); the

first element can be seen in Arc. μέστε (**7** 30) and Hom. μέσφα (for -ποδ- cf. on ποκκί 12), and cf. Chadwick (1996: 195–8).   **ἕτερος, ἀξίος**: acc. plur. (§23.9).   **ἐπινοείσουμεν** (Att. ἐπινοήσωμεν): 1 plur. aor. subj.   **πὰρ ἀμμέ**: the acc. rather than the dat. after παρά is characteristic of Thess., Boe. and NW Gk.; occurs sporadically elsewhere (Colvin 1999: 224), incl. Att.-Ion.

14. **ἔτ**: < ἐπ (ἐπί).   **κρεννέμεν**: pres. act. inf. In north-eastern Thessaly (Pelasgiotis) and in Boe. the -μεν ending of the athematic inf. spread to thematic verbs. The stem κριννω (Att. κρῑνω) < *krin-yō (§23.7); ι is often written ε after ρ in Thess., indicating a more open sound.   **ψᾱφίξασθειν** (Att. ψηφίσασθαι): infinitives in -σαι and -σθαι turn up at Larisa with an ending -ειν (with final -ν perhaps triggered to avoid ambiguity with finite forms: §34.3b and García Ramón 1975: 67).   **ο(ὗ)ς κε** (with υ added by editors): corresponds to ὅπως in the koiné of Philip's letter; for ὡς κε in a final relative clause cf. **13** 2.   **κατοικέντεσσι**: pres. ptcpl. (dat. plur.) of an athematic verb (§24.1): Att. κατοικέω.   **Πετθαλοῦν** (Att. Θετταλῶν): the aspiration of the Aeolic form Φετταλός (for Φ- see §35.1) has been transferred from the labial to the dental.

15. **δοθεῖ** (Att. δοθῆι): 3 sing. aor. pass. subj.   **τοίνεος**: gen. sing. of a demonstr. pronoun ὅ-νε, both parts of which are declined (Lejeune 1943).   **συν-μεννάντουν** (Att. -μεινάντων): aor. ptcpl. of συν-μένω. For the aor. stem μενν- < *μενσ- cf. §23.6.

16. **πεπείστειν** (Att. πεπεῖσθαι): perf. pass. inf.   **ἄλλα τε**: the phrase is repeated from Philip's letter; it seems unlikely that τε < *kʷe is native to Thess. (§35.1).   **ἔσσεσθειν** (Att. ἔσεσθαι): fut. inf. **εὐτοῦ** (Att. αὐτῶι): dat. sing. (ε-αυτο > ηυτο > ευτο: the first vowel in a long diphthong is occasionally shortened in Greek, Lejeune 1972: §376).

17. **ἐξεργασθείσεσθειν** (Att. ἐξεργασθήσεσθαι): fut. pass. inf. **ἐψᾱφιστει** (Att. ἐψήφισται): 3 sing. perf. pass. For ει in place of αι cf. ψᾱφίξασθειν 14.   **πρασσέμεν**: pres. act. inf. (cf. κρεννέμεν 14). **τούννεουν**: gen. plur. (see τοίνεος 15).

18. **δεδόσθειν** (Att. δεδόσθαι): perf. pass. inf.
19. **ἐσγόνοις**: for ἐς 'from' see on **9** 10.   **ὑπαρχέμεν**: pres. act. inf.   **Λασαίοις**: syncope (Λαρισαίοις).
19–20: **φυλᾶς ... βέλλειτει**: ἑκάστου is dat. in apposition to

ἐλομένοις (which agrees with Λασαίοις); φυλᾶς has been attracted into the gen. of ποίας (understand 'to be').
20. **βέλλειτει** (Att. βούληται): 3 sing. pres. subj. (cf. βολόμενον **7** 24 for the stem; ἐψάφιστει 17 for the ending). **κύρρον** (< κύριον): see on ἀργύρ[ρου] **10** 9. **ἐσδόμεν** (Att. ἐκδοῦναι): aor. act. inf. (cf. ἐσγόνοις 19).
21. **ὀνγράψειν** (Att. ἀναγράψαι): aor. act. inf. For ὀν-: see §28.9. **ἐν**+acc., the usual construction in Thess. and Boe. (§28.8). **στάλλας**: < *stal-nā or *sta-slā (cf. §23.6), Att. στήλη. **λιθίας**: adjs. of material are usually built with -ινος in Gk. (Att. λίθινος 'made of stone'). For the suffix -ιος, a general adjectival suffix, see Chantraine (1933: 34–7): however, it may also represent -εος (which usually denotes material) in dialects such as Thess. where ε > ι before a vowel. **δύας**: a rare example of a fem. acc. of δύο, 'two'. **ὀνύματα**: the usual form outside Att.-Ion. (**10** 10). **πολῖτο-γραφειθέντουν**: gen. plur., aor. ptcpl. (Thess. rendering of the koiné verb πολιτογραφέω). **κατθέμεν** (Att. καταθεῖναι): aor. act. inf.
22. **τάμ**: τάν (§23.4). **ἴαν**: fem. form of 'one' found in all Aeolic dialects; or perhaps ἴαν (assuming μία → ἴα under the influence of masc. ἔν-ς, neut. ἔν). **Ἄπλουνος**: gen., cf. on **10** 20. **μά**: see on **10** 5. **ὀνάλᾱν**: ā-stem corresponding to Att. ἀν-άλ-ωμα, 'expense' (§28.9). **γινύειτει** (Att. γίγνηται): 3 sing. pres. subj.; for γινυ- cf. γινυμέναι **10** 5, for the ending -τει cf. ἐψάφιστει 17.
23. **ἐν τάνε**: Att. ἐς τάδε (§28.8 and τοίνεος 15).

BOEOTIAN
(Aeolic)

For Boeotian phonology and spelling see §34.

12. Dedication in two dactylic hexameters on a bronze statuette of Apollo (probably from Thebes). Early VII cent. BC. *LSAG* 90, 94 no. 1. *CEG* 326. ▶▶ Powell (1991: 167–9), *NAGVI* §303.

Μάντικλός μ' ἀνέθεκε Ϝεκαβόλοι ἀργυροτόξσοι
τᾶς {δ}δεκάτας· τὺ δέ, Φοῖβε, δίδοι χαρίϜετταν ἀμοι[βάν].

Mantiklos dedicated me to the Far-darter with silver bow out of the tithe; and you, Phoibos, grant a gracious recompense.

1. Two Homeric epithets of Apollo are joined in a single expression (see Risch 1974: 220 for ἑκη-βόλος). Μάντικλος is a hypocoristic of a name such as Μαντι-κλείδας. **ἀργυροτόξσōι**: the letter here transcribed ξ is written <X>, the normal 'red' alphabet sign for [ks] (§18); the first letter of χαρίϝετταν is written <Ψ>.

2. **δεκάτᾱς** (μερίδος): 'tenth (part), tithe.'   The final phrase is found with epic colouring at *Od.* 3. 58, δίδου χαρίεσσαν ἀμοιβήν. δίδοι has been explained as a 2 sing. opt. of δίδωμι, with imperatival force (and unusual morphology); but 2 sg. imper. is more likely, formed on the 2 sg. indic. δίδοις (cf. *Il.* 9. 164) of the Aeolic poetic tradition (see Strunk 1961). The form is also found in Pindar (**79** 85).   **χαρίϝετταν**: adj. contains the *-*went*- suffix seen in Myc. *pe-ne-we-ta* **1** (§13). The fem. is built on *-*wn̥t-ya*, where *ty > ττ in Boe. and Attic (§31.4), σσ in the other dialects.

13. Graffito on a vase of unknown provenance: one word *extra metrum* followed by two iambic trimeters. V cent. BC. *IG* VII 3467. Buck 38–5. Schwyzer 441. *CEG* 446.

> Μογέα   δίδōτι τᾶι γυναικὶ δῶρον Εὐχάρῑ
> τēὐτρētιφάντō κότυλον, ὅς χ᾿ ἄδαν πίε̄.

Mogea(s) gives a cup as a gift to his wife Eucharis, the daughter of Eutretiphantos, that she may drink her fill.

1. **Μογέα**: masc. *a*-stems were recharacterized in Gk. with nom. sing. -ς. Forms in -α found occasionally in Boe. and NW Gk. are probably old vocatives, as in Hom. ἱππότᾰ (Méndez Dosuna 1982).

2. **Εὐχάρῑ** < Εὐχάρι: dat.

3 **τēὐτρētιφάντō**: crasis (τᾶι + Εὐ-).   **ὅς χ᾿ ἄδαν πίε̄**: purpose clause (ὡς generally takes the potential particle in Hom. purpose clauses).   **ὡς**: apparently unaspirated (the inscription could have written the aspirate *H*).   **χ᾿** = κα (§36.7) with elision and aspiration (χ᾿ denotes *KH*, so the breathing on ἄδαν is typographic convention).   **πίε̄**: 3 sing. aor. subj. of πίνω (the original ending: Att. -ηι is due to the analogy of indic. -ει).

14. Stone from Orchomenos giving details of an agreement between Orchomenos and Chaironea to conduct joint mounted patrols. The first few lines of the inscription are

damaged. Early III cent. BC. Étienne-Roesch (1978). *SEG* 28.
461. ▶▶ Étienne-Roesch (1978).

... ὁμολογὰ τοῖς ἱππότης τοῖς Ἐρ|χομενίων κὴ Χηρωνείων ὑπὲρ
τᾶν | στροτειιάων. Τὰς μὲν προτεινὶ στρο‖¹⁰τειίας Θιογνειτίδαο
ἄρχοντος Ἐρχο|μενίοις, Βοιωτοῖς δὲ Φιλοκώμω, ἀφι|[εμ]ένας
εἶμεν, ἄρχεμεν δὲ τὰς στρο|[τε]ιίας τὰς ἐπὶ Θιογνειτίδαο ἄρχον|-
[τος] Ἐρχομενίοις, Βοιωτοῖς δὲ Φιλο‖¹⁵[κώ]μω· στροτευθεῖμεν δὲ
ἐχθόν|[δ]ε τᾶς Βοιωτίας πράταν τὰν Σαυκλ|[ία]ο, δευτέραν τὰν
Πουθοδώρω, τ|[ρ]ίταν τὰν Χηρωνείων Εὐμειλίαν, | [π]ετράταν
Ἀριστίωνος, ἐν δὲ τῇ ‖²⁰ [Βο]ιωτίῃ πράταν τὰν Ἀριστίωνος, |
[δ]ευτέραν Πουθοδώρω, τρίταν | [Χ]ηρωνείων Εὐμείλω, πετράταν |
[Σ]αυκλίαο· ἠ δέ κά τινες Fίλη Fίσα | [στρ]οτευθείωνθι, κλαροέτω
ὁ ἴπ‖²⁵[πα]ρχος τὰς Fίσα ἐσστροτευμέ|νας Fίλας· τιθέσθη δὲ τὰς
στροτειιίας τάς τε ἐν τῇ Βοιωτίῃ κὴ τὰς ἐ|χθόνδε τᾶς Βοιωτίας
χωρὶς ἑκατέ|[ρ]ας ἇς κα τὰ ἐφόδια λάβωνθι.

An agreement between the cavalry of Orchomenos and that of
Chaironea pertaining to military expeditions. The previous
expeditions (10) under the archonship of Theognetidas at
Orchomenos and Philokomos in Boeotia are released from duty:
the expeditions (constituted) under the archonship of Theognetidas at Orchomenos and Philokomos in Boeotia are (hereby)
inaugurated (15). First to exercise outside of Boeotia shall be the
(squadron) of Saukleas; second that of Pythodoros; third that of
the Chaironians of Eumeilos, fourth that of Aristion. And within
(20) Boeotia, first shall be that of Aristion, second that of Pythodoros, third that of the Chaironians of Eumeilos, fourth that of
Saukleas. In the case that some of the squadrons spend an equal
amount of time on exercise, the Hipparch (25) is to draw lots
(*sc.* for extra service) among those squadrons which have spent an
equal amount of time on exercise. One should account separately
exercises in Boeotia and exercises outside Boeotia, (and the
accounting should be) for the time that they are drawing their
daily allowance.

7. **ὁμολογά**: Att. ὁμολογία.   **ἱππότης**: dat. plur.   **Ἐρχομενίων**:
the form *Orchomenos* is the result of vowel assimilation.

8. **ὑπέρ**: see **15** 4.   **τᾶν**: -ᾱ-ων contracts in the article, but not in nouns (Att. τῶν < τέων < τή-ων): §30.2.

9. **στροτειάων**: < *strt̥- (§34.1). The Boe. reflex of *r̥ is mixed, perhaps a result of its WGk./Aeol. history (cf. πετράταν 19). The spelling -ειιά- suggests that a glide -y- has emerged from the diphthong ει (§34.4) before another vowel.   **προτεινί**: elsewhere spelled προτηνί (~ Att. προταινί), 'earlier'.

10. **Θιογνειτίδαο**: the name is an old patronymic form of Θεόγνητος.   **ἄρχοντος**: construction with the dat. is found in Homer, but very rare in Att. (occasionally in tragedy).

11. **ἀφι[εμ]ένας**: pass. ptcpl. of ἀφίημι, here a technical term.

12. **εἶμεν**: < ἦμεν < *es-men (§36.3).

13. **ἐπί**: with gen. 'in the time of', regular in Boe. archon formulae (cf. Attic ἐπὶ κινδύνου 'in time of danger', etc.).

15. **στροτευθεῖμεν**: aor. pass. infin.   **ἐχθόν[δ]ε**: 'outside', *hapax*. ἐχθός < *ἐχτός (assimilation) < *ἐκσ-τος (cf. **7** 6 ἐσδοτῆρες). For the final -ν cf. ἔνδον (Buck §133.3).

16. **πράταν**: Att. πρῶτος, WGk./Boe. πρᾶτος (§38.2).   **Σαυκλίαο**: gen. of *Σαο-κλεας. In Boeotia -κλεας replaced -κλος in the hypocoristic form of *kleos* names (cf. on **12** 1).

18. **Εὐμειλίαν**: 'of Eumelos'. The adj. performs the same function as a gen., and is an extension of the Boe. patronymic adj. in -ιος which substitutes for the gen. of the father's name. Names in μῆλον were popular in Boeotia.

19. **πετράταν**: for the labial (*kʷetwr̥-tos) see §35.1.   **τῆ**: < ταῖ < τᾶι.

23. **ἠ δέ κά**: Att. ἐὰν δέ (note different order).   **Fίλη**: nom. pl. of Fίλα, 'squadron'.   **Fίσα**: neut. plur., adverbial. For initial F- see ἇς **29** (§35.2).

24. **στροτευθείωνθι**: aor. subjunct. pass., 3 plur. (uncontracted θη: in Att. θῶ < θέω < θηω). For -νθι see on ἐγένονθο **11** 12.

25. **ἐσστροτευμένας**: s is often doubled before consonants in Boe., indicating 'spread' across the syllable boundary.

29. **ἇς**: < *ἇ̄Fος (Att. ἕως < ἧος). Internal -F- has now disappeared from Boe. (cf. χαρίFεττα **12** 2); initial F- remains (§35.2).

---

15. Stone from Akraiphia regulating the price of fish. The first text on the stele deals with sea fish, the second with freshwater fish. The first 11 lines (out of 41) of the first text are given here. Late III cent. BC. *SEG* 32. 450. ▶▶ Vatin (1971), Roesch (1974), Thompson (1947).

1 Τὺ ἀγώναρχυ τὺ ἐπ' Ἀριστοκλεῖος ἄρχοντος
  Ἀμινίας Διονουσίω, Δικῆος Διονουσίω,
  Ἰαροκλεῖς Ἐγχόρμαο, ἐσταλοκόπεισαν τὰ δεδο[γμένα]
  οὐπὲρ τῶ θαλαττήω·   Κουνοπρείστιος *H*
5 τὼς δὲ τὸ θαλαττῆον   5a Κουνὸς καρχαρίαο *Π*
  πωλίοντας πωλῖμεν   Κανθάρω παντό[ς] *H*
  σταθμῦ[ς] κο[θ]αροῖς.   Κοκκούκων *ΙΠΧ*
  Ἀλφειστᾶο [.]*XX*   Κορακίνων [   ]
  Ἀμία[ς.]*XX*   Καλλιωνούμω [   ]
10 Ἀγνάθω [10a Λάβρακος [   ]
  Ἀρκάνω [..]*XX*   τῶ μίονος τῶ μναιήω [ ]
  (30 more lines in 2 columns, much mutilated)

The market-commissioners in the archonship of Aristokles— Aminias son of Dionysios, Dikaios son of Dionysios, Hierokles son of Enkhormas—had the stele cut for the decisions concerning seafood.

5 Those selling seafood
  are to sell it with honest
  measures as follows:
  • wrasse *2 coppers*
  • bonito tuna *2 coppers*
10 • lamprey (?) [
  • bass (?) [..]*2 coppers*

• sawfish *½ obol*
• spiny dogfish *5 coppers*
• black bream *each ½ obol*
• gurnard *1½ obols*
• corb [   ]
• white scorpion fish [   ]
• sea-bass [   ]
the smaller type, per *mna* [ ]

Money. X = Att. χαλκοῦς, Boe. χάλκιος (bronze coin: 12 to an obol in Boeotia). Π = 5 χ. I = 1 obol. H for ἡμι-, 'half' (Att. ἡμιωβέλιον). Prices are apparently per *mna*.

1. **τύ**: i.e. τοί, nom. plur. (Boe. and WGk., §32.6). **ἀγώναρχυ**: Att. ἀγορανόμοι (officials who regulated the business of the market). **Ἀριστοκλεῖος**: < *-κλεϜεσ-ος.

2. **Ἀμινίας Διονουσίω**: from around the mid III cent. the Aeolic patronymic adj. gives way to the genitive of the koiné (§36.7).

4. **οὐπέρ**: ὑπέρ in the sense of περί was also a feature of colloquial Attic (in the IV cent. orators, and epigraphic after *c*.300).

θαλαττήω: neut. noun made from an adj. meaning 'of the sea' (Att. θαλάττιος, but Pindar's θαλασσαῖος has the stem seen here).

5. **τώς**: 'thus'. Corresponds to Att. οὔτως.

6. **πωλίοντας**: synizesis (§34.9).   **πωλῖμεν**: from πωλε + εμεν (with [i:] < [e̤:]).

7. **σταθμῦ[ς] κο[θ]αροῖς**: inconsistencies in the spelling of the old diphthongs are not unusual in inscriptions. κοθαρός: found in WGk. dialects and Lesbian: the variation α ~ ο is unexpected.

8. **ἀλφειστᾶο**: ἀλφηστής, *Labrus cinaedus* (see Athen. 7. 281 for an explanation of the Latin name); the Greek term is obscure. Fish are listed in the gen. (of cause, as at Ar. *Clouds* 31), both sing. and plur.

9. **ἀμία[ς]**: bonito (*Sarda sarda*), a fish closely related to skipjack tuna.

10. **ἀγνάθω**: not previously attested. The modern class of *agnatha* (jawless fish) has only two extant examples, one of which is the the lamprey (genus *petromyzon*), an eel-like fish which may be meant here.

11. **ἀρκάνω**: not elsewhere attested, but probably a type of bass: cf. (*a*) ἀκάρναξ, a type of *labrax* (bass) according to Hesych.; and (*b*) ἄχαρνος, a fish apparently identified with bass by Aristotle.

4*a*. **κυννοπρείστιος**: sawfishes (*pristidae*) are closely related to sharks, which would explain the compound (not elswhere attested) in κυνο-. Cf. Attic πρῖστις or πρῆστις (πρίω 'saw'): refers to the shape of its snout.

5*a*. **κυννὸς καρχαρίαο**: καρχαρίας from κάρχαρος 'jagged' (i.e. with saw-like teeth). A small shark, called 'dog(-fish)' across the Mediterranean (*Squalus acanthias*).

6*a*. **κανθάρω**: a word borrowed from the Near East (Szemerényi 1974: 148) for a type of drinking-cup: then 'dung beetle, scarab' (here *Spondyliosoma cantharus*).

7*a*. **κοκκούκων**: κόκκυξ, 'cuckoo'. From the noise it makes when caught, according to Aristotle (*Hist. Anim.* 535b). One of the gurnard family (e.g. *Aspitrigla cuculus*).

8*a*. **κορακίνων**: lit. 'raven fish' < κόραξ 'raven' (*Corvina nigra*).

9*a*. **καλλιωνούμω**: the name may be euphemistic (reflecting the appearance or poisonous spikes of the fish). A member of the *scorpaeidae* or *trachinidae* (said to be the Fr. *rascasse blanche*, an important ingredient in bouillabaisse).

10*a*. **λάβρακος**: the name suggests its reputation as an aggressive predator (*Dicentrarchus labrax*).
11*a*. **τῶ μίονος**: μείων. A comparative of ὀλίγος, rare in Attic (modifies λάβρακος). **μναιήω**: apparently < μναϊαῖον (Attic μνᾶ), a measure of weight. A loanword from Semitic (probably Phoenician).

LESBIAN
(Aeolic)

For the accentuation of Lesbian see §34.10.

16. Epitaph on a stone monument from the neighbourhood of Kebrene in the Troad. V cent. BC. Buck 24. Schwyzer 638. Hodot (1990), #TRO 302.

σ[ᾶμ]α 'πὶ Σθενείαι ἔμμι τὸ Νικιαίδι τὸ Γαυκίō.

I am the monument upon Stheneias the son of Nikias the son of Gaukos.

σ[ᾶμ]α: some editors read σ[τάλ(λ)]α (cf. στάλλας **11** 21).   **(ἐ)πί**: prodelision.   **ἔμμι** < *ἐσμί (Att. εἰμί): § 38a.   **τō**: dat. sing. The loss of -ι from long diphthongs happened first in the article. **Νικιαίδι**: dat. sing. of a patronymic adj., which Aeolic uses in preference to gen. of the father's name (§ 35).   **Γαυκίō**: another patronymic adj., if the reading is correct, but it may not be a complete word (Bechtel suggests Γ(λ)αυκίō[νος]).

17. Stone from Mytilene, recording a monetary agreement between that city and Phokaia on the mainland. Late V or early IV cent. BC. *IG* XII 2. 1. Buck 25. Schwyzer 619. Hodot (1990), #MYT 01. ▶ Heisserer (1984), Engelmann (1985).

- - - - - - - - - - - - - - - - - [ὄττι | δέ κε αἰ] πόλις [ἀ]μφότ[εραι - - - -
- - - - - - - | - - - -]γράφωισι εἰς ταὶ[ς στάλλαις ἢ ἐ|κκόπ]τωισι,
κύ[ρ]ιον ἔστω. τ[ὸν δὲ κέρναν‖⁵τα τὸ] χρύσιον ὑπόδικον ἔμ[μεναι
ἀμφο|τέρ]αισι ταῖς πολίεσσι· δικ[ά]σ[ταις δὲ | ἔμ]μεναι τῶι μὲν
ἐμ Μυτιλήναι κ[έρναν|τι] ταὶς ἄρχαις παίσαις ταὶς ἐμ Μ[υτιλ]ήναι
πλέας τῶν αἱμίσεων, ἐμ Φώκαι δ[ὲ τ]‖¹⁰αὶς ἄρχαις παίσαις ταὶς ἐμ

Φώκαι πλ[έ]|ας τῶν αἰμίσεω[ν]· τὰν δὲ δίκαν ἔμμεναι | ἐπεί κε
ὠνίαυτος ἐξέλθηι ἐν ἒξ μήννε|σι. αἰ δέ κε καταγ[ρέ]θηι τὸ χρύσιον
κέρ|ναν ὐδαρέστερο[ν] θέλων, θανάτωι ζαμιⁱ|¹⁵ώσθω· αἰ δέ κε
ἀπυφ[ύ]γηι μ[ὴ] θέλων ἀμβρό|την, τιμάτω τὸ̣ δικαστήριον ὄττι
χρὴ αἶτ<ο>ν πάθην ἢ κατθέ[μ]εναι. ἀ δὲ πόλις ἀναί|τιος καὶ
ἀζάμιος [ἔσ]τω. ἔλαχον Μυτιλή|ναοι πρόσθε κόπτην. ἄρχει πρότανις
ὀ ||²⁰ πεδὰ Κόλωνον, ἐ[μ Φ]ώκαι δὲ ὀ πεδὰ ᾽Αρίστ̣|αρχον.

Whatever the two cities [—————] inscribe on the [stone] or
delete from it, that is to be valid. A person who alloys (5) the
gold (coinage) is to be responsible to both cities. For one who
makes the alloy in Mytilene the judges are to be all the magistrates in Mytilene, (constituting) more than half; and in Phokaia
all the (10) magistrates in Phokaia, (constituting) more than
half: the trial is to be held within six months of the end of
the year. If anyone is convicted of wilfully debasing the gold, let
him be punished with death (15); but if anyone is acquitted of
wilful wrongdoing, let the court decide what he should suffer
or what fine he should pay. And let the city be free from blame
or penalty. The Mytilenaians drew the lot to strike (the
currency) first. The agreement begins with the magistrate (20)
after Kolonos, and at Phokaia with the magistrate after
Aristarchos.

2. **πόλῑς**: nom. plur., most likely extended from the acc. -ῑς < -ινς.
3. **]γράφωισι**: 3 plur. pres. subj. < -ωνσι (§34.11). Probably a
compd. with προσ-, 'add'. **εἰς**: note that this is a real diphthong
in Lesb., unlike Attic εἰς = [ẹːs].
4. **[κέρναντα]**: pres. ptcpl. of κέρνᾱμι (Att. κεράννυμι), 'mix', so
(here) 'make an alloy': but this (hypothetical) form could be
thematic (see κέρνᾶν 13).
5. **ὐπόδικον**: an item borrowed from Att. legal language (López
Eire 1993: 54 f.). **ἔ[μμεναι]**: athematic inf. (§36.3).
6. **πολί-εσσι**: Aeolic -εσσι attached to an *i*-stem (§36.4).
δικ[άσταις]: acc. plur. (§34.11), so also ταὶς ἄρχαις 8, etc.
8. **παίσαις**: παίσα < *pansa < *pant-ya (§34.11).
9. **πλέας**: < *πλέοας with hypheresis (cf. δαμιοργόντōν 37 1).
Forms of this comparative are built on *plē-yos- (Szemerényi 1968a:
33–6), with the diphthong in Att. πλείους, etc. probably analogical

on superl. πλεῖστος. Cf. Hom. πλέες, πλέας, and *a-ro₂-a* **1** (a).
αἰμίσεων: αι for η in αἰμι- < *sēmi*- is hard to account for, unless
the confusion is evidence for [ai] > [ε:] as in Boe. and later in
Att. (Hodot 1990: 71): also found in Sapph. and Alk. (αἰμιθέων,
Alk. 42.13). **Φώκαι**: dat. < Φωκαίαι by reduction of the -ι- and
contraction.

12. **κε**: §36.7. **ὠνίαυτος**: crasis (ὁ ἐνίαυτος). **μήννεσ(σ)ι**:
the stem is *μηνσ- (cf. Lat. *mēns-is*). Lesb. μῆννος < *μηνσός (§23.6),
Att. μηνός. The *s*-stem dat. plur. in Sapph. and Alk. is always -εσι
(cf. §36.4).

13. **αἰ δέ κε**: Att. ἐὰν δέ (note different order). **καταγρέθηι**:
Lesb., Thess., Elean have ἀγρέω for αἱρέω (and Myc. *a-ke-re-
se*=ἀγρήσει); cf. the fossilized imper. ἄγρει in Homer. **κέρνᾶν**:
*κερνάων, pres. ptcpl. masc. with καταγρέθηι, for which cf. θέλων
with ἀπυφύγηι **15** (Heisserer 1984: earlier editors took it as an
athem. pres. infin. of κέρνᾱμι). Contrast athem. κέρναις **75** b4 (Alk.):
a them. ~ athem. doublet is already attested in Hom.
κιρνάω ~ κίρνημι).

14. **ὑδαρέστερον**: lit. 'too watery', so 'debased'. **ζᾱμιώ-σθω**:
denominative: athematic endings are added to a long-vowel stem
throughout the paradigm (*ζᾱμίω-μι).

15. **ἀμβρότην**: aor. inf. (Att. ἀμαρτεῖν): *amr̥t- > *ἀμροτ- (for
ρο < *r̥ see §34.1); then -β- is inserted as a glide between μ and ρ
(cf. ἀνδρός < *ἀνρός). Inf. ending -ην < *-ε-εν (§36.3).

16. **ὄττι**: < *okkʷi < *yod-kʷid (Att. ὅτι remodelled on the basis of
ὅστις).

17. **κατθέμεναι**: athematic aor. inf. (§36.3), apocope of κατα-.

19. **πρότανις**: Att. πρύτανις. Fluctuation in the vowel points to
borrowing from a non-Greek source (cf. *di-pa* **5e**).

20. **πεδά**: prep. equivalent to (unrelated) μετά, found in Lesb.,
Boe., and a few other dialects (and Myc., which has μετά
also).

18. Stone from Mytilene, much damaged at the left, recording
a settlement adopted by the city after Alexander's forces
retook it from the Persians in 332 BC. The returning exiles
are presumably pro-Macedonian elements who had fled the
Persians. (Only the first part of the inscription is given

110   *Dialect Inscriptions*   **18**

here.) *c*.332 BC. *IG* XII 2. 6. Buck 26. Schwyzer 620. Hodot
(1990), #MYT 04. Rhodes–Osborne (2003, no. 85*b*). ▶▶
Heisserer (1980: 118–39), Hodot-Heisserer (1986: 120–28).

1 - - - - - - - - - - [καὶ οἱ β]ασί[ληες προστί]θησ[θον τῶι
κατεληλύθον-
[τι ὡς τέχναν τεχνα]μέν[ω] τῶ ἐ[ν τᾶι] πόλι πρόσθε [ἔοντος.
αἰ δέ κέ τις
[τῶν κατεληλυθόν]των μὴ ἐμμένη ἐν ταῖς διαλυσί[εσ]σι
ταύτ[αισι,
[μὴ - - - - - - - - - - -]ζέσθω πὰρ τᾶς πόλιος κτήματος μήδενος
μη[δὲ στ-
5 [ειχέτω ἐπὶ μῆ]δεν τῶμ παρεχώρησαν αὔτωι οἱ ἐν τᾶι πόλι
πρό[σθε
[ἔοντες, ἀλλὰ σ]τείχοντον ἐπὶ ταῦτα τὰ κτήματα οἱ
παρχωρήσαν[τ-
[ες αὔτωι ἐκ τῶν] ἐν τᾶι πόλι πρόσθε ἐόντων. καὶ οἱ στρόταγοι
εἰσ-
[αῦθις ἀπυφέρο]ντον ἐπὶ τὸν ἐν τᾶι πόλι πρόσθε ἔοντα τὰ
κτήματα,
[ὡς μὴ συναλλαγ]μένω τῶ κατεληλύθοντος· καὶ οἱ βασίληες
προστί-
10 [θησθον τῶι ἐν τ]ᾶι πόλι πρόσθε ἔοντι ὡς τέχναν τεχναμένω τῶ
κα-
[τεληλύθοντος]· μηδ᾽ αἴ κέ τις δίκαν γράφηται περὶ τ[ο]ύτων,
μὴ εἰσά-
[γοντον οἱ περί]δρομοι καὶ οἱ δικάσκοποι μηδὲ ἄ[λλ]α ἄρχα
μηδέϊα.

And let the magistrates favour him who has returned on the
ground that the party who remained in the city has committed
fraud. But if any of the returned exiles does not abide by these
agreements, let him not————receive any property from the
city, nor let him take possession (5) of any of the properties which
those who remained in the city made over to him; but let those
of them who were previously in the city take possession of any
property which they made over to him; and let the *strotagoi* deliver
back the property to the person who remained in the city, on
the ground that the returned exile has not entered into the

reconciliation; and let the magistrates favour (10) him who remained in the city, on the ground that the returned exile has committed fraud; and if anyone brings an action regarding these matters, neither the circuit-judges nor the recorders nor any other official are to admit the case.

1. The function of the *βασιλῆες* ('magistrates') at Mytilene is discussed by Carlier (1984: 457–8). ***προστί]θησ[θον***: 3 plur. mid. imperat., §36.9 (Att. *-τιθέσθων*). The long vowel of the stem has been generalized from the active *τίθημι*. **[*κατεληλύθοντι*]**: perf. ptcpl. conjugated like the pres. (§36.2).

2. **[*τέχναν τεχνα*]*μέν*[*ω*]**: gen. absolute, 'plotting a plot'. Subject is [*τ*]*ῶ*, '(any-)one who' (gen. absolute). ***πόλῑ***: < *πόλιι*, dat. sing. (cf. §32.4, and *πόλιος* 4).

3. ***ἐμ-μένη***: 3 sing. pres. subj. (final *-ι* is lost in long diphthongs from the IV cent.). ***διαλυσί-εσσι***: dat. plur. (§36.4).

4. *-]ζέσθω*: Heisserer (1980: 126) suggests *ἀπυκομιζέσθω*. ***πάρ***: §24.5. ***πόλιος***: §32.4.

5. ***τῶμ***: *τῶν* with labial assimilation. Attic would have *ὦν* (§32.13).

6. **[*σ*]*τείχοντον ἐπί***: 3 plur. imper., 'walk upon', so 'take possession of'.

7. ***ἐόντων***: the expected form < **ἐσ-οντ-*, etc. (§32.11). ***στροτᾱγοί***: *στροτ-* < **strt-* (§34.15, and *ἀμβρότην* **17** 15).

9. **[*ὡς*] ... *κατεληλύθοντος***: gen. absolute.

12. **[*περί*]*δρομοι, δικασκόποι***: these two terms are not known outside of Lesbos. ***μηδε-ία***: for *ἴα = μία* see *ἴαν* **11** 22.

IONIC
(Attic-Ionic)

19. Four-sided block from Chios (broken at the top), inscribed on each side (only the first is given here): a decree fixing the boundaries of Lophitis. V cent. BC. Buck 4. Schwyzer 688. *LSAG* 344 no. 48.

ἀπὸ τούτō μέχρι [*τῆς*] | *τριόδō, ἢ ̔ς Ἑρμώνοσσαν* [*φ*]|*έρει, τρὲς· ἀπὸ τῆς τριόδō ἄ*[*χ*]|*ρι Ἑρμωνόσσης ἐς τὴν τρίοδ*||⁵*ον, ἔξς· ἀπὸ τούτō μέχρι τὸ* | *Δηλίō, τρὲς· σύνπαντες ὅρ*|*οι ἑβδομήκοντα πέντε*. | *ὅση τῶν ὅρων τούτων ἔἰσω πᾶσα Λοφῖτις. ἤν τίς τ*||¹⁰*ινα τῶν ὅρων*

τούτων | ἢ ἐξέληι ἢ μεθέληι ἢ ἀ|φανέα ποιήσει ἐπ᾽ ἀδικί|ηι τῆς
πόλεως, ἑκατὸν σ|τατῆρας ὀφειλέτω κά|τι||¹⁵μος ἔστω, πρηξάντων δ᾽
ὁ|ροφύλακες· ἢν δὲ μὴ πρή|ξοισιν, αὐτοὶ ὀφειλόντω|ν, πρηξάντων δ᾽
οἱ πεντε|καίδεκα τὸς ὀροφύλακας· ||²⁰ ἢν δὲ μὴ πρήξοισιν, ἐν ἐπ|αρῆι
ἔστων.

From here as far as the fork in the road which leads to
Hermonossa, three (stones); from the fork up to Hermonossa
to the fork, six (stones); from here as far as Delion, three (stones);
in all seventy-five boundary-stones. What is within these
boundaries is all Lophitis. If anyone takes out or removes or
destroys any of these stones to the harm of the city, let him be
fined one hundred staters and deprived of civic rights, and let the
boundary-wardens exact (the fine); and if they do not exact it, let
them owe (the fine) themselves, and let the Fifteen exact it from
the boundary-wardens; and if they do not exact it, let them be
under a curse.

1. **τούτō**: ō [ǫ:] is kept distinct from the inherited diphthong *ου*
in this inscription (§23.1); so also ē [ẹ:] and *ει*, except for ὀφειλ-
(where the digraph represents lengthened ē [ẹ:]).
2. **(ἐ)ς**: prodelision. **τρês**: i.e. [trẹs:] < *trey-es*.
3. **ἄχρι**: synonym of μέχρι, with α- < *m̥- (zero-grade of initial
*me-).
5. **ἔξς**: probably a confused spelling. Since the word ends a
phrase it seems unlikely that the -s had an extended articulation
(cf. ἐξξανακάδēν 9 8).
6. **ὄροι**: [ǫ:ros] < (ϝ)όρϝος. Loss of -w- after a liquid caused compensatory lengthening (§30.6).
9. **ἤν**: contraction of εἰ + ἄν (cf. Att. ἐάν, §32.8).
12. **ἀδικίηι**: Att. -ίᾱι (cf. ἐπαρῆι 8): §§30.1, 30.3.
14. **κάτιμος**: crasis (καὶ ἄτιμος).
16. **πρήξοισιν**: 3 plur. fut., the clearest indication that Chian
contains elements from the neighbouring Aeolic region: Ionic stem
πρηξ- (§30.1), Lesbian ending -οισι (< -ονσι, §34.11), Ionic moveable
-ν (§32.7).

20. Two stones from Teos, cursing public and private
malefactors. *c.*475–450 BC. Buck 3. Schwyzer 710. *LSAG* 340,

345 no. 62. Meiggs–Lewis 30. *Nomima* i. 104. ▶️ Herrmann (1981), Merkelbach (1982).

A ὅστις φάρμακα δηλητή-
ρια ποιοῖ ἐπὶ Τήιοισι-
ν τὸ ξυνὸν ἢ ἐπ᾽ ἰδιώτηι κ-
ênον ἀπόλλυσθαι καὶ α-
5 ὐτὸν καὶ γένος τὸ κêνō.
ὅστις ἐς γῆν τὴν Τήιην κ-
ωλύοι σῖτον ἐσάγεσθαι
ἢ τέχνηι ἢ μηχανῆι, ἢ
κατ-
ὰ θάλασσαν ἢ κατ᾽
ἤπειρο-
10 ν, ἢ ἐσαχθέντα ἀνωθεοίη,
κêν-
ον ἀπόλλυσθαι καὶ αὐτ-
ὸν καὶ γένος τὸ κέ̄νō.

B *2 lines mutilated*
3 ὅστις Τηίων [- - - - - - - -]
  2 lines mutilated
6 [- - - - -]ἀπόλλυσθαι καὶ
αὐτὸν καὶ γένος τὸ κείν-
ō. ὅστις τὸ λοιπō αἰσυμ-
νῶν ἐν Τέωι ἢ γῆι τῆι Τη-
10 ίηι [- - - - - - - - - - - - -]
[- - - - - - - - - - - - - εἰδ-]
ὡς προδο[ίη - - - -] τὴ[ν]
πό-
λ[ιν καὶ γῆν] τὴν Τηί-
ων ἢ τὸ[ς] ἄνδρας [ἐν ν-]
15 ήσωι ἢ θα[λάσσηι] τὸ

μετέ[πειτ᾽ ἢ τὸ] ἐν
Ἀρο[ί]ηι περιπό[λιον ἢ
τô]
λοιπô προδο[ίη ἢ κιξα-]
λλεύοι ἢ κιξάλλας ὑπο-
20 δέχοιτο ἢ ληίζοιτο ἢ λ-
ηιστὰς ὑποδέχοιτο εἰ-
δὼς ἐκ γῆς τῆς Τηίης ἢ
[θ-]
αλάΤης φέροντας ἤ [τι κ-]
ακὸν βōλεύοι περὶ Τ[ηί-]
25 ων τὸ ξυνὸ εἰδὼς ἢ π[ρὸς]
Ἕλληνας ἢ πρὸς βαρβάρο-
υς, ἀπόλλυσθαι καὶ αὐ-
τὸν καὶ γένος τὸ κέ̄νō.
οἵτινες τιμōχέοντες
30 τὴν ἐπαρὴν μὴ ποιήσεα-
ν ἐπὶ Δυνάμει καθημένō-
ō τὠγῶνος Ἀνθεστηρίο-
ισιν καὶ Ἡρακλέοισιν
καὶ Δίοισιν, ἐν τῆπαρῆ-
35 ι ἔχεσθαι. ὃς ἂν τὰ(ς)
στήλ-
ας ἐν ἧισιν ἡπαρὴ γέγρ-
απται ἢ κατάξει ἢ φοιν-
ικήια ἐκκόψει ἢ ἀφανέ-
ας ποιήσει, κêνον ἀπόλ-
40 λυσθαι καὶ αὐτὸν καὶ γ-
ένος [τὸ κέ̄νō].

A. Whoever shall manufacture poisonous drugs against the Teans—either as a community or against an individual—that man is to die, both himself (5) and his family. Whoever shall prevent grain from being imported to the territory of Teos by any device or means, either by sea or by land (10), or inflates the price of (re-exports?) grain that has been imported, that man is to die, both himself and his family.

B. . . . Whoever of the Teans [. . .], that man is to die, both himself and his family. Whoever in the future shall be *aisumnêtês* in Teos or the territory of Teos (10) and [. . .] or shall knowingly betray [. . .] the city and territory of Teos or her men on (15) the island or at sea hereafter or the suburb at Aroia; or in the future shall behave treacherously or engage in banditry or (20) harbour bandits; or shall engage in piracy or knowingly harbour pirates bearing (booty) from the territory of Teos or the sea; or shall knowingly plot evil concerning the community of the Teans (25), either with Greeks or barbarians; that man is to die, both himself and his family. Whichever magistrates (?) do not pronounce (30) the curse at the statue of Dynamis during the assembly at the Anthesteria, and at the festivals of Herakles and Zeus, they are to be (35) cursed. Whoever breaks the steles on which the curse is written, or knocks out the letters or makes them illegible, that man is to die (40), both himself and his family.

Colons (not reproduced here) divide the inscription into accentual units (Wachter 1999: 366).

A2. **ποιοῖ**: < ποι-ε-οι (Att. ποι-ε-οιην > ποιοίην). Although ε + οι are usually uncontracted outside Attic, exceptions occur after a vowel: cf. ἀνωθεοίη 10. **Τήιοισιν**: §32.14. Moveable -ν is common before a consonant in inscriptions (§32.7).

3. **ξυνὸν**: ξῦνός < ξυν-yος (cf. ξύν). Semantically equivalent to Att. κοινός < κομ-yος (cf. Lat. *cum*).

4. **ἀπόλλυσθαι**: inf. in imperative sense.

5. **κένō**: gen. sing. (Att. κείνου): §23.1.

6. **ἐς**: Ionic has ἐς < *ἐνς before a consonant (§32.10). In the case of *ἐνς + V (e.g. ἐσαχθέντα 10) εἰς ~ [e:s] was maintained in some areas: but the spelling of [e̞:] with *E* makes this difficult to detect (§23.1).

10. **ἀνωθεοίη**: athem. inflection of a vowel-stem verb in the opt., characteristic of Attic and found occasionally elsewhere (cf. §24.1).

B3–5. The discovery of a new stone in 1976 (*SEG* 31. 984 and

Herrmann 1981) undid earlier attempts to read these lines. The general sense is 'Whoever conspires to install a tyrant (*aisumnêtês*) . . .'

8. **αἰσυμνῶν**: an 'elected dictator' according to Aristotle (*Pol.* 1285a31). The city clearly had bad memories from the Persian occupation.

22. **[θ]αλάΤης**: <*T*> stands for the sign 'sampi', found sporadically along the Ionian coast (*LSAG* 38), and perhaps borrowed from the Karian alphabet. It was used between *c.*550 and 450 BC to write a sibilant (the result of **ky*, **ty*, **tw* in the case of words of Greek origin), perhaps an affricate such as [ts].

30. **ποιήσεαν**: an intervocalic -*i*- occasionally becomes a weakly articulated glide and is omitted from the writing (ViV > Vi̯V > VV).

35. **τὰ(ς) στήλας**: i.e ταστηλας on the stone, with single writing of double *s*.

37. **κατάξει**: short-vowel subjunctive. Notice the switch from opt. to subj. The clause deals with more mundane wrongdoing (vandalism as opposed to high treason), and the mood is therefore less 'remote'. **φοινικήια**: see Hdt. 5. 58 for the introduction of writing by the Phoenicians, and **52** below for the Cretan word ποινικαστάς, 'scribe'.

21. Letter written on lead from Achillodorus to his son Protagoras. Found at Berezan near the Milesian colony of Olbia on the Black Sea. *SEG* 26. 845. Dubois (1996: no. 23). *Nomima*, ii. 72. Trapp (2003: no. 1). Late VI cent. BC. ▶▶ Chadwick (1973), Merkelbach (1975), Wilson (1998).

A. ὦ Πρωταγόρη, ὁ πατήρ τοι ἐπιστέλλε. ἀδικέται | ὑπὸ Ματασυος, δόλοται γάρ μιγ καὶ τὸ | φορτηγεσίō ἀπεστέρεσεν. ἐλθὼμ παρ' Ἀναξαγόρην | ἀπήγησαι· φησὶ γὰρ αὐτὸν Ἀναξαγόρεω ||⁵ δōλον ἔναι μυθεόμενος· «Τἄμ' Ἀνα<ξα>γόρης ἔχε̄, | καὶ δο̄λōς καὶ δόλας κοἰκίας.» ὁ δὲ ἀναβῶι τε | καὶ οὔ φησιν ἔναι οὐδὲν ἑωυτῶι τε καὶ Ματασιν | καὶ φησιν ἔναι ἐλεόθερος καὶ οὐδὲν ἔναι ἑωυτ<ῶ>ι | καὶ Ματ{ατ}ασυ. ε̄ δέ τι αὐτῶι κἀναξαγόρη, αὐτοὶ ||¹⁰ οἴδασι κατὰ σφᾶς αὐτός. ταῦτ' Ἀναξαγόρη λέγεν | καὶ τῆ γυναικί. ἕτερα δέ τοι ἐπιστέλλε. τὴμ μητέρα | καὶ τὸ̄ς ἀδεφεὺς <ο>ἵ ἐσ{σ}ιν ἐν Ἀρβινάτηισιν ἄγεν ἐς τὴμ πόλιν, | αὐτὸς δὲ †εονεορος ἐλθὼμ παρά †μιν θυωρα καταβήσεται.

B Ἀχιλλοδώρō τὸ μολίβδιον παρὰ τὸμ παῖδα | κἀναξαγόρην

A12. *Εονεορος* Chadwick; ἐς *Νεορο(υ̇)ς* Merkelbach; δέ γ' ὁ νεορὸς Bravo *apud* Dubois.

Protagoras, your father sends you these instructions. He is being treated unjustly by Matasys, who is holding him as a slave and confiscated his equipment. Go to Anaxagoras and tell him, since he (Matasys) claims that he is the (5) slave of Anaxagoras, saying 'Anaxagoras has my stuff—both male and female slaves, and houses'. But he (your father) protests, and denies that there is anything to do between him and Matasys, and declares that he is a free man, and that there's nothing to do between him and Matasys. But if there's some business between him and Anaxagoras, they (10) themselves between them know what it is. Tell this to Anaxagoras, and his wife. And he sends these further instructions: your mother and your brothers who are in Arbinatai, take them to the town. And [. . .]self, going [. . .] will travel down to the coast at Minthyora (?).

The lead tablet of Achillodorus, to his son and Anaxagoras.

Features characteristic of private letters (but not exclusive to them) include: repetition (see Dover 1997: 59, who compares Lysias i. 17), paratactic style (use of connectives such as τε καί, δέ to structure the sentences), and confusing switches in grammatical subject.

1. **ἐπιστέλλε̄**: Achillodorus refers to himself in the third person throughout the letter. Use of <ε> for the verbal ending (historically a diphthong) indicates that [ei] and [ẹ:] had already fallen together in this Ionic dialect (§23.1).   **τοι**: enclitic dat. of σύ (as in Hdt., who has a tonic dat. σοί). In Att. τοι was fossilized as a particle.

2. **Ματασυος**: a non-Gk. name. The writer makes limited attempts to inflect it with Gk. case-endings. Merkelbach concludes that Matasys is 'ein halb-hellenisierter Skythe'. The Scythians were a semi-nomadic Iranian people who inhabited the southern steppes north of the Black Sea.   **δō̄λō̂ται**: mid. 'enslave'. A connection with δολόω 'trick' would also be possible, but makes difficult sense.   **μιγ**: [min], assimilated to the following velar. An isolated Ionic pronoun (3 sing., acc. only), found in Homer and Hdt. (also in Myc.).

3. **φορτηγεσίō**: *hapax*, clearly related to φορτ-ηγέω (Hdt.), 'carry cargo'. The exact meaning has been disputed: may refer to the ship itself, or the business in a wider sense.   **ἀπεστέρēσεν**: perhaps ἀπεστέρεσεν, given *Od.* 13. 262 στερέσαι (orig. from *στέρε-μι, Ruijgh 1992: 446).

4. **ἀπήγησαι**: aor. imper. of an Ionic vb. (Att. ἀφηγέομαι is not used in this sense).   **Ἀναξαγόρεω**: gen. ending < -ηο < *-āο. Probably a monosyllable (cf. Δεινοδίκηο **23** 2): §§30.2, 30.7.

5. **μυθεόμενος**: not a verb used in Att. prose (or Hdt.). Perhaps 'his story is . . .'.

7. **ἐωυτῶι**: < ἑοῖ αὐτῶι (Att. ἑαυτῶι is the result of 'etymological' contraction, i.e. desire to leave the main element recognizable in crasis outweighs the normal phonological rule).   **Ματασιν**: dative. Chadwick emends Ματασ<υι>.

8. **ἐλεόθερος**: this spelling for ἐλεύθερος suggests that εο and ευ had fallen together (cf. Χαλκίδευ **22** 2). The spelling of μυθεόμενος would be helped by its morphological transparency.   **ἐωυτ<ῶ>ι** : tablet has εωυται.

9. **Ματ{ατ}ασυ**: dative, with dittography.   **κἀναξαγόρη**: καὶ Ἀναξαγόρη (dat.), with final -ηι apparently simplified already to -η (cf. 10, τῆ 11).

10. **οἴδασι**: 3 pl. found also in Hdt. Morphological regularity came early to this vb. in Ionic: οἶδας *Odyssey* 1. 337.   **σφᾶς αὐτός**: the reflexive (later ἑαυτούς, both forms in Hdt.) emphasizes the author's lack of involvement.

11. **γυναικί**: not completely clear whether this is the wife of Achillodorus or Anaxagoras.

12. **ἀδεφεύς**: i.e. ἀδελφε-ός (cf. **24** 26). Printing ἀδε<λ>φεύς implies that the writer mistakenly omitted λ, but it may be a phonetic spelling: e.g. ἀδευφεύς (attested in Crete, and cf. the change Lat. *alter* > Fr. *autre*), with dissimilation of the first υ.   **Ἀρβινάτηισιν**: perhaps 'among the Arbinatai', given Steph. Byz. Ἀβρινάται· Ποντικὸν ἔθνος.

13. **αὐτὸς δέ**: should refer either to the author or to εονεορος. **εονεορος**: suggestions include a new name 'Euneuros' (but *neur* is a puzzling onomastic element); ἐς Νεορούς 'to the Neuroi' (a Scythian tribe mentioned at Hdt. 4. 17); ὁ νεορός 'the captain' (*νᾱϜ-ορος). **μιν θυωρα**: perhaps a name 'Minthyora'; otherwise μιν, 'him' plus a

second word difficult to analyse. **καταβήσεται**: often with the sense 'towards the coast'.

22. Stone from Erythrai: proposal to place restrictions on the holding of the office of scribe. *c*.400 BC. *I. Erythrai* 1. Schwyzer 702. *Nomima*, i. 84. ▶▶ Garbrah (1978).

Ἀπελλίας εἶπεν· ὅσοι ἤδη ἐγρα|μμάτευσαν ἀπὸ Χαλκίδευ ἔκαθ|εν, τούτων μὴ ἐξεῖναι γραμματ|εῦσαι ἔτι μηδενὶ μηδεμιῆι ἀρ||⁵χῆι, μηδὲ τὸ λοιπὸν γραμματεύ|εν ἐξεῖναι μηδενὶ πλέον ἢ ἅπα|ξ τῆι αὐτῆι ἀρχῆι μηδὲ ταμίηι | πλέον ἢ ἐνί, μηδὲ δύο τιμαῖς τὸ|ν αὐτόν. ὃς δ᾽ ἂγ γραμματεύσηι ||¹⁰ ἢ ἀνέληται ἢ εἴπηι ἢ ἐπιψηφίσ|ηι, κατάρητόν τε αὐτὸν εἶναι κ|αὶ ἄτιμον καὶ ὀφείλεν αὐτὸν ἐ|κατὸν στατῆρας. ἐκπρηξάσθων | δὲ οἱ ἐξετασταὶ ἢ αὐτοὶ ὀφειλ||¹⁵όντων. ἄρχεν δὲ τούτοις μῆνα Ἀ|ρτεμισιῶνα ἐπ᾽ ἱροποιὸ Πόσε|ος.

Apellias proposed: those who have already held the office of scribe, from (the time of) Chalkides onwards, should no longer be allowed to act as scribe for any magistracy, and should not be allowed in future to act as scribe more than once for the same magistracy nor for more than one treasurer, nor the same scribe for two magistracies. Now whoever acts as scribe [10] (a second time) or chooses (someone) to act as his scribe, or makes a proposal, or puts it to the vote, is to be accursed and deprived of civic rights and fined one hundred staters. Let the auditors exact this sum or be fined [15] themselves. The beginning of these provisions to be the month Artemision in the priesthood of Posis.

Compare the complexity of the syntax with the preceding passage. The preposed relatives (ὅσοι . . . etc.) with resumptive pronoun recall the structure of **20**. These and other features (e.g. 'polar' or universalizing expressions coordinated with ἤ) point to the early development of a technical legal style in Ionia.

1. **Ἀπελλίᾱς**: the name may be borrowed from neighbouring Aeolic, since it is built (*a*) on the *e*-grade of *Apollo* (cf. on **10** 20), and (*b*) with suffix -ίᾱς rather than -ῆς < -έης < -έᾱς.

2. **Χαλκίδευ**: gen. of Χαλκίδης. Final -ευ < -εω < *-ηο < *-ᾱο (cf. §30.7, and Szemerényi 1956). **ἔκαθεν**: found in the meaning 'from afar' in Homer; here it is equivalent to Herodotean ἀνέκαθεν, 'from the beginning, starting with'.

3. **γραμματεύεν**: pres. inf. with *E* denoting [e̩:] < *-*e(h)en* (§23.1).
4. **μηδεμιῆι**: η < ā (§30.1).
9. **ἄγ**: [aŋ] < ἄν, with assimilation of the nasal to the following velar.
10. **τιμαῖς**: short dat. plur. ending (replaces older -ῃσιν, §32.14). By the late V cent. E. Ionic had started to shorten dat. plur. endings: influenced perhaps by Attic (and central/W. Ionic), where -αις prevailed by at least 425, and by the Doric area around Halicarnassos.
15. **ἄρχēν δὲ τούτοις**: ἄρχω takes a partitive gen. when a real agent is to start something. In this case μῆνα is not the agent: ἄρχēν is absolute and and τούτοις an indirect object ('the beginning for these things is to be the month . . .').
16. **ἱροποιô**: gen. sing. The form ἱρο- occurs in Ionic inscriptions only in places close to the Aeolic region (ἱερο- elsewhere in the Ionic speech-area). **Πόσεος**: gen. of Πόσις. The *i*-stem gen. sing. at Erythrai generally ends in -ιος (or Att. -εως, §30.2): but forms such as πόλεος are found elsewhere in Ionia, and doubtless reflect remodelling under the influence of *u*-stems (cf. ἄστεος in Homer) or *s*-stems.

23. Naxian hexameter dedication (boustrophedon) on the statue of a woman found at Delos. Late VII cent. BC. Buck 6. Schwyzer 758. *LSAG* 303 no. 2. *CEG* 403. ▶▶ Lejeune (1971), *LSAG* 291.

Νικάνδρη μ' ἀνέθēκεν h(ε)κηβόλōι ἰοχεαίρηι,
Ϙόρη Δεινοιδίκηο τô Ναξσίō, ἔξσοχος ἀλήōν,
Δεινομένεος δὲ κασιγνέτη, | Φηράξσō δ' ἄλοχος μ[

Nikandre dedicated me to the Far-darter, shooter of arrows, daughter of Deinodikes the Naxian, exalted above other women, sister of Deinomenes, wife of Phraxos.

1. **Νικάνδρη**: in this inscription <*H*> is used to write the sound (perhaps [ä:]) which had developed from original long *a*; but <*E*> is used to write original long *e* (e.g. ἀνέθēκεν): §30.1. **h(ε)κηβόλōι**: Hom. epithet of Apollo (cf. **12** 1), here applied to his sister Artemis. h(ε)κη- is written *HKH*-; <*H*> for [he] is not uncommon in early inscriptions (central Ionic retained the aspirate into the epigraphic period). **ἰοχεαίρηι**: traditionally understood as a compd. of ἰός

'arrow' and χέω 'pour out' (but the second element may historically be the word for 'hand'). A standard Hom. epithet of Artemis.

2. ϙόρη: i.e. κούρη (§23.1). The letter *qoppa* (§17.2) was used for κ before a back vowel, in line with the Semitic distinction between back and front velars. Since the distinction is not phonemic in Gk. the letter was dropped at an early date.   *Δεινοδίκηο*: gen. -ηο is scanned as a single syllable (cf. *Χαλκίδεν* **22** 1 and §§30.2, 30.7). The spelling is conservative (cf. Szemerényi 1956): it it not necessary to assume with Ruijgh (1968: 315) a hyper-correct spelling by an Athenian scribe on Delos.   *Ναξσίο*: the letter transcribed here as <ξ> looks like a rectangular box (so also *ἔξσοχος*, *Φηράξσō*). Buck (ad loc.) suggests that it is a form of <Ξ> (cf. on **19** 5 *ἔξς*); it is more probably a by-form of <H> created to write [h] after original <H> was in use for [ε:]. The writing *hσ* for ξ is reminiscent of the Gk. preference for χσ over κσ, and points to an acoustic effect exercised by *s* on a preceding stop (§18.2).   *ἀλήōν*: simplex writing of -λλ-. For -ηον (scanned as a single syllable) cf. *Δεινοδίκηο* above.

3. *Δεινομένεος*: -εος is scanned as a single syllable.   At the end, the cutter seems to have begun a word with *M*, but never completed it; perhaps he intended to write *N* (*νῦν* is the only obvious word that would scan).

24.   Stone from Keos, inscribed with a law regulating funeral ceremonies. Late V cent. BC. *IG* XII 5. 593. Buck 8. Schwyzer 766. Sokolowski (1969) no. 97. ▶ Parker (1983: 34–41), Garland (1985).

οἵδε νόμοι περὶ τῶγ καταφθιμ[έ]νω[ν· κατὰ | τ]άδε θά[π]τēν τὸν
θανόντα· ἐν ἑματίο[ις τρι]σὶ λευκοῖς, στρώματι καὶ ἐνδύματι [καὶ |
ἐ]πιβλέματι, ἐξεῖναι δὲ καὶ ἐν ἐλάσ[σ]οσ[ι, μ‖⁵ἐ] πλέονος ἀξίοις
τοῖς τρισὶ ἑκατὸν δρ[αιχ]μέων· ἐχφέρēν δὲ ἐγ κλίνηι σφηνόπο[δ]ι
[κ]λαὶ μὲ καλύπτēν, τὰ δ' ὀλ[ο]σ[χ]ερέα τοῖ[ς ἑματ]ίίοις· φέρēν δὲ
οἶνον ἐπὶ τὸ σῆμα, μὲ π[λέον] | τριῶν χῶν, καὶ ἔλαιον, μὲ πλέο[ν]
ἑνό[ς, τὰ δὲ ‖¹⁰ἀ]γγεῖα ἀποφέρεσθαι· τὸν θανό[ν]τα [φέρēν |
κ]ατακεκαλυμμένον σιωπῆι μέχρι [ἐπὶ τὸ | σ]ῆμα· προσφαγίωι
[χ]ρêσθαι κατὰ τὰ π[άτρια· τ]ὴγ κλίνην ἀπὸ το[ῦ] σ[ήμ]ατο[ς]
καὶ τὰ σ[τρώ]|ματα ἐσφέρēν ἐνδόσε· τῆι δὲ ὑστεραί[ηι ἀ‖¹⁵π]οραίνēν

τὴν οἰκίην ἐλεύθερον θαλά[σσηιι] πρῶτον, ἔπειτα δὲ ὑσώπωι
ο[ἰκ]έτη[ν τὰ π]|άντα· ἐπὴν δὲ διαρανθῆι, καθαρὴν ἔναι τὴν οἰκίην
καὶ θύη θύε̄ν ἐφί[στιια]. τὰς γυναῖκας τὰς [ἰ]ούσας [ἐ]πὶ τὸ κῆδ[ος] |
ἀπιέναι προτέρας τῶν {αν}ἀνδρῶν ἀπὸ [τοῦ] ||²⁰ σήματος. ἐπὶ τῶι
θανόντι τριηκόστ[ια μὲ̄ | π]οιε̄ν. μὲ̄ ὑποτιθέναι κύλικα ὑπὸ τὴγ
[κλίν]ην με̄δὲ τὸ ὕδωρ ἐκχε̄ν με̄δὲ τὰ καλλύ[σμα]|τα φέρε̄ν ἐπὶ τὸ
σῆμα. ὅπου ἂν θάνηι, ἐπὴ[ν ἐ]|ξενιχθε̄ι, μὲ̄ ἰέναι γυναῖκας π[ρὸ]ς
τ[ὴν οἰ]||²⁵κίην ἄλλας ἒ̈ τὰς μιαινομένας· μια[ίνεσθ]|αι δὲ μητέρα καὶ
γυναῖκα καὶ ἀδε[λφεὰς κ|α]ὶ θυγατέρας. πρὸς δὲ ταύταις μὲ̄ π[λέον
πί]έντε γυναικῶν, παῖδας δὲ τ[ὦν θ]υγ[ατρῶν κὰ]|νεψιῶν, ἄλλον δὲ
μ[ε̄]δένα.

These are the laws concerning the dead. Bury the deceased as
follows: in three white cloths, one beneath, one around, and one
above—it is permitted to use even fewer—the cost of the three
not (5) to exceed one hundred drachmas; carry out (the corpse)
on a bier with wedge-shaped legs, and do not cover (the bier
with a separate cloth), but the whole with the cloths (already
specified); carry wine to the grave, not more than three measures, and oil, not more than one (measure), and carry away the
(10) receptacles; bear the deceased, shrouded, in silence as far as
the grave; perform the sacrifice in the ancestral manner; the bier
and the coverings carry indoors from the grave; and on the following day (15) let a free man first sprinkle the house with sea-
water, then a slave is to come in and sprinkle with hyssop; and
when it has been sprinkled, let the house be (regarded as) purified, and sacrifices made at the hearth. Women who come to the
funeral are to depart before the men from the (20) tomb. Do not
hold ceremonies for the deceased on the thirtieth day. Do not
place a cup under the bier (?), nor pour out water, nor bring
sweepings to the tomb. Where a person dies, when he is carried
out, women are not to come to the (25) house except for those
who are polluted. Those polluted are the mother and the wife
and the sisters and the daughters. In addition to these, no more
than five women, plus the children of the daughters and cousins,
and no one else.

1. **τῶγ**: [to:ŋ] < τῶν, with assimilation of the nasal to the following velar. Cf. ἐγ 6, τήγ 13.   **καταφθιμ[έ]νω[ν]**: aor. ptcpl. The

verb is poetic in Attic, and probably had a formal feel in Ionic also (death is often subject to linguistic displacement).

2. **θάπτε̄ν**: the first of a series of infinitives used in imperatival sense.　**ἑματίοις**: woollen covers. Dimin. of εἷμα (**wes-mn̥*, as in Skt. *vásman-*, cf. Lat. *uestis*).

5. **πλέονος**: gen. of value with ἀξίοις.

6. **ἐχ-φέρε̄ν**: the final consonant of the prefix has been assimilated to the initial consonant of the stem.

7. **ὁλο-σχερέα**: Ionic *s*-stem adj., uncontracted neut. plur. The second element is formed to σχε (root **seg^h*- as in ἔχω): cf. Hom. ἐπισχερώ, 'in a row' (for orig. **σχερός*, a -*ro*- adj., see Chantraine 1933: 224).

9. **χῶν** < χόϝων: gen. plur., with loss of -ϝ- and contraction: cf. χέ(ϝ)ω, 'pour'.

12. **προ-σφαγίωι**: dat. sing. with χρέσθαι (προ- is not temporal 'before'; perhaps 'on behalf of [others]').　**[χ]ρε̂σθαι**: from χρή-εσθαι (cf. on ἀποχρεωμένων **83** 1).

14. **ἐνδόσε**: 'inside', with motion (*hapax*); formed from ἔνδον with the rare allative suffix -σε (cf. ἄλλοσε). Att. εἴσω.　**τῆι δέ**: the sentence is arranged chiastically.

17. **διαρανθῆι**: 3 sing. aor. pass. subj. of δια-ραίνω, the prefix conveying the idea of sprinkling 'completely' or 'thoroughly'.
θύη < θύϝεα: acc. plur. neut., 'sacrifices'; loss of -ϝ- and contraction. **ἐφί[στια]**: neut. plur., lit. 'things at the hearth'; all dialects except Att. (which has ἑστία, cf. Lat. *Vesta*) have ἱστία, perhaps by vowel assimilation.

20. **ἐπὶ τῶι θανόντι**: presumably with the implication 'at the grave-side'.　**τριηκόστ[ια]**: adj. (not otherwise attested) derived from τριᾱκοστός (for the long ā see Palmer 1980: 290). Here a neut. plur. substantive, 'thirtieth-day rituals' (cf. Garland 1985: 39f.).

22. **καλλύ[σμα]τα**: from καλλύνω, 'beautify', hence 'sweep clean'. Throwing out water and dirt from the house may have symbolized the banishing of death pollution (cf. Parker 1983: 36).

23. **ἐξ-ενιχθε̂ι**: aor. pass. (suppletive) of ἐκ-φέρω. Most dialects have aor. ἠνικ-/ἤνεικ- corresponding to Att. ἤνεγκ-.

26. **ἀδε[λφεάς]**: most dialects have ἀδελφε-ός, -ά (Att. ἀδελφός is a simplified form).

29. **ἄλλον**: the masc. is 'general': in this case the (unspecified) referent seems to be female.

EUBOEAN
(Attic-Ionic)

Also known as West Ionic, Euboean occupies an intermediate position between Attic and Ionic.

25. Retrograde inscription on a Geometric vase found in 1954 in a grave at Pithecusae, a Euboean colony on Ischia. Late VIII cent. BC. *LSAG* 235, 239 no. 1; Meiggs–Lewis 1; *CEG* 454 (but '535–520' should read '735–720'). Arena (1994: no. 2). Dubois (1995: no. 2). ▶▶ Hansen (1976), Risch (1987), Powell (1991: 163–7), Cassio (1994).

Νέστορος ἐ[γόμ]ι εὔποτ[ον] ποτέριον.
hὸς δ᾽ ἂ\<ν\> τόδε πίεσι ποτερί[ō] αὐτίκα κένον{ν.}
hίμερος hαιρέσει καλλιστε[φά]νō Ἀφροδίτες.

I am Nestor's cup, good to drink from. Whoever drinks from this cup, him straightway shall the desire of fair-crowned Aphrodite seize.

Lines 2–3 are hexameters: line 1 is either prose or an iambic trimeter with an unusual licence in the first foot (*Νέστορος*: – ◡ ◡ has to stand for – –). The whole looks like a *skolion* (a song in which friends tried to cap each other) from a drinking party. It plays with the 'standard' formula 'I belong to *x*, and if anyone [damages or steals] me, then *y*' (for which compare Tataie **26**).

1. **Νέστορος**: generally thought to be a humorous allusion to Nestor's δέπας in the *Iliad* (11. 632).   **ἐ[γόμ]ι**: crasis (ἐγὸ ἔμι); the restoration is that of Risch (1987), since the gap is too wide for a single *mu*. An obvious alternative is ἐ[ἰμ]ι, 'I am': for the (real) diphthong ει see §23.1 (but **26** below).   **ποτέριον**: not a word found in epic diction, but it survives into Mod. Gk. (ποτήρι).

2. **hὸς δ᾽ ἂν**: Homeric epic always has ὅς δέ κε in this position

(Cassio 1994). This indicates that the lines are not simply borrowed from epic, but (much like archaic hexameter epigrams) were created in epic style using elements of the local dialect (and cf. ποτήριον 1). **τόδε ... ποτερί[ō]**: genitive (partitive), with <o> spelling the sound which resulted from the contraction of *o + o*. **πίεσι**: an aor. subj. in which -σι (from the athematic conjugation) has been added to the personal ending (in Hom. the ending has a secondary iota 'subscript', -ηισι). **κ̂ενον**: Homeric epic would have (αὐτίκ᾽) ἐκεῖνον at the end of the line (see hὸς δ᾽ ἄν 2 and Cassio 1994). Euboean has κεῖνος.   3. **hίμερος haιρέσει**: a variation of ἵμερος αἱρεῖ at *Il.* 14. 328 (the erotic context of the 'Deception of Zeus'). **καλλιστε[φά]νō Ἀφροδίτēς**: she is ἐϋστέφανος (a regular variant) just once in Homer (*Od.* 8. 267), in the tale of Ares and Aphrodite (Cassio 1994); the erotic reference is again significant.

26. Graffito on a vase from Cumae, a Euboean colony near Naples. Mid VII cent. BC. *IG* XIV 865. Schwyzer 786. Buck 10. *LSAG* 240 no. 3. Arena (1994: no. 16). Dubois (1995: no. 12).

Ταταίε̄ς ἐμὶ λḗϙυθος· hὸς δ᾽ ἄν με κλέφσ|ει, θυφλὸς ἔσται.

I am the oil-flask of Tataie; whoever steals me shall become blind!

Ταταίε̄ς: female names in *Tata-* are common in Asia Minor (so-called *Lallnamen*), but there is plenty of evidence for *tata-* as an element in subliterary Gk. appellatives. For examples see Headlam's commentary (Cambridge 1922) on Herodas 1. 60, ταταλίζειν. **κλέφσει** (Att. κλέψηι): 3 sing. aor. short-vowel subj. <φσ> is the regular spelling in alphabets which did not employ <ψ> in this function (§18.2): cf. Ναξσίō **23** 2. **θυφλός** (Att. τυφλός): initial stop aspirated by anticipation of -φ-.

27. Stone from Eretria honouring Hegelochos for his part in detaching the city from the Athenian alliance in 411 BC. *IG* XII 9. 187. Buck 13. Schwyzer 804. Meiggs-Lewis 82.

θεοί. | ἔδοξεν τε̂ι βουλῆι Ἡγέλοχον | τὸν Ταραντῖνον πρόξενον εἶναι καὶ εὐεργέτην καὶ αὐτὸν ||⁵ κ[α]ὶ παῖδας, καὶ σίτηριν εἶνα|ι καὶ αὐτῶι καὶ παιρίν, ὅταν ἐ|[π]ιδημέωριν, καὶ ἀτελέην καὶ |

προεδρίην ἐς τὸς ἀγῶνας, ὡς σ|υνελευθερώραντι τὴμ πόλιν ‖¹⁰ ἀπ᾽ Ἀθηνάων.

Gods. The Council decided that Hegelochos the Tarentine should be *proxenos* and benefactor, himself and his sons, and that meals (at the public expense) should be available to him and his sons, whenever they are in the city, and also exemption from taxes and an honoured place at the Games, because of his help in freeing the city from the Athenians.

2. **ἔδοξεν**: for -ν see §32.7.   **τεῖ**: Euboean shortened the long diphthong -ηι to -ει (probably [ẹ:] via [eⁱ]) at an early date, and -ωι to -οι (cf. §28.10). Attic also has -ει sporadically in the IV cent. (cf. Threatte 1980: 368). βουλῆι may be a conservative spelling, or may reflect the generally slower change of nominal endings compared to the article.

5. **σίτηριν**: the typical Eretrian developement of intervocalic -σ- to -ρ- (rhotacism, as in Lat. *honos, honōris*) is seen here and in παιρίν 7, ἐπιδημέωριν 7–8, and συνελευθερώραντι 8–9. Plato (*Cratylos* 434c) says that final -s in Eretria also became -r, but there is no epigraphic evidence for this.

6. **ἐπιδημέωριν**: pres. subj. of ἐπιδημέω (uncontracted).

7. **ἀτελέην**: a fem. abstract was formed in Gk. with the suffix -ία (ἀδικία type). Ionic preserves this pattern with s-stems (-είη/-έη < -εσ-ία); Att. ἀτέλειᾰ is the result of contamination with -ειᾰ from (derived) fem. substantives (type ἡδεῖα < *ἡδεϝ-yᾰ, with fem. suffix -yᾰ).

ATTIC
(Attic-Ionic)

28. Vase-inscription from the Dipylon cemetery at Athens, published in 1880. A hexameter followed by some letters which are difficult to make sense of. Widely considered the oldest comprehensible alphabetic Greek inscription. *c*.740–730 BC. Schwyzer Appendix I, no. 1. *LSAG* 68, 76 no. 1. *CEG* 432. *Nomima*, ii. 99. ▶▶ Watkins (1976), Powell (1991: 158–63).

hὸς νῦν ὀρχεστὸν πάντον ἀταλότατα παίζει,
τοτοδεκλλμιν

(*a*) Whoever of all the dancers now dances most friskily

(*b*) ... [*he is to receive this*?]

The vocabulary (especially ἀταλότατα) and composition are Homeric. Various attempts have been made to read the second line and make the vase a prize for the dancer: τοτο has been taken as τούτου ('of him'); or τοτοδε as τοῦ τόδε ('of him this ...'). Watkins compares the syntax and structure of *Il.* 23. 805–7: ὁππότερός κε φθῆισιν ... τῶι μὲν ἐγὼ δώσω τόδε φάσγανον, 'Whoever comes first ... to him I shall give this sword'. Wachter (*NAGVI* 50) argues persuasively that the original meaning of παίζω is 'dance'; Chadwick (1996: 218–21) suggests sexual innuendo in both this and ὀρχεστόν (cf. Ar. *Lys.* 409).

29. Stele found near the 'Theseion' at Athens: decree regulating the conduct of the Eleusinian Mysteries. Inscribed on three sides: the second (least damaged) side is given here. *c.*460 BC. *IG* I³ 6 B4–47. Schwyzer Appendix I, no. 8. Sokolowski (1962), no. 3. ▶ Rougemont (1973: 95–9), Dover (1981), (1997: 82).

...]τ|[ὰ μ]ὲν hακόσι[α | h]απλêι, τὰ δὲ h|[ε]κόσια διπλ[êι· σ]πονδὰς εἶν||⁵[αι] τοῖσι μύστι[εσιν] καὶ το[ῖς | ἐπ]όπτεισιν [κ|αὶ τ]οῖς ἀκολ[ο|ύθ]οισιν καὶ [χ||¹⁰ρέμα]σιν τὸν [ὀ|θ]ν[ε]ίον καὶ ['Αθ|ē]ν[α]ίοισιν [há|]πασιν· ἄρχε[ν δ]|ὲ τὸν χρόνο[ν τ]||¹⁵ὸν σπονδὸν [τô] | Μεταγειτνι[ô]|νος μēνὸς ἀπ[ὸ] | διχομēνίας [κ|α]ὶ τὸν Βοēδρ[ο]||²⁰μιôνα καὶ τô [Π]|υανοφσιôνος | μέχρι δεκάτēς hισταμένō· τ|ὰς δὲ σπονδὰς ||²⁵ εἶναι ἐν τêισι πόλεσιν hό[σ]|αι χρôνται τôι hιερôι, καὶ 'Αθēναίοισιν ἐ||³⁰κεῖ ἐν τêισιν | αὐτêσι πόλεσ|ιν. τοῖσι δὲ ὀλείζοσι μυστē|ρίοισιν τὰς [σ]||³⁵πονδὰς εἶνα[ι] | τô Γαμēλιôνο|ς μēνὸς ἀπὸ δ[ι|χ]ομēνίας κα[ὶ] | τὸν 'Ανθεστē-[ρ||⁴⁰ι]ôνα καὶ τô 'Ελαφēβολιôνος | μέχρι δεκάτēς hισταμένō.

...] unintentional (injuries must be paid for) by an equivalent (amount), intentional (injuries) by a double (amount); a truce is to be in force for the initiates and for the observers and for their attendants and for the property of (15) foreigners and for all Athenians; and the time of the truce is to begin at the full moon in the month of Metageitnion, and (to extend through the month of) Boedromion, and up to the tenth (day) after the beginning of (25) Pyanopsion; and the truce is to apply in those cities which participate in the rite, and to Athenians (resident) there in the same cities. (35) And for the Lesser Mysteries the truce is to be in force from the full moon in the month of Gamelion, and (to extend through the month of) Anthesterion, and up to the tenth (day) after the beginning of Elaphebolion.

This stele once stood in the Eleusinion, and may be the one referred to by Andocides, *On the Mysteries* 116 (ἡ δὲ στήλη παρ᾽ ἧι ἕστηκας . . . κελεύει).

2. **hāκόσια**: a derivative in -ιος from ἀ-έκων, giving an adj. used of actions (ἀ-έκων of people). *ἀ-Ϝεκόντ-ια > *ἀ-Ϝεκόνσια (assibilation of τ before ι) > ἀ-εκούσια (loss of ν before σ with compensatory lengthening). The aspiration is secondary, arising by analogy with positive *h*εκ-. A technical legal term in classical Attic (cf. Antiph. 3.2.6).

3. **[h]απλ͂ει**: ἁπλόος is related to Lat. *simplex* (**sṃ*, 'once' + **pel*, 'fold'), but the contracted ending in Gk. is puzzling. ἁπλῆι is an old advb. of manner (κοινῆι, πανταχῆι, etc.).

5–6. **τοῖσι . . . τοῖς**: of the three instances of τοῖσι in the V cent., two are in this inscription (Threatte 1996: 29). Although -οῖσι more or less disappears from Att. inscriptions by the mid V cent. (§32.14), earlier public inscriptions hesitate between -οῖς and -οῖσι, indicating that the latter is due to the pressure of the 'official' chancellery language.

5–7. **μύστ[εσιν] . . . ἐπόπτεισιν**: dat. plur. masc. *a*-stems. Although the long forms in -ησι were kept in official documents until the 420s, the appearance of Ionic -ηισιν here suggests that the author was not used to these endings (§32.14, and cf. Dover 1981: 4). Final -ν is found in the earliest Att. inscriptions, before both vowel and consonant (§32.7); but since the 'normal practice' is to omit it in the V cent. (Threatte 1980: 641), its abundance here may be evidence of an Ionicizing chancellery style.

10. **[ὀθ]νεῖον**: cf. ἔθνος. The word may have been intended to make it clear that all foreigners were included: there is some evidence that ξένος implied citizens of allied (mostly Ionian) states (see Gauthier 1971).

17. **μ̄ενός**: from *μηνσ-ος, without apparently undergoing Osthoff's Law (§23.3): contrast μείς **42** 2.

18. **διχομ̄ενίας**: the full moon split the month in two (months began with a new moon).

20. **Πυανοφσιο͂νος**: for φσ in the old Att. alphabet see §18.2.

23. **hισταμένō**: gen. sing. (with Πυανοφσιο͂νος), the normal expression for the beginning of a period of time in Hom. and later Greek.

27. **χρο͂νται**: from *χρέωνται < *χρή-ονται (cf. on ἀποχρεωμένων **83** 1).

32. **ὀλείζοσι**: dat. plur. of ὀλείζων (< *ὀλείγ-γων, §23.8) 'lesser', old Attic comp. of ὀλίγος. Attic literature uses ἐλάττων exclusively, and ὀλείζων disappears from inscriptions around 420. Wilamowitz restored ὀλείζους to (appropriately) the Old Oligarch (c.425) at ps.-Xen. *Ath. Pol.* 2.1 (where μείζους codd. does not make sense: scribes were puzzled by an unfamiliar form). See Dover (1981: 4).

30.   Stone from the Athenian acropolis regulating future relations between Athens and Chalcis in Euboea after the revolt of the island from the Athenian League (Thuc. 1. 114). The first provision is given here. 446/5 BC; though Mattingly (1961) argued for 424/3. *IG* I³ 40, Meiggs–Lewis 52. Schwyzer Appendix I, no. 11. ▶▶ Balcer (1978), López Eire (1999: 95–8).

ἔδοχσεν τε͂[ι β]ōλε͂ι καὶ τōι δέ̄μōι, Ἀντιοχὶς ἐ[πρυτ]άνευε, Δρακ-
[ον]τίδε͂ς ἐπεστάτε̄, Διόγνετος εἶπε· | κατὰ τάδε τὸν hόρκον ὀμόσαι
Ἀθεναίōν τ|ὲν βōλὲν καὶ τὸς δικαστάς· οὐκ ἐχσελō̂ Χαl|⁵λκιδέας
ἐχ Χαλκίδος οὐδὲ τὲν πόλιν ἀνά|στατον ποέ̄σō οὐδὲ ἰδιότε̄ν οὐδένα
ἀτιμ|ṓσō οὐδὲ φυγε͂ι ζε̄μιṓσō οὐδὲ χσυλλέφσο|μαι οὐδὲ ἀποκτενō̂
οὐδὲ χρέματα ἀφαιρέ|σομαι ἀκρίτō οὐδενὸς ἄνευ τō δέ̄μō τō
Ἀθ|l¹⁰εναίōν, οὐδ' ἐπιφσε̄φιō̂ κατὰ ἀπροσκλέτō | οὔτε κατὰ τὸ κοινὸ
οὔτε κατὰ ἰδιότō οὐδ|ὲ ἑνός, καὶ πρεσβείαν ἐλθōσαν προσάχσō | πρὸς
βōλὲν καὶ δε͂μον δέκα ἑμερōν hόταν | πρυτανεύō κατὰ τὸ δυνατόν.
ταῦτα δὲ ἐμπl|¹⁵[ε]δṓσō Χαλκιδεῦσιν πειθομένοις τōι δέ|[μ]ōι τōι
Ἀθεναίōν. hορκōσαι δὲ πρεσβεία|[ν] ἐλθōσαν ἐχ Χαλκίδος μετὰ
τὸν hορκōτō|ν Ἀθεναίōς καὶ ἀπογράφσαι τὸς ὀμόσαντ|ας. hόπōς δ'
ἂν [ὀ]μόσōσιν hάπαντες ἐπιμελl|²⁰όσθōν hοι στ[ρ]ατεγοί.

The Council and People resolved, in the prytany of Antiochis and the presidency of Drakontides, on the motion of Diognetos: the Council and jurors of the Athenians are to swear the oath as follows: 'I shall not expel (5) the Chalcideans from Chalcis nor lay waste their city nor deprive any individual of his civic rights nor punish him with exile nor arrest him nor put him to death nor deprive him of property, unless sentence has been passed by the Athenian (10) People; nor shall I put to the vote (a motion) against either the community or any individual without his having been summoned (to trial), and when an embassy has come I shall conduct it to the Council and People within ten days when I hold the prytany, so far as possible. These provisions I shall ratify (15) upon the Chalcideans' submission to the Athenian People.' The Athenians shall impose the oath on the embassy when it comes from Chalcis, with the officers responsible for oaths, and shall register the names of those who have sworn. Let the generals see to it (20) that all swear the oath.

1. **ἔδοχσεν**: for χσ in the old Att. alphabet see §18.2; for -ν see §32.7.

2. **ἐπ-εστάτε̄**: 3 sing. imperf. -ε̄ < -εε (§23.1), 'was president' (ἐπι-στάτης).

4. **ἐχσελô**: < -ελάω (the Att. pres. stem ἐλαυν- is anomalous and may be an old denominative: Benveniste 1935: 112, Sihler §465.6).

5. **ἀνά-στατον**: 'destroyed', a word frequently applied to cities by Athenian writers (from ἀν-ίστημι in its sense of 'break up an assembly of people': of a meeting, a house, or a *polis*).

6. **ποέσō**: intervocalic -ι- tends to disappear in certain common words in Att., esp. ποεῖν (from the VI cent. on). The diphthong [oi-] became [oʸ -], i.e. [o] plus glide, and the glide was then liable to deletion (not having phonemic status in Gk.).

7. **χσυλλέφσομαι**: i.e. ξυν- (normal in public inscriptions till *c*.425, and perhaps an 'official' spelling). σύν/ξύν is not in any case found outside of compounds in Attic, having replaced by μετά. For the mid. future see §24.2*b*.

8. **ἀποκτενô**: contracted future < -έω (§24.2*a*).

9. **ἀκρίτō**: 'unjudged' (cf. κρίνω), gen. after ἀφαιρήσομαι. Formally identical to Lat. *in-cer-tus.*

10. **ἐπιφσέφιō**: both ψηφίσω and ψηφιῶ are found in Attic (§24.2*a*). **ἀπροσκλέτō**: gen. sing., 'un-summoned (to trial)' (cf. προσ-καλέομαι).

13. **ἔμερον**: omission of the *h*- is normal in Attic inscriptions until the second half of the V cent. (Threatte 1980: 500, and cf. on ἀμέραν **76** 38).

19. **hόπōs**: normal in an Attic object clause (whereas in a purpose clause evidence suggests that ἵνα was more common in the spoken language, and that ὅπως may have been 'official sounding': Dunbar on Ar. *Birds* 1457). Cf. Dover (1997: 82).

31. Curse tablet from Attica, probably deposited in a grave. The curses appear to be directed against commercial competition. Folded lead with a line (*b*) written on the reverse. *c.*400–350 BC. *IG* III 3. 3: *Defixionum tabellae* 87. Gager (1992) no. 62. ▶ Faraone (1991: 10–17).

(*a*) καταδῶ Καλλίαν τὸν κάπηλον τὸν ἐγ γειτόνων καὶ τὴν γυναῖκα αὐτοῦ | Θρᾶϊτταν καὶ τὸ καπηλεῖον τὸ φαλακροῦ καὶ τὸ Ἀνθεμίωνος καπηλεῖον τὸ πλησίον [.....] | καὶ Φίλωνα τὸν κάπηλον· τούτων πάντων καταδῶ ψυχὴν ἐργασίαν | χεῖρας πόδας· τὰ καπηλεῖα αὐτῶν. ‖⁵ Καταδῶ Σωσιμένην τ[ὸν] ἀδελφόν, καὶ Κάρπον /τὸν οἰκότην αὐτοῦ/ τὸν σινδο[νο]πώλην καὶ Γλύκανθιν ἣν καλοῦσι | Μαλθάκην, καὶ Ἀγάθωνα τ[ὸ]ν κάπηλον | [τ]ὸν Σωσιμένους /οἰκότην/· τούτων πάντων καταδῶ ψυχὴν ἐργασία[ν β]ίον χεῖρας πόδας·| καταδῶ Κίττον τὸν γείτονα τὸν καν<ν>αβιōργὸν καὶ τέχνην τὴν Κίττου καὶ ἐργασίαν καὶ ψυχὴν καὶ νōν | καὶ γλῶτταν τὴν Κίττου. ‖¹⁰ καταδῶ Μανίαν τὴν κάπηλιν τὴν ἐπὶ κρήν<η>ι καὶ τὸ καπηλεῖον τὸ Ἀρίστανδρος Ἐλευσινίου | καὶ ἐργασίαν αὐτοῖς καὶ νōν. | ψυχὴν χεῖρας γλῶτταν πόδας νōν. τούτους πάντας καταδῶ ἐμ μνήμασι ασφαραγιαι | πρὸς τὸν κάτοχον Ἑρμῆν.

(*b*) τοὺς Ἀριστάνδρου οἰκέτας

(*a*) I bind Kallias the tavern-keeper, the one who's my neighbour, and his wife Thratta, and the bald man's tavern, and the tavern of Anthemion next door [....] and Philo the tavern-keeper. All of them, I bind their soul, business, hands, feet, their taverns. (5) I bind Sosimenes [his] brother, and Karpos (his slave) the linen-seller and Glykanthis, the one they call Princess. And Agathon the tavern-keeper, (the slave) of Sosimenes. All of them, I bind their soul, work, life, hands, feet. I bind Kittos my neighbour, the rope-maker, and Kittos' craft, and the business and soul and mind and tongue of Kittos. (10) I bind Mania, the woman who runs the tavern by the spring, and the tavern of Aristander from Eleusis, both their business and their mind. Soul, hands, tongue, feet, mind. I bind all of them in *unsealed* (?) tombs to Hermes the restrainer.

(*b*) The slaves of Aristander.

The tablet is unusually well written (both calligraphically and linguistically).

1. **καταδῶ**: a regular verb of curse tablets (Lat. *defīgō*). **κάπηλον**: often a tavern, but also the word for shop.   **ἐγ**: [eg], from ἐκ (by assimilation to the following γ-).

2. **Θρᾶιτταν**: lit. 'Thracian'. All the women mentioned appear (from their names) to be non-citizens (either slaves or free *pallakai*). **πλησίον**: the five missing letters may have specified what was next door.

5. **Σωσιμένην**: the 'correct' acc. is -μένη (< *-μένεα < *-μενεσ-α), but s-stem names often acquired an acc. in -ην on the analogy of 1st decl. names.   **οἰκότην**: agent noun built to οἶκος, elswhere οἰκέτης. The *o* vowel between root and suffix is analogical on forms such as δημότης, τοξότης, etc. (Between slash brackets because written above the words it explains: so also at 7.)   **σινδο[νο]πώλην**: σινδών is a borrowing from Semitic (see Szemerényi 1965: 5 for Phoen. **sidd-* > Gk. *sind-*).

6. **Μαλθάκην**: 'soft' (cf. Lat. *mollis*), often metaphorical 'soft-living', etc.

8. **καν<ν>αβιōργόν**: compd. of κάνναβις, 'hemp', a foreign loan into Gk. (whence it reached Lat.): cf. Engl. *hemp* < OE *hoenep* < *cannabis*. The second element is taken from words such as δημιουργός < δημιο-(ϝ)οργός (Hom. δημιο-εργός is by diektasis of the contracted form under the influence of ἔργον when (ϝ)οργός 'worker' had been lost).   **νōν**: i.e. νοῦς < νόος (§23.1). Our author uses *ou* in productive morphological categories such as

the gen. sing. (αὐτοῦ): note that τούτων contains a historical diphthong.

10. **κρήν(η)ι**: a slip, perhaps facilitated by the movement of η towards [i:]. **Ἀρίστανδρος**: if a nom. denoting the name of the tavern, then the following gen. is odd. Perhaps a slip (regular gen. on side *b*).

12. **ασφαραγιαι**: reading and interpretation unclear. Some compd. of ἀ- + σφραγίς, 'seal', is possible: curses were often slipped into unsealed graves (so as to reach the underworld gods?).

(*b*) The line appears to be an afterthought: the curser includes the entire household of his victim in his curse (in this case abbreviated, but listed by name on side *a*).

LACONIAN
(West Greek)

32. Dedication around the rim of a bronze *aryballos* from the 'Menelaion' at Sparta, *c*.675–650 BC. Probably a hexameter, but the line on the inner rim is corroded and difficult to read. Catling–Cavanagh (1977). *SEG* 26. 457. *LSAG* 446 no. 3*a*.

Δεῖνι[ς] τά<ν>δ' ἀνέθēκε χα	outer rim
ρι[.] Ϝελέναι	inner rim (retrograde)
Μενελάϝō	handle

Deinis dedicated this . . . to Helen (wife) of Menelaos.

χαρι[.]: reading uncertain: perhaps χαρ[ι]ν.

Helen here appears with a digamma (the reading is confirmed by a VI cent. dedication from the same site, with which it was published: τᾶι Ϝελέναι, *SEG* 26. 458): but in archaic inscriptions from Corinth the expected Ϝ- is absent from the name (for Ϝ at Corinth cf. Δϝενία **40**). It may be that the form *Helena* at Corinth is a foreign literary import (i.e. the name comes from poetry, not the local dialect): see *NAGVI* §§251, 504. If not, Helen is either an amalgam of two separate deities *sel- and *swel- (Skutsch 1987), or both forms derive from *swel- (De Simone 1978): for the phonology of *sw- see Lejeune (1972: §128) and cf. hικάδι **50** 2. The name Menelaos is also spelled with digamma (μεν- + λᾱϝο- 'withstander of the host'); later it contracts to Μενέλᾱς.

33. Inscription on a stone stele found at Mistra (originally in the temple of Athena on the Spartan acropolis), recording the victories of Damonon in various chariot-races: only the first part is given here. The first six lines of the inscription comprise two hexameters. *c.*450–400 BC. *IG* V 1. 213. Schwyzer 12. Bourguet (1927), no. 6. Buck 71. *LSAG* 196, 201 no. 52. *CEG* 378.

Δαμόνōν | ἀνέθēκε Ἀθαναίᾱ<ι> | πολιάχōι,
νικάhας | ταυτᾶ hᾶτ' οὐδὲς ‖⁵ πέποκα τōν νῦν. |
τάδε ἐνίκαhε Δαμ[όνōν] | τōι αὐτō τεθρίππō<ι> | αὐτὸς ἀνιοχίōν· |
ἐν ΓαιαϜόχō τετράκι<ν> ‖¹⁰ καὶ Ἀθάναια τετ[ράκιν] | κέλευhύνια
τετ[ράκιν]. | καὶ Ποhοίδαια Δαμόνō[ν] | ἐνίκē hέλει, καὶ ho κέλ[εξ |
hαμ]ᾶ αὐτὸς ἀνιοχίōν ‖¹⁵ ἐνhēβόhαις hίπποις | hεπτάκιν ἐκ τᾶν
αὐτō | hίππōν κἐκ τō αὐ[τ]ō [hίππō]. | καὶ Ποhοίδαια Δαμόνōν |
[ἐ]νίκē Θευρίαι ὀκτά[κ]ι[ν] ‖²⁰ αὐτὸς ἀνιοχίōν ἐν|hēβόhαις hίπποις |
ἐκ τᾶν αὐτō hίππōν | κἐκ τō αὐτō hίππō. | κἐν Ἀριοντίας ἐνίκē ‖²⁵
Δαμόνōν ὀκτάκιν | αὐτὸς ἀνιοχίōν | ἐνhēβόhαις hίπποις | ἐκ τᾶν αὐτō
hίππōν | κἐκ τō αὐτō hίππō, καὶ ‖³⁰ ho κέλεξ ἐνίκē h[αμᾶ]. | καὶ
Ἐλευhύνια Δαμ[όνōν] | ἐνίκē αὐτὸς ἀνιοχίōν | ἐνhēβόhαις hίπποις |
τετράκιν.

Damonon made a dedication to Athena *Poliakhos*, having won victories in a way which none of the men of today (has equalled). Damonon was victorious as follows with his own four-horse chariot, he himself driving: in the Games of the Earth-shaker four times (10) and in the Games of Athena four times and in the Eleusinian Games four times. And Damonon won the Games of Poseidon at Helos, and his courser on the same occasions, he himself driving, seven times, with fillies from his own mares and by his own stallion. And Damonon won the Games of Poseidon at Theuria eight times (20), he himself driving, with fillies from his own mares and by his own stallion. And Damonon won the Games of Ariontia eight times, he himself driving, with fillies from his own mares and by his own stallion, and (30) his courser won on the same occasions. And Damonon won the Eleusinian Games four times with his fillies, he himself driving.

1. **Δαμώνων**: a hypocoristic in -ων of a name such as Δαμῶναξ or Δαμώνυμος.

3. **Πολιάχōι**: 'holder of the city' < πολιάοχος, with the stem πολιᾱ- extracted from forms such as πολι-ᾱτᾱς (Att. πολι-οῦχος with vowel from κληροῦχος, etc.). For -οχος (ἔχω) cf. κάτοχος **31** 13. **νικάhας**: aor. ptcpl. with intervocalic -s- > -h- (§39.6).

4. **ταυτᾶ hᾱτ(ε)**: adv. formed from an old instr. in -ᾱ (cf. on hαμᾶ 14). There are examples from Att. (cf. ἁπλῆι **29** 3), but the type seems to have been more productive in WGk.   **οὐδέs**: i.e. οὐδής < *οὐδ(ε)-ένς with compensatory lengthening (§38.3).

5. **πέποκα**: 'ever', πη being a WGk. indef. particle (cf. Att.-Ion. πω). For -κα see §40.7.

6. **ἐνίκαhε**: §39.6.

7. **αὐτô**: reflexive sense, 'his own'. There were various ways of expressing the distinction (Lat. *suus/eius*) in the dialects; reflexive use of αὐτοῦ (with the article) is not uncommon outside classical Attic (West 1974: 101). Cf. *Il.* 9. 341–2, ὅς τις ἀνὴρ ἀγαθὸς ... τὴν αὐτοῦ (ἄλοχον) φιλέει.   **τεθρίππō<ι>**: with four (the combining form *k^wetr̥-) horses yoked abreast. From *tetra-hippos* (the *a* is elided and the *h* attaches itself to the beginning of the new syllable).

8. **ἀνιοχίōν** (Att. ἡνιοχέων): 'holding the reins', a denominative vb. from ἀνι-όχος (cf. Πολιάχōι 3). Lac. like Att. generally keeps the aspirate: however, presence of *h*- is less predictable in cases where it started in the middle of the word and got transferred to the initial vowel by 'anticipation' (§10.4): *ansiai > *ānhiai > (h)āniai (cf. on *a-ni-ja-pi* 2). For ε > ι see §23.2.

9. **ΓαιᾱϜόχō**: gen., with a word for 'games' understood. An epithet of Poseidon. It is difficult to tell whether this is a re-modelling of epic γαιήοχος, 'earth-holder' (for intrusive -Ϝ- cf. Ποτεδά-Ϝ-ονι **39**), or represents the original form: in which case Ϝόχος might come from *wegh-, 'put in motion' (hence 'earth-shaker'). Like Engl. *drive*, *wegh- can signify 'put in motion' or 'be conveyed' (Lat. *uehō*).   **τετράκι<ν>**: the engraver may have intended τετράκι. Lac. and Cretan use -ιν to form numeral adverbs (e.g. hεπτάκιν 16 and ὀκτάκιν 25), in contrast to the -ις of other dialects; but -ι is also found (τετράκι at Argos, and cf. πολλάκι in choral sections of tragedy).

11. **κἐλευhύνια**: crasis (καὶ Ἐλευ-). The vowel in -*hυν*- has been assimilated to the preceding diphthong.

12. **Ποhοίδαια**: adj. formed from Lac. *Ποhοιδάν* (cf. Arc. *Ποσοιδάν*). Most WGk. dialects have forms in -τ- (*Ποτει*-, etc.): for assibilation in the other dialects cf. §§27.3, 31.3. Lac. **Ποσ*- may (therefore) be due to the influence of neighbouring or substrate dialects: cf. Myc. *Po-se-da-o* (Pylos), Arc. *Ποσοιδᾶν* (-*οι*- is the result of vowel assimilation).

13. **ἐνίκε̄**: note the switch from aor. to imperf. (-*ε̄* < -*αε*, §38.4): *ἐνίκαhε* 6 is foregrounded, and focuses attention on important information (the point of the inscription); in the list that follows it is the number and location of the victories that is important (the fact of victory is established), and the imperf. performs this back-grounding function.   **κέλ[ἐξ]**: Att. *κέλης*, with a velar extension of a type associated with WGk. (cf. *ὄρνιξ*, 'bird', Pindar). It is found in Att. with *a*-vocalism (*ἄνθραξ, δέλφαξ, κόραξ*), mostly in sub-literary vocabulary: the suffix became extremely productive in Mod. Gk. as a 'diminutive' (Chantraine 1933: 377).

14. **[haμ]ᾶ**: Att. *ἅμα*, with short final (cf. *ταυτᾶ* 4). The vowel length is known from literary Doric (Ar. *Lysistrata*, Pindar, Theokritos). Restored from examples later in the inscription.

15. **ἐνhε̄βόhαις**: 'mares in their prime' (*ἥβη*): from *ἡβα-ωσα*-.

17. **κἐκ**: crasis (καὶ ἐκ).

24. **Ἀριοντίας**: gen. of the name of a goddess, with word for 'games' understood.

34. Dedication on a throne from Sparta, *c*.400–375 BC. Three hexameters. <*H*> is used for both the aspirate and *eta*. Ed. pr. Kourinou-Pikoula (1992–8). *SEG* 46. 400. ▶▶ Cassio (2000).

Μνᾶμα γεροντείας hιππανσίδας | τοῦτ᾽ ἀνέσηκε
τᾶι hαλέαι καὶ σᾶ|τρον· ha μὲν κα λῆ hώστ᾽ ἀπὸ τούτω |
σᾶσθαι, τὼς δὲ νέως τοῖς περγυ‖⁵τέροις hυποχάδδην.

As a memorial of his service in the Council, Hippanthidas dedicated this to (Athena) Halea, and seating for spectators: so, whatever you want you can watch from this—but young men are to yield to their elders.

1. **γεροντείας**: i.e. *γεροντίας*, confirmation of the existence of this

form in Lac. (cf. Cassio 1998, Colvin 1999: 235–6). The Spartan council of elders (Att. γερουσία). **hιππανσίδας**: the spelling <σ> for <θ> indicates that [tʰ] had moved to [θ] (§39.7). Note that the name Hippanthidas cannot be accommodated in regular hexameters (in the fourth foot -δας has to count as a short syllable).

2. **τοῦτ(ο)**: the throne, which is separate from the seating (καὶ σᾶτρον) which Hipp. has also paid for. **hαλέαι**: the aspirated form is found only once in Arcadia (the home of Athena Alea). Dubois ad loc. (1986: II, 12) assumes it to be a hypercorrect spelling (which implies weak articulation of the aspirate). **σᾶτρον**: i.e. θᾶτρον < *θᾱ(ϝ)ᾱ-τρον (Att. θεᾶτρον < *θηᾱ-τρον). Here apparently 'a place for spectators [to sit]'. **κα λῆ**: ed. pr. takes this to be καλῆ ('calls', a mistake for καλεῖ), but Cassio (2000) shows that λῆ (< λῆι) is subj. (3 sing., indefinite subject unexpressed) of λῆν 'wish' (cf. λέι 44 2). hα is then neut. plur. (acc.).

4. **σᾶσθαι**: < θᾱ(ϝ)ᾱ-εσθαι. θ following σ has not been changed (§39.7): presumably because it retained its quality as a stop in this cluster (a position in which aspiration was often lost). **περγυτέροις**: Att. πρεσβυτέροις. For WGk. -γ- in the stem of this word cf. πρείγυντας (Crete). An early variant *περσγυς is suggested by σπέργυς· πρέσβυς Hesych.

5. **hυποχάδδην**: χάζομαι, 'withdraw' is found in epic and other poetry (compds. in ἀνα-, δια- in Xen., in military contexts where they may be borrowings from Lac.). In WGk. δδ for ζ is found in Lac., Crete, Elis, and elsewhere: the etymology of this word is uncertain, but δδ/ζ implies an earlier *dy or *gy (§23.8).

HERAKLEA
(West Greek)

35. Two bronze tablets from Heraklea, a colony of Taras (itself a Spartan colony) in Lucania: a record of the measurement and apportionment of lands sacred to Dionysos (Table I) and Athena (Table II): part of Table I is given here. Late IV cent. BC. IG XIV 645. Buck 79. Schwyzer 62. Ionic alphabet, with digamma and with Ⱶ for the aspirate. ▶ Uguzzoni–Ghinatti (1968).

συνεμετρήσαμες δὲ ἀρξάμελνοι ἀπὸ τῶ ἀντόμω τῶ hυπὲρ Πανδοσίας

ἄγοντος, τῶ διατάμνοντος τώς τε hιαρὼς χώ|ρως καὶ τὰν Fιδίαν γᾶν,
ἐπὶ τὸν ἄντομον τὸν ὀρίζοντα τώς τε τῶ Διονύσω χώρως καὶ | τὸν
Κωνέας ho Δίωνος ἐπαμώχη. κατετάμομες δὲ μερίδας τέτορας· ||¹⁵
τὰν μὲν πράταν μερίδα ἀπὸ τῶ ἀντόμω τῶ πὰρ τὰ hηρώιδεια ἄγον-
τος | εὖρος ποτὶ τὰν τριακοντάπεδον τὰν διὰ τῶν hιαρῶν χώρων
ἄγωσαν, | μᾶκος δὲ ἄνωθα ἀπὸ τᾶν ἀποροᾶν ἄχρι ἐς ποταμὸν τὸν
Ἄκιριν, καὶ | ἐγένοντο μετριώμεναι ἐν ταύται τᾶι μερείαι ἐρρηγείας
μὲν δι|ακάτιαι μία σχοῖνοι, σκίρω δὲ καὶ ἀρρήκτω καὶ δρυμῶ
Fεξακάτιαι ||²⁰ τετρώκοντα Fὲξ σχοῖνοι.

We carried out the measurement, beginning with the fence that
leads beyond Pandosia, which separates the sacred lands and the
private property, up to the fence which separates the lands of
Dionysos and the land which Koneas the son of Dio possessed.
And we divided it into four parts: (15) the first part from the fence
which runs beside the Heroideia, (extending) in width to the
thirty-foot (way) leading through the sacred lands, and in length
down from the drainage-area (?) as far as the river Akiris; and
there were measured in this division two hundred and one *schoinoi*
of arable and six hundred and (20) forty-six *schoinoi* of non-arable
scrub-land with thickets.

11. **συνεμετρήσαμες**: WGk. 1 plur. in -μες (§40.1).
12. **ἀντόμω**: gen. sing. of an apocopated form (ἀνα-) meaning
'that which dissects' (τομός), i.e. 'divider'.   **διατάμνοντος**: WGk.,
Ion. τάμνω < *tm̥-n- (a nasal infix present): Att. τέμνω takes its vowel
from aor. ἔτεμον.   **τώς ... hιαρὼς χώρως**: acc. plur. (ἱαρός §38.1).
13. **Fιδίαν**: initial F- retained (§39.1).
14. **τόν**: use of the 'article' stem as a rel. pron. is relatively rare in
WGk. (§32.13). It may represent the penetration of a koiné feature
into the dialect.   **ἐπᾱμώχη**: imperf. of the WGk. verb πᾱμωχέω,
'possess' (πᾱμο-οχέω): for the stem cf. πέ-πᾱμαι (86 41), and
πολυπάμων, Il. 4. 443.   **τέτορας**: < *kʷetwor-, with o-grade in the
second syllable and, apparently, dissimilation of -w- (see Lillo 1988
for a different analysis).
15. **πρᾱ́τᾱν**: §38.2.
16. **ποτί**: in WGk., Thess., Boe. (§40.8).   **τριακοντάπεδον**: sc.
ὁδόν.
17. **ἄνωθα**: 'from above'; WGk. adverbial suffix -θα, 'from'

(Att.-Ion. -θε/-θεν). **ἀποροᾶν**: < ἀπορο(ι)άων (cf. ποεῖν 32 6), lit. 'that which flows off', here 'watershed' (Schwyzer 1928: 229). **ἄχρι**: see on 19 3. 18. **μετριώμεναι**: < μετρεόμεναι. The lengthened vowel raises a question about what the (graphic) change of ε to ι denotes (§23.2): the [i] has probably lost most of its syllabicity, leading to a compensatory lengthening of the [o]. **μερείᾱι**: derived from μέρος (*μερεσ-ιᾱ); equivalent to Att. μερίς (a dimin. of μέρος). **ἐρρηγείᾱς** (sc. γᾶς): perf. ptcpl. of ῥήγνυμι (Att. ἐρρωγυίᾱς), i.e. land 'broken (by ploughing)', with -η- by analogy with ῥήγνυμι. The fem. ptcpl. in -ει- occurs in late Attic and the koiné, probably taken from fem. *u*-stem adjs. (ἡδεῖα). **διακάτιαι**: < *-kn̥tiai (§§32.9, 39.4). 19. **σκίρω**: lit. 'hard' (perhaps 'rocky'). **ἀρρήκτω**: 'unbroken, non-arable', in opposition to ἐρρηγείᾱς. **Fεξακάτιαι**: Fέξ < *sweks (Fεξα- in compds. is modelled on ἑπτα-, etc.). 20. **τετρώκοντα**: WGk. τετρω- is perhaps from *k^wetr̥- (cf. Lat. *quadrāginta*) with *o*-vocalism imported from the numeral τέτορες (other possibilities discussed by Szemerényi 1960: 15–20).

WEST ARGOLIC
(West Greek)

36. Hexameter dedication on a bronze vessel. Late VII cent. BC. *IG* V 1. 231. Schwyzer 77. *LSAG* 156, 168 no. 3. *CEG* 363.

ΧαλϘοδάμανς με ἀνέθεκε θιοῖν, περικαλλὲς ἄγαλμα.

Chalkodamas dedicated me to the two goddesses, a gift of surpassing beauty.

ΧαλϘοδάμανς: see 23 2 on qoppa (§17.2). The dialect of Argos retains final -νς (§23.9): -δάμανς is built with the adj. suffix *-nt-s found also in the ptcpl. **με**: note the *scriptio plena* for μ'. **θιοῖν**: in this dialect an [i] followed by another vowel seems to have given rise to a particularly marked glide (cf. Ἀθᾱναίᾱς 37 2). The scansion ˘ – points to raising of ε rather than synizesis (§23.2). **περικαλλὲς ἄγαλμα**: is a Hom. formula at verse-end (cf. *Od.* 18.300, and *NAGVI* §303). The two goddesses are Demeter and Persephone.

37. Boustrophedon inscription from the acropolis at Argos listing officials who have presided over important work in the temple of Athena, and giving rules for the use of sacred objects. Mid VI cent. BC. Buck 83. *SEG* 11. 314. Sokolowski (1962), no. 27. *LSAG* 158, 168 no. 8. *Nomima*, i. 88.

ἐπὶ τōνδεōνὲν δαμιοργόντōν τὰ ἒ|[ν] Ἀθαναίας ἐπ[ο]ιϜέθε̄· ταδέν τὰ
ποιϜέ| ματα καὶ τὰ χρέ̄ματά τε καὶ τὸν [- - - - - - | - - - - -] ἀ[νέθεν]
τᾶι Ἀθαναίαι τᾶι Πολιάδι·||

5 Συλεύς τε   τοῖσι χρέ̄μασι τοῖσι χρε̄στέρ-
   καὶ Ἐράτυιιος   ίιοισι τοῖσι τᾶς θιιō μὲ χρέ̄-
   καὶ Πολύϙτōρ   [σ]θō Ϝhεδιέστας [ἐ]χθὸς
   καὶ Ἐξάκεστο[ς]   τō τεμένεος τō τᾶς Ἀ[θαν-]
   καὶ Ηαγί[ας]   [αίιας] τᾶς Πολιάδος. δαμόσ-
10 καὶ Ἐρύϙο[ιρος].   ιον δὲ χ[ρ]όνσθō προ[τὶ τὰ
   ἱαρά]. αἰ δὲ σίναιτο, ἀφ[α]κεσ-
άσθō, hοῖζ δὲ δαμιορ[γὸς ἐπ]α[να]νκασσάτō.
hο δ᾽ ἀμφίπολος μελεταινέτō τούτōν.

During the time that the following held office as *demiourgoi* the work was carried out in (the temple) of Athena; these works and the precious objects and the [...] they dedicated to Athena Polias:

Syleus and Eratyios and Polyktor and Exakestos and Hagias and Erykoiros.

The precious objects that are utensils of the goddess let no private citizen use outside the precinct of Athena Polias. But the state may use them for the sacrifice. If (anyone) damages (them), let him make restitution: in what amount, let the *demiourgos* impose. And the temple-servant is to see to these matters.

1. **τōνδεōν-έν**: gen. plur. of ὅδε, with both elements declined and with the addition of -ην (for which cf. Lat. deictic *ēn*): so also ταδέν, nom. plur. **δαμιοργόντōν**: < δαμιοργε-οντ-. Simplification of εο in a closed syllable by dropping the ε (hypheresis) is common in Argos and Crete (sporadic elsewhere). **τά**: perhaps some renovation or new decorative work. Edd. have generally punctuated after ταδέν, which is awkard both for the syntax and the sense (no list of 'works' follows).

2. **Ἀθᾱναίᾱς**: gen. depending on a word for 'temple' understood.

The second ι indicates a glide (cf. θιιοῖν **36**, and Πολιιάδι below). ἐποιϜέθε: aor. pass., with preservation of -Ϝ- (§39.1).

4. ἀ[νέθεν]: restored, but the normal 3 plur. secondary ending in WGk. (§40.1).

5. τοῖσι: the disyllabic ending of the dat. plur., familiar from Ionic (§32.14), is found in early inscriptions from Argos.

6. χρέ[σ]θō: < χρη-έσθω (imper. 3 sing.): cf. on ἀποχρεωμένων **83** 1.

7. Ϝhεδιέστας: cognate with Att. ἰδιώτης. From *Ϝhέδιος, an adj. formed to the pronoun Ϝhε ('oneself', Hom. ἕ): in this case Att. ἴδιος must be the result of vowel assimilation (cf. ἐφίστια **24** 17). A similar derivation for Lat. *sodālis* (Sihler §42.2). For -έστας cf. τελεστάς ('official', i.e. the semantic opposite). ἐχθός: < *ἐχτός < *ἐκσ-τός (Att. ἐκτός).

9. δαμόσιον: either a collective (§24.4) with plur. verb, or an advb. (Att. δημοσίαι, 'in public service') with a plur. of general agency.

10. χρόνσθō: imper. 3 plur. in -όνσθω (the ending is found in various WGk. dialects), with preservation or restoration of -νσ- (§23.9). From χρεόνσθω: for εο > ο in Arg. in closed syllables cf. διατελοντι etc. in Thumb–Kieckers (1932: 115): §23.2. For the stem cf. ἀποχρεωμένων **83** 1. προ[τί] (restored here on the basis of προτ᾿ in another inscription): elsewhere ποτί in WGk., apart from Cretan πορτί (§40.8).

11. [ἱαρά]: for the smooth breathing on the restored word cf. on ἱερόν **49** 4. ἀφακεσάσθō: 3 sing. imper. (aor.), compd. of ἀκέομαι (cf. ἄκος 'remedy, cure').

12. hοῖζ: dat. plur. (neut.), with partial assimilation of -ς to the following δ- shown by the writing -ζ (= *zd*). [ἐπ]ανανκασσάτō: mid. imper. (aor.) of ἐπ-αναγκάζω. Arg. avoids the usual WGk. stem -ξ- when a velar precedes (§40.4): for the sporadic doubling of s in inscriptions cf. ἐσστροτευμένας **14** 25.

13. μελεταιν-έτō: a form of μελεδαίνω, influenced by μελέτη, etc. (not found elsewhere).

38. Block of stone found at Argos, giving part of a treaty the city had arbitrated between two of her (supposed) colonies, the Cretan cities of Knossos and Tylissos: the dialect is largely Argolic. The first half is given here. *c.*450 BC. Buck 85. Schwyzer

83a. Meiggs–Lewis 42B. *LSAG* 165, 170 no. 39*a*. *Nomima*, i.
54, 2. Another copy was set up at Tylissos, of which fragments
survive, and probably at Knossos also. ▶ Vollgraff (1948).

[... τôι Τυλισίοι ἐξêμ]εν ξύλλεσθαι πλὰ[ν] τ|[ὰ μέρē τὰ Κνōσίōν
συν]τέλλοντα ἐνς πόλιν. hότ[ι ‖⁵ δέ κα ἐκ δυσμενέ]ōν hέλōμες συνα-
νφότεροι, δα[σ|μôι τôν κὰτ γ]ᾶν τὸ τρίτον μέρος ἔχεν πάντōν, τôι[ν
δὲ κὰτ] θάλασαν τὰ hέμισα ἔχεν πάντōν· τὰν δὲ [δ|εκ]άταν τὸνς
Κνōσίονς ἔχεν, hότι χ᾽ ἔλōμες κοι[ν|â]ι. τὸν δὲ φαλύρōν τὰ μὲν
καλλ<ι>στεῖα Πυθôδε ἀπ[ά]‖¹⁰γεν κοινᾶι ἀμφοτέρονς, τὰ δ᾽ ἄλλα
τôι[Ἄρει Κνōσ]|οῖ ἀντιθέμεν κοινᾶι ἀμφοτέρονς. ἐξ[αγōγὰν δ᾽ ê]|μεν
Κνōσόθεν ἐνς Τυλισὸν κὲκ Τυλι[σô Κνōσόνδ]|ε· α[ἰ] δὲ πέρανδε
ἐξάγοι, τελίτō hόσσα[περ hοι Κν] |όσιοι· τὰ δ᾽ ἐκ Τυλίσō ἐξαγέσθō
hόπυ[ί κα χρêι. τô]‖¹⁵ι Ποσειδᾶνι τôι ἐν Ἰυτôι τὸν Κνōσίō[ν ιαρέα
θύ]|εν. τᾶι Hέρāι ἐν <H>εραίōι θύεν βôν θέλει[αν ἀμφοτ]|ι έρον[ς
κ]οινᾶι ...

[... It is permitted to the Tylissians] to plunder [...], except
those areas which pay taxes to the city of the Knossians. Whatever (5) we take together from enemies, in the division of the
(spoils taken) by land, (the Tylissians) are to have a third of
the whole, while (in the division) of the (spoils taken) by sea (the
Tylissians) are to have a half of the whole; and the Knossians are
to have one-tenth of whatever we take in common. And of the
spoils both parties are to send the choicest in common to Pytho,
(10) and the rest both parties are to dedicate in common to
Ares at Knossos. There is to be right of export from Knossos to
Tylissos, and from Tylissos to Knossos; if (a Tylissian) exports
abroad, let him pay whatever the Knossians (pay), but let
goods from Tylissos be exported wherever he wishes. The priest
of the Knossians is to sacrifice to (15) the Poseidon at Iytos.
Both parties are to sacrifice a heifer in common to Hera in the
Heraion ...

3. [ἐξêμ]εν: athematic inf. ending -μεν (§40.3): Att. ἐξεῖναι.
ξύλλεσθαι: apparently the mid. of σκύλλω ('tear out' > 'harass'), with
metathesis of σκ- to κσ- (a connection with συλάω has also been
suggested). The connection with σκῦλα, 'spoils' (whether historical
or popular) may have influenced the semantic development.

4. [συν]τέλλοντα: τέλλω < *τελ-yω (a doublet of Att. τελέω): found also in Crete, and Att.-Ion. compds. (ἀνατέλλω 'rise'). **ἐνς**: -νς retained (§23.9).

5. [δυσμενέ]ον̄: restored from a fragment found at Tylissos (Schwyzer 84*b*). Strikingly poetic in Attic, it may have been less unusual in Argolic (found also in Crete, Gortyn Law Code). **hέλο̄μες**: regular 1 plur. ending in WGk. (§40.1).   **δα[σ]μο̂ι**: for the sense cf. *Il.* 1. 166 (means 'tribute, levy' in classical literature).

6. **ἔχεν**: thematic infin. (§40.3), found also in neighbouring Arc. (§28.2).

7. **θάλασαν**: writing of single consonant for double (common in early inscriptions).   **hέμισα**: probably another single for double *s* (*ἡμιτϝ-, cf. ἡμίσσοι 7 25).

8. **hότι χ'**: ὅτι κα, 'whatever' (§40.6).

9. **φαλύρο̄ν**: from λαφύρων, 'spoils' by metathesis.   **καλλιστεῖα**: noun (neut. plur.) meaning 'offering of the finest' (as at Eurip. *IT* 23).

11. **ἀντιθέμεν**: ἀνα- (apocope) and athem. infin. in -μεν (§40.3).

13. **πέρανδε**: advb. formed to a noun πέρα [sc. χώρα] 'the land outside, beyond'. Cf. Aesch. *Ag.* 190, Χαλκίδος πέραν ἔχων. **τελίτō̄**: < *τελε-έτω (imper.), with ῑ < [ẹ:] arising from the contraction.   [**hοι**]: restored from l. 34 hοι Κνόσιοι, where the Cretan form of the article has crept into the text when attached to the word for Knossians (Arg. τοί, §40.5).

14. **hόπυι**: loc. of an old *u*-stem, for which cf. Sappho τυίδ' ἔλθ(ε), 'come hither' (**74** A5): Att. ὅποι comes from a thematic variant of the same stem.

15. **Ποσειδᾶνι**: perhaps due to the influence of neighbouring or substrate dialects: cf. Ποhοίδαια **33** 12.

16. **βο̂ν**: < *gʷōm (< *gʷoum already in late IE), the usual WGk. form of the acc. sing. (Att.-Ion. βοῦν was re-modelled on nom. βοῦς: cf. βόας **88** 77).

SARONIC: CORINTH
(West Greek)

39. Dedication to Poseidon on a painted clay tablet from Corinth: hexameter. *c*.650–625 BC. Buck 92*a*. Schwyzer 123: 2. *CEG* 357. *LSAG* 131 no. 8. *NAGVI* COP 3.

Ποτεδά̄[ν]   Σιμίōν μ' ἀνέθ<ε>κε Ποτε̄δᾱϜο̄ν[ι Ϝά]ϝακτι
Poseidon   Simion dedicated me to Lord Poseidon

Ποτε̄δά̄[ν]: label on a figure. WGk. form (cf. on *Ποhοίδαια* **33** 12), with contraction (not part of the hexameter). The sign transcribed ε̄ in the word for Poseidon is a special form of the letter <*E*> reserved for [ẹ:] < [ei] (§23.1). **Σιμίōν**: the second *i* (short) has to be counted long for the hexameter. **Ποτε̄δά̄Ϝο̄ν[ι]**: uncontracted form, with intrusive -Ϝ- to avoid hiatus. That this was dictated by the metre is shown by other dedications in the same series: e.g. *NAGVI* COP 13 μ' ἀνέθε̄κε Ποτε̄δᾶνι.

40. Hexameter epitaph (boustrophedon) on a stone at Corinth. *c.*650 BC. Buck 91. Schwyzer 124. *LSAG* 131 no. 6. *CEG* 132.

ΔϜε̄νία τόδε [σᾶ ι μα] τὸν ὄλεσε πό ι ντος ἀναι[δέ̄ς

This is the tomb of Deinias: him the pitiless ocean destroyed

ΔϜε̄νίᾱ: Ϝ retained (§39.1), and ε̄ for [ẹ:] as in *Poseidon* **39** (Att. *Δεινίου*). Gen. -ᾱ < -ᾱο (§24.3). The name is a hypocoristic of some form such as *Deinomenes* **72**.   **τόν**: 'whom' or 'him' (cf. **35** 14 and τὸν λεῖπε **67** 144). The line is modelled on a number of epic phrases: for a 'pitiless' or 'shameless' object as the cause of human destruction cf. the λᾶας ἀναιδής of *Il.* 4. 521.

SARONIC: CORINTHIAN (COLONIAL)
(West Greek)

41. Lead tablet recording a delivery of wooden beams and clay tiles: from Corcyra, a colony of Corinth. *c.*475–450 BC. Ed. pr. A. Choremis (1992–8). *IG* IX 1² 4. 874. *SEG* 48. 604.

  δοϙοὶ πὰρ 'Αλκίμου· σέλματα—ΔΠ|·
2 ἄλλοι Ϝίκατι ποδο͂ν—δυοῖν Δ||||·
  ἄλ<λ>οι δεκάπεδοι—τετόρων πλε͂θος—ΔΠ||||·
4 πλίνθοι πὰρ Φιλότα πλατεῖαι ΗΗΗΗΗΗΔΔΔΔΔ
  καλυπτρίδες ΗΗΗΗΗΗΔΔΔΔΔ.
        vacat
  ὀνικίνδιοι{οι} κατέϜαξαν |||| πλίνθους.

The original line ordering on the tablet is too complicated to replicate in transcription:
Beams from Alkimos: long beams—16.
Others, 20 feet—pairs: 14. Others, 10 feet—bundles of four: 19.
Large tiles from Philotas: 660 Roof tiles: 660.
The carriers broke 4 tiles.

1. **δοκοί**: noun to δέκ-ομαι, 'supporting beams'. **πάρ**: rather than παρ' (apocope, as at 4). **Ἀλκίμου**: an early spelling ου = [o̩:], from ο + ο in Saronic dialects (§38.3): cf. πλίνθους 6. **ΔΠΙ**: semi-acrophonic, i.e. δέκα + πέντε + 1.
2. **Fίκατι**: < IE *wikm̥ti (Lat. uīgintī): §32.9.
3. **δεκάπεδοι**: evidence for *e*-vocalism in a near derivative of πούς. Att. δεκάπους (Ar. *Eccl.* 652) is secondary (its formation suggests 'with ten feet'). **τετόρων**: see τέτορας 35 14.
4. **Φιλότα**: gen. -ā < -āo (§24.3). **πλίνθοι ... πλατεῖαι**: lit. 'flat (and/or broad) bricks'. The ed. pr. suggests that these are joists.
5. **καλυπτρίδες**: form not elsewhere attested (Att. καλυπτήρ).
6. **ὀνικίνδιοι**: i.e. ὀνο-κίνδιοι (vowel assimilation), 'donkey drivers'. For κινδ- cf. Hesych. κινδάνει· κινεῖται. **κατέΓαξαν**: aor. of κατ(α)-Γάγ-νυμι, 'break'.

42. Bronze tablet containing a proxeny decree from Corcyra, a colony of Corinth. Late IV cent. BC. *IG* IX 1² 4. 786. Schwyzer 136.

πρύτανις Στράτων. | μεὶς Ψυδρεύς· ἀμέρα τε|τάρτα ἐπὶ δέκα· προστάτας | Γνάθιος Σωκράτευς. ||⁵ πρόξενον ποεῖ ἁ ἁλία | Διον-ύσιον Φρυνίχου | Ἀθηναῖον, αὐτὸν καὶ | ἐκγόνους. δίδωτι δὲ καὶ | γᾶς καὶ οἰκίας ἔμπασιν. ||¹⁰ τὰν δὲ προξενίαν γράψαν|τας εἰς χαλκὸν ἀνθέμεν, | εἴ κα προβούλοις καὶ προ|δίκοις δοκῆι καλῶς ἔχειν. | Διονύσιον ||¹⁵ Φρυνίχου |Ἀθηναῖον.

Prytanis: Straton. Month of Psydreus, fourteenth day. President: Gnathios son of Socrates. (5) The assembly makes Dionysios son of Phrynichos from Athens a *proxenos*, himself and his descendants; and it bestows the right to own both land and real estate. (10) Those who draw up the proxeny decree are to put it up on a bronze tablet, wherever seems best to the council members and advocates. Dionysios (15) son of Phrynichos from Athens.

2. **μείς**: < *μένς < *μήνς (by Osthoff's Law: §23.3): lengthened ε > ει [e:] in Saronic dialects (§38.3).

4. **Σωκράτευς**: < Σωκράτεος. This synizesis of *o* is normal in Saronic (§23.2*b*, and cf. ἐλεόθερος **21** 8).

5. **πρόξενον**: earlier ξένϝος at Corinth and Corcyra (the ϝ has now disappeared without compensatory lengthening, as in Att.): §39.1. **ποεῖ**: see ποήσω **30** 6.   **ἀλία**: the WGk. term corresponding to Att. ἐκκλησία. Without initial aspiration (cf. ἀλίαι **55** 41, where *h*- is noted).

7. **Φρυνίχου**: for ου [o̜:] from *o + o* cf. μείς above.

8. **δίδωτι**: all WGk. dialects retain inherited -τι (§39.4).

9. **ἔμπασιν**: Att. ἔγκτησις (for WGk. πάομαι in place of Att. κτάομαι, cf. on ἐπᾱμώχη **35** 14).

11. **ἀνθέμεν**: athematic infin. in -μεν (§40.3), with apocope of preverb (§24.5).

12 **εἶ**: Att. οὖ (see **44** hοπείō 3 hόπē 6).

SARONIC: MEGARA
(West Greek)

43. Epitaph on a marble stele from the Megarid. A phrase identifying the deceased followed by a hexameter. *c.*480–470 BC. *SEG* 41. 413. ▶▶ Ebert (1996).

λέγō Πόλλις Ἀσōπίχō φίλος hιυιός·
ὁ κακὸς ἐὸν ἀπέθνασκον | hυπὸ στ[ί]κταισιν ἐγόνε

I, Pollis, beloved son of Asopichos, speak: *Proving no coward I died from the tattooers' wounds.*

1. **λέγō**: Ebert (1996) suggests the reading ΑΙ]ΑΙ ΕΓΟ, 'woe is me'. In this case the line could be made into an irregular hexameter. **Ἀσōπίχō**: name formed to the Theban river Asopus (the suffix -ιχος is characteristic of Boeotian names). It is not unusual for names to spread into adjacent territories.

2. **ὁ**: negative οὐ (early evidence for pronunciation [o̜:] of a historical diphthong: §23.1).   **ἐὸν**: scanned with synizesis, i.e. [ʲo:n] (§32.11).

3. στ[ί]κταισιν: disyllabic dat. plur. and -ν are epic (§32.14): the Hom. vulgate has the *a*-stem dat. plur. in -ησι/-αις, but Lesb. has -αισι and this form may have been in the version known to the composer (or he may have 'extended' the local form -αις). Hdt. (7. 233) says that Thebans were branded with στίγματα βασιλήια (the King's mark) after the battle of Thermopylae: Pollis may have suffered similar treatment from an enemy. ἐγόνε̄: emphatic form, attested (in the grammarians) for WGk. and Boe. Aristophanes' Megarian (*Ach.* 736 etc.) has ἐγών. Cf. §36.5.

SARONIC: MEGARIAN (COLONIAL)
(West Greek)

44. Lead tablet with instructions for sacrifice and purification: from Selinous, Sicily (a colony of Megara). Two columns, of which B. 1–7 is given here. *c.*460–450 BC. Ed. pr. Jameson– Jordan–Kotansky (1993). *SEG* 43. 630. [▶] Dubois (1999*b*).

[...] ἄνθρο̄πος [......... ἐλ]αστέρο̄ν ἀποκα[θαίρεσθαι], προειπὸν hόπο̄ κα λε̣ι̣ κ̣αὶ τὸ Ϝέ[τ]ε̣ος hοπ<εί>ο̄ κα λε̂ι καὶ [τὸ με̄νὸς]Ι hοπείο̄ κα λε̂ι καὶ <τᾶι> ἀμέραι hοπείαι κα λ<ε̂>ι, προειπὸν hόπυι κα λε̂ι, καθαίρεσθο̄, [...hυ]Ιποδεκόμενος ἀπονίψασθαι δότο̄ κἀκρατίξασθαι καὶ hάλα το̂ι αὐ[το̂ι Ⅱ⁵ κ]αὶ θύσας το̂ι Δὶ χοῖρον ἐξ αὐτο̂ ἴτο̄ καὶ περιστ{ι}ραφέσθο̄ Ι καὶ ποταγορέσθο̄ καὶ σῖτον hαιρέσθο̄ καὶ καθευδέτο̄ hόπε̄ κ̣ⅠΙα λε̂ι.

[If ...] a man [wishes] to be purified of avenging spirits, announcing this from wherever he wishes, and in whatever year he wishes, and in whatever [month] he wishes, and on whatever day he wishes, and announcing it in whatever direction he wishes, let him purify himself: and admitting (the spirit) let him provide the means for ablution and food and salt to it; (5) and sacrificing a piglet to Zeus let him leave that place, and turn in a circle: and let him be addressed, and take food, and sleep wherever he wishes.

1. [ἐλ]αστέρō̄ν: the word ἀλάστωρ is familiar from tragedy, and is traditionally connected with λανθάνειν ('the unforgetting one'). This form (restored here from l. 9) may have been influenced by ἐλάω ('drive, persecute'). Denotes the indignant spirit of the deceased:

the missing text may have specified a man 'who has committed homicide' (ed. pr.).

2. **hópō**: 'whence' (Att. ὁπόθεν), with old abl. ending.　**λε̑ι**: subj. of the WGk. verb λῶ, infin. λῆν (cf. **34** 2).　**Fέ[τ]εος**: digamma retained in Selinous (had probably already disappeared in Megara at this date, §39.1).

3. **hοπείō̄**: gen. of an adj. apparently formed to WGk. ὅπει, 'where'. **hópυι**: as at **38** 14.　**[hυ]ποδεκόμενος**: the subject has to purify himself by confronting the spirit and taking certain actions. δεκ- is the original form of the root (cf. δοκεῖ, L. *decet*), with Att. δεχ- coming from infin. δέχθαι (where κ assimilated to following θ).

4. **κἀκρατίξασθαι**: καί+aor. infin. of ἀκρατίζομαι, 'have a meal' (from ἄκρατος, unmixed wine). For -ξ- see §40.4.

5. **ἐξ αὐτō̄**: presumably the shrine of Zeus in which the sacrifice took place.

6. **ποτᾱγορέσθō̄**: < -ᾱγορεέσθω, with preverb WGk. ποτ/ποτί (§40.8). The subject can now return to normal society.　**hόπε̄**: WGk. inherited a tendency to use -ει (an old loc.) and -η (an old instr.) in advbs. of place.

SARONIC: EPIDAUROS
(West Greek)

45. Stele from the Asclepieion at Epidauros, inscribed on two sides with twenty miraculous stories of healing, of which the second is given here. Late IV cent. BC. *IG* IV² 1. 121. Edelstein (1945, no. 423). Buck 90. Rhodes–Osborne (2003, no. 102). ▶▶ LiDonnici (1995).

Ἰθμονίκα Πελλανὶς ἀφίκετο εἰς τὸ ἱαρὸν ὑπὲρ γενεᾶς. ἐγ[κατα-
|κοι]μαθεῖσα δὲ ὄψιν εἶδε· ἐδόκει αἰτεῖσθαι τὸν θεὸν κυῆσαι κό[ραν],
τὸν δ' Ἀσκλαπιὸν φάμεν ἔγκυον ἐσσεῖσθαί νιν, καὶ εἴ τι ἄλλο |
α[ἰτ]οῖτο, καὶ τοῦτό οἱ ἐπιτελεῖν, αὐτὰ δ' οὐθενὸς φάμεν ἔτι
ποι|δε[ῖ]σθαι. ἔγκυος δὲ γενομένα ἐγ γαστρὶ ἐφόρει τρία ἔτη ἔστε
παⁱⁱ¹⁵ρέβαλε ποὶ τὸν θεὸν ἱκέτις ὑπὲρ τοῦ τόκου. ἐγκατακοιμαθεῖσα |
δὲ ὄψ[ι]ν εἶδε· ἐδόκει ἐπερωτῆν νιν τὸν θεόν, εἰ οὐ γένοιτο αὐτᾶι |
πάντα ὅσσα αἰτήσαιτο καὶ ἔγκυος εἴη· ὑπὲρ δὲ τόκου ποιθέμεν | νιν
οὐθέν, καὶ ταῦτα πυνθανομένου αὐτοῦ, εἴ τινος καὶ ἄλλου δέ|οιτ[ο],

λέγειν ὡς ποιησοῦντος καὶ τοῦτο. ἐπεὶ δὲ νῦν ὑπὲρ τούτου ||²⁰ παρείη ποτ᾽ αὐτὸν ἱκέτις, καὶ τοῦτό οἱ φάμεν ἐπιτελεῖν. μετὰ δὲ | τοῦτο σπουδᾶι ἐκ τοῦ ἀβάτου ἐξελθοῦσα, ὡς ἔξω τοῦ ἱαροῦ ἦς, ἔτε|κε κόραν.

[10] Ithmonika of Pellene arrived at the temple (with a request) about having children. Going to sleep, she saw a vision: she dreamed that she requested the god that she might conceive a daughter, and Asclepios said she would become pregnant, and that if she made any further request this too he would fulfil for her— but she said that she desired nothing more. She became pregnant, and carried (the child) in her womb for three years, until [15] she came to the god as a suppliant (with a request) about giving birth. Going to sleep, she saw a vision: she dreamed that the god asked her whether she had not got all that she had wanted, being now pregnant; she had not added anything about giving birth, even though he had asked her, if there was anything else that she wanted, to speak up, so that he could bring that about as well. But since it was for this reason [20] that she was now before him as a suppliant, he said he would fulfil this too for her. Thereupon she hurried out of the shrine, and when she was outside the temple she gave birth to a daughter.

Much of the diction of these stories is formulaic (ἀφίκετο . . . ὄψιν εἶδε . . . ἐδόκει, etc.): the structure is paratactic and repetitive.

10. **Ἰθμονίκā**: 'victorious at the Isthmus', i.e. the Isthmian games. Ἰθμός (with simplification of the consonant cluster) is also attested at Delphi.   **Πελλāνίς**: a woman of Pellene, in Achaea.   **ἱαρόν**: §38.1.   **ἐγ[κατακοι]μαθεῖσα**: a technical term for sleeping in a temple in the hope of seeing a vision ('incubation'). Lengthened ε is written <η> and <ει> in eastern Argolic: interaction with the 'mild' Doric of Megara and Corinth encouraged the spread of close [ẹ:] even before koiné influence (§23.1).

12. **φάμεν**: regular WGk. athematic infin. in -μεν (§40.3). **ἐσσεῖσθαι**: fut. infin. (§40.2).   **νιν**: WGk. enclitic 3 sing. personal pron. (acc.).   **εἰ**: koiné form (from Att.-Ion.): §40.6.

13. **οἱ**: enclitic 3 sing. pron., dative (indirect reflexive: refers to subject of ἐδόκει).   **οὐθενός**: a form which appears sporadically from the IV cent. and is standard in the koiné, remade with

aspiration from εἶς and devoicing [dh] > [th]. There will have been pressure (from οὐδέ, οὐδεμία) to restore οὐδείς (cf. Mod. Gk. δέν [ðen] < οὐδέν). **ποιδε[ῖ]σθαι**: Att. προσ-δέομαι, 'need in addition' (cf. ποί 15).

14. **ἐγ**: [eŋ], with assimilation of the nasal to the following velar. **ἔστε**: < *ἐνς-τε. WGk. and Ion. (poetic in Attic, apart from Xenophon).

15. **ποί**: Att. πρός. Usual WGk. form is ποτί, as in prevocalic ποτ' 20 (§40.8). **ὑπέρ**: close to meaning to περί (cf. οὐπέρ **15** 4).

16. **ἐπερωτῆν**: WGk. contraction of α + ε to η (§38.4).

17. **ποιθέμεν**: aor. infin. of ποι-τίθημι (§40.3).

19. **ποιησοῦντος**: < ποιη-σέ-οντος (§40.2).

21. **ἐξελθοῦσα**: ἐνθεῖν < ἐλθεῖν is found in some WGk. dialects, including Corcyra (a colony of Corinth): but it may never have existed in this area. **ἦς**: 3 sing. imperf. from *ēs-t (replaced in Attic by ἦν, the old 3 plur. < *ēs-ent: §32.2).

SARONIC: AEGINA
(West Greek)

46. Stone slab (in fragments) from the temple of Aphaia on Aegina recording construction work at the temple. Aegina was settled from Epidauros (the inhabitants were expelled by Athens in 431 BC). Mid VI cent. BC. *IG* IV 580, rev. Williams (1982). *LSAG* 112 no. 4, 439. *SEG* 32. 356.

[ἐπὶ Θ]εοίτᾱ ἱαρέος ἐόντος, τᾱφαίᾱι hοῖϘος | ἐπ[οι]έθē χὄ βōμὸς χὄλέφας ποτεποιέθē· | χὄ [θρίγϘο]ς περιποιέθē.

In the priesthood of Theoitas the temple was built to Aphaia, and the altar; and the ivory was added, and the coping was put around.

1. **[Θ]εοίτᾱ**: gen. -ᾱ < -ᾱο (§24.3). **ἱαρέος**: gen. sing. < *ἱαρήϜ-ος (cf. §30.2). **ἐόντος**: cf. §32.11. **τᾱφαίᾱι**: crasis with τᾶι. **hοῖϘος**: crasis (hο οῖϘος), the word being used in the sense of 'temple'. See **23** 2 on *qoppa* (§17.2).

2. **χὄ**: crasis, καί + hο. **χὄλέφας**: crasis, καί + hο + ἐλέφας. This may refer to the ivory (chryselephantine) cult statue. **ποτεποιέθē**: aor. pass. with WGk. preverb ποτ/ποτί (Att. πρός): §40.8.

3. [θρίγϘο]ς: refers (if correctly restored) to the wall of the sanctuary (Williams 1982).

RHODES
(West Greek)

47. Vase inscription from Rhodes. Mid V cent. BC. Schwyzer 276*a*. *LSAG* 357 no. 30. *CEG* 461. *NAGVI* DOH 3. The relation between the two parts is not clear (there are no figures on the vase).

(*a*) καλλίστα γᾶς ha Βρασία | hως ἐμὶν δοκεῖ
(*b*) Δεὺς Ηερμᾶς | Ἄρταμις Ἀθαναία

(*a*) The girl from Brasos is the finest in the world (?), in my opinion.
(*b*) Zeus, Hermes, Artemis, Athena.

1. **καλλίστᾱ**: if this is an adj., then the subject could be a place or a person: perhaps *ha Βρασία*, 'the woman from Brasos' (or with Wachter ad loc., *haβρὰ Ἀσία* 'the delightful Asia'). To make an orthodox trimeter the final vowel must be short: this would make it an advb., which would mean *haβρασία* must be a woman, and a courtesan (given the nature of the verb likely to be understood).
2. **ἐμίν**: the WGk. tonic form of *μοι* (same ending as plur. *ἁμίν*, Att. *ἡμῖν*).
3. **Δεύς**: δ/δδ from *dy (§23.8). In most dialects the sound is written ζ, though the pronunciation is much disputed (see *τόζ'* **48** 1). Not attested elsewhere on Rhodes.
4. **Ἄρταμις**: normal WGk. form of the name.

48. Boustrophedon hexameter dedication on a stone found near Kameiros. Early VI cent. BC. <*H*> for the aspirate and *eta*. *IG* XII 1. 737. Schwyzer 272. Buck 100. *LSAG* 356 no. 5. *CEG* 459.

σᾶμα τόζ' Ἰδα|μενεὺς ποίη|σα hίνα κλέος | εἴη· ||⁵ Ζεὺ δέ νιν, ὅστις | πημαίνοι, λειō|λη θείε.

I, Idameneus, set up this tombstone so that fame should be (mine); and if anyone harms it, may Zeus curse him !

1. **τόζ(ε)**: indicates that inherited [d] > a fricative [ð] as in Mod. Gk. As at Elis (cf. **58** 2), the change coincides with the development (at least at some sociolinguistic levels) of δ/δδ < *dy* (§23.8, **47** 3 above): the new *d* is written δ, leading to sporadic occurrences of ζ for 'old' *d* (see Méndez Dosuna 1991, and cf. *hιππανσίδας* **34** 1). That ζ does not here represent a double consonant is shown by the scansion σᾱμᾰ τόζ̆. **Ἰδαμενεύς**: cf. Hom. Ἰδομενεύς and the Myc. (fem.) name *i-do-me-ne-ja*; the a/o alternation suggests a non-Greek origin for the stem. **ποίησα**: epic-style unaugmented aor.

3. **hίνα**: the aspirate does not prevent elision in Homeric verse.

5. **Ζεύ**: nom. Ζεύς > Ζεύδ by assimilation (both consonants are now fricatives); the resulting δδ is written as a single consonant. **νιν**: cf. **45** 12.

6. **λειόλη**: same as παν-ώλης 'accursed', with first element from λεῖος, 'uniform, without break', corresponding to παν-. Such grave-curses are common in neighbouring Lycia, an area which had much contact with Rhodes.

49. Decree on a stone from Ialysos regulating conduct in the temple precinct (the first part is given here). IV/III cent. BC. *IG* XII 1. 677. Buck 103. Schwyzer 284.

ἔδοξε τοῖς μαστροῖς καὶ Ἰαλυσίοις, | Στρατῆς Ἀλκιμέδοντος εἶπε· | ὅπως τὸ ἱερὸν καὶ τὸ τέμενος | τᾶς Ἀλεκτρώνας εὐαγῆται κα||⁵τὰ τὰ πάτρια, ἐπιμεληθήμειν | τοὺς ἱεροταμίας, ὅπως στᾶλαι | ἐργασθέωντι τρεῖς λίθου Λαρτ[ί]|ου καὶ ἀναγραφῆι ἐς τὰς στάλαις τό τε ψάφισμα τόδε καὶ ἃ οὐχ ὅ||¹⁰σιόν ἐντι ἐκ τῶν νόμων ἐσφέ|ρειν οὐδὲ ἐσοδοιπορεῖν ἐς τὸ τέ|μενος, καὶ τὰ ἐπιτίμια τῶ[ι] πράσ|σοντι παρὰ τὸν νόμον· θέμειν δὲ | τὰς στάλας μίαμ μὲν ἐπὶ τᾶς ἐσό||¹⁵δου τᾶς ἐκ πόλιος ποτιπορευομέ|νοις, μίαν δὲ ὑπὲρ τὸ ἱστιατόριον, | ἄλλαν δὲ ἐπὶ τᾶς καταβάσιος τᾶ[ς]| ἐξ Ἀχαίας πόλιος.

The magistrates and people of Ialysos decided, on the motion of Strates the son of Alkimedon: in order that the shrine and precinct of Alektrona should be well managed in accordance (5) with ancestral custom, the temple-stewards are to see to it that three steles of Lartian marble are prepared; and that there be inscribed upon the stelai both this decree and those things (10) which—

according to the laws—one may not take into the precinct, and those who may not enter; and the penalties for a person who transgresses the law; and to set up the steles, one in the (15) entrance which (is used by) those making their way in from the city, one above the banqueting-hall, and the other on the descent from the Achaean citadel.

1. **μαστροῖς**: title of an official (**μασ-τρο-*, cf. *μαίομαι*, 'seek, investigate') in several Dorian cities (Att. *μαστήρ*).

4. **ἱερόν**: koiné form (WGk. *ἱαρ-*, §38.1). The word was apparently without the initial aspirate in Rhodian (cf. on *i-je-ro-jo* **4** and §10.4), even after the koiné form had penetrated the dialect (*ἐπ᾽ ἱερέως*, SEG 3. 674.2, II cent. BC). So also in Argolic.   **Ἀλεκτρώνᾱς**: daughter of Helios and Rhodos. *ἠλέκτωρ*, 'shining' is an epithet of the sun at *Il.* 19.398 (for a fem. name cf. *Ἠλέκτρα*). This form may be the result of contamination with the stem *ἀλεκ-*, 'defend' (cf. *Ἀλέκτωρ*, *Od.* 4.10).

5. **ἐπι-μελεθήμειν**: aor. pass. infin. (§40.3).

7. **ἐργασθέωντι**: aor. pass. subj. (Att. *ἐργασθῶσι*). For uncontracted *-θε-* cf. *στροτευθείωνθι* **14** 24. Inherited *-τι* preserved (§39.4).

8. **ἀναγραφῆι**: aor. pass. subj., sing. agreeing with the nearest subject (technically the grammatical subjects are neuter, but *ἐσοδοιπορεῖν* implies an antecedent at odds with *ἅ*).

10. **ἐντι**: 3 plur. for 3 sing. (neut. plur. subject *ἅ*). Confusion between *ἐντι* and *ἐστι* in later WGk. inscriptions (and Theokritos: e.g. 1. 17, 5. 21) may have originated in the imperf., where WGk. (inherited) 3 plur. *ἦν* was identical to the koiné 3 sing. form (cf. on *ἦς* **45** 21).

13. **θέμειν**: see *ἐπιμελεθήμειν* 5.

15. **πόλιος**: see *πόλιος* 7 12.   **ποτι-πορευομένοις**: WGk. preverb *ποτί* (Att. *πρός*): §40.8.

16. **ἱστιᾱτόριον**: from *ἑστιάω*, 'entertain' (denominative vb. to *ἑστία*): cf. *ἐφί[στια]* **24** 17.

THERA
(West Greek)

50. Rock inscription from Thera referring to the Karneian festival: two iambic trimeters followed by two words *extra*

metrum. Early V cent. BC. <*H*> for the aspirate and *eta.*
Buck 111. Schwyzer 219. *LSAG* 323 no. 16. *CEG* 457.

Ἀγλōτέλης πράτισ|τος ἀγοράν hικάδι |
Καρνήια θεὸν δεί|πνιξεν· hὸν[ι]παντίδα ||⁵ καὶ Λακαρτôς.

Agloteles, foremost in the Assembly, on the twentieth (of the
month *Karneia*) honoured the god with a Karneian banquet:
the (son) of Enipantidas and Lakarto.

1. **Ἀγλōτέλης**: < *Ἀγλα*ϝ*ο*- with loss of digamma and contraction.
πράτιστος: to be taken with ἀγοράν as acc. of respect (*πρᾶτος* §38.2).
2. **ἀγοράν**: in Att.-Ion. this would imply 'at public speaking'
(cf. the Theran name *Πρᾱταγόρᾱς*): here it might refer to some com-
petitive event of the festival (the vb. ἀγείρω can also have a religious
connotation, 'collect [offerings]'). **hικάδι**: dat. sing. < ϝικάς
(cf. **11** 10). It is not possible to define the conditions under which
IE *w- gave Gk. h- (as opposed to the 'normal' development ϝ-
then zero). There was probably confusion in early Gk. between
w- < *w- and ʰw- < *sw- (sometimes written ϝH- epigraphically).
3. **Καρνήια**: neut. plur. of an adj. in -ηιος. A festival of Apollo in
the Dorian world which gave its name to a month. **δείπνιξεν**:
unaugmented aor. in a verse-inscription (cf. **48** 1). For the velar stem
see §40.4.
4. **hὸν[ι]παντίδᾱ**: crasis (*ho Ἐνιπ-*); gen. sing. < *-ᾱο (§24.3).
5. **Λακαρτôς**: fem. name in -ω (< ωι, cf. λεχώι **52** 16): gen.
sing. < *-οι-ος. A compd. name built to masc. *λαϝο-κράτης (cf.
καρτερόν **53** 24).

CYRENE
(West Greek)

51. A list of religious laws from Cyrene (settled from Thera
*c.*630 BC), formulated as an oracular response by Apollo
(paras. 4–6 of nineteen given here). Early IV cent. BC. Buck
115. *SEG* 9. 72. Sokolowski (1962) no. 115. Rhodes–Osborne
(2003, no. 97). Dobias-Lalou (2000: 299–303). ▶▶ Brunel
(1984), Parker (1983: 332–51).

IV. [ἀ] λεχὼι ὄροφομ μιανεῖ· τὸμ μ[ὲν ὑπώροφομ μιανεῖ, τὸν | δ' ἐ]ξόροφον οὐ μιανεῖ, αἴ κα μὴ ὑπένθηι. ὁ δ' ἄ[νθρ|ω]πος, ὅ κα ἔνδοι ἦι, α<ὐ>τὸς μὲν μιαρὸς τέντα[ι ἀμ|έρα]ς τρῖς, ἄλλον δὲ οὐ μιανεῖ, οὐδὲ ὅπυι κα ἔνθ[ηι ὁ]‖²⁰ὗτος ὁ ἄνθρωπος.|

V. [Ἀ]καμαντίων ὁσία παντὶ καὶ ἀγνῶι καὶ βαβάλῳ[ι]·| πλὰν ἀπ' ἀνθρώπω Βάττω τῶ {τω} ἀρχαγέτα καὶ | Τριτοπατέρων καὶ ἀπὸ Ὀνυμάστω τῶ Δελφῶ{ι},| ἀπ' ἄλλω ὅπη ἄνθρωπος ἔκαμε, οὐκ ὁσία ἀγνῶ<ι>· ‖²⁵ τῶν δ' ἱαρῶν ὁσία παντί.

VI. αἴ κα ἐπὶ βωμῶι θύσηι ἱαρήιον, ὅ τι μὴ νόμος θύεν, τ[ὸ]| ποτιπίαμμα ἀφελὲν ἀπὸ τῶ βωμῶ καὶ ἀποπλῦν|αι καὶ τὸ ἄλλο λῦμα ἀνελὲν ἐκ τῶ ἱαρῶ, καὶ τὰν ἴκ|νυν ἀπὸ τῶ βωμῶ καὶ τὸ πῦρ ἀφελὲν ἐς καθαρόν,‖³⁰ καὶ τόκα δὴ ἀπονιψάμενος καθάρας τὸ ἱαρὸν καὶ | ζαμίαν θύσας βοτὸν τέλευν, τόκα δὴ θυέτω ὡς νόμ<ος>.

IV. A woman who has given birth will pollute a roof: she will pollute him who lives under the roof, but she will not pollute him who is outside, unless he comes in. Any person who is inside will himself remain polluted for three days, but he will not pass on the pollution to another, nor to the place from which this person comes.

V. Participation in the feast of the Akamantia (is) permitted to everyone, both purified and unpurified, except when (the honor-and is) a human being—Battos the first founder and the Ancestors and Onymastos the Delphian, (and) in any other case in which a person has died—(then) participation is not permitted to the purified. But with regard to the sacred feast (of the Akamantia), the right to participate (belongs) to everyone.

VI. If anyone sacrifices upon an altar a victim which it is not legitimate to sacrifice, take the residue of fat from the altar and cleanse (the altar) and remove the remaining defilement from the temple, and take the ashes and the fire from the altar to a purified (place). Then, having washed himself, purified the temple, and sacrificed in recompense an unblemished animal, then let him carry out the sacrifice according to the law.

16. **λεχώι**: fem. noun in -ωι (an *i*-stem: the final -ι was lost in Att.-Ion.). For the root cf. Hom. λέκτο, 'lay down'. **ὄροφομ**: final -ν > -μ, §23.4 (for the meaning 'roofed building' cf. Lat. *tectum*).

17. **ὑπένθηι**: < ὑπέλθηι, an assimilatory sound-change that occurred sporadically in WGk.

18. **ὅ (κα)**: article with relative function (§32.13).   **ἔνδοι**: WGk. form of ἔνδον (re-modelled on οἴκοι).   **τέντα[ι]**: Att. ἔσται (form found only at Cyrene). Probably from *τέλται (cf. ὑπένθηι 17) < τέλεται by syncope (Szemerényi 1964: 165–7). This was a defective (suppletive) fut. to εἰμί in Cretan (the middle may imply futurity, since its reflexive force becomes associated with volition: §24.2b). Hom. πέλομαι (with Aeolic treatment of *kʷel-) has present function.

19. **τρῖς**: inherited acc. < τρίνς (Att. generalized the nom. τρεῖς < *trey-es, perhaps influenced by i-stem nouns like πόλεις).   **ὅπυι**: see **38** 14.

21. The interpretation of ll. 21–4 is difficult and disputed (the translation follows Brunel).   **Ἀκαμαντίων**: nom. ἀκαμάντια, a festival named for the *Akamantes* (heroes whose cult is also attested in Attica).   **βαβάλωι**: 'profane', perh. derived from βέβηκα (normal WGk. form is βέβαλος: βα- here by assimilation to the adjacent vowel), orig. 'that which may be stepped on'.

22. **ἀπ' ἀνθρώπω**: ἀπό with the gen. (=abl.) 'deriving from' implies the source, reason, or funding of one type of *akamantia*. The ritually pure cannot participate in a feast or ritual with funerary associations. Gen. -ω (§38.3).   **ἀρχāγέτā**: gen. sing. (§24.3); the ἀρχηγέτης is the legendary founder of a city.

23. **Τριτοπατέρων**: τριτο-, lit. 'third generation back' (i.e. great-grandparents), came to mean 'original' or 'earliest' ancestors (cf. Aesch. τριγέρων, 'very old'). Three is a conventional designator of 'many'.   **Ὀνυμάστω**: cf. ὀνύματα **10** 10.

24. **ὅπη**: 'where' for 'in which' (cf. hόπε̄ **44** 6 for the form). **ἔκαμε**: cf. Hom. οἱ καμόντες, 'the dead'.

26. **θύεν**: thematic infin. (§40.3).

27. **ποτιπίαμμα**: fat (πίαμμα < *πιαν-μα, cf. πῖαρ, §24.4) which '(still) adheres to' (ποτι-) the altar.   **ἀφελέν** etc.: aor. infin. (§40.3), imperatival.

30. **τόκα**: §40.7.

31. **τέλευν**: < τέλεον (cf. Σωκράτευς **42** 4).

CRETE
(West Greek)

52. Boustrophedon inscription on both sides of a piece of bronze armour (a semicircular plate), probably from Aphrati: a contract, in the form of a decree, between the scribe Spensitheos and the community (the opening lines of side A are given here). *c.*500 BC. Ed. pr. Jeffery–Morpurgo Davies (1970). *SEG* 27.631. *LSAG* 468 no. 14b. *Nomima*, i. 22. ▶▶ Van Effenterre (1973), Edwards & Edwards (1974), Beattie (1975).

θιοί. ἔϝαδε Δαταλεῦσι καὶ ἐσπένσαμες πόλις | Σπενσιθίωι ἀπὸ πυλᾶν πέντε ἀπ᾽ ἑκάστας θροπάιν τε καὶ ἀτέλειαν πάντων αὐτῶι τε καὶ γενιᾶι ὤισκα πόλι τὰ δαμόσια τά τε θιήια καὶ τἀνθρώπινα ||⁵ ποινικάζεν τε καὶ μναμονευϝην. ποινικάζεν δὲ |[π]όλι καὶ μναμονεῦϝεν τὰ δαμόσια μήτε τὰ θιήιλα μήτε τἀνθρώπινα μηδέν᾽ ἄλον αἰ μὴ Σπενσίθ[ιιο]ν αὐτόν τε καὶ γενιὰν τὀνυ, αἰ μὴ ἐπαίροι τ|ε καὶ κέλοιτο ἢ αὐτὸς Σπενσίθεος ἢ γενιὰ ||¹⁰ [τ]ὀνυ ὅσοι δρομῆς εἶεν τῶν [υἱ]ῶν οἱ πλίες· | μισθὸν δὲ δόμεν τὸ ἐνιαυτὸ τῶι ποινι[κ|α]στᾶι πεντήϟοντά τε πρόϟοος κλεύκιος . . .

Gods. The Dataleis decided and we the city, five men from each of the tribes, pledged to Spensitheos subsistence and freedom from all taxes, both to himself and to his descendants, on condition that he act for the city in public matters, both sacred and secular (5), as scribe and recorder. No one other than Spensitheos and his descendants is to be scribe and recorder for the city in public matters, either sacred or secular, unless either Spensitheos himself should initiate and support (this), or his offspring (10), (that is) the majority of his sons, as many as are adults. As payment (the city) is to give annually to the scribe fifty measures of new wine and . . .

1. **θιοί**: §23.2.   **ἔϝαδε**: aor. of ϝανδάνω, 'please', equivalent in function to Att. ἔδοξε.   **Δαταλεῦσι**: either the name of the community, or (edd. pr.) a ruling elite or clan within it.   **ἐσπένσαμες**: aor. of σπένδω (with retention of secondary -νσ- < *ἔσπενδσα-): orig. 'pour a drink-offering (in ratification of a promise)', Lat. *spondeō*. WGk. 1 plur. -μες agreeing in sense with πόλις.

2. **πυλᾶν**: Att. φυλῶν (§30.2). The archaic script of Crete lacked the signs φ, χ. This is not evidence of deaspiration (θ is used): π was used for both π and φ, κ for κ and χ.   **ἐκάστας**: initial F- has disappeared from this word (Fέκαστον at Gortyn, **53** 41). **θροπάν**: metathesis or anticipation (θροφάν) of the aspirate (Att. τροφήν).

3. **ἀτέλειαν**: cf. **9** 5.   **ὦσκα**: Att. ὦστε (§40.7).

4. **πόλῑ**: < πόλι-ι (cf. §32.4).   **θιήια**: usually ε > ι before a back vowel. In this case the adj. suffix -ηιος was added to the stem θι- of θιός (edd. pr.): §23.2.

5. **ποινικάζεν**: pres. infin. of a verb previously unknown; if formed to the stem φοινικ-, it could mean 'write Phoenician letters' (cf. Hdt. 5. 58–9), or 'write red letters' (letters cut on stone were often coloured red to improve legibility). Cf. φοινικήια, 'letters' at Teos (**20** 37).   **μνᾱμονευFην**: vb. formed to μνάμων, 'recorder' (the position is scribe and public archivist). The infin. ending is probably a scribal error: cf. -εν in the next line.

7. **ἄλον**: single writing of a double consonant (archaic scribal practice).

8. **τὀνυ**: Att. τούτου (refers back). These pronouns in -νυ are known from Arc.-Cyp. and may represent survivals of an Achaean substrate dialect in Crete (Brixhe 1991: 65–7).   **ἐπαίροι**: or 'induce' with 'the city' as unexpressed object.

9. **κέλοιτο**: κέλομαι, 'order, urge' is found in WGk. inscriptions, literary Doric, and epic (Att. κελέυω).

10. **δρομῆς**: < δρομῆες, nom. plur. of δρομεύς, 'runner, one admitted to the public gymnasium (δρόμος)', i.e. 'one who has come of age'.   **οἰ**: τοί usual in WGk. (§40.5). Perhaps a substrate feature (Achaean).   **πλίες**: 'more [than half]'; see πλέας **17** 9 (with ε > ι extended from the oblique cases: cf. θιήια 4).

11. **δόμεν**: WGk. athem. infin. as elsewhere in Crete (except for -ην at Gortyn): §40.3.   **τὀ ἐνιαυτὀ**: gen. with the article may be distributive (as in Att.-Ion.), 'per year'.

12. **πρόFοος**: orig. 'jugs' (Att. πρόχους), uncontracted acc. plur. < *προ-χοFονς (-ος < -ονς before C-, §23.9). See **23** 2 on *qoppa* (§17.2). The unit was perhaps equivalent to the Attic χοῦς (3¼ litres). **κλεύκιος**: gen. sing. of neut. κλεῦκος, 'must, new wine', which occurs at Gortyn in the form γλεῦκος (cf. γλυκύς, 'sweet'): edd. pr. (ad loc.)

suggest 'a neutralization of voiced and voiceless consonants before liquid'. Damaged text after this word contained another component of the payment (signalled by τε here).

53. Boustrophedon wall inscription at Gortyn, codifying a number of laws (the eighth provision, occupying part of Column IV, is given here). Mid V cent. BC. *Inscriptiones Creticae*, IV, 123–71. Buck 117. Schwyzer 179. Meiggs–Lewis 41. *Nomima*, ii. 49. The inscription has only one sign *E* for all *e*-vowels (other texts from Gortyn have both *E* and *H*). ▶▶ Willetts (1967), Sealey (1994: 37–43), Dubois (1999*a*).

τὸν πατέρα τὸν | τέκνōν καὶ τὸν κρēμάτōν κ‖²⁵αρτερὸν ἔμēν τᾶδ
δαίσιος, | καὶ τὰν ματέρα τὸν Ϝὸν αὐ|τᾶς κρēμάτōν. ἇς κα δόōντι, | μὲ
ἐπάνανκον ἔμēν δατεῖθθαι· αἰ δέ τις ἀταθείε͂, ἀποδ‖³⁰άτταθθαι τōι
ἀταμένōι ἇλι ἔγ̣ραττ̣αι. ἒ δέ κ᾽ ἀποθάνει τις, | (σ)τέγανς μὲν τὰνς ἐν
πόλι κἄ|τι κ᾽ ἐν ταῖ(ς) στέγαις ἐνεῖ, αἶ|ς κα μὲ Ϝοικεὺς ἐνϜοικεῖ
ἐπ‖³⁵ὶ κόραι Ϝοικίōν, καὶ τὰ πρόβατα καὶ κ̣αρται|ποδα, ἅ κα μὲ
Ϝοικέος εῖ, | ἐπὶ τοῖς υἰάσι ἔμēν, τὰ δ᾽ ἄλ|λα κρέματα πάντα
δατεῖθθαι κ̣αλōς, καὶ λανκάνεν τὸς μ‖⁴⁰ἐν υἰύνς, ὁπόττοι κ᾽ ἴōντι,
δύ|ο μοίρανς Ϝέκαστον, τὰδ δὲ θυγατέρανς ὁπότται κ᾽ ἴōν|τι,
μίαν μοῖραν Ϝεκάσταν. δ|ιατεῖθ[θ]αι δὲ καὶ τὰ ματρōια, εῖ‖⁴⁵ κ᾽
ἀποθά[νε͂]ι, ἇιπερ τὰ [πατρō]ι᾽ | ἔ[γρατ]τ̣αι. αἰ δὲ κρέματα μὲ εῖ|λε͂,
στέγα δέ, λακὲν τὰθ θ[υ]γατέ|ρας ἇι ἔγραττ̣αι. αἰ δέ κα λεῖλι ὁ πατὲρ
δōòς ἰὸν δόμēν τᾶ‖⁵⁰ι ὀπυιομέναι, δότō κατὰ τ|ὰ ἐγραμμένα, πλίονα
δὲ μέ.

The father is to have power over the children and over the division of the estate, and the mother (is to have power over the division) of her own estate. So long as they are alive, there is no obligation to make a division; but if anyone should be fined, (30) the person fined shall have his share apportioned to him, as is prescribed. And if a man should die, the houses in the city and whatever is in the houses—excluding any in which a serf in the (35) country is living—and the animals, both small and large—except those belonging to a serf—are to descend to the sons; and they are to divide all the rest of the estate fairly, and the (40) sons, as many as there may be, are to get two parts each, and the daughters, as many as there may be, are to get one part each. And the estate of the mother, when (45) she dies, is to be divided in the same way as is prescribed for the father's estate. If there is no property but a building, the daughters are to get their share as is prescribed. If the father wishes, while he is alive, to make a gift to his married daughter, let him make the gift according to what is prescribed, but not more.

24. **κρēμάτōν**: the archaic script of Crete lacks the signs χ and φ (see **52** 2 πυλᾶν). **καρτερόν**: adj. built to the neut. κράτος/κάρτος (for the vocalic *r̥ cf. δαρχμάς **7** 23).
25. **ἔμēν**: i.e. ἤμην, 'to be' (§40.3): cf. Rhodian -μειν **49** 5. **τᾶδ**: τᾶς, with assimilation of -s to the following dental. **δαίσιος**: gen. of Cretan noun δαῖσις, 'division' (cf. Hom. δαίομαι).
26. **Ϝôν**: Ϝός (ὅς) < *swo-, 'own' (cf. Lat. *suus*).
27. **ᾶς**: see **14** 29. **κα**: §40.6. **δόōντι**: δ- < *gʷy- (§23.8: Att. ζῶσι with contraction): pres. subj.
28. **δατēθθαι**: mid. infin. < δατέεσθαι, with σ assimilated to the following θ, i.e. [s+tʰ] > [t+tʰ], for which cf. the regular assimilation of -s to δ- (τᾶδ 25).
29. **ἀταθείē**: pass. opt. (aor.) of ἀτάω (< ἀϜατάω), here in the narrow sense of 'financial distress'. An advance may be given to pay a creditor and avoid the danger of debt bondage (bonded labour); the opt. expresses a more remote contingency than that envisaged by the preceding subj. (for 'urbane' remoteness cf. note on διακωλύσει **7** 6). **ἀπο-δάτταθθαι**: mid. infin. to aor. stem δαττ- < *δατ-σ-.
30. **ᾶι**: characteristic advb. of WGk., an old dat.-loc. (cf. ταυτᾶ hᾶτε **33** 4); Att. ὥσπερ (ἧι is rare and poetic).
31. **ἔγραπται**: perf. pass. < ἔγραπται with assimilation of π to τ. Verbs beginning with a cluster stop + liquid generally form a perf. by reduplicating the initial stop (Att. γέ-γραμμαι): in some cases dialects have ἐ- on the analogy of consonant clusters starting with s- (where e.g. στέλλω → *σέ-σταλκα > *ἔσταλκα, remodelled as ἔσταλκα). **ἔ**: 'when', here with κα and the subj. 'in the case that, in the event that . . .' (close in meaning to αἰ, 'if'). **τις**: i.e. τιστέγανς on the stone, with the double s written as a single (cf. στέγα **47**).
32. **(σ)τέγανς**: acc. plur. of the word for 'roof' (cf. ὄροφομ **51** 16);

note that Gortyn retains final -*νς* in nouns (contrast πρόϟοος **52** 12).
τάνς: §23.9.   **πόλῑ**: < πόλι-ι (§32.4).   **κἄτι**: crasis, καὶ ἄτι neut.
plur. (cf. Att. indef. ἄτινα, re-modelled).

34. **Ϝοικεύς**: a class of non-citizen peasants (possibly remnants of
the pre-Dorian population) with very restricted rights (Arist. *Politics*
1264a).   35. **κόραι**: i.e. χώραι, the countryside, as opposed to πόλι.
Ϝοικίον: pres. ptcpl. (§23.2); 'houses inhabited by serfs belonged,
like the serfs themselves, to the soil, being regarded as part of the
property producing income, of which the daughters had their share'
(Willetts 1967: 65). The sacrifice of elegance for clarity is a feature of
all legal language.   36. **καρταίποδα**: 'stout-footed' beasts (cf. καρτερόν 24), i.e. herds
of larger animals, opposed to the πρόβατα (sheep and goats).
Ϝοικέος: < gen. *Ϝοικήϝ-ος. η> ε in hiatus after (relatively recent) loss
of -Ϝ-.   37. **υἱάσι**: a *u*-stem in archaic Gk. (cf. gen. ὑυιός **9** 11), later transferred to the thematic declension. The dat. plur. (for which cf.
δάκρυσι) has been re-modelled after forms such as πατράσι (υἱάσι
already in Homer).   39. **λανκάνεν**: thematic infin. (§40.3).
40. **υἱύνς**: acc. plur., original form (Palmer 1980: 276).
ὀπόττοι: *-ty- > -ττ- in Crete (§§23.8, 39.2). The treatment of *-ts- is
identical (δάττασθαι 29).   **ἴοντι**: subj. of the verb 'be' (Ion. ἐῶσι):
§§23.2, 32.11.   42. **θυγατέρανς**: the -νς ending has been analogically extended
from them. and *a*-stem nouns (cf. στέγανς 32): but not at 47–8.
48. **λεῖ**: pres. subj. of λῶ (**44** 2).   49. **δōός**: 'alive' (Att. ζωός: cf. δōōντι 27).   **ἴον**: cf. ἴοντι 40.

PHOKIS
(North-west Greek)

54. Wall inscription at the stadion at Delphi prohibiting the
removal of (sacred) wine. Early/mid V cent. BC. *CID* I 3.
Buck 50. Schwyzer 321. *LSAG* 104 no. 17. Sokolowski (1969)
no. 76. *Nomima*, ii. 97.

τὸν Ϝοῖνον μὲ̄ φάρεν ἐ̄ς τοῦ δρ|όμου· αἰ δέ κα φάρēι, ἱλαξάστō | τὸν

θεὸν hôι κα κεραίεται, καὶ | μεταθυσάτō κἀποτεισάτō πέν||⁵τε
δραχμάς· τούτου δὲ τôι καταⁱγορέσαντι τὸ hέμισσον.

Do not take the wine away from the stadium. If one does remove
(it), he is to propitiate the god for whom it is mixed, and make a
sacrifice in place of it, and he is to be fined five drachmas; and of
this the half (is to go) to the accuser.

The inscription, the language of which appears archaic, was found in
a wall dated to the late IV cent. BC. It may be a copy of an older text:
this would explain (a) why ϜΟΙΝΟΝ 1 is written *EOINON* (the
engraver was unfamiliar with an old letter), and (b) the appearance
of the digraph *ου* for [ǫ:] (unlikely to have been in use in the first half
of the V cent. BC).

   1. **Ϝοῖνον**: initial *w*- preserved (§39.1): Lat. *uīnum*.   **φάρεν**: pres.
infin. (φέρειν), with ε > α (§38.5). Infin. -εν (§40.3) is characteristic
of Phocis, but not of NW Gk. in general.   **ἐς**: for ἐς < ἐκς
cf. ἐσδοτῆρες **7** 6.   **τοῦ δρόμου**: §38.3.
   2. **hιλαξάστō**: imper. (aor. mid.) of ἱλά-σκομαι. The Hom. aor. is
ἱλασσ- (§40.4 for the stem in -ξ-). Imper. -σθω > -στω (§39.5).
   3. **κεραίεται**: κεραίω (also in Hom.) and κεράννυμι are both built
to the aor. stem ἐκέρασα (cf. κέρναντα **17** 4). For the root *krH₂, 'mix'
cf. κράτηρ < *kreH₂.
   4. **μετα-θυσάτō**: compd. not attested elsewhere.   **κἀποτεισάτō**:
crasis, καὶ ἀπο-.
   6. **hέμισσον**: see ἡμίσσοι **7** 25.

55. Block from Delphi, inscribed on all four sides, giving the
rules of the so-called 'phratry of the Labyadai' (a kinship
group, perhaps on a Thessalian model, with some procedures
analogous to an Athenian phratry): part of the first side is
given here. IV cent. BC. *CID* I 9. Rhodes–Osborne (2003, no. 1).
Buck 52. Schwyzer 323. ▶▶ Bousquet (1966), Kearns (1994).

ἔδοξε Λαβ[υ]ᾴδαις Βουκατ||²⁰ίου μηνὸς δεκ[ά]ται ἐπὶ Κ[ά]|μπου ἐν
τᾶι ἀ[λί]αι σὺμ ψά[φ]|οις ἑκατὸν ὀγδοήκοντ[α] | δυοῖν· τοὺ[ς]
ταγοὺς μὴ δέκⁱεσθαι μήτε δαρατᾶν γάμε||²⁵λα μήτε παιδηῖα μήτ᾽
[ἀπελ]ⁱλαῖα, αἰ μὴ τᾶς πατριᾶς ἐπⁱαινεούσας τᾶς πληθύος ἐⁱξ ἆς
κα ἦι. αἰ δέ τί κα πὰρ ν[ό]|μον κελεύσωντι, τῶν κελε||³⁰υσάντων ὁ

κίνδυνος ἔστ[ω].Ι τὰ δ[ὲ] ἀπελλαῖα ἄγεν Ἀπέ[λ]Ιλαις καὶ μὴ ἄ[λλ]αι
[ἀ]μέρᾳ[ι], Ι μήτε ἄγεν τοὺς ἄγο[ν]τας μ̣ήτε τοὺς ταγ[ο]ὺς
δέκεσθαιΙΙ³⁵ι· αἰ δέ κα ϝέξωνται ἄλλαι Ι [ἀ]μέραι ἢ Ἀπέλλαις,
ἀποτεΙ[ι]σάτω ϝέκαστος δέκα δραΙχμάς· ὁ δὲ χρήζων καταγορΙεῖν
τῶν δεξαμένων ἐπὶ τῶΙΙ⁴⁰ν hυστέρων ταγῶν καταγοΙρείτω ἐν τᾶι
ἀλίαι τᾶι μεΙ[τ]ὰ Βουκάτια, αἴ κ᾽ ἀμφιλλέΙγωντι τοὶ ταγοὶ τοὶ
δεξάΙμενοι. ἄγεν δὲ τἀπελλαῖα ΙΙ⁴⁵ ἀντὶ ϝέτεος καὶ τὰς δαράΙτας
φέρεν. hόστις δέ κα μὴ Ι ἄγηι τἀπελλαῖα ἢ τὰν δαρΙάταν μὴ φέρηι,
ἀμμόνιον κΙατθέτω στατῆρα ἐπὶ ϝεκαΙΙ⁵⁰τέρωι, τῶι δὲ hυστέρωι
ϝέΙτει ἀγέτω τἀπελλαῖα καὶ Ι τὰν δαράταν φερέτω· αἰ δέ Ι κα μὴ
ἄγηι, μηκέτι δεκέσθΙων ἀμμόνια, ἀλλ᾽ ἢ ἀ<γ>έτω ἀπΙΙ⁵⁵ελλαῖα ἢ
ἀποτεισάτω ϝίϙΙατι δραχμὰς ἢ hυπογραψάΙμενος τόκιομ φερέτω.

The Labyadai decided, on the tenth of the month (20) Boukatios,
in the presidency of Kampos, in the assembly by 182 votes: the
tagoi are not to accept either *daratai* (*gamela* or *paideia*) or
apellaia except with the approval of the majority of the *patria* of
which (the party) is a member. Now if they give instructions con-
trary to the law, let it be at the risk of those (30) who give the
order. One is to bring the *apellaia* during the Apellai, and on no
other day are the candidates to bring them or the *tagoi* to accept
them; if they accept them on any day other than the Apellai, each
is to pay ten drachmas. A person wishing to accuse them of
(unlawfully) accepting (offerings) is to make the charge during
the period of office of the (40) next *tagoi* in the assembly following
the Boukatia, if the *tagoi* accused of accepting dispute the charge.
One is to bring the *apellaia* in the same year, and (likewise) offer
the *daratai*. Whoever does not bring the *apellaia* or does not
offer the *daratai*, he is to deposit a pledge of a stater in either
case (50), and in the following year he is to bring the *apellaia*,
and offer the *daratai*. If he (still) does not bring (them), they are
not to accept any more pledges, but he must either bring the
apellaia or pay twenty drachmas, or give a promissory note and
pay interest.

19. *Λαβ[υ]άδαις*: the name has the form of a patronymic (cf.
Θιογνειτίδαο **14** 10), appropriately for a social group predicated on
descent from a putative common ancestor: the Bassaidai at **10** 2 may
be a parallel.

20. **ἐπὶ Κάμπου**: cf. the Boeotian use at **14** 13.   **ἀ[λί]αι**: see on **42** 5.

23. **ταγούς**: known from Thessaly as the title of an official (e.g. **10** 3).   **δέκεσθαι**: cf. *hυποδεκόμενος* **44** 3.

24. **δαρατᾶν**: two kinds of baked offering (*δαράται*) are specified: those which marked a wedding (*γάμελα*) and those which marked the enrolment of an infant (*παιδῆια*). The *ἀπελλαία* were sacrificial offerings which marked a young man's majority, and hence full entry into the clan. Offerings were made at the *Apellai*, a festival corresponding to the Athenian *Apatouria*.

26. **πατριᾶς**: a subdivision of the kinship group (partitive gen. dependent on *τᾶς πληθύος* in the following gen. absolute).

28. **πάρ**: apocope (§24.5).

29. **κελεύσωντι**: aor. subj. (inherited *-τι* preserved, §39.4).

30. **ὁ κίνδυνος**: the article is without aspiration in this inscription (as in Locrian), probably indicating a generally weak articulation of *h-* in the dialect (so also *ὁ δὲ* 38). Cf. on **62** 2 and §23.10.

31. **ἄγεν**: pres. inf. (§40.3) with imper. force.

37. **Ϝέκαστος**: initial *w-* preserved (§39.1).

38. **χρήζων**: a vb. confined to poetry in Attic (which in prose uses *ὁ βουλόμενος* in this context).

42. **ἀμφιλλέγωντι**: a compd. of *ἀμφίς + λέγω*, with assimilation of *-ς* to *λ-* (the Att. form is a compound of *ἀμφί + λέγω*).

43. **τοί**: definite article (§40.5).

45. **ἀντὶ Ϝέτεος**: i.e. within a year of the event (this sense is supported by the contrast with *τῶι δὲ hυστέρωι Ϝέτει* 50).

48. **ἀμμόνιον**: formed to *ἀναμένω*, 'wait for' (*ἄν* §24.5 > *ἀμ-* §23.4). A *hapax*: perhaps a deposit indicating an intention to act (and returnable when the pledge is made good).   **κατθέτω**: aor. imper. (*κατ-* §24.5).

55. **Ϝίκατι**: §32.9.

57. **τόκιομ**: local form of *τόκος*. Nouns denoting payment are often formed with the suffix *-ιον* (cf. *ἀμμόνιον*, and Chantraine 1933: 58). Final *-ν > -μ* §23.4.

LOKRIS
(North-west Greek)

56. Bronze tablet from western Lokris, with a boustrophedon inscription regarding the settlement of a new tract of land (first paragraph given here). Late VI cent. BC. *IG* IX 1² 3. 609. Buck 59. *LSAG* 105, 108 no. 2. Meiggs–Lewis 13. *Nomima*, i. 44. ⏭ Vatin (1963), Link (1991).

A. τεθμὸς ὅδε περὶ τᾶς γᾶς βέβαιος ἔστō κὰτ τὸν | ἀνδαιθμὸν πλακὸς Ὑλίας καὶ Λισκαρίας, καὶ τὸν ἀ|ποτόμōν καὶ τὸν δαμοσίōν. ἐπινομία δ' ἔστō γο|νεῦσιν καὶ παιδί· αἰ δὲ μὲ παῖς εἴε̄, κόραι· αἰ δὲ μὲ κόρα εἴε̄, ‖⁵ ἀδελφεȭι· αἰ δὲ μὲ ἀδελφεὸ<ς> εἴε̄, ἀνχιστέδαν ἐπινεμέσθō κὰ τὸ | δίκαιον· αἰ δὲ μέ τοι ἐπινόμοι [*erasure: c.* 4]. hό τι δέ κα φυτεύσεται | ἄσυλος ἔ{ι}στō, αἰ μὲ πολέμōι ἀνανκαζομένοις δόξξαι ἀ|νδράσιν hενὶ κε̄κατὸν ἀριστίνδαν τōι πλέ̄θει ἄνδρας δια|κατίōς μεῖστον ἀξξιομάχōς ἐπιϝοίκōς ἐφάγεσθαι· hόστ‖¹⁰ις δὲ δαιθμὸν ἐνφέροι ἒ ψᾶφον διαφέροι ἐν πρείγαι ἒ'ν πόλι ἒ'ν ἀποκλ- ε̄σίαι ἒ στάσιν ποιέοι περὶ γαδαισίας, αὐτὸς μὲ|ν ϝερρέτō καὶ γενεὰ ἄματα πάντα, χρέματα δὲ δαμευόσθōν | καὶ ϝοικία κατασκαπτέσθō κὰτ τὸν ἀνδρεφονικὸν τετθμ|όν.

This law concerning land is to be valid in the apportioning of the Hylian and the Liscarian plain, both the reserved and the public (land). The line of inheritance shall be both to parents and to son. If there is no son, to a daughter. If there is no daughter, (5) to a brother. If there is no brother, let it pass to the nearest kin in accordance with the law; if the legal heirs *do not* (?) . . . [*erasure, c.* 4]. Whatever (land) is planted, let it be exempt from seizure, unless, under constraint of war, a hundred and one men from the best families decide by majority vote to settle at least two hundred men of military age as colonists. Whoever (10) proposes a motion for a distribution (of the land) or casts his vote (for this) in the council of elders, or before the people, or in the select assembly, or agitates for a land distribution, let him be exiled, himself and his family for ever, and let his property be confiscated, and let his house be pulled down in accordance with the law concerning homicide.

1. **τεθμός**: 'that which is laid down', from θε- plus a suffix -θμος (first aspirate dissimilated, §23.5). Att. θεσμός is formed with a suffix -σμος (Chantraine 1933: 136–40).   **κὰτ τόν**: κατά undergoes apocope (§24.5) in Lokr. only before the article. In common phrases (e.g. κὰ τὸ δίκαιον 5) it appears as κά by dissimilation, or haplology.

2. **ἀν-δαιθμόν**: ἀνά + δαιθμός (10 below). From δαίω with suffix -θμος; for the suffix in Att. δασμός (< *δατ-σμος, cf. δατέομαι) see τεθμός/θεσμός 1.   **πλακὸς Ὑλίας**: the designation seems to entail an adj. ὕλιος, 'wooded' (*hapax*); editors differ in their capitalization of the phrase. It is conceivable that λισκαρίας meant 'cleared' (cf. τὸ λισγάριον, 'hoe, spade').

2.–3. **ἀποτόμōν . . . δᾱμοσίōν**: the lands 'cut off' (cf. τέμνω and τέμενος) are distinguished from those still within the jurisdiction of the community (δᾶμος).

3. **ἐπι-νομίᾱ**: could also mean 'right of pasturage', but the relationship with ἐπινεμέσθō 5 makes it more attractive to assume that the clause specifies inheritance rules for the new allotments slightly different from those in general force in the city.   **γονεῦσιν**: note the final -ν, probably on the analogy of the pronominal dat. plur. (ἀμίν, etc.): §32.7. So ἀνδράσιν 7.

4. **παιδί . . . κόραι**: παῖς in the sense 'son' is also found at **57** 7, and may have replaced υἱός in Lokr. (cf. *ko-wo* **3**). So also κόρα (poetic in Att.) for θυγάτηρ.

5. **ἀδελφεōι**: for the form see ἀδελφεάς **24** 26. On the dat. sing. in NW Gk., §40.10.   **ἀνχιστέδᾱν**: adv. formed from a verb *ἀγχιστέω (cf. ἀγχιστεία 'close kinship') with the suffix -δᾱν (Fraenkel 1932).   **κά**: see κὰτ τόν 1.

6. **τοι ἐπίνομοι**: the sentence appears to break off before the erasure. The top line of the reverse side *may* contain the 'insertion': κομίζοιεν, ἀξιοδότας ἔστō τὰν αὐτô ὅτινι χρέζοι, 'if the heirs do not take possession, one shall be entitled to gift one's land to whoever one wishes' (useful discussion in Meiggs–Lewis).   **φυτεύσεται**: short vowel aor. subjunctive (pass.).

7. **δόξξαι**: 3 sing. aor. opt. of δοκέω. For the writing with double -ξ- cf. ἐξξανακάδēν **9** 8.

8. **κἒκατόν**: crasis, καὶ ἑκατόν (for the erratic appearance of *h*- cf. on ἐφάγεσθαι 9 and ὁ **55** 30).   **ἀριστίνδᾱν**: adv. formed with the extended suffix -ιν-δᾱν (for -ιν cf. τετράκιν **33** 9).   **διακατίōς**: §§32.9, 39.4.

9. **μεῖστον**: superl. of μεῖον (advb.).   **ἐπιϝοίκōς**: retention of intervocalic *w* (contrast κόρα 5 < κόρϝα).   **ἐφ-άγεσθαι**: the 'hypercorrect' aspiration of ἐπ- is a sign that *h*- was disappearing from the spoken language.

10. **ἐνφέροι**: the compound reflects NW Gk. ἐν+acc. instead of εἰς < ἐν-ς (§28.8). **πρείγᾱι**: Att. πρεσβείᾱ. The γ ~ β alternation in WGk. πρει(σ)γ-, Att. πρεσβ- points to an earlier labiovelar *gʷ (cf. Lac. περγυτέροις 34 3). For the vowel cf. πρεισβείας 11 12. 11. **ἀποκλἒσίᾱι**: i.e. a committee of ἀπόκλητοι, 'chosen delegates' (a noun parallel in formation to Att. ἐκ-κλησίᾱ). **γᾱ-δαισίᾱς**: 'land-division' (δαίω). 12. **Ϝερρέτō**: ἔρρω, 'go' always has a perjorative sense in Gk. (Aristophanes ἔρρ' ἐς κόρακας!); here in a technical sense 'go into exile' (Att. φευγέτω, cf. Elis 58 2). **ἅματα**: acc. plur. of ἇμαρ, formulaic in curses (§24.4b for the morphology). ἁμάρα < *ἁμέρα is the normal form (for vowel assimilation cf. βαβάλωι 51 21). **δαμευόσθōν**: the 3 pl. imper. in -ōσθōν (< *-ονσθōν) is common in V cent. Attic inscriptions (Threatte 1996: 465). 13. **ἀνδρ-ε-φονικόν**: the unusual liaison vowel -ε- (Att. -ο-) in this word was considered a peculiarity of Doric by ancient grammarians. **τετθμόν**: syllabification [te.tʰmo-] and [tetʰ.mo-] led to this hybrid form in which the θ appears as a double consonant. Cf. δόξξαι 7.

57. Bronze tablet found at Oianthea in western Lokris, inscribed on both sides with the conditions under which eastern Lokrians are to go to Naupaktos in western Lokris, to keep their colony up to strength (the opening paragraph is given here). Early V cent. BC. *IG* IX 1² 3. 718. Buck 57. *LSAG* 106, 108 no. 3. Meiggs–Lewis 20. Schwyzer 362. *Nomima*, i. 43. ▶▶ Beck (1999), Wachter (1999).

ἐν Ναύπακτον κὰ τόνδε hἀπιϜοικία. ΛοϘρὸν τὸν hυποκναμίδιον,
ἐπleί κα Ναυπάκτιος γένēται, Ναυπάκτιον ἐόντα, hόπō ξένον ὅσια
λανχάνlειν καὶ θύειν ἐξεῖμεν ἐπιτυχόντα, αἴ κα δείλēται· αἴ κα
δείλēται, θύειν καὶ λιανχάνειν κὲ δάμō κὲ Ϙοινάνōν αὐτὸν καὶ τὸ
γένος κατ' αἰϜεί. τέλος τοll⁵ὺς ἐπιϜοίκους ΛοϘρὸν τὸν hυποκνα-
μιδίōν μὲ φάρειν ἐν ΛοϘροῖς τοῖς hυποκναμιδίοις φρίν κ' αὖ τις
ΛοϘρὸς γένēται τὸν hυποκναμιδιōν. αἰ l δείλēτ' ἀνχōρεῖν, κατα-
λείποντα ἐν τᾶι ἱστίαι παῖδα hēβατὰν ἒ 'δελφεόν, ἐξleῖμεν ἄνευ
ἐνετēρίον. αἰ κα hυπ' ἀνάνκας ἀπελάōνται ἒ Ναυπάκτō ΛοϘροὶ τοὶ
hυποκναμίδιοι, ἐξεῖμεν ἀνχōρεῖν, hόπō Ϝέκαστος ἐν, ἄνευ ἐll¹⁰νετēρίον.
τέλος μὲ φάρειν μēδὲν hότι μὲ μετὰ ΛοϘρὸν τὸν Ϝεσπαρίōν.

The colony to Naupaktos on these (terms). A Hypoknemidian Lokrian, when he has become a Naupaktian, being a Naupaktian may participate as a guest in civil affairs and in sacrifices when he is here, if he wishes; if he wishes, he may sacrifice and participate (in civil affairs), both those of the state and those of the communities, himself and his descendants for ever. (5) The colonists of the Hypoknemidian Lokrians are not to pay tax among the Hypoknemidian Lokrians, unless a man becomes a Lokrian of the Hypoknemidians again. If he wishes to return home, so long as he leaves by his hearth a grown-up son or brother, he may (return) without (payment of) entry-dues. If the Hypoknemidian Lokrians are forcibly driven out of Naupaktos, they may return (to the places) they were severally from, without (payment of) entry-dues. (10) They are not to pay any tax at all except in common with the western Lokrians.

Colons (not reproduced here) divide the inscription into phrases, which appear to be partly accentual and partly syntactic (see Wachter 1999).

1. **ἐν**: §28.8 and ἐνφέροι **56** 10.   **κὰ τὸνδε**: cf. κὰτ τόν **56** 1. **hἀπιϜοικία**: crasis < hā + ἐπιϜοικία.   **Λοϟρὸν τὸν hυποκναμίδιον**: i.e. from eastern Lokris, separated from western Lokris by the Phokians (presumably later arrivals). A copy of the text (the 'original' ?) must have been put up in eastern Lokris: it is uncertain whether the dialect reflects this.

2. **ἐόντα**: §32.11.   **hόπō**: most likely from hόπōs, 'as', by simplification of the cluster -sks- (contrast line 9).   **ὅσια**: 'secular, profane', as opposed to ἱαρά.

3. **ἐξεῖμεν**: athem. infin. (§40.3), imperatival ('he is to be able'). **δείλεται**: pres. subj. (cf. βολόμενον **7** 24, βέλλειτει **11** 20 for the stem).

4. **κἒ̄**: i.e. καὶ ἐκ, with assimilation of ἐξ or ἐς (cf. τὲς **9** 10) to the following cons., and single writing of the ensuing geminate δ and κ. **ϟοινᾱ̈ὸν**: see **23** 2 on qoppa (§17.2). For κοινᾱ(ϝ)ον- > κοινᾱν- cf. **7** 21: gen. plur.   **κατ' αἰϜεί**: αἰϜεί (Att. ἀεί) is an old loc., frozen here in an advb. phrase.

5. **φάρειν**: ε > α before ρ, §38.5.

6. **φρίν**: i.e. πρίν (for erratic aspiration in Lokr. cf. ἐφάγεσθαι **56** 9).

7. **ἀνχōρεῖν**: ἀν- §24.5.   **ἱστίᾱι**: cf. ἐφίστια **24** 7. Initial h- has

disappeared (the root probably started with *w*-, cf. *hικάδι* **50** 2).
παῖδα: see **56** 4.   **(ἀ)δελφεόν**: for the form see ἀδελφεάς **24** 26.
8. ἐνετērίōν: 'entry taxes', from ἐν-ε- (ἐν-ίημι 'cause to
enter') + -τηρ-ιον (agent with 'payment suffix' -ιον, for which cf.
τόκιον **55** 57).   **ἀπελάōνται**: pass. subj. of ἀπελάω, a form of
ἀπελαύνω (cf. ἐπελασάσθων **7** 23).   **ἒ**: i.e. ἐκ (as at 4).
9. hόπō: 'from where' (with old abl. ending), Att. ὁπόθεν.
10. Γεσπαρίōν: Att. ἑσπέριος (for the aspirate cf. *hικάδι* **50** 2),
Lat. *uesper*. For ε > α before ρ §38.5.

ELIS
*Traditionally grouped with North-west Greek, the dialect of
Elis also shows affinities with Arcadian*

58. Bronze tablet from Olympia with an inscription
concerning the immunity of the scribe Patrias. Early V cent.
BC. Buck 61. Schwyzer 409. *LSAG* 220 no. 15. *Nomima*, i. 23.
▶▶ Koerner (1981: 190–4).

ἀ Γράτρα τοῖς Γαλείοις. Πατρίαν θαρρεν καὶ γενεὰν καὶ ταὐτō.| αἰ ζέ
τις κατιαραύσειε, Γάρρεν ὄρ Γαλείō. αἰ ζὲ μἐ̓πιθείαν τὰ ζί|καια ὄρ
μέγιστον τέλος ἔχοι καὶ τοὶ βασιλâες, ζέκα μναῖς κα | ἀποτίνοι
Γέκαστος τὸν μἐ̓πιποεόντōν καθυταῖς τοῖ Ζὶ 'Ολυν||⁵πίοι· ἐπενπōι ζέ
κ' Ἑλλανοζίκας, καὶ τἆλλα ζίκαια ἐπενπ|έτō ἀ ζαμιοργία· αἰ ζὲ
μἐ̓νπōι, ζίφυιον ἀποτινέτō ἐν μαστράλαι. αἰ ζέ τις τὸν αἰτιαθέντα
ζικαιōν ἱμάσκοι, ἐν τᾶι ζεκαμναίαι κ' ἐἰνέχο[ιτ]ο, αἰ Γειζὸς ἱμάσκοι.
καὶ Πατρίας ὁ γροφεὺς ταὐτά κα πάσκοι, |[αἴ τ]ιν' [ἀζ]ικέοι. ὁ
π[ί]ναξ ἱαρὸς 'Ολυνπίαι.

The decree of the Eleians. Patrias is to enjoy legal protection, and
so are his family and his property. If anyone brings a charge
(against him), he is to be prosecuted as (though he were) an
Eleian. If the highest magistrate and the kings do not uphold his
rights, let each of those who fail to uphold (them) pay ten minas
dedicated to Olympian Zeus (5); and let the *Hellanodikas* enforce
this, and let the board of magistrates enforce his other rights. If
one does not enforce it, let him be fined double the amount at his
public audit. If a person, having laid a charge against him, deprives
him of his rights, that person is to be held to a ten-mina fine,
if he does this knowingly. And let Patrias the scribe suffer the

same (penalty) if he wrongs anyone. The tablet (to be) sacred at Olympia.

1. **ἂ**: *h-* has dropped from the dialect.   **Ϝρά̄τρā**: see **59** 1 below. **Ϝαλείοις**: initial digamma (§39.1); ἄ < ε as very commonly in the dialect (before ρ, λ, and nasals): §38.5.   **Πατρίαν**: in view of **52** above, this is probably the name of a scribe (either a foreigner or former slave) who was offered privileges to work for the city. Earlier editors took it to be a noun meaning 'clan', which makes the interpretation difficult.   **θαρρῆν**: in Att.-Ion. the verb means 'be confident, cheerful'; here it is used in a technical sense, 'be immune, enjoy legal rights' (for the semantic shift cf. φεύγω, 'flee' > 'be prosecuted').   **ταὐτό**: crasis < τὰ αὐτό.

2. **ζέ**: the spelling of initial <Δ> with <Ζ> in Elis is the result of two intersecting phonological developments (Méndez Dosuna 1991): (i) the cluster *dy* (§23.8) > δδ, initial δ-; (ii) the stops *b*, *d*, *g* became fricatives (as in Mod. Gk.). The Eleans therefore used <Δ> for [d-] (from *dy-*), and then, since <Ζ> was freed up, used it for [ð] (from *d*). Cf. τόζ **48** 1.   **κατ-ιαραύ-σειε**: lit. 'imprecate against' (Att. καθιερεύειν), here 'bring an accusation against' (Ϝαλείō in the gen.).   **Ϝάρρῆν**: cf. Lokr. Ϝερρέτō **56** 12. Here it has a technical sense, 'stand trial' (Att. φεύγω).   **ὄρ**: i.e. ὡς, with rhotacism (cf. τοῖρ **59** 1).   **μὲ̄πιθεῖαν**: crasis < μή/μά + ἐπι-, 3 plur. opt. (for the ending cf. ἀποτίνοιαν **59** 6).

3. **ὄρ**: ὅς (with rhotacism), with ἔχοι attracted into the opt. by ἐπιθεῖαν.   **τοί**: §40.5.   **βασιλᾶες**: < -η(Ϝ)ες, local magistrates. **μναίς** < μνάνς: acc. plur. As in Lesb. (§§23.9, 34.11), -*Vns* > -*Vis* (but note that this is attested in Elis only at word end). The acc. plur. thus became identical to the dat. plur. in *a*- and *o*-stems.

4. **ἀποτίνοι**: see ἔᾱ **59** 2.   **μὲ̄πιποεόντōν**: crasis (μὲ̄πιθεῖαν 2). For ποι- > πο- cf. Ion. ποιήσεαν **20** 30.   **καθυταίς**: adj., acc. plur. < -άνς. καθ- spells the result of καταθ- > κατθ- (apocope): the cluster (originally [ttʰ]) would have been pronounced [tθ], since it seems likely (πάσκοι 8) that [tʰ] had developed into a fricative [θ]. **τοῖ ... Ὀλυνπίοι**: dat. sing. with shortened diphthong (§40.10). **Ζί**: i.e. Δί < ΔιϜί.

5. **ἐπενπōι**: 3 sing. pres. opt. of a verb ἐπ-εμπάω, not apparently attested in other dialects. Cf. Hom. ἐμπάζομαι, 'pay attention to' (for

doublets in -άω/-άζω cf. δαμάω/δαμάζω, etc.). ἐπενπέτō is 3 sing. imper. of the same verb (αε > ē, §38.4).   **Ἑλλᾱνοζίκᾱς**: an official with special jurisdiction at the Olympic Games.

6. **ζᾱμιοργία**: < *δᾱμι-Fοργία (orig. *δᾱμιο-Fοργία, shortened by haplology).   **ζίφυιον**: by the IV cent., koiné διπλάσιον had expelled the local word.   **μαστράᾱι**: < *μαστρέα < μαστρεία (cf. μαστροῖς **49** 1). The examination of a magistrate on the expiry of his term of office (Athenian εὔθυναι).

7. **ἱμάσκοι**: the vb. (not attested elsewhere) may be related to ἱμάς, 'leather strap'. The interpretation here assumes a semantic development 'bind' (δέω ἱμᾶσιν, *Il.* 21. 30) > 'hinder, keep from' (δέω, *Od.* 4. 380, with *Od.* 1. 195, τόν γε θεοὶ βλάπτουσι κελεύθου).

8. **γροφεύς**: there is no reason why the dialect of this region should not have had both *a*- and *o*-coloured reflexes of the syllabic resonants (γράφεα **59** 7, and cf. §26.3). In this case analogy may be a factor (cf. τροφεύς?).   **πάσκοι**: -σκ- for -σχ- can be compared to -στ- for -σθ-, also found in Elis. If we assume an early development of [kʰ], [tʰ] to fricatives [x], [θ] (as in Laconia, and cf. our account of ζέ 2), then -σκ- would indicate that *s* inhibited the development of χ from stop to fricative. See Méndez Dosuna (1985: 348–66).

59. Bronze tablet from Olympia recording the conclusion of an alliance between Elis and Eua in Arcadia. *c.*500 BC. Buck 62. Schwyzer 413. *LSAG* 220 no. 6. Meiggs–Lewis 17. *Nomima*, i. 52. ▶ Dubois (1985), Wachter (1999).

ἁ Fράτρα τοῖρ Fαλείοις καὶ τοῖς Ἐυ|Fά{οι}οις. συνμαχία κ' ἔα ἑκατὸν Fέτεα, | ἄρχοι δέ κα τοΐ. αἰ δέ τι δέοι, αἴτε Fέπος αἴτε Fλάργον, συνέαν κ' ἀλάλοις τά τ' ἄλ<α> καὶ πᾶ||⁵ρ πολέμō. αἰ δὲ μὰ συνέαν, τάλαντόν κ' | ἀργύρō ἀποτίνοιαν τοῖ Δὶ Ὀλυνπίοι τοὶ κα|δαλέμενοι λατρειόμενον. αἰ δέ τιρ τὰ γ|ράφεα ταῖ καδαλέοιτο, αἴτε Fέτας αἴτε τ|ελεστὰ αἴτε δᾶμος, ἐν τξπιάροι κ' ἐνέχ||¹⁰οιτο τοῖ 'νταῦτ' ἐγραμένοι.

The agreement of the Eleians and the people of Eua. Let there be an alliance for a hundred years, and let this (year) begin (it). And if there should be need of anything, whether word or deed, let them stand by each other in all matters, and especially (5) in war. But if they do not stand by (each other), let those in violation pay a talent of silver consecrated to Olympian Zeus. And if anyone violates this inscription, whether a private citizen or a magistrate or the community, let him be liable to the penalty written here.

Colons (not reproduced here) divide the inscription into phrases, which appear to be partly accentual and partly syntactic (see Wachter 1999).

1. **Ϝρᾱ́τρᾱ**: cf. Cyp. εὐϝρητάσατυ **8** 4. In Elis η was opened to ᾱ (cf. the general NW Gk. ε > α before ρ).   **τοῖρ**: sporadic rhotacism of -ς (later it becomes general), in this text generally before a voiced cons. (τιρ 7 shows it in the process of being generalized). **Ἐυϝά{οι}οις**: was read ’Ερϝ- in earlier editions (‘Heraians’), but see Dubois (1985).

2. **ἔᾱ**: 3 sing. opt. of εἰμί. The intervocalic -i- became a weakly articulated glide and dropped (ViV > Vi̯V > VV), for which cf. Ion. ποιήσεαν **20** 30. Note opt. + κ(α) in prescriptive sense (Arc. also uses the opt., without particle).   **ἑκατόν**: the dialect has lost *h*-.

3. **τοί**: τό + deictic -ί (a demonstr. pron., Att. τόδε), picking up Ϝέτος.   **Ϝάργον**: §38.5.

4. **συν-έαν**: cf. ἔα 2.   **ἀλάλοις**: single writing of double conson-ant (and throughout).   **τά τ’ ... καί**: this idiom puts the emphasis on the second clause, introduced by καί.   **πάρ**: from περί (§§24.5, 38.5).

5. **μᾱ́**: μή (cf. Ϝράτρα 1).

6. **ἀπο-τίνοιαν**: 3 pl. opt. (in Elis ε > α before final nasal as well as r).   **τοῖ ... Ὀλυνπίοι**: cf. **58** 4 (§40.10).   **τοί**: §40.5. **καδαλέμενοι**: i.e. καδ-δαλ-ήμενοι (Att. κατα-δηλ-ούμενοι), with apocope (καδ-, assimilation) and η > ᾱ in -δαλ-. The vowel in the mediopass. ptcpl. is analogical (§40.9).

7. **λατρειόμενον**: the pres. in -είω in Elis < *-εϝγω (by regular sound change): Attic -εύω is re-modelled on the aor. (ἐλατρεύσα, etc.).   **γράφεα**: uncontracted plur. of a neut. noun γράφος (also in Arc.), probably formed to the vb. γράφειν (cf. πάθος: παθεῖν, earlier πένθος).

8. **ταῖ**: cf. τοί 3.   **Ϝέτᾱς**: formed to the pron. Ϝhε (‘oneself’, Hom. ἕ): cf. Ϝhεδιέστας **37** 7 (Hom. ἔτης ‘companion’).   **τελεστά**:

for masc. forms in -α found occasionally in Boe. and NW Gk. cf. *Μογέα* **13** 1.

9. **τἐπιάροι**: crasis < τôι ἐπιάροι (dat. sing. as at 6). From ἐπ- and ἰαρο- (no *h*-).

10. **᾿ῦταῦτ᾿**: prodelision and elision. ἐνταῦτα < ἐνθαῦτα: Elean and Ionic preserve the earlier form (built to ἔνθα). Att. ἐνταῦθα is the result of metathesis. The replacement of θ by τ in the spelling of ἐνταῦτα indicates that [tʰ] remained an obstruent after [n], rather than becoming a fricative [θ] (see πάσκοι **58** 8, and Méndez Dosuna 1985: 368). **ἐγραμένοι**: perf. pass. ptcpl. (cf. **53** 31 ἔγρατται), dat. sing. Double -μμ- written with a single.

EPIRUS
North-west Greek

60. Lead tablet from Dodona with an enquiry from Hermon addressed to the oracle. Boustrophedon. Late VI cent. BC. Parke (1967: 264 no. 5). *LSAG* 230 no. 13.

*h*έρμōν· τίνα | κα θεὸν ποτθέμ|ενος γενεά Ϝοι γένοιτο ἐκ Κ||ρεταίας ὀνά|σιμος πὸτ τᾶι ἐλάσσαι;

Hermon: applying himself to which of the gods would offspring be born to him from Kretaia, a useful (child) in addition to the girl we (already) have?

2. **ποτθέμενος**: apocope (§24.5) of preverb ποτι- (§40.8).
3. **Ϝοι**: dat. < *swo- (Hom. οἱ): cf. Cret. Ϝôν **53** 26.
6. **ἐλάσσαι**: fem. ptcpl. of 'be'. To masc.-neut. *H₁s-ont- (§32.11) a fem. *H₁s-ṇt-ya was formed, with (expected) zero-grade of root and ptcpl. suffix (as in Skt. *satí*): resulting **ά̆σσα* was recharacterized with ἐ- from the masc.-neut. Also in Arc. and some WGk. (cf. Myc. *a-pe-a-sa*, ἀπεάσσαι).

NORTH-WEST GREEK IN SICILY AND ITALY

61. Gold leaf from the tomb of a woman in Hipponion, a Lokrian colony in southern Italy (renamed Vibo Valentia by the Romans): a text in hexameters gives information about the afterlife. *c.*400 BC. Ed. pr. Pugliese Carratelli (1974), revised Pugliese Carratelli (2003). *SEG* 26.1139. ▶▶ Janko (1984), Sacco (2001), Pugliese Carratelli (2003).

Μναμοσύνας τόδε ἔργον, ἐπεὶ ἂμ μέλλεισι θανε̃σθαι.
εἰς Ἀΐδαο δόμōς εὐέρεας ἔστ᾽ ἐπὶ δ<ε>ξιὰ κρε̃να,
πὰρ δ᾽ αὐτὰν ἑστακῦα λευκὰ κυπάρισ<σ>ος·
ἔνθα κατερχόμεναι ψυχ{κ}αὶ νεκύōν ψύχονται.
5 ταύτας τᾶ<ς> κράνας με̃δὲ σχεδὸν ἐνγύθεν ἔλθεις·
πρόσθεν δὲ ͱευρέσεις τᾶς Μναμοσύνας ἀπὸ λίμνας
ψυχρὸν ὕδōρ προρέον· φύλακες δὲ ἐπύπερθεν ἔασι,
ͱ]οι δέ σε εἰρέσονται ἐν<ὶ> φρασὶ πευκαλίμαισι
ὅτ<τ>ι δὲ ἐξερέεις Ἀϊδος σκότος †ορορεεντος.
10 εἶπον· Γε̃ς πα̃ι <ς> ἐμι καὶ ὀρανō ἀστερόεντος,
δίψαι δ᾽ ἐμὶ αὖος καὶ ἀπόλλυμαι· ἀλ<λ>ὰ δότ᾽ ο̃κα
ψυχρὸν ὕδōρ πιὲν αὐτε̃ς Μνēμοσύνēς ἀπὸ λίμ[νε̃]ς.
καὶ δέ τοι ἐρέōσιν ὑποχθονίōι βασιλε̃ϊ·
καὶ δέ τοι δόσōσι πιὲν τᾶς Μναμοσύνας ἀπὸ λίμνα[ς.
15 καὶ δὲ καὶ σὺ πιὸν ͱοδὸν ἔρχεα<ι> ͱάν τε καὶ ἄλλοι
μύσται καὶ βάχχοι ͱιερὰν στείχōσι κλεινοί.

5 τᾶ<ς> edd., ταρ on leaf.   9 ορορεεντος: ὀρφ<ν>ήεντος Pugliese Carratelli (2003); ἠερόεντος (*EEPOENTOΣ*) cj. Cassio (1987).

This is the task of remembrance, when one's time has come to die. Approaching the sturdy halls of Hades there is on the right a spring, and rising up next to it a shining cypress. Entering here the souls of the dead are brought back to life. (5) These springs you should not even go near. But further on you will find the cold water which flows from the lake of remembrance. Guardians there are above it, who will ask in the wisdom of their hearts why you search into the darkness of gloomy (?) Hades. (10) Say: 'I am a child of the earth and the starry heavens, but I am dry with thirst and I perish: give me quickly cold water to drink from this lake of remembrance.' And so they will ask the king of the Underworld; and they will give you to drink from the lake of remembrance. (15) And you, having drunk, enter the road with the other initiates, the holy road which the glorious bacchants are taking.

Around ten such 'Orphic' leaves are known from IV cent. Magna

Graecia and Thessaly (the texts are very similar). This text seems to be an effort to produce epic diction by a speaker of West Greek. Lines 2 and 14 have seven feet.

1. **ἔργον**: by remembering these instructions the initiates will avoid earthly reincarnation (a line or more may have dropped before **εἰς**). The leaf appears to have **EPION**. Conjectures include ἠρίον, <h>ιερόν. **ἄν**: the Att.-Ion. form (§23.4) reflects the epic diction of the poem. **μέλλεισι**: for the 3 sing. subj. ending (in this case borrowed from epic) cf. πίεσι **25** 2. **θανέσθαι**: the digraph <*EI*> (§23.1) is confined to epic glosses: the use of plain <*E*> for lengthened ε in unmarked (non-epic) words suggests that it had fallen together with inherited η (§38.3), as in the founding city Locri Epizephyrii. This is shared by Laconian and Achaean colonies in south Italy, and is no doubt an areal feature (mainland Lokrian has ει, ου). The digraph <*OY*> is not in use in this text.

2. **εἰς**: epic, < *ἐν-ς (NW Gk. and Arc. typically have ἐν + acc.). **Ἀΐδᾱο**: a Hom. (Aeolic) gen. which is at home also in WGk. **εὐέρεας**: epic adj. with Ion. vocalism (*εὐ-ᾱρ-, root as in ἀραρίσκω). **κρένᾱ**: Ion. vocalism in the first syllable; contrast κράνας 5 (Att. κρήνη < κρᾱ- is anomalous, perhaps simple vowel assimilation).

3. **πάρ**: apocope (§24.5), but also Homeric (*Od.* 1. 132, πὰρ δ' αὐτός, line beginning). **ἐστακῦα**: aspiration is erratic: probably absent by now from much of NW Gk. (cf. ἐφάγεσθαι **56** 9), and in any case absent from Ionic. For -ῦα < -υῖα cf. ἕᾱ **59** 3. The final short -α is unmetrical (Janko 1984: 93 shows that this is because the author has changed the syntax of the phrase: in parallel texts the word is acc. as the object of εὑρήσεις).

4. **ψύχονται**: probably from ψύχω 'blow, breathe' (and hence 're-animate'), with a pun on the meaning 'be chilled, be refreshed' (i.e. the uninitiated refresh themselves here, but then experience the deathly chill of forgetfulness and earthly reincarnation).

6. **δέ**: note the *scriptio plena*.

7. **ἐπ-ύπερθεν**: aspiration would be indicated by ἐφ-. **ἔᾱσι**: an epic form, not attested in any dialect (Att. ἴᾱσι from εἶμι): §32.12.

8. **[h]οι**: or [τ]οι, or οἰ. **εἰρέσονται**: epic form (initial Ϝ- would avoid hiatus, §46.2*a*). **φρασὶ πευκαλίμαισι**: epic formula (πευκάλιμος is confined to it). φρασί is the orig. form < *pʰr̥si (Hom.

φρεσί remodelled on the other cases). For the 'epic' dat. plur. in -αισι cf. στίκταισιν **43** 3 (§32.14).

9. **ἐξερέεις**: an epic verb (< *ἐξ-ερέϝεις), though not in Hom. in this form.   **ορρεεντος**: a difficult sequence (ὀρφνήεντος here translated).

10. **εἶπον**: 2 sing. imper. (as at Theokr. 14. 11, and cf. Alkman 106 *PMG*, Ϝείπατέ μοι): probably a WGk. element, esp. given evidence for the form in Sicily (see Thumb–Kieckers 1932: 215 f.). Not common in Att. till New Comedy.

12. **πιέν**: short-vowel infin. This is attested locally in Croton, and in Phokis and Arcadia (cf. §40.3): Lokrian inscriptions have -ειν. Cassio (1996a) defends the reading πιέναι τές of Pugliese Carratelli (2003): the thematic infin. -έναι would be an innovation of western Ionic (Euboea and colonies). This would give the line a caesura. **αὐτᾶς Μνᾱμοσύνᾱς**: epic vocalism (contrast 14).

13. **ἐρέōσιν**: epic future (Att. ἐρῶ), with Ion. -ōσι < -οντι and final -ν.

15. **σύ**: generally τύ in WGk. (attested in Epicharmus and Sophron).

16. **hιεράν**: epic form (§38.1).   **κλεινοί**: epic form < *κλεϝεσ-νός.

62. Retrograde inscription on a bronze tablet from the hinterland (Francavilla Marittima) of Sybaris, an Achaean colony in Calabria. Late VI cent. bc. Edd. pr. Stoop–Pugliese Carratelli (1966). *CEG* 394. *LSAG* 456 no. 1a. Arena (1996: no. 2). Dubois (2002: no. 5). ▶▶ Hornblower (2007).

Δο· Κλεόμροτος | ὁ ΔεξιλάϜō ἀνέθēκ' | Ὀλυνπίαι νικάσας | Ϝίσο(μ) μᾶκός τε πάχος τε ‖⁵ τἀθάναι, ἀϜέθλōν | εὐξάμενος δεκάταν.

Kleomrotos the (son) of Dexilaos, having won at Olympia, dedicated (a statue), equal in height and size (to himself), to Athena, having vowed a tithe of his prizes.

1. **Δο**: an abbreviation of the phratry name of Kleomrotos (Guarducci 1965: 394).   **Κλεόμροτος**: the absence of a β-glide between μ and ρ has a few parallels in archaic inscriptions from across the Gk. world (contrast Lesb. ἀμβρότην **17** 15): it may be a mere spelling variant. There is no reason to think (with McDevitt

1968) that this indicates a Thessalian. Hornblower notes that this is the earliest known inscription naming an Olympic victor. 2. **ὀ**: when *h*- started to disappear from the dialects it was typically lost first in the article (cf. 55 30). **ΔεξιλάϜō**: intervocalic -*w*- retained (as in Lac. *ΜενελάϜō* 32): **ἀνέθēκ'**: the object (understood) is the statue, which was probably erected at Olympia out of prize money (*ἀϜέθλōν*) paid to Kl. by his home city (so Hornblower): he tells his fellow-citizens that he has fulfilled his obligations. 4. **Ϝίσο(μ)**: neut. sing. (agreeing with e.g. τοῦτο understood). The final -*ν* has undergone assimilation (§23.4): the double consonant is written as a single. Note loss of post-consonantal -*w*- (*ϜίσϜο-). **μᾶκός τε πάχος τε**: a formula, apparently, for impressive size: cf. Pind. *Pyth.* 4. 245, ὃς πάχει μάκει τε πεντηκόντερον ναῦν κράτει. 5–6. The last two lines form a pentameter, and the preceding two lines have a dactylic rhythm approximating to a hexameter.

PAMPHYLIAN
(Unclassified dialect)

63. Wall inscription from Sillyon (gulf of Antalya): it records an attempt to bring to an end a period of civil strife by the foundation of a social organization open to all parties. The longest extant Pamphylian inscription but much worn, especially at the right, and difficult to understand; only the the first half is given here. Early IV cent. BC. Schwyzer 686. Brixhe (1976: 167, no. 3). ▶ Luria (1959), Brixhe (1976).

σὺ ΔιϜία καὶ ἱιαροῖσι Μάνē[ς .]υ ἀνhêλε ΣελύW[ι]ιυς [..? hι-
†ια[ρ]ά Ϝίλσιιος ὕπαρ καὶ ἀγίιας ὅσα περ(ι)ί[στα-]
τυ Woικ[...]ισ[.....]τυ καὶ ΣελυWίιōς †πᾶ[σ]ι ρα[..]π[...
ισ'† απα κεκραμένōς, ἐξ ἐ[πι]τέρύια ἰς πόλιν [...
5 διὰ πέδε καὶ δέκα Ϝέτ[ι]ια, πόλι μhε[ι]άλα [...
οσα καὶ τιμάϜεσά πōς ἄβατι ἀφιέναι κα[.]ιλλ [...
ἀτρόποισι περτ(ὶ) ἴρēνι ἀWταῖσι hēWόταισι [...
ἐβολάσετυ ἀδριιόνα καταστᾶσ[αι ...
ραιε hῖκαι Μhειάλēτι καὶ ἐφ[ι]ιēWόται[σι ...

10 †πᾶς Μάνētυς <u>κ</u>αὶ Μhειά[λē]τυς καὶ <u>δ</u>ι[. . .

    <u>οεϜε</u> ἰ πόλιι ἐφιέλοδυ [. .]<u>ι</u> δικαστέρεσσ[ι καὶ ἀργυρō-

    ταῖσι καί νι σκυδρὺ κατεϜέρξοδυ καὶ [. . .

    κάθεδυ καὶ hάιι(α) ἀνεῖε̣ <u>κ</u>αὶ ὺ βōλέμενυς [. . .

    κ]αί νι Ϝοῖκυ π[ό]λι<u>ς</u> ἐχέτō καί †hô κα <u>δ</u>ε [. . .

15 <u>ας</u> Ϝρυμάλι(α) ἀνhαγλέσθō. h(ὰ) ἀτρέκαδι [. . .

    δικαστêρες καὶ ἀργυρōταὶ μὲ̀ ἐξάγōδι <u>κ</u>[. . .

With the help of Diwia and the priests, Manes [son of ...] of Sillyon ordered sacrifices on account of the oppression and distress which afflicted the dwellings [...] and the Sillyonians, who had been devastated [by ...], because of his solicitude for the city, [troubled] (5) for fifteen years: to release in some way the city, which was (formerly) great [...] and honoured, from its misfortune [...] For the adult men, with a view to peace, together with the youth [...] he decided to establish a men's club-house [...] for Megales and the young men to come [...] (10) every [follower] of Manes and of Megales [...] in the city let them elect both judges and treasurers, and let them quell anger and [...] restore [...] and put an end to sacrilege; and anyone who wishes [...] And the city is to own the building, and whoever [...], that party (15) is to undertake the responsibility for its upkeep. The matters they have examined [...], the judges and treasurers are not to release ...

No interpretation/reconstruction has been offered for under-lined letters: cruces warn that the reconstruction is especially doubtful.

1. **σύ**: final -ν is omitted when a consonant follows (§42.5). **ΔιϜία**: female deity formed from Διϝ-, the stem of Ζεύς (a goddess spelled *di-u-ja/di-wi-ja* is found in Myc.). Dat. -ᾱ < -ᾱι. **hιαροῖσι**: the second ι marks a glide between ι and another vowel (cf. Ἀθᾱναίᾱς **37** 2). Pamph. shares ἱαρός with Boe. and WGk. (§38.1). **Μάνē[ς]**: Anatolian personal name.   **ἀνhêλε . . . hιαρά**: Brixhe's suggestion ad loc. (ἀνhêλε is aor. of ἀναιρέω, 'appoint, ordain'). **ΣελύϜυυς**: ethnic adj., though oddly separated; if -υς is the right reading it illustrates the characteristic lack of distinction between ο and υ in final syllables. <W> here transcribes <Η>, the original Pamph. form of <Ϝ> (digamma). Pamph. then took over <Ϝ> as well:

there is no clear pattern to the distribution of the two signs in this text (see Brixhe 1976: 53–6 and ἄβατι 6).

2. **Fίλσιιος**: gen. sing. of an unattested noun Fίλσις, the stem of which may be that of the Hom. verb (F)εἰλέω 'press hard, confine'. **ὕπαρ**: postposition, with usual opening of ε to α (§42.3). **ὄσᾶ**: relative (fem. sing.), agreeing with ἀνίας. **περ(ι)ί[στᾱ]τυ**: 3 sing. imperf. of περ-ίστᾱμι, a simplified form of περι-ίστᾱμι, 'stand round', so 'afflict'.

3. **Woικ[**: seems to refer, in some sense, to the fabric of the city. **ΣελυWίιὸς**: acc. plur.

4. **]ισ̣**: on this reading a dat. plur. (in -οισι/-αισι, §44.1), taken with πᾱ[σ]ι (perhaps an adverbial phrase modifying κεκραμένὸς). **κεκραμένὸς**: perf. pass. ptcpl. (acc. plur.), probably of κείρω (root *ker, zero grade here -κρα-). **ἐξ ἐ[πι]τερίιᾶ**: dat. sing. of a noun formed from ἐπιτηρέω, 'watch out for' (§28.5). **ἰς**: < ἐν-ς (§§26.1, 28.8).

5. **πέδε**: τ > δ after ν (i.e. the opposition t ~ d was neutralized after a nasal, as in Mod. Gk.); the ν then disappeared before the following stop (§43.3). **Fέτ[ι]ια**: cf. Cyp. Fέπιja 8 26 (§26.6). **πόλι**: acc. sing., with loss of -ν as in σύ(ν) 1. **μhε[ι]άλᾶ**: acc. sing. (Att. μεγάλην). μh- (i.e. ʰm < *sm-) is not etymological in this root, but has spread analogically from other words beginning *sR- (e.g. μοῖρα < *smor-); found in other dialects also (e.g. Att. μhεγάλō). After a front vowel intervocalic g > y in a development reminiscent of Mod. Gk. (see Wallace 1983, and for Att. cf. Threatte 1980: 440).

6. **τῑμάFεσα**: acc. sing. (Hom. τιμήεσσαν). For the form (§13) cf. *pe-ne-we-ta* 1 (a). **πōς**: on this reading an enclitic advb. 'in some manner or other'. **ἄβατι**: dat. of a by-form of ἀFάτᾱ (> Att. ἄτη), 'ruin', dat. (§28.5). The spelling of earlier [w] with <β> (as well as F, W) suggests that the sound had become a fricative and had merged with [v] < inherited *b (as in Lac., where the same β/F spelling fluctuation is attested at this period).

7. **ἀτρōποισι**: i.e. ἀνθρ-, with loss of nasal (§43.3). The spelling <τ> indicates that inherited [tʰ] maintained its quality as a stop before [r], rather than becoming a fricative [θ] (cf. πάσκοι 58 8): whether the aspiration remained distinctive is difficult to say. **περτ(ί)**: περτί has a parallel in Cretan πορτί (cf. §28.7). **ἱρēνι**: dat.

of a form ἱρέν ? (Brixhe): variation in this word (Att. εἰρήνη) across the dialects is unpredictable (Colvin 1999: 237). **ἀWταῖσι**: the second element of αυ may have developed from semivowel to fricative before the following stop (cf. Mod. Gk. αὐτός [aftós]). **hēWόταισι**: apparently the dat. of a collective noun ἡβότᾱς (cf. ἥβᾱ), which may have had a specific social implication similar to *ephebe* at Athens. For the spelling cf. ἄβατι 6. The syntagm (also in Hom. and classical Gk.) implies a special connection between the ἄνθρωποι and the youths (members of the same civic or kinship group?).

8. **ἐβōλάσετυ**: aor. (3 sing.) of βōλάομαι (cf. Arc. βολόμενον 7 24): §44.4.   **ἀδριōνα**: the basic meaning is 'room or building for men' (Ion. ἀνδρεών): §43.3.

9. **hῖκαι**: athematic aor. inf. of ἵκω.   **MhειάλΞτι**: personal name (dat.): cf. μhειάλᾱ 5.   **ἐφ[ι]ιΞWόται[σι]**: compd. of ἐπι+ἡβοτ- (for which cf. hΞWόταισι 7), with ἐπι- > ἐφι- by anticipation of the aspirate (Lejeune 1972: §367, and cf. τεθρίππōι 33 6). Is this the faction of Megales?

10. **ΜάνΞτυς**: gen. sing. (cf. ΣελύWιιυς 1): §42.2.

11. **ἰ πόλιι**: ἰ< ἰν< ἐν (ἰς 4). For πόλι-ι cf. πόλῑ 18 2 (§32.4). **ἐφιέλοδυ**: aor. imper. (3 plur.) < *ἐπι-hέλοντον (§44.3): Att. ἐλέσθων. For ἐφι- cf. ἐφιιΞWότ- 9 (note lack of expected glide here); for -ντ- > -δ- in -έλοδυ cf. πέδε 5; plus ο > υ and loss of final -ν. **δικαστέρεσσ[ι]**: the only example so far in Pamph. of the dat. plur. -εσσι. Either an independent development in Pamph. (ἀργυρωταί : ἀργυρωταῖσι :: δικαστῆρες : x), or a reflection of Aeolic influence (§36.4).

12. **καί νι**: this formula introduces a prescription with imperative. The νι is perhaps related to enclitic νυ (emphatic particle in Homer). **σκυδρύ**: < *σκυδρόν (cf. Att. σκυθρός, 'angry', Hom. σκύζομαι). **κατεFέρξοδυ**: aor. imper. (3 plur.) < *κατ-εFέρξοντον (κατ-εFέργω, Att. κατείργω): cf. ἐφιέλοδυ 11.

13. **κάθεδυ**: aor. imper. (§44.3) < *κάθεντον (καθ-ίημι), 'they are to restore'. Brixhe (ad loc.) suggests that the object is some such quality as ὁμόνοια (in the preceding lacuna).   **hάυι(α)**: a disputed word. Brixhe's interpretation (ἄγεα, acc. plur. of an aspirated form ἄγος with development ε > ι) is translated here: it entails the change γ > ι before a front vowel (but after α), for which cf. μhειάλᾱ 5.   **ἀνεῖε**:

aor. opt. (3 plur.) of ἀν-ίημι, 'put an end to' is plausible in context, though -h- is kept elsewhere in the inscription in compds. of ἀν(α): ἀνhêλε 1, ἀνhαγλέσθō 15. **ὐ βōλέμενυς**: rare, perhaps unique, attestation of the article (Att. ὁ) in Pamph. The phrase, common in Att. legal language, was perhaps borrowed *in toto* from a foreign source. ἐβōλάσετυ 8 points to pres. βōλάομαι. The ē of βōλέμενυς (pres. ptcpl.) is most easily explained as the influence of the infin. βōλέσθαι < βōλά-εσθαι, for which cf. καδαλέμενοι 59 6 (Elis).

14. **Woîκυ**: < *Ϝοîκον (acc. sg.). Presumably a reference to the ἀνδρεών. **hô κα**: the sequence *HOKA* is ambiguous. This reading assumes that *HO* is a relative (dat. sing.), and *KA* is the potential particle (i.e. ὧι ἄν, Thumb–Scherer 1959: 192).

15. **Wρυμάλι(α)**: if the stem is *wru- (as in Hom. ἔρυμαι) the word might mean the 'protection' or 'upkeep' of the ἀνδρεών (Brixhe): neut. plur. acc. **ἀνhαγλέσθō**: mid. imper. (3 sing.). Brixhe suggests that the vb. hαγλέω (Att. αἱρέω) is the result of contamination between pres. (h)αγρέω (cf. καταγρέθηι 17 13 with García Ramón 1999: 543) and aor. εἷλον. **ἀτρέκαδι**: perf. (3 plur.) of ἀθρέω (from *ἀθρήκαντι). For the spelling with <τ> cf. ἀτρόποισι 7.

16. **ἐξάγōδι**: pres. subj. (3 plur.) in prohibitive sense, from ἐξάγōντι.

KOINÉ AND NORTH-WEST GREEK KOINA

64. Two letters from Ptolemaic Egypt. Both are addressed to the same person, and date to the middle of the III cent. BC. The first seems to have been written by a Greek or Greek-trained scribe, and is composed quite elegantly. The second seems to have been written by an Egyptian scribe: the spelling and composition are more informative about contemporary spoken koiné.

(a) Letter on papyrus from Aunkhis to Zenon, petitioning him to intervene in the abduction of her daughter by Demetrios. Philadelphia, 253 BC. Zenon archive: *P. Lond.* VII 1976.
▶▶ Rowlandson (1998: no. 209).

Αὖγχις Ζήνωνι χαίρειν. | λαμβάνουσα ζῦτον ἐκ | τοῦ μεγάλου

ζυτοπω‖λίου διατίθημι τὴν ‖⁵ ἡμέραν Ⱶ δ, καὶ εὐτακτῶ.‖ Δημ-
ήτρ[ι]ος δέ μου ὁ ἀμ‖πελουργὸς ἀπατήσας | τὴν θυγατέρα
ἐξαγα‖γὼν κρύπτει, φάμενος ‖¹⁰ συνοικήσ[ε]ιν αὐτῆι ἄνευ | ἐμοῦ.
αὕτη δέ συνέ‖νεμε | τὸ ἐργαστήριον καὶ ἐμὲ | ἔτρεφεν πρεσβυτέραν
οὖ‖σαν. νῦν οὖν ζημίαν ποι‖¹⁵ῶ ταύτης ἐξελθούσης, καὶ | αὐτὴ δὲ τὰ
δέοντα οὐκ ἔ‖χω. ἔχει δὲ καὶ γυναῖκα ἑτέραν καὶ παιδία ὧδε | ὥστε
οὐ δύναται συνοικεῖν ‖²⁰ ἧι ἠπάτησεν. ἀξιῶ οὖν βο‖ηθῆσαί μοι διὰ τὸ
γῆρας | καὶ παραδοῦναί μοι αὐτήν. ἔρρωσο.
Label   L λβ, Μεχείρ | Αὖγχις

Aunkhis to Zenon: greetings. Taking beer from the large whole-
saler I dispose of four drachmas' worth per day, and I pay my
account regularly. But Demetrios the vineyard-worker deceived
and abducted my daughter and now hides her, saying (10) that
he will set up house with her without my consent. She used to
manage the business with me, and provided for me now that I am
older. So now I make a loss since she has gone, and I don't have the
bare necessities for myself. He has another woman, and children,
so he can't set up house with (20) the girl he's deceived. I call on
you to come to my help, on account of my age, and restore her to
me. Be well.
Year 32, (month of) Mekheir. Aunkhis.

    1. **Ζήνωνι**: the estate manager of Ptolemy II's chief minister
(Apollonius).
    2. **ζῦτον**: regular spelling in papyri, but ζῦθον in literary texts.
Although a connection with ζύμη, 'leaven' is possible, Gk. writers
regarded the word as Egyptian (cf. Theophrastos, *Plants* 6.11). The
θ/τ variation could be explained by supposing that Greeks first came
across the word in the Delta region, which had a slightly different
dialect from the interior (where these and most other papyri come
from).
    3. **ζυτοπωλίου**: brewing beer was a royal monopoly.
    4. **διατίθημι**: distribute, i.e. retail.
    5. **εὐτακτῶ**: not found with this meaning before the koiné (but
this may be an accident).
    6. **μου**: oddly separated from τὴν θυγατέρα.
    10. **ἄνευ**: this sense is attested also in the classical period (e.g.
Thuc. 8. 5. 3).

16. **δέ**: it is not impossible that δή was meant (cf. ἐνήτυχ[ον] b1 below): but cf. on καὶ τοῦ δέ b9).

20. **ἦι**: corrected by the scribe from ἦν (cf. on συνοικῆσαι **65** 29).

21. **διά**: see on **65** 110.

(b) Letter on papyrus from Senkhons to Zenon, petitioning him to make Nikias return her donkey. Philadelphia, 256 BC. Zenon archive: *P.Mich.* I 29. Written with a brush (as Egyptians wrote), not a reed pen (as did Greeks). ▶▶ Clarysse (1993). Rowlandson (1998: no. 162).

Ζήνωνι χαίρειν Σενχῶνς. ἐνήτυχ[όν] | σοι περὶ τῆς ὄνου μου ἦν ἔλαβεν Νικί[ας]. | ἴ μοι ἔγραψας περὶ αὐτῆς, ἀπέστ[ιλά] | <σοι> ἄν αὐτήν. ἴ σοι δοκεῖ, σύνταξαι ἀποδο[ῦ]ǁ5ναι αὐτήν, ἵνα τὰ ζμήνεα μεταγ[ά]|γωμεν ἐπὶ τὰ νομάς, μέ σοι παρα|πόλωνται μέτε σοὶ μέτε τῶι βα[σι]|λεῖ. καὶ ἐὰν ἐπιζετῆς τὸ πρᾶγμα, | πεισθήσεις ὅτι χρήσιμοί σοί ἱμεν. κᾳ[ὶ] ǁ10 τοῦ δὲ πώλου αὐτῆς ἀποστηλῶ [σοι] | αὐτόν. δέομαι ὂν σοι καὶ εἰκετεύω | μέ με παραελκύσῃς. γυνή ἱμι χέ[ρα]. | εὐτύχι.
Label   L λ, Παχὼνς κ[.] | Σενχῶνς ὄνου.

Senkhons to Zenon: greetings. I petitioned you concerning my donkey, which Nikias has taken. If you had written to me about her, I would have sent her to you. If it please you, order him to return (5) her, so that we can move the beehives to the pastures, and they won't prove a loss to you, neither to you nor to the king. And if you look into the matter, you'll find that we're good for your profits. As for (10) her foal, I'll send it to you. So I beg and implore you not to put me off. I am a widow. Be prosperous.
Year 30, (month of) Pakhons 2[.]   Senkhons, about a donkey.

1. **Ζήνωνι**: see on a1.   **Σενχῶνς**: 'sister of Khons' according to ed. pr. She leases beehives from a Greek estate, apparently one that Zenon owns or administers.   **ἐνήτυχ[ον]**: this sense only in the koiné (Att. 'meet with, talk to'). Confusion of ε ~ η is common in III cent. Ptol. koiné (Teodorsson 1977: 103, 216): it indicates that η still had an open quality. It is markedly less frequent from the late III cent., as η becomes closer ([ε:] > [e:]). Clarysse (1993), noting that many instances come from texts written by Egyptian scribes, argues

that since the mistake is rare in Attica it may reflect substrate influence.

3. *ἶ̈*: Att. εἴ (the vowel [ẹ:] was clearly indistinguishable from [i:] to many speakers).

4. *<σοι>*: written above the line.   *σύνταξαι*: this sense typical of the koiné (but already in IV cent. Attic). Middle imper., though the vb. is active elsewhere in Ptol. koiné; ed. pr. assumes a mistake for σύνταξον (not certain, as the mid. is found in IV cent. Attic prose).

5. *ζμήνεα*: usually spelled σμῆνος. The writing ζ for σ before μ (and β) is not uncommon in Ptol. koiné (Teodorsson 1977: 190, 243): it indicates that ζ had become a voiced sibilant [z], and that the opposition [s] ~ [z] was liable to be neutralized before a voiced cons. This *may* reflect substrate influence (lack of phonemic opposition between [s] and [z]), but ζ had become [z] in at least some varieties of Attic by the late IV cent. (Threatte 1980: 548).

6. *τὰ νομάς*: final -s (before C-) in Ptol. koiné seems to have been feeble: in general, however, the articulation remained robust and survived into Mod. Gk.   *μέ*: i.e. μή (cf. ἐνήτυχον 1).   *σοι*: a dative of interest ('ethic').   *παρ-απόλωνται*: aor. subj. of παραπόλλυμαι (once in Aristophanes, then starts to compete with ἀπόλλυμαι, itself a strengthened form of the simplex).

8. *ἐπιζετῆς*: i.e. ἐπιζετῆις, §53.6 (so also παραελκύσης 12).

9. *πεισθήσεις*: πεισθήσει (fut. pass.), recharacterized with 2 sing. -s.   *ἰμεν*: εἴμεν, for ἐσμεν.   *καὶ τοῦ δέ*: an odd sequence of connectives in Gk.

10. *τοῦ δὲ πώλου*: a gen. expressing relation, Engl. 'regarding' (cf. Pl. *Gorg.* 470e, οὐ γὰρ οἶδα παιδείας ὅπως ἔχει [*sc.* ὁ βασιλεὺς] καὶ δικαιοσύνης). Ed. pr. emends to τὸν δὲ πῶλον. Fronting is a normal mode of topicalization in Gk. (and, probably, contemporary Egyptian): but the following anaphoric αὐτόν may reflect substrate influence (required, for example, in Coptic syntax after fronting). *ἀποστηλῶ*: i.e. ἀποστελῶ.

11. *δέομαι ... σοι*: δέομαι takes the gen. in Gk. of all periods. A scribal slip.   *ὃν*: i.e. οὖν. There is sporadic confusion of [o] and [u] in Ptol. koiné, esp. next to a nasal or in unstressed position (Horrocks 1997: 62).

12. *παραελκύσης*: the sense as at *Od.* 21. 111, though not in

classical Att. The 'scriptio plena' of the preverb is perhaps an instance of hypercorrection. **ἴμι**: i.e. εἶμι.

65. Inscription from Xanthos (Lycia), containing an appeal for help from the people of Kytenion in central Greece and the response of the Xanthians. 205 BC. Ed. pr. Bousquet (1988). *SEG* 38. 1476.

A. Decree of the Xanthians (first 42 lines only): koiné

Βασιλεύοντος Πτολεμαίου τοῦ Πτολεμαίου καὶ | Βερενίκης θεῶν
εὐεργετῶν καὶ τοῦ υἱοῦ Πτολεμαίlου (ἔτους) ιζ΄, ἐφ᾽ ἱερέως θεῶν
εὐεργετῶν καὶ βασιλέως | Πτολεμαίου Ἀνδρονίκου τοῦ Περλαμου,
πρὸ πόλεως ||⁵ δὲ Τληπολέμου τοῦ Ἀρταπάτου, μηνὸς Αὐδναίου β΄,|
ἐκκλησίας γενομένης, ἔδοξεν Ξανθίοις τῆι πόλει | καὶ τοῖς ἄρχουσιν.

ἐπειδὴ ἀπὸ τοῦ κοινοῦ τῶν Αἰτωλῶν | παραγεγόνασιν πρεσβευταὶ
Δωριεῖς ἀπὸ Μητροπόλιος | ἐκ Κυτενίου Λαμπρίας, Αἴνετος,
Φηγεύς, ψήφισμά ||¹⁰ τε παρ᾽ Αἰτωλῶν φέροντες καὶ ἐπιστολὴν παρὰ
Δωριέlων, δι᾽ ἧς, τὰ συμβεβηκότα τῆι πατρίδι αὐτῶν ἀπολογισάl
μενοι, καὶ αὐτοὶ διαλεγέντες ἀκολούθως τοῖς ἐν τῆι ἐπιlστολῆι
γεγραμμένοις μετὰ πάσης σπουδῆς καὶ φιλοτιlμίας, παρακαλοῦσιν
ἡμᾶς ἀναμνησθέντας τῆς πρὸς ||¹⁵ αὐτοὺς ὑπαρχούσης συγγενείας
ἀπό τε τῶν θεῶν καὶ | τῶν ἡρώων μὴ περιιδεῖν κατεσκαμμένα τῆς
πατρίδος | αὐτῶν τὰ τείχη. Λητοῦν γαρ, τὴν τῆς πόλεως ἀρχηγέτιν |
τῆς ἡμετέρας, γεννῆσαι Ἄρτεμίν τε καὶ Ἀπόλλωνα παlρ᾽ ἡμεῖν.
Ἀπόλλωνος δὲ καὶ Κορωνίδος τῆς Φλεγύου τοῦ ἀπὸ ||²⁰ Δώρου γεν-
έσθαι ἐν τῆι Δωρίδι Ἀσκληπιόν. τῆς δὲ συγγεlνείας ὑπαρχούσης
αὐτοῖς πρὸς ἡμᾶς ἀπὸ τῶν θεῶν τούlτων, προσαπελογίζοντο καὶ τὴν
ἀπὸ τῶν ἡρώων συμπλοκὴν | τοῦ γένους ὑπάρχουσαν αὐτοῖς, ἀπό τε
Αἰόλου καὶ Δώρου | τὴν γενεαλογίαν συνιστάμενοι, ἔτι τε παρε-
δείκνυον ||²⁵ τῶν ἀποικισθέντων ἐκ τῆς ἡμετέρας ἀπὸ Χρυσάορος
τοῦ | Γλαύκου τοῦ Ἱππολόχου πρόνοιαν πεποιημένον Ἀλήτην, ὄντα |
τῶν Ἡρακλειδῶν. ὁρμηθέντα γὰρ αὐτὸν ἐκ τῆς Δωρίδος βοηlθῆσαι
πολεμουμένοις καὶ τὸν περιεστηκότα κίνδυνον | λύσαντα συνοικῆσαι
τὴν Ἄορος τοῦ Χρυσάορος θυγατέll³⁰ρα. καὶ δι᾽ ἄλλων δὲ πλειόνων
παραδεικνύοντες τὴν ἐκ | παλαιῶν χρόνων συνωικειωμένην πρὸς
ἡμᾶς εὔνοιαν διὰ συγγένειαν, ἠξίουν μὴ περιιδεῖν τὴν μεγίσlτην
πόλιν τῶν ἐν τῆι Μητροπόλει ἐξαλειφθεῖσαν, ἀλλὰ βοηθῆσαι εἰς τὸν
τειχισμὸν καθ᾽ ὅσον ἂν δυνατὸ[ν] ||³⁵ ἡμῖν ἦι, καὶ φανερὰν ποιῆσαι

τοῖς Ἕλλησι τὴν εὔν[οιαν] | ἣν ἔχομεν πρός τε τὸν κοινὸν τῶν
Δωριέων καὶ τὴν Κ[υτε]|νίων πόλιν, συναντιλαβομένους ἀξίως τε
πρ[ογό]|νων καὶ ἡμῶν αὐτῶν, χαριεῖσθαι τε ἡμᾶς ὑπακούσαν|τας εἰς
ταῦτα οὐ μόνον αὐτοῖς ἀλλὰ καὶ Αἰτωλοῖς καὶ ‖⁴⁰ τοῖς ἄλλοις
Δωριεῦσι πᾶσιν, καὶ μάλιστα τῶι βασιλεῖ Πτ[ο]|λεμαίωι ὄντι συγ-
γενεῖ Δωριέων κατὰ τοὺς βασιλεῖς | τοὺς ἀφ᾽ Ἡρακλέους Ἀργεάδας.

B. Decree of the Aitolians

Ἔδοξε τοῖς Αἰτωλοῖς | πρεσβείας δόμεν τοῖς Δωριέοις ποτί τε τὰς
πόλεις τὰς ‖⁷⁵ συγγενεῖς καὶ τοὺς βασιλεῖς τοὺς ἀπὸ Ἡρακλέος
Πτολε|μαῖον καὶ Ἀντίοχον. τοὺς δὲ ἀποσταλέντας διαλεγέσ|θαι
ὅπως καὶ διὰ τὰν ποτὶ Δωριεῖς συγγένειαν καὶ διὰ τὰν ποτ᾽ Αἰτω-
|λοὺς συναντιλάβωνται τοῦ τειχισμοῦ τᾶς πόλιος τῶν Κυτε|νιέων
ὅπως συνοικισθῆι τὰν ταχίσταν.

C. Letter of the Aitolian magistrates to Xanthos

Ἀγέλαος, Πανταλέ‖⁸⁰ων, Μόλοσσος καὶ οἱ σύνεδροι τῶν Αἰτωλῶν
Ξανθίων τᾶι βουλ|λᾶι καὶ τῶι δάμωι χαίρειν. Λ[α]μπρίας, Αἴνετος,
Φηγεύς, οἱ ἀπο|δεδωκότες ὑμῖν τὰν ἐπιστολάν, ἐντὶ μὲν Δωριεῖς ἐκ
Κυ|τενίου, παραγεγόναντι δὲ ποθ᾽ ὑμὲ πρεσβεύοντες παρὰ | τῶν
Αἰτωλῶν περὶ τειχισμοῦ τᾶς τῶν Κυτενιέων πόλιος. κα‖⁸⁵λῶς οὖν
ποιήσετε καὶ ἕνεκεν ἁμῶν καὶ τοῦ κοινοῦ τῶν Αἰτωλ|λῶν καὶ τᾶς
ποτὶ Δωριεῖς οἰκειότατος ὑμῖν ὑπαρχούσας, | διακούσαντες αὐτῶν
μετὰ φιλανθρωπίας καὶ ἐν τὰ ἀξιούμε|να προθύμως ὑπακούσαντες.
ἔρρωσθε.

D. Letter of the Kytenians to Xanthos

Δωρ[ι]έων τῶν ἀπὸ | Ματροπόλιος οἱ πόλιν Κυτένιον οἰκέοντες
Ξανθίων τᾶι βουλ‖⁹⁰λᾶι καὶ τῶι δάμωι χαίρειν. ἀπεστάλκαμες ποθ᾽
ὑμὲ πρέσ|βεις καὶ ἁμεῖς καὶ τοὶ Αἰτωλοὶ Λαμπρίαν [Π]αγκλέος,
Αἴνετον | Πολύτα, Φηγέα Σωτίωνος τοὺς διαλεγησομένους περὶ ὧν |
ἔχοντι τὰς ἐντολάς. συμβαίνει γὰρ ἁμῶν, καθ᾽ ὃν καιρὸν | ὁ βασιλεὺς
Ἀντίγονος ἐνέβαλε ἐν τὰν Φωκίδα, τῶν τε ‖⁹⁵ τειχέων μέρη τινὰ
καταπεπτώκειν ὑπὸ τῶν σεισμῶν πα|σᾶν τᾶμ πολίων καὶ τοὺς
νεωτέρους εἰσβοαθοήκε<ι>ν ἐν τὸ ἱερὸ[ν]| τοῦ Ἀπόλλωνος τοῦ ἐν
Δελφοῖς. παραγενόμενος δὲ ὁ βασιλεὺς ἐν τὰν Δωρίδα τὰ τε τείχη
ἁμῶν κατέσκαψε πασᾶν | τᾶμ πολίων καὶ τὰς οἰκίας κατέκαυσε.
ἀξιάζομες οὖν ὑμὲ ‖¹⁰⁰ μνασθέντας τᾶς συγγενείας τᾶς ὑπαρχούσας
ἁμῖν | ποθ᾽ ὑμὲ μὴ περιιδεῖν τὰμ μεγίσταν τᾶν ἐν τᾶι Ματροπόλ[ι

πό]|λιν Κυτένιον ἐξαλειφθεῖσαν, ἄλλα βοαθοῆσαι ἁμῖν ἐν [τὸν| τει-
χισμὸν τᾶς πόλιος καθ᾽ ὅ κα δυνατὸν ὑμῖν φαίνηται ε[ἶ]|μεν, καὶ
φανερὰν ποιῆσαι τοῖς Ἑλλάνοις τὰμ παρ᾽ ὑμῶν εὔνοια[ν] ||¹⁰⁵ ποτί τε
τὸ ἔθνο<ς> ἁμῶν καὶ τὰμ πόλιν, συναντιλαβομένους ἀξίως | καὶ τῶν
προγόνων καὶ ὑμῶν αὐτῶν καὶ τοῦ Ἡρακλέος καὶ τῶν ἀπογό|νων
αὐτοῦ. καὶ ἁμεῖς δὲ χάριτας ἀποδωσεῖμες καθ᾽ ὅ κα παρακάλητε.
γινώσκετε δὲ οὐ μόνον ἁμῖν εὐχαριστῆς ἐόντες ἀλλὰ καὶ | [το]ῖς
Αἰτωλοῖς καὶ τοῖς ἄλλοις Δωριέοις πᾶσι καὶ μάλιστα βασιλεῖ ||¹¹⁰
Πτολεμαίωι διὰ τὸ συγγενῆ ἁμῶν εἶμεν κατὰ τοὺς βασιλεῖς.

[A.] In the 17th year of the reign of Ptolemy (IV Philopator), son
of Ptolemy (III Euergetes) and Berenike divine benefactors, and of
his son Ptolemy (V Epiphanes); with Andronikos son of Perlamos
priest of the divine benefactors and of the king Ptolemy; with
Tlepolemos son of Artapates priest of the civic cult: on the second
day of the month Audnaios an assembly was held and the people
and magistrates of Xanthos resolved as follows. Whereas: Ambassadors from the Aitolian League, Dorians from Metropolis, have
presented themselves: Lamprias, Ainetos, Phegeus from Kytenion.
(10) Bringing a decree from the Aitolians and a letter from the
Dorians, by means of which they recounted what has befallen their
country, and giving a detailed and powerful elaboration of the
letter's contents, they call upon us to remember our kinship with
them, which descends from a line of gods and of heroes, and not
to remain indifferent to the destruction of the walls of their homeland. For Leto (they point out), the founder of our city, gave birth
to both Artemis and Apollo in our country; and Asklepios was
born in Doris to Apollo and Koronis, daughter of Phlegyas, des-
cendant of (20) Doros. In addition to the kinship which exists
between them and us from these gods, they also recounted their
connections in heroic genealogy, establishing their descent from
Aiolos and Doros. They described, furthermore, the kindness
shown by Alêtês, one of the Herakleidai, to our colonists under the
command of Chrysaor, son of Glaukos, son of Hippolochos: for
he set out from Doris and came to their aid as they were being
attacked, and heading off the danger which threatened them he
married the daughter of Aor, son of Chrysaor. (30) And demon-
strating with many other arguments the goodwill which has,

through kinship, bound them to us since ancient times, they begged us not to remain indifferent to the obliteration of the biggest city in Metropolis, but to help them in the rebuilding of the walls as far as we are able and to make clear to the Greeks the goodwill we bear towards the Dorian League and city of Kytenion, by assisting in a manner worthy both of our ancestors and of ourselves; and in responding positively we would be obliging not only them, but also the Aitolians and (40) all the other Dorians, and especially King Ptolemy on account of his kinship with the Dorians through the Argead kings descended from Herakles . . .

[B.] The Aitolians resolved to grant to the Dorians embassies to cities (75) linked by kinship and to the kings descended from Herakles, Ptolemy and Antiochos. Those who are sent are to petition them, on account of their kinship with both the Dorians and the Aetolians, to assist in the rebuilding of the city walls of Kytenion, so that the city may be re-established as quickly as possible.

[C.] Agelaos, Pantaleon, (80) Molossos and the magistrates of the Aitolians, to the council and people of Xanthos, greetings. Lamprias, Ainetos, and Phegeus, who have given you this letter, are Dorians from Kytenion, and have come before you as ambassadors from the Aitolians in the matter of the reconstruction of the city of the Kytenians. We request that you be kind enough, for our sake, and for the sake of the Aitolian League and your kinship with the Dorians, to grant them a kind hearing and to entertain their requests with a gracious spirit. Be well.

[D.] From the Dorians in Matropolis who inhabit the city of Kytenion, to the council (90) and people of Xanthos, greetings. We and the Aitolians have sent to you, as ambassadors, Lamprias son of Pankles, Ainetos son of Polutas, and Phegeus son of Sotion: they are to enter into discussions with you according to their instructions. This is what has befallen us: when King Antigonos invaded Phokis, parts of the walls of all of our cities had fallen down as a result of the earthquakes, and our young men had gone to the help of the temple of Apollo in Delphi. When the king arrived in Doris he destroyed the walls of all of our cities and burned the houses. We therefore call upon you (100) to remember your kinship with us, and not to remain indifferent to the obliteration of the biggest city in Metropolis, but to help us in the rebuilding of the city as far as seems possible to you, and to make clear to the Greeks the extent of the goodwill you have towards our people and our city, by assisting us in a manner worthy both of your ancestors and of you yourselves, and of Herakles and his descendants. For our part, we shall render thanks in whatever way you call for. And you should know that you will not only be obliging us, but also the Aitolians and all the other Dorians, and in particular King Ptolemy, on account of his kinship with us through the kings.

The documents from Kytenion are in North-west Greek koina: the Xanthian decree is in elegant chancellery-style Hellenistic koiné. The Lycians were a people of Anatolian (Luwian) origin, who had had a long history of interaction with the Greek world, and were hellenized at an early date. Their language was probably still spoken at this period, but few traces of interference are detectable in texts written in Greek.

A. *Hellenistic koiné*

1. **βασιλεύοντος Πτολεμαίου**: great-grandson of Ptolemy I, a Macedonian general of Alexander who took control of Egypt after Alexander's death in 323 and founded a Greek dynasty there. Lycia was under Ptolemaic control until 197.

2. **Βερενίκης**: in standard Gk. this would be Φερε-. Details of Macedonian phonology are scarce, since little survives except names.

3. **θεῶν εὐεργετῶν**: i.e. the deified Ptolemy III and Berenike.

4. **Περλαμου**: Lycian name.   **πρὸ πόλεως**: i.e. the cult of the patron (protecting) god(s) of the city of Xanthos (Robert and Robert 1983: 171): cf. the title πολιοῦχος (note on **33** 3).

5. **Ἀρταπάτου**: Persian name. The Persians controlled Lycia (and Egypt) until Alexander's conquest.

7. **ἐπειδή**: introduces 35 lines of background explanation, until ἔδοξεν 6 is picked up by δεδόχθαι at 42 (not given here) which gives the response of the Xanthians: the people are sympathetic, but the city's finances are in ruins: the archons are authorized to borrow 500 drachmas to give to the ambassadors.   **τοῦ κοινοῦ**: the Aitolian

League, a federal organization which controlled much of central Greece in the III cent. (including Doris).

8. **Δωριεῖς ... Μητροπόλιος**: in the narrow sense, people from Doris, a valley north of Delphi. Some Dorian Greeks claimed this as their original home (μητρόπολις: Thuc. 1. 107). *Μητροπόλιος*: a hybrid form (koiné -πόλεως).

12. **διαλεγέντες**: ptcpl. of διελέγην (aor. pass.): classical Att. διελέχθην. **ἀκολούθως**: 'almost exclusively confined to the koiné' (Welles 1934: 310): a tech. term in diplomatic letters.

13. **φιλοτιμίας**: in classical Att. this has the negative sense implied by its constituent elements; in the koiné it acquires a positive sense of public-spiritedness (of a wealthy elite who perform philanthropic services for their city).

14. **παρακαλοῦσιν**: in the sense 'exhort', probably alien to classical Att. before Xenophon.

17. **Λητοῦν**: acc. formed from the gen. Λητοῦς < *Λᾱτόγος (earlier Λητῶ < *Λᾱτόγα, cf. λεχώι **51** 16): so already Ἰοῦν Hdt. 1. 2. Leto was the chief deity at Xanthos, and corresponded to an indigenous Lycian/Luwian goddess (the 'mother of the gods').

19. **ἡμεῖν**: a rare slip. [ẹ:] had doubtless fallen together with [i:] by this time.   **Κορωνίδος**: the story is told at Pind. *Pyth.* 3.

20. **Δώρου**: eponymous ancestor of the Dorians (Hesiod frag. 9 in Merkelbach–West 1967); his brothers were Aiolos (Aeolians) and Xouthos (Ionians).

23. **προσαπελογίζοντο**: the use of multiple preverbs is a feature of koiné Gk., and may be connected with the development of technical or specialist styles in the Hellenistic period (ἀπολογίζομαι, 'recount', esp. of ambassadors, is not an idiom of classical Att.).

25. **ἡμετέρας**: sc. γῆς.

26. **Γλαύκου**: Glaukos and Sarpedon led the Lycians at Troy (*Il.* 6. 144 ff. for the family history). Chrysaor, however, is a Carian hero, which makes Bousquet (1988: 36) suspect that the ambassadors had also stopped in Caria.   **Ἡρακλειδῶν**: the Dorians claimed to be descendants of Herakles (for the formation cf. Λαβυάδαις **55** 19).

29. **συνοικῆσαι**: elsewhere takes the dat.

30. **παραδεικνύοντες**: classical Att. -δεικνύντες, but Hdt. 3. 79

δεικνύοντες. The athem. inflection is gradually abandoned in the IV cent.

37. **συναντιλαβομένους**: cf. προσαπελογίζοντο 22. A koiné usage (Welles 1934: 314).

42. **Ἀργεάδας**: the Argeadai, ruling clan of Macedonia who claimed kinship with the royal house of Argos, founded by Herakles (cf. Hdt. 5. 22).

B–D. North-west Greek koina

73. **ἔδοξε**: note absence of -ν (compare the Xanthian text): §32.7.

74. **δόμεν**: athematic infin. (§40.3). **Δωριέοις**: NW Gk. typically replaced the -σι ending of C-stem nouns with -οις (cf. Δωριεῦσι 40). **πόλεις**: koiné influence (earlier πόλιες).

75. **συγγενεῖς**: nom. for acc. -εας is a feature of Attic (from the mid IV cent.) and koiné, but also of NW Gk. from an early date (Méndez Dosuna 1985: 465–8). So also βασιλεῖς.

77. **ὅπως . . . ὅπως**: marked increase in the use of this conjunction is a feature of koiné Gk. (Horrocks 1997: 45): in this case the first ὅπως introduces an object clause, the second a purpose (final) clause.

79. **πόλιος**: non-Att. inflection (§32.4, and contrast πόλεις 74). **τὰν ταχίσταν**: sc. ὁδόν.

80. **οἱ**: koiné form (§40.5).

82. **ἐντί**: WGk. form (§39.4).

83. **παραγεγόναντι . . . παρά**: apocope (§24.5) is missing from the koina (cf. πάρ 59 5). For the ending of παραγεγόναντι cf. ἐντί, but note that -αντι has been recharacterized (earlier NW Gk. 3 plur. -ατι < *-n̥ti): cf. §32.12. **ὑμέ**: WGk. (cf. §32.5).

85. **ποιήσετε**: koiné form (cf. ἀποδωσεῖμες 107, §40.2). **ἕνεκεν**: characteristic of Ionic and koiné Gk. (no evidence for the form in NW Gk.).

87. **διακούσαντες**: a tech. term in the koiné for listening to envoys. **ἐν**: NW Gk. (cf. §28.8).

90. **ἀπεστάλκαμες**: resultative perfect. A koiné form with WGk. verbal ending (§40.1). **πρέσβεις**: koiné form (cf. Lokr. πρείγᾱι 56 10): acc. plur. (συγγενεῖς 75).

91. **τοί**: WGk. (§40.5): contrast οἱ 80.

92. **Πολύτᾱ**: WGk. gen. sing. < -ᾱο (§24.3).

93. **ἔχοντι**: cf. ἐντί 82.   **ἐντολάς**: rare in classical Att., the word becomes common in the koiné (Welles 1934: 331).   **ἀμῶν**: probably a slip for ἀμῖν (ed. pr.).

94. **ἐνέβαλε ἐν**: for NW Gk. ἐν + acc. cf. 87 and Lokr. ἐνφέροι **56** 10.

95. **καταπεπτώκειν**: a perf. infin. created with a thematic infin. ending (as in Thess. and Delphi, and sporadically in WGk.). **πασᾶν**: WGk. -ᾶν < -άων (§30.2).

96. **εἰσβοαθοήκε<ι>ν**: Bousquet emends -εν to match καταπεπτώκειν (either ending would in theory be acceptable), and notes also the lack of reduplication. The preverb εἰσ- stands in contrast to ἐνέβαλε 94. See βοαθοῆσαι 102.

99. **ἀξιάζομες**: ἀξιάζω for ἀξιόω is not attested elsewhere, though ἀξιάω is found in Lesb. (ἀξίαισι, 3 plur. indic., Eresos): cf. τιμάω/τιμάζω/τιμόω.

102. **βοαθοῆσαι**: βοᾱθοέω is attested in Aitolian (Att. βοηθέω by hypheresis), formed to βοᾱθό(ϝ)ος.

103. **ε[ἶ]μεν**: athem. infin. (§40.3) < *es-men.

104. **Ἑλλάνοις**: cf. Δωριέοις 74 (and Ἕλλησι 35 < *Ἑλλᾱν-σι).

105. **ἔθνο<ς>**: ed. pr. for ἔθνον on stone.

107. **ἀποδωσεῖμες**: strange ending. The 'Doric' future -σε-ομες (suffix + ending) could not give -σεῖμες. The vowel must be analogical (e.g. from the 2 plur. -σεῖτε < -σε-ετε).

108. **γινώσκετε**: forms in γιν- are normal in NW Gk. (this is not a sign of koiné influence): cf. on γίνηται 7 2.   **εὐχαριστῆς**: apparently nom. plur. (*-ήϝ-ες) of a noun in -εύς, 'benefactor'. **ἐόντες**: §32.11.

109. **πᾶσι**: koiné form (NW Gk. πάντοις: cf. Δωριέοις 74).

110. **διά**: διά with the articular infin. was destined to play an important role in the syntax of the koiné, as participle constructions became less common (Horrocks 1997: 46). The Xanthian version avoids it.

LITERARY TEXTS

EPIC

66. Homer, *Iliad* 22. 93–125: Hektor's soliloquy before his duel with Achilles. Text: ed. M. L. West (Teubner: Leipzig 2000). Date: probably some time in the VIII cent. BC (when and how it was written down is a matter of debate). Hexameters.
▶▶ Chantraine (1953: 362–4), Fenik (1978), Sharples (1983), De Jong (1987: 129–30).

ὡς δὲ δράκων ἐπὶ χειῆι ὀρέστερος ἄνδρα μένησιν
βεβρωκὼς κακὰ φάρμακ᾽, ἔδυ δέ τέ μιν χόλος αἰνός,
95 σμερδαλέον δὲ δέδορκεν ἑλισσόμενος περὶ χειῆι,
ὣς Ἕκτωρ ἄσβεστον ἔχων μένος οὐχ ὑπεχώρει,
πύργωι ἔπι προύχοντι φαεινὴν ἀσπίδ᾽ ἐρείσας.
ὀχθήσας δ᾽ ἄρα εἶπε πρὸς ὃν μεγαλήτορα θυμόν·
«ὤι μοι ἐγών, εἰ μέν κε πύλας καὶ τείχεα δύω,
100 Πουλυδάμας μοι πρῶτος ἐλεγχείην ἀναθήσει,
ὅς μ᾽ ἐκέλευεν Τρωσὶ ποτὶ πτόλιν ἡγήσασθαι
νύχθ᾽ ὕπο τήνδ᾽ ὀλοήν, ὅτε τ᾽ ὤρετο δῖος Ἀχιλλεύς·
ἀλλ᾽ ἐγὼ οὐ πιθόμην· ἦ τ᾽ ἂν πολὺ κέρδιον ἦεν.
νῦν δ᾽ ἐπεὶ ὤλεσα λαὸν ἀτασθαλίηισιν ἐμῆισιν,
105 αἰδέομαι Τρῶας καὶ Τρωιάδας ἑλκεσιπέπλους,
μή ποτέ τις εἴπησι κακώτερος ἄλλος ἐμεῖο,
῾Ἕκτωρ ἦφι βίηφι πιθήσας ὤλεσε λαόν.᾽
ὣς ἐρέουσιν· ἐμοὶ δὲ τότ᾽ ἂν πολὺ κέρδιον εἴη
ἄντην ἢ Ἀχιλῆα κατακτείναντα νέεσθαι
110 ἠέ κεν αὐτῶι ὀλέσθαι ἐϋκλείως πρὸ πόληος.
εἰ δέ κεν ἀσπίδα μὲν καταθείομαι ὀμφαλόεσσαν
καὶ κόρυθα βριαρήν, δόρυ δὲ πρὸς τεῖχος ἐρείσας
αὐτὸς ἰὼν Ἀχιλῆος ἀμύμονος ἀντίος ἔλθω
καί οἱ ὑπόσχωμαι Ἑλένην καὶ κτήμαθ᾽ ἅμ᾽ αὐτῆι
115 πάντα μάλ᾽, ὅσσα τ᾽ Ἀλέξανδρος κοίληις ἐνὶ νηυσίν
ἠγάγετο Τροίηνδ᾽, ἥ τ᾽ ἔπλετο νείκεος ἀρχή,
δωσέμεν Ἀτρεΐδηισιν ἄγειν, ἅμα τ᾽ ἀμφὶς Ἀχαιοῖς
ἀλλ᾽ ἀποδάσσεσθαι, ὅσα τε πτόλις ἥδε κέκευθεν·
Τρωσὶν δ᾽ αὖ μετόπισθε γερούσιον ὅρκον ἕλωμαι
120 μή τι κατακρύψειν, ἀλλ᾽ ἄνδιχα πάντα δάσεσθαι—

122 ἀλλὰ τίη μοι ταῦτα φίλος διελέξατο θυμός;
μή μιν ἐγὼ μὲν ἴκωμαι ἰών, ὃ δέ μ᾽ οὐκ ἐλεήσει
οὐδέ τί μ᾽ αἰδέσεται, κτενέει δέ με γυμνὸν ἐόντα
125 αὔτως ὥς τε γυναῖκα, ἐπεί κ᾽ ἀπὸ τεύχεα δύω.»

As a snake in the mountains waits for a man by its den, having fed
on poisonous herbs, and a terrible anger has entered it: dreadfully
its eyes glitter as it twists around its den. So Hektor, full of
unquenchable fierceness, did not give ground, but leant his bright
shield against a projecting battlement. With turbulent feelings he
addressed his mighty spirit: 'Ah me, if I enter within the gates and
the wall, (100) Polydamas will be the first to lay reproach upon me:
he was the man who bade me lead the Trojans to the city during
this fatal night when glorious Achilles roused himself. But I did
not listen: that indeed would have been far better. As it is, now that
I have destroyed the host with my reckless folly, I feel shame before
the Trojan men and the long-robed Trojan women, in case
someone else, a man of lower rank than I, should say, "Hektor, by
putting faith in his own strength, has destroyed the host". So they
will say; but for me it would be far better to meet Achilles face to
face, slay him, and return home, (110) or die gloriously at his
hands in front of the city. Perhaps if I were to lay down my bossed
shield and mighty helmet, and leaning my spear against the wall
were to go just as I am to meet blameless Achilles and promise him
Helen and, along with her, all the treasure which Alexander
brought in his hollow ships to Troy (which was the cause of the
dispute), and give it to Atreus' sons to carry away, and at the same
time divide up amongst the Achaeans all the rest that this city
contains, and later take from the Trojans an oath sworn by the
elders (120) not to hide anything but to divide everything in
two—but why does my heart hold converse with me like this? No,
I must not go and approach him, for he will not pity me nor show
me any respect, but will kill me there and then like a woman,
without defence when I have taken off my armour.'

93–5. Hom. simile. The comparison is both timeless and immedi-
ate, hence the non-temporal aorist ἔδυ (Chantraine 1953: 185), in
which aor. aspect (achievement of the predicate), rather than past
tense, is important. Note the coordination of pres. subjunctive,

non-temporal aor. and perf. (intrans., indicating the snake's appearance).

93. **ὥς**: E. Ionic was psilotic (§31.6). If, as is commonly thought, the poem assumed its final form in this region, rough breathings and other signs of aspiration must reflect the influence of Athens on the history of the text (§23.10).　　**δράκων**: < *dr̥kōn (root *derk-, 'look'): poetic term derived from the unnerving eyes of a reptile. A play with δέδορκεν 95.　　**μένησιν**: the 3 sing. subj. of thematic vbs. in Homer is often extended with the marker -σι (earlier -τι, as in WGk. athem. δίδωτι); the 1 and 2 sing. less frequently have -μι, -θα added. Some MSS have μένηισιν (cf. Arc. τυγχάνη 7 11).

94. **ἔδυ δέ τέ μιν**: enclitic pronouns and particles in Indo-European follow the first accented unit in the phrase (phenomenon known as Wackernagel's Law: cf. Ruijgh 1990); in post-Hom. Gk. this pattern is weakened. (Gk. δέ is semi-clitic.)　　**τέ**: with generalizing force, common in similes.　　**μιν**: cf. μιγ 21 2.

98. **εἶπε πρὸς ὃν μεγαλήτορα θυμόν**: direct speech (which comprises about two-thirds of the *Iliad*) is always clearly introduced in epic with formulas such as this (Bers 1997: 15–17).　　**ὅν**: < *swos (with doublet ἑός < *sewos). Cf. Lat. *suus*.

99. **ὤι μοι ἐγών**: introduces a 'type scene', the monologue of an isolated warrior. All four such scenes in *Iliad* start with this lament (Fenik 1978).　　**ἐγών**: §36.5.　　**κε**: Hom. epic uses κ(ε), κεν, and ἄν. The most common is κε/κ' (also found in Lesb., E. Thess. and Cypr.). Cf. §36.7. Here with the pres. subj. δύω.

100. **Πουλυδάμας**: <ου> in our text represents ō, lengthened for metrical convenience. This licence grew out of poetically useful doublets such as μόνος ~ μῶνος (μοῦνος) < *μόνϝος, which reflect the different dialectal elements which contributed to epic language: compensatory lengthening in some dialects such as E. Ionic (§30.6) but absent from others (such as Lesb.).　　**ἐλεγχείην**: for the formation of this fem. abstract (elsewhere neut. ἔλεγχος) see on ἀτελέην 27 7 (Eretria).

101. **ποτί**: πρός is most frequent in Hom. epic, and often seems to have replaced ποτί (Janko 1982: 177). προτί and ποτί look like metrically useful archaisms from mainland Gk. (with early Aeolic ποτί replacing Achaean ποσί: §28.7, and Janko 1982: 90).　　**πτόλιν**: found in Cypr. (cf. on 8 1).

102. **νύχθ᾽**: cf. ὥs 93 (and on ἐπιστᾶσα **83** 38.1). **ὕπο**: rare use, perhaps restricted to Ionic (also in Hdt., and on Thasos). **τ(ε)**: following a specific temporal relative, appears to give 'a causal colour' to the relative (Denniston 1954: 522). **ὥρετο**: aor. (intrans.) of ὄρνυμαι, 'arise'. A thematic version of athem. ὦρτο, it makes a dactyl and was perhaps confected for metrical reasons (root as in Lat. *ortus*). **δῖοs**: adj. < *diw-yos*, 'relating to Zeus/the sky'. Frequent epithet of Hom. heroes; may also have a sense 'shining' (cf. particularly the use with 'dawn', 'sea', and 'upper air': García Ramón 1999: 549).

103. **πιθόμην**: them. aor. (intrans.) of πείθομαι, 'obey'. The augment may be omitted in Hom. epic: descriptively a poetic licence, the historical reasons are obscure (§14.2). **ἦ τ᾽**: ἦ is emphatic, τ(ε) may be due to the tendency in Gk. syntax for negative propositions (here an unfulfilled apodosis) to be marked as indefinite (see also Ruijgh 1971: 54 f.). **ἦεν**: 3 sing. imperf. (> Att.-Ion. ἦν): §32.2.

104. **λᾱόν**: < earlier epic λᾱϝόν, retained by bards in Ionia in spite of the change ā > η, since Ion. *ληόν had become λεών (not metrically equivalent). **ἀτασθαλίηισιν**: a-stem abstracts may be used in the plur. in Hom., most often the dat. plur. (Hainsworth 1957). §32.14 for the ending.

105. **Τρῶας**: acc. plur. of Τρώs. The adj. 'Trojan' is Τρώϊος, of which Τρωϊάς (here contracted Τρωιάς) is the fem. **ἑλκεσιπέπλους**: compd. adj., in which the second member (a noun) is determined by the first, here a verbal stem (ἑλκε-): the linking suffix -τι- (assibilated -σι-) is characteristic of such compds.

106. **τις**: long because of following (ϝ)εἴπηισι (for the subj. cf. μένησιν 93). **ἐμεῖο**: gen. sing., built on acc. ἐμέ on the analogy of thematic nouns in -οιο.

107. **ἧφι**: dat.-instr. (fem.) of possess. adj. ὅs < *swos. βίηφι could in origin be sing. or plur. (Hainsworth 1957: 6). For the ending -φι see §11.4. **πιθήσας**: see on **68** 671.

109. **ἠ᾽**: i.e. ἠϝ (preventing hiatus). For ἠ-ϝέ cf. the Lat. particle -ue. **Ἀχιλῆα**: a poetic liberty for Ἀχιλλ-, perhaps deriving from forms such as ἔλλαβε (ἔλαβε), in which root-initial λ- < *sl- could count (metrically) as single or double. **κατακτείναντα**: the need for a dat. in agreement with ἐμοί 108 yields to the need for an acc. as the subject of inf. νέεσθαι.

110. **κεν**: modal particle with infin. (very rare): it seems to be carrying the hypothetical force of ἄν 108 into the dependent clause. Epigraphic evidence for κεν is extremely feeble, suggesting that the form may be an epic innovation (different view in Forbes 1958*b*). **αὐτῶι**: dat. pron. involving Achilles in the action (as agent). **ἐϋκλείως**: or ἐϋκλε(F)έως (cf. *Il.* 17. 415, ἐϋκλεές, neut. sing. as advb.). **πόληος**: §32.4.

111–21. A long and complex sentence by Hom. standards. Formally it takes the syntax of an incomplete conditional: protasis, then interruption. 111. **καταθείομαι**: aor. subj. of κατα-τίθεμαι, formed by adding them. vowel and ending to the long grade of the stem (θη-): instead of expected θή-ο-μαι the MSS here and elsewhere give θεί- before *o*-vowels (i.e. in contexts where -ηο- underwent metathesis to -εω- in post-Hom. Ionic and Attic). The bards, for whom -ηο- was obsolete, may have tried to make a long *e* vowel (required by the metre) by lengthening the ε they were familiar with (giving ε̄, later written ει). Att. θῶμαι < θέωμαι < θήομαι. **ὀμφαλόεσσαν**: for the suffix see §13.

114. **καί οἱ**: hiatus caused by loss of *w* (cf. on **72** 79). ὑπόσχωμαι has a long final in hiatus, which is unusual: the reason is probably the caesura (not F- before Ἑλένην, which is not found in epic: cf. on **32**). 115. **ὅσσα**: *yotyo-* > Lesb. Thess. ὄσσο-, Ion. ὄσο- (§23.8), creating a useful poetic doublet (cf. ὅσα 118). **κοίληις**: i.e. κοίληισ’ (κοίληις before C- is a poetic extension of κοίληισ’, and extremely rare). For -ηισ(ι) §32.14. **ἐνί**: this doublet of ἐν was inherited from IE. **νηυσίν**: dat. plur. of ναῦς (Hom. νηῦς), stem *νᾱF-. In the nom. sing. and dat. plur. ᾱ > α in early Gk. (§23.3), restored as η in Hom. on the analogy of nom. plur. νῆες, etc. Has undergone synizesis here.

116. **ἥ**: refers to the clause (the abduction, with neut. ὅ attracted into the gender of ἀρχή) rather than Helen in 114. **ἔπλετο**: aor. of πέλομαι, 'be' (the form is Aeolic: *kʷel-, lit. 'turn'). Cf. τέντα[ι] **51** 18. 117. **δωσέμεν**: 'Aeolic' infin., characteristic of Boe. and Thess. (§36.3). **Ἀτρείδηισιν**: -ίδης is a productive patronymic suffix in epic language (cf. Νεστορίδης **67** 155). Note metrical shortening: orig. *Ἀτρη-ίδης cannot go into a hexameter line. **ἄγειν**: an infin. of purpose (also possible in Att. with verbs of giving). **ἀμφίς**:

adv., 'apart (from that)'. The form with -ς is restricted to Hom.
Ἀχαιοῖς: guaranteed short form at line end (contrast κοίλης 115).
These are rare in *Iliad*, less so in *Odyssey*, and common in Hes. *Works and Days* (where over 60% of short dat. plur. forms are guaranteed short: Janko 1982: 57).

118. **ἀποδάσσεσθαι**: mid. infin. to fut. stem δασσ- < *δατ-σ- (cf. ἀποδάττασθαι 53 29). For δάσεσθαι 120, cf. ὄσσα 115 (*-ts- is subject to the same development as *-ty-).

120. **ἄνδιχα**: 'into two', ἀνά (syncopated) + δίχα (advb. built to δίς 'twice').

122. **τίη**: interrog. τί + emphatic particle ἦ (as in classical Att.).
φίλος: the semantic relationship between 'dear' and 'own' (both meanings in Hom.) is not difficult, but the details (and direction) of the shift are hard to pin down (useful discussion by Hooker 1987).
διελέξατο: an instantaneous aor. (see the note on ἔδυ 93–5), which typically expresses the sudden onset of an emotion, or an abrupt reaction (characteristic of but not confined to dialogue).

123. **μὲν ... δέ**: the two eventualities are presented para-tactically (rather than with γάρ, or a conditional clause).   **ἵκωμαι**: approach as ἱκέτης.

124. **κτενέει**: uncontracted fut. (§24.2).   **ἐόντα**: §32.11.

125. **ἀπὸ ... δύω**: tmesis (§24.6).

67. Homer, *Odyssey* 4. 136–67: Helen recognizes Telemachus. Text: ed. T. W. Allen (2nd edn., Oxford 1917). Generally dated a little later than the *Iliad*. Hexameters.

> ἕζετο δ᾽ ἐν κλισμῶι, ὑπὸ δὲ θρῆνυς ποσὶν ἦεν.
> αὐτίκα δ᾽ ἥ γε ἔπεσσι πόσιν ἐρέεινεν ἕκαστα·
> «Ἴδμεν δή, Μενέλαε διοτρεφές, οἵ τινες οἵδε
> ἀνδρῶν εὐχετόωνται ἱκανέμεν ἡμέτερον δῶ;
> 140 ψεύσομαι, ἦ ἔτυμον ἐρέω; κέλεται δέ με θυμός.
> οὐ γάρ πώ τινά φημι ἐοικότα ὧδε ἰδέσθαι
> οὔτ᾽ ἄνδρ᾽ οὔτε γυναῖκα, σέβας μ᾽ ἔχει εἰσορόωσαν,
> ὡς ὅδ᾽ Ὀδυσσῆος μεγαλήτορος υἷι ἔοικε,
> Τηλεμάχωι, τὸν λεῖπε νέον γεγαῶτ᾽ ἐνὶ οἴκωι
> 145 κεῖνος ἀνήρ, ὅτ᾽ ἐμεῖο κυνώπιδος εἵνεκ᾽ Ἀχαιοὶ
> ἤλθεθ᾽ ὑπὸ Τροίην, πόλεμον θρασὺν ὁρμαίνοντες.»

Τὴν δ᾽ ἀπαμειβόμενος προσέφη ξανθὸς Μενέλαος·
«οὕτω νῦν καὶ ἐγὼ νοέω, γύναι, ὡς σὺ ἐΐσκεις·
κείνου γὰρ τοιοίδε πόδες τοιαίδε τε χεῖρες
150 ὀφθαλμῶν τε βολαὶ κεφαλή τ᾽ ἐφύπερθέ τε χαῖται.
καὶ νῦν ἦ τοι ἐγὼ μεμνημένος ἀμφ᾽ Ὀδυσῆϊ
μυθεόμην, ὅσα κεῖνος ὀϊζύσας ἐμόγησεν
ἀμφ᾽ ἐμοί, αὐτὰρ ὁ πυκνὸν ὑπ᾽ ὀφρύσι δάκρυον εἶβε,
χλαῖναν πορφυρέην ἄντ᾽ ὀφθαλμοῖιν ἀνασχών.»
155 τὸν δ᾽ αὖ Νεστορίδης Πεισίστρατος ἀντίον ηὔδα·
«Ἀτρεΐδη Μενέλαε διοτρεφές, ὄρχαμε λαῶν,
κείνου μέν τοι ὅδ᾽ υἱὸς ἐτήτυμον, ὡς ἀγορεύεις·
ἀλλὰ σαόφρων ἐστί, νεμεσσᾶται δ᾽ ἐνὶ θυμῶι
ὧδ᾽ ἐλθὼν τὸ πρῶτον ἐπεσβολίας ἀναφαίνειν
160 ἄντα σέθεν, τοῦ νῶϊ θεοῦ ὣς τερπόμεθ᾽ αὐδῆι.
αὐτὰρ ἐμὲ προέηκε Γερήνιος ἱππότα Νέστωρ
τῶι ἅμα πομπὸν ἕπεσθαι· ἐέλδετο γάρ σε ἰδέσθαι,
ὄφρα οἱ ἤ τι ἔπος ὑποθήσεαι ἠέ τι ἔργον.
πολλὰ γὰρ ἄλγε᾽ ἔχει πατρὸς πάϊς οἰχομένοιο
165 ἐν μεγάροις, ὧι μὴ ἄλλοι ἀοσσητῆρες ἔωσιν,
ὡς νῦν Τηλεμάχωι ὁ μὲν οἴχεται, οὐδέ οἱ ἄλλοι
εἴσ᾽ οἵ κεν κατὰ δῆμον ἀλάλκοιεν κακότητα.»

She sat down on a chair, with a footstool under her feet. At once she spoke, and began to question her husband on each matter. 'Do we know, Menelaus, cherished by Zeus, who these men say that they are who have come to our house? Shall I hide or say what I believe to be true? My spirit urges me on. I declare that I have never seen such a resemblance, in either man or woman—amazement seizes me as I look—as this man looks like the son of great-hearted Odysseus, Telemachus: him he left as a newborn baby in his house (145) when the Achaeans went to Troy for the sake of shameless me, intending bold war.' In reply fair-haired Menelaus addressed her: 'Now I too see the truth of your comparison, wife. He has similar feet and hands; his eyes have the same glance; his head and hair above are the same. And just now, indeed, I was recalling Odysseus and recounting how much he suffered and toiled on my account; and this man shed a large tear from under his eyebrows, holding up his purple cloak in front of his eyes.' (155) Then Nestor's son Peisistratos answered him: 'Menelaos, son of Atreus, cherished by Zeus, leader of the host, this is truly his son, as you say; but he is a man of restraint, and on his first coming here he is ashamed to speak rashly before you, in whose voice we take pleasure as in a god's. I was sent by the Gerenian horseman Nestor to be an escort for him; for he hoped to see you, in case you might offer him some helpful word or deed. Many are the sorrows that a son has in his house in the absence of his father, (165) when there are no others to help him; as now Telemachus' father is gone, and there are no others among the people to avert harm from him.'

136. **ἕζετο**: imperf., < *sed-yo- §23.8 (cf. Lat. sedeō < *sedē-yo-, §24.1, b (ii). **θρῆνυς**: richly decorated footstools (Myc. *ta-ra-nu*, θρᾶνυς) are listed in the Pylos Ta tablets (palace inventory, cf. 5). **ποσίν**: < *ποτσί (*pod-): cf. ἀποδάσσεσθαι 66 118. **ᾗεν**: cf. 66 103.

137. **ἔπεσσι**: hiatus caused by initial *w*- in (F)ἔπος (*wekʷ-, cf. Lat. *uox*): for the ending see §36.4. The MSS also offer the reading γ' ἐπέεσσι, which represents an attempt to refashion the phrase (avoiding hiatus) in a period/region which was unfamiliar with digamma. ἐπέεσσι is an entirely artificial form.

139. **ἀνδρῶν**: partitive gen. with οἵ τινες, 'who?' **εὐχετόωνται**: from εὐχετάομαι by diektasis. The verb is a product of the epic tradition: a metrically convenient by-form of εὔχομαι. **ἱκανέμεν**: cf. δωσέμεν 66 117. **δῶ**: always acc., with one exception, and mostly after a poss. adj. (as here): traditionally interpreted as a by-form of δῶμα. Most likely it was a form of the suffix -δε ('place to which'): ἡμέτερόν-δω would be *chez nous* in origin (cf. Hom. ὑμέτερόνδε, Lat. *endo*). Risch (1974: 359 f.).

141. **ἐοικότα**: < *Fε-Foικ-, isolated perf. (root as in εἰκών). ἐΐσκεις 148, 'compare' is a factitive pres. built to this perf. stem (*FεFίκ-σκω). **ἰδέσθαι**: hiatus caused by initial *w*- in (F)ιδ- (Lat. *uideō*).

142. **εἰσορόωσαν**: diektasis of εἰσορῶσαν < *-ορα-ōσαν.

143. **υἷι**: < *suiw-i, dat. of a *u*-stem υἱύς < *suyu-s (later made into an *o*-stem υἱός, as at 157).

144. **τόν**: personal pron., 'him'. **γεγαῶτ(α)**: perf. ptcpl. of γίγνομαι. Forms a zero-grade perf. stem in γεγα- as though to a root

*gen (instead of *genH₁-): cf. μεμαώς < **me-mn̥-wōs* (root *men).
The acc. -ῶτα instead of -ότα is unexpected: may conceal an earlier
Aeolic ptcpl. in -οντα, §36.2 (cf. Thess. ἐπεστάκοντα **9** 8). **οἴκωι**:
hiatus caused by initial *w*- in (ϝ)οικ- (cf. Lat. *uīcus*).

145. **κυνώπιδος**: lit. 'dog-faced' or 'dog-eyed' (*okʷ-), with the *o*
lengthened in 'composition' (regular when the second element of a
compd. starts with a vowel).   **εἴνεκ(α)**: see on *e-ne-ka* **4**.

148. **ἔϊσκεις**: see ἐοικότα 141.

149. **κείνου**: in most cases (around 60%) the gen. ending -ου *may*
(as here) be resolved into earlier uncontracted -οο (or -ο᾽/-οι᾽ before
vowels); in a few cases it *must* be resolved (for the metre: resolution is
the replacement of one long syllable by two short ones). Figures in
Janko (1982: 54).

151. **Ὀδυσῆϊ**: a poetic liberty for Ὀδυσσ-, perhaps deriving from
doublets such as μέσος ~ μέσσος, where the phonology reflects dialect
differences (§23.8).

152. **ὀϊζύσας**: onomatopoeic (built to οἰζύς, a cry οἴ).

153. **εἶβε**: doublet of λείβω (cf. Lat. *lībāre*) created by the epic
tradition. The sequence adj. + δάκρυον εἴβω (always at line end) is
a formulaic reworking of δάκρυα λείβω (and note that δάκρυον is a
secondary sing. formed to δάκρυα). See Haslam (1976).

154. **πορφυρέην**: adj. of 'material' in *-*eyos* from πορφύρα (cf. Myc.
po-pu-re-jo of textiles).   **ὀφθαλμοῖϊν**: the Hom. dual in -οῖϊν is
no better understood than other oblique-case dual endings (Att.
-οιν). A disyllabic ending is attested in Arc. Διδύμοιυν (Dubois 1986:
I, 101).

155. **Νεστορίδης**: see on **66** 117.   **ηὔδā**: imperf. of αὐδάω
'speak': perhaps an old athematic imperf. (as in Att. ἐτίθη < ἐτίθη-τ,
i.e. stem + ending *-*t*).

156. **Ἀτρείδη**: cf. Ἀτρείδηισιν **66** 117. The earliest form of the voc.
was in -ă (cf. ἱππότα 161): the masc. form in -ā/-η may be a borrowing from the fem. *a*-stems (where it would represent substitution of
the nom. sing.).

158. **σαόφρων**: of sound (σάϝος) mind (φρήν), contracted in Att.-
Ion. to σώφρων.

159. **ὧδ(ε)**: 'hither', the 'directive' of pronominal *so (cf. Lat. *quō*,
eō and Sihler §259.6) plus suffix -δε.   **ἐπεσβολίας**: lit. 'word-
throwing' (ἔπος + βάλλω): initial *w- is ignored in the scansion.

Neglect of digamma runs at less than 18% in both *Il.* and *Od.* (Janko 1982: 47).   160. **σέθεν**: attested in Sappho and Alkaios, so perh. Aeolic in origin: formed by adding the abl. suffix -θεν to the acc. σέ.   **τοῦ**: rel. 'whose' §32.13 (and cf. κείνου 149).   **νῶϊ**: the classical Att. dual is νώ (exact cognates in Indo-Iranian). The final -ι/-Ϝι of the Hom. form is obscure.   **θεοῦ**: can be resolved into θεοι᾽ before ὡς. 161. **προέηκε**: aor. of προΐημι, with -έηκα < *e-yē-k- < *e-yeH₁-k- (cf. Lat. *iēc-ī*), contracted in Att. to ἧκε.   **Γερήνιος**: epithet of Nestor, of uncertain origin (the later tradition may have connected it with γέρων).   **ἱππότᾰ**: epithet, generally regarded as an old voc. (ἱππότης is impossible metrically). Cf. Μογέα **13**. 162. **πομπὸν ἔπεσθαι**: acc. (Peisistratos) and final infin. (cf. ἄγειν **66** 117).   **ἐέλδετο**: probably from *H₁weld- (the less common ἔλδετο looks like the result of re-analysing the first ἐ- as an augment). **ἰδέσθαι**: cf. 141.   163. **ὄφρα**: here with the fut. instead of the usual subj./opt. (perhaps influenced by ὅπως).   **οἱ ... ἔπος ... ἔργον**: hiatus before original Ϝοι, Ϝέπος, Ϝέργον.   164. **πάϊς**: both this and contracted παῖς are found in Hom.   165. **μεγάροις**: cf. κοίλης **66** 115.   **μὴ ... ἔωσιν**: subj. without modal particle is normal in indef. rel. clauses of a very general nature.   **ἀοσσητῆρες**: derived from *ἄοσσος (*sm̥-sokʷ-, root as in ἕπομαι, Lat. *socius*), apparently via the denom. ἀοσσέω (not, however, attested until the Hellenistic period, which is suspicious).   166. **οἱ**: pronoun (Ϝοι).   167. **ἀλάλκοιεν**: opt. of a reduplicated aor. ἀλαλκεῖν built to the stem ἀλκ- (cf. ἀλέξω, built to ἀλεκ-).

68. Hesiod, *Works and Days* 663–94. Advice to seafarers. Text: M. L. West (Oxford 1978). Hexameters. ▶▶ West (1978), Rosen (1990).

> ἤματα πεντήκοντα μετὰ τροπὰς ἠελίοιο,
> ἐς τέλος ἐλθόντος θέρεος, καματώδεος ὥρης,
> 665 ὡραῖος πέλεται θνητοῖς πλόος· οὔτε κέ νῆα
> κανάξαις οὔτ᾽ ἄνδρας ἀποφθείσειε θάλασσα,
> εἰ δὴ μὴ πρόφρων γε Ποσειδάων ἐνοσίχθων

ἢ Ζεὺς ἀθανάτων βασιλεὺς ἐθέλησιν ὀλέσσαι·
ἐν τοῖς γὰρ τέλος ἐστὶν ὁμῶς ἀγαθῶν τε κακῶν τε.
670 τῆμος δ' εὐκρινέες τ' αὖραι καὶ πόντος ἀπήμων·
εὔκηλος τότε νῆα θοὴν ἀνέμοισι πιθήσας
ἑλκέμεν ἐς πόντον φόρτόν τ' ἐς πάντα τίθεσθαι.
σπεύδειν δ' ὅττι τάχιστα πάλιν οἶκόνδε νέεσθαι,
μηδὲ μένειν οἶνόν τε νέον καὶ ὀπωρινὸν ὄμβρον
675 καὶ χειμῶν' ἐπιόντα Νότοιό τε δεινὰς ἀήτας,
ὅς τ' ὤρινε θάλασσαν ὁμαρτήσας Διὸς ὄμβρωι
πολλῶι ὀπωρινῶι, χαλεπὸν δέ τε πόντον ἔθηκεν.
ἄλλος δ' εἰαρινὸς πέλεται πλόος ἀνθρώποισιν·
ἦμος δὴ τὸ πρῶτον, ὅσον τ' ἐπιβᾶσα κορώνη
680 ἴχνος ἐποίησεν, τόσσον πέταλ' ἀνδρὶ φανήηι
ἐν κράδηι ἀκροτάτηι, τότε δ' ἄμβατός ἐστι θάλασσα·
εἰαρινὸς δ' οὗτος πέλεται πλόος. οὔ μιν ἔγωγε
αἴνημ'· οὐ γὰρ ἐμῶι θυμῶι κεχαρισμένος ἐστίν·
ἁρπακτός· χαλεπῶς κε φύγοις κακόν· ἀλλά νυ καὶ τά
685 ἄνθρωποι ῥέζουσιν ἀιδρίηισι νόοιο·
χρήματα γὰρ ψυχὴ πέλεται δειλοῖσι βροτοῖσιν.
δεινὸν δ' ἐστὶ θανεῖν μετὰ κύμασιν· ἀλλά σ' ἄνωγα
φράζεσθαι τάδε πάντα μετὰ φρεσὶν, ὡς ἀγορεύω.
μηδ' ἐν νηυσὶν ἅπαντα βίον κοίλῃσι τίθεσθαι,
690 ἀλλὰ πλέω λείπειν, τὰ δὲ μείονα φορτίζεσθαι·
δεινὸν γὰρ πόντου μετὰ κύμασι πήματι κύρσαι,
δεινὸν δ' εἴ κ' ἐπ' ἄμαξαν ὑπέρβιον ἄχθος ἀείρας
ἄξονα καυάξαις καὶ φορτία μαυρωθείη.
μέτρα φυλάσσεσθαι· καιρὸς δ' ἐπὶ πᾶσιν ἄριστος.

For fifty days after the solstice, at the tiresome season when summer is coming to an end, it is the right time for mankind to set sail; neither will you wreck your ship nor will the sea destroy the crew, unless Poseidon the earth-shaker or Zeus king of the immortals is intent on bringing them to ruin; for with them rests the issue alike of good things and bad. But at that season the breezes are steady and the sea is harmless: then, free from anxiety, trust in the winds and drag your swift ship down to the sea, putting on board all your cargo; make best speed to return home again, and do not wait for the new wine and autumn rains, the

onset of storms and the dreadful blast of the south wind which
stirs up the waves with the heavy autumnal rain of Zeus and makes
the sea dangerous. Another time for men to sail comes in the
spring: when on the very top of the fig-tree a man first sees a leaf
the size of the print made by a crow's foot, then the sea is fit for
sailing; this is the springtime sailing-season. For my part, I do not
recommend it; it is not agreeable to my spirit, having to be
snatched as opportunity offers. With difficulty will you escape
disaster; but even that people do in the ignorance of their mind,
for wealth is as life for wretched mortals. It is a terrible thing to
lose one's life among the waves; but I bid you take thought in your
mind of all these things that I am telling you. Do not consign your
entire livelihood to hollow ships: leave behind the larger portion,
and put on board the smaller. For it is a terrible thing to meet with
calamity among the waves of the deep; terrible too, if by
overloading a waggon you break the axle and the freight is spoiled.
Observe due measure; there is an appropriate time for all things.

663. **ἤματα**: acc. plur. of ἦμαρ (§24.4). Not found in Ionic: the
word may be part of the Achaean strand in epic (i.e. a metrically
useful archaism from mainland Gk.). It survives into Arc. in the set
phrase ἄματα πάντα.   **τροπάς**: see §46.6 for the short-vowel
acc. plur. (so also δεινάς 675).

664. **καματώδεος**: the suffix -ώδης, extracted from adjs. such as
εὐώδης (root *od-, 'smell' with lengthening in composition: κυνώπιδος 67 145), lost its original signification and became increasingly
productive in adj. derivation. See Chantraine (1933: 429–32). Gen.
sing. fem. with ὥρης.

665. **πέλεται**: equivalent to ἐστί (cf. ἔπλετο 66 116).
νῆα: < *νῆFα < *nāwm̥ (Att. ναῦν formed after the nom. sing.).
θνητοῖς: see on Ἀχαιοῖς 66 117.

666. **κανάξαις**: *κατ-Fάξαις (aor. opt. of κατ-άγνυμι) >
*καFFάξαις (assimilation) > κανάξαις with (Aeolic) vocalization of
w. The opt. with κε is 'potential' (dependent on a circumstance),
but here (as often, and also in Att.) virtually equivalent to a
fut.

668. **ἀθανάτων**: the word can only be accommodated in a
hexameter with metrical lengthening of the initial ἀ-.   **ἐθέλησιν**:

cf. μένησιν **66** 93.   **ὀλέσσαι**: built to a stem ὀλε-, the double σ being motivated by forms such as τελέσσαι (stem τελεσ-). This is observable in Lesb. (lit. and epigraphic) and Boe.

671. **πιθήσας**: aor. of πιθόμην (old aor. of πείθομαι): sigmatic form built with the stative marker ē (§24.1, and Palmer 1980: 302). Hexameters would not admit πιθόμενος.

672. **ἐλκέμεν**: cf. δωσέμεν **66** 117.   **ἐς ... τίθεσθαι**: tmesis (§24.6).

673. **ὅττι**: < *yod-kʷid, indef. relative. Cf. **17** 16 (Lesb.).   **πάλιν**: lengthening due to original w- in Ϝοικ-.

674. **ὀπωρινόν**: adj. built to ὀπώρη, 'following-summer': ὀπί (o-po-qo 2a) + ὥρη.

675. **δεινάς**: see on τροπάς 663.

676. **ὥρινε**: this and ἔθηκεν 677 are 'gnomic' aorists, expressing a timeless or general observation (cf. on **66** 93–5), and associated with generalizing τε.

678. **εἰαρινός**: metrical lengthening of ἐαρινός, built to ἔαρ (*wesr-, cf. Lat. *uernus* to *uēr*).

680. **ἐποίησεν**: gnomic aor. The use of -ν to lengthen a syllable (rather than prevent hiatus) is markedly rarer in Hes. than in Hom. (22%∶36%), which Janko (1982: 66) takes as a reflection of a mainland epic tradition where this feature was not part of the bards' own dialect.   **τόσσον**: cf. ὅσσα **66** 115.   **φανήηι**: aor. subj. (to ἐφάνην): the thematic -ηι replaces an earlier athem. short-vowel subj. *φανήει (κατάξει **20** 37): cf. 1 plur. forms such as στήομεν, where introduction of them. -ωμεν is prevented by metre. Found several times in Hom. (and contracted at *Il.* 9. 707 to φανῆι). All medieval MSS of Hesiod have φανείη (editors correct on the basis of the Homeric text). *φανήει itself looks secondary: before the replacement of the athem. endings in Gk. one could imagine a form *φανη-ε-τι (cf. Rix 1976: 71 on Hom. δῶσι, Skt. *dāti* < *deH₃-e-ti*).

681. **ἄμβατος**: ἀν (i.e. ἀνά) + verbal adj. βατός (stem as in βαίνω).

683. **αἴνημ(ι)**: athem. inflection of a vowel-stem verb (Ion. αἰνέω): §24.1. The 1 sing. of this type does not occur in Hom. (only the infin. and dual are well attested, though there are other 'ghost' forms: cf. ηὔδα **67** 155).

684. **τά**: demonstr. (anaphoric), 'those things'.

685. **ῥέζουσιν**: (Ϝ)ρέζω comes from *wṛg-yō via *Ϝράζω (replace-

ment of *a*- by *e*-vocalism on the analogy of aor. ἔϜερξα). There is a doublet (Ϝ)έρδω < *Ϝέρζω (with regular CsC > CC), which was backformed to aor. ἔϜερξα (cf. Ϝέργον). Orig. zero grade of the pres. stem is seen in Myc. 3 sing. *wo-ze* < *wr̥g-y-*.   **ἀϊδρίηισι**: ἀ(Ϝ)ιδρῖα is built to ἄϊδρι-ς with the suffix -ία. For the plur. cf. ἀτασθαλίηισιν **66** 104.

687. **ἄνωγα**: old perf. with pres. force. Attested only in Cyp. (ἄνωγον **8** 2), which suggests it may be part of the Achaean strand in epic. Preverb ἀν(ά) with a stem seen in the Att. imperf. ἦ < *ēg-t, 'he said' (root *H₁g-, as in Lat. *aiō* < *ag-yō).

688. **φρεσίν**: cf. φρασί **61** 8.

689. **νηυσίν**: cf. **66** 115.

690. **πλέω ... μείονα**: parallel older and younger comparatives (neut. plur. acc.): cf. §12, and *a-ro₂-a* **1** (a). For πλέω see on πλέας **17** 9.

691. **πόντου**: around two-thirds of the contracted gen. sing. forms cannot (as here) be resolved in *Works and Days* (Janko 1982: 54). Contrast Hom. κείνου **67** 149.

692. **ἄμαξαν**: from ἁμ- and ἀξ- (as in ἄξων, 'axle'). Aspirated (like ἅμα) in Attic, but not apparently elsewhere (uncertain aspiration is reflected in other compds. with copulative ἁ-/ἀ- < *sm̥-).

693. **φορτία μαυρωθείη**: perhaps from false division of φορτί᾽ ἀμαυρωθείη (the adj. is ἀμαυρός in *Odyssey*): but either form could be derivative.

IONIC ELEGY AND IAMBOS

69. Archilochos of Paros, frag. 196a *IEG* (*P. Köln* 58). From a papyrus (I–II cent. AD) published in 1974. Mid VII cent. BC. A seduction scene. Metre: epodic 'couplets' (*a* iambic trimeter, *b* dactylic hemiepes + iambic dimeter). ▶▶ Van Sickle (1976), Slings (1987), Van Sickle (1989).

«... εἰ δ᾽ ὦν ἐπείγεαι καί σε θυμὸς ἰθύει,
    ἔστιν ἐν ἡμετέρου ἣ νῦν μέγ᾽ ἱμείρε[ι γάμου
καλὴ τέρεινα παρθένος· δοκέω δέ μι[ν
5   εἶδος ἄμωμον ἔχειν· τὴν δὴ σὺ ποίη[σαι φίλην.»
τοσαῦτ᾽ ἐφώνει· τὴν δ᾽ ἐγὼ ἀνταμει[βόμην·
«Ἀμφιμεδοῦς θύγατερ, ἐσθλῆς τε καὶ [μακαρτάτης
γυναικός, ἣν νῦν γῆ κατ᾽ εὐρώεσσ᾽ ἔ[χει,
τ]έρψιές εἰσι θεῆς πολλαὶ νέοισιν ἀνδ[ράσιν

10 παρὲξ τὸ θεῖον χρῆμα· τῶν τις ἀρκέσε[ι·
    τ]αῦτα δ' ἐπ' ἡσυχίης εὖτ' ἂν μελανθῆ[ι– ‿ –
    ἐ]γώ τε καὶ σὺ σὺν θεῶι βουλεύσομεν.
    π]είσομαι ὥς με κέλεαι· πολλόν μ' ἐ[ποτρύνει πόθος.
    θρ]ιγκοῦ δ' ἔνερθε καὶ πυλέων ὑποφ[θάνειν
15 μ]ή τι μέγαιρε, φίλη· σχήσω γὰρ ἐς ποη[φόρους
    κ]ἠπους· τὸ δή νυν γνῶθι. Νεοβούλη[ν μὲν ὦν
    ἄ]λλος ἀνὴρ ἐχέτω· αἰαῖ, πέπειρα δ.[– ‿ –
    ἄν]θος δ' ἀπερρύηκε παρθενήϊον
    κ]αὶ χάρις ἣ πρὶν ἐπῆν· κόρον γὰρ οὐ κ[ατέσχε πω,
20 ἤβ]ης δὲ μέτρ' ἔφηνε μαινόλις γυνή.
    ἐς] κόρακας ἄπεχε· μὴ τοῦτ' ἐφοῖτ' ἀν]ὴρ φίλος·
    ὅ]πως ἐγὼ γυναῖκα τ[ο]ιαύτην ἔχων
    γεί]τοσι χάρμ' ἔσομαι· πολλὸν σὲ βούλο[μαι πάρος·
    σὺ] μὲν γὰρ οὔτ' ἄπιστος οὔτε διπλόη,
25 ἡ δ]ὲ μάλ' ὀξυτέρη· πολλοὺς δὲ ποιεῖτα[ι φίλους·
    δέ]δοιχ' ὅπως μὴ τυφλὰ κἀλιτήμερα
    σπ]ουδῆι ἐπειγόμενος τὼς ὥσπερ ἡ κ[ύων τέκω.»
    τοσ]αῦτ' ἐφώνευν· παρθένον δ' ἐν ἄνθε[σιν
    τηλ]εθάεσσι λαβὼν ἔκλινα· μαλθακῆι δ[έ μιν
30 χλαί]νηι καλύψας, αὐχέν' ἀγκάλης ἔχω[ν,
    δεί]ματι †παυ[σ]αμένην† τὼς ὥστε νέβρ[ον εἱλόμην
    μαζ]ῶν τε χερσὶν ἠπίως ἐφηψάμην
    ἧιπε]ρ ἔφηνε νέον ἥβης ἐπήλυσιν χρόα·
    ἅπαν τ]ε σῶμα καλὸν ἀμφαφώμενος
35 λευκ]ὸν ἀφῆκα μένος, ξανθῆς ἐπιψαύ[ων τριχός.

.. 'But if you are in a hurry, and your spirit drives you, there is at home a girl who is eager for [marriage], a pretty and delicate maiden. She seems a fine-looking creature to me: so make her your [beloved]!' Such were her words, and I answered her: 'Daughter of Amphimedo, that splendid and wise woman whom now the dank earth holds below: many are the pleasures that the goddess gives to young men, (10) beside the divine deed. One of these will suffice. These things you and I shall decide at our leisure with the god's help when [——] has grown dark. I shall do as you tell me. A great [desire drives] me. Do not begrudge me, beloved, to go as far as the cornice gates: I shall halt at the grassy gardens. Now, be sure of this: another man can have Neoboule. Oy veh! She [is] over-ripe, the flower of her maidenhood has perished, and the grace she once had. She [could never get] enough, (20) and now she has displayed the limits of her youth, crazed woman. To hell with her! May [a friend] never recommend this—that I should take such a woman to wife and be a laughing-stock to my neighbours. You are the one I have long preferred: you are neither faithless nor two-faced. Her ardour, on the other hand, is all too keen, and many are the [men friends] she makes. I am afraid that if I got carried that far by my excitement I would [give birth— like the bitch] to blind monsters.' Such were my words; and taking the girl I set her down amid the blooming flowers. (30) Covering her with a soft cloak and cradling her neck in my arm, I took hold of her as she hesitated [nervously] like a fawn, and caressed her breast gently with my hands ... the onset of her prime was revealed in the bloom of her skin. Stroking the beautiful girl [all over] I released my white force, lightly grazing her blonde [hair].

Note: The supplements adopted illustrate the general flow of the narrative, but are not, of course, the only possibilities.

2. **ὦν**: Ionic (e.g. Hdt.) and WGk. (οὖν in the text of Homer may be an Atticism): etymology uncertain.

3. **ἐν ἡμετέρου**: as in Hdt. (cf. *Od.* 2. 195, ἐς πατρός, sc. οἶκον).

4. **καλή**: the papyrus has κᾱλη (< καλϝή), the makron denoting the long vowel expected in Ionic (guaranteed by the metre at 34). **μιν**: cf. μιγ **21** 2.

5. **τήν**: pronominal. Archil. does not seem to use the article (cf. its extreme rarity in epic). [**φίλην**]: if correct, this illustrates the slippage between 'own' and 'beloved' (cf. on φίλος **66** 122).

6. **ἐγὼ_ἀνταμει[βόμην]**: written ἐγὼντ̄αμει[βόμην]. Note the epic-style absence of augment.

7. **Ἀμφιμεδοῦς**: for the morphology see λεχώι **51** 16.

8. **κατ'** ... **ἔ[χει]**: epic-style tmesis (§24.6). **εὐρώεσσ(α)**: for the form (§13) cf. *pe-ne-we-ta* **1** (a). An epic adj. of the underworld.

9. [**τ**]**έρψιες**: §32.4. **θεῆς**: gen. of θεά, a word found in Hom. (alongside θέαινα) and generally supposed to be Aeolic in origin (elsewhere ἡ θεός is normal). A ref. to Aphrodite.

10. **τὸ θεῖον χρῆμα**: Hesychius paraphrases ἔξω τῆς μίξεως, 'apart

from intercourse'. τό is apparently demonstr., 'that' (cf. on τήν 5); τῶν is anaphoric.

11. **ἐπ' ἡσυχίης**: an isolated spelling. The text of Archil. generally ignores Ionic psilosis (§31.6; cf. [δέ]δοιχ' ὅπως 26, ἐφηψάμην 32). **εὖτ(ε) ἄν**: Hom. locution. **μελανθῆ[ι]**: supplements include μοι γένυς, 'my beard', and various phrases meaning 'the evening'. 13. **κέλεαι**: cf. κέλοιτο 52 9. **πολλόν**: a mixed u-stem and thematic declension in class. Attic. In Hom. both types are found; the thematic decl. generally prevails in literary Ionic. 14. **[θρ]ιγκοῦ ... πυλέων**: hendiadys. θριγκός is a protective border of stones (or prickly bushes at Od. 14. 10) on top of a wall. πυλέων (with synizesis, §23.2) < πυλήων < πυλάων. 15. **σχήσω**: fut. built to the aor. stem -σχ- (zero grade of *segʰ-, pres. ἔχω), with the affix -η- (cf. πιθήσας 68 671). To end a journey, or (of ships) 'put in (at)'. **ποη[φόρους]**: for the reduction of the first syllable ποι- cf. ἐπιποεόντον 20 30. 16. **Νεοβούλη[ν]**: Archilochos' attacks on a girl called Neoboule (name implies 'changes her mind') are part of his poetic signature: elsewhere he complains that she jilted him. 17. **πέπειρα**: Hom. masc. πέπων, 'ripe' (of figs) > 'soft, bad' (of fighting-men). The fem. is analogical on inherited πίων : πίειρα (§24.4). **δ.[...]**: supplements include δὴ πέλει and similar (for which cf. ἔπλετο 66 116). 18. **ἀπερρύηκε**: perf. of ἀπο-ρρέω (root *sreu-), built to the old (pass.-intrans.) aor. ἐρρύην (affix -η- as in σχήσω 15). **παρθενήϊον**: in Ion. and other non-Att. dialects the suffix -ήϊος was productive and could be added to any stem (orig. a u-stem ending < *-ηϝ-ιος). 20. **[ἥβ]ης δὲ μέτρ' ἔφηνε**: if the supplement is correct, the phrase is modelled on the Hom. ἐπεί ῥ' ἥβης ἐρικύδεος ἵκετο μέτρον (Il. 12. 225), where μέτρον has a meaning close to 'peak, prime'. **μαινόλις**: see on μαινόλαι 74 (a) 18. 21. **[ἐς] κόρακας**: colloquial expression, attested in Athenian Old Comedy (and cf. Theognis 833, ἐν κοράκεσσι). **τοῦτ'**: papyrus has τοῦτο (scriptio plena). **ἐφοῖτ(ο)**: aor. opt. mid. of ἐφίημι (secondary thematized form); some editors read ἐφεῖτ' (the regular athem. form < *ἐ-ῑ-το). 22. **[ὅ]πως**: the forms familiar from Hom. are generally used by

Archil. (as opposed to E. Ion. ὅκως etc.): so also 26. The conjunction explains τοῦτ᾽ 21.

25. **μάλ(α)**: reinforces the change of subject in [ἡ δ]έ.

26. **ἀλιτήμερα**: missing or offending against (ἀλιτέσθαι) the day (ἡμέρη), so 'untimely born, monstrous'. In crasis with καί.

27. **ὥσπερ ἡ κ[ύων τέκω]**: a proverbial expression (a scholion on Ar. *Peace* 1079 has ἡ κύων σπεύδουσα τυφλὰ τίκτει). τώς (as at **15** 5) reinforces ὥσπερ.

28. **ἐφώνευν**: contraction of ἐφώνεον (§30.7). *IEG* restores the uncontracted form.

29. **[τηλ]εθάεσσι**: for adjs. of the form τηλεθάεις cf. εὐρώεσσα 8. A variation of the Hom. participial τηλεθάων (as at *Hom. Hymn* 7. 41, ἄνθεσι τηλεθάων): the analogy may explain the unexpected short ᾰ in τηλεθάεσσι (Risch 1975: 224). Stem as in θάλλω, τέθηλα, 'flourish' (τηλε-θα- by dissimilation from θηλε-θα-).

33. **ἐπήλυσιν**: taken here as the acc. sing. of 'approach, onset', in apposition to νέον χρόα.

34. **καλόν**: cf. καλή 4 for the long vowel. **ἀμφαφώμενος**: ἀφάω is a denom. to ἀφή, 'touch' (cf. ἅπτω < *ἄφ-γω).

70. Kallinos of Ephesos, frag. 1. 1–9 *IEG* (21 lines survive in a quotation by Stobaios). Mid VII cent. BC. A call to arms: the danger is probably invading Kimmerians from southern Russia. Metre: elegiac couplets. Also in Campbell (1982: 8). ▶▶ Verdenius (1972), Bowie (1990).

> μέχρις τέο κατάκεισθε; κότ᾽ ἄλκιμον ἕξετε θυμόν,
>   ὦ νέοι; οὐδ᾽ αἰδεῖσθ᾽ ἀμφιπερικτίονας
> ὧδε λίην μεθιέντες; ἐν εἰρήνηι δὲ δοκεῖτε
> 4   ἧσθαι, ἀτὰρ πόλεμος γαῖαν ἅπασαν ἔχει
> . . .
> καί τις ἀποθνήσκων ὕστατ᾽ ἀκοντισάτω.
> τιμῆέν τε γάρ ἐστι καὶ ἀγλαὸν ἀνδρὶ μάχεσθαι
>   γῆς πέρι καὶ παίδων κουριδίης τ᾽ ἀλόχου
> 8 δυσμενέσιν· θάνατος δὲ τότ᾽ ἔσσεται, ὁππότε κεν δή
>   Μοῖραι ἐπικλώσωσ᾽. . .

For how long are you going to lie idle ? When will you have a warlike spirit, young men? Do you not feel shame before the people who live around you, living such an over-relaxed life? You think you recline in peace, but war has a grip on the whole country [. . .] and a dying man should throw his spear one last time. An honourable and glorious thing it is for a man to fight for his country, his children, and his wife against enemies. Death will come whenever the Fates ordain . . .

1. **μέχρις**: final -ς apparently to close the syllable: in Hom. μέχρι and ἄχρι are used before cons., with final -ς only before a vowel. **τέο**: with synizesis (spelled τεῦ in the MSS), Att. του. The regularized declension of τίνος etc. is built to the old acc. τιν (the original indef. stem must have alternated *k^wi-/*k^we-). **κότ(ε)**: Kallinos uses E. Ion. κ-forms (as opposed to Hom. π-forms: cf. ὅπως **68** 22): §31.7.

2. **ἀμφιπερικτίονας**: one of only two words in the surviving text which is not found in Homer.

4. One or more lines has dropped out of the text.

6. **τιμῆεν**: for the form (§13) cf. *pe-ne-we-ta* **1** (a). **τε . . . καί**: copulative: joins τιμῆεν and ἀγλαόν.

7. **κουριδίης**: adj. derived from κούρη, implying 'pertaining to [respectable] girls', and thus making clear that the consort in question is legitimate (i.e. the mother of legitimate children), rather than a concubine. **ἀλόχου**: bedmate, from ἀ- (*$sm̥$-) + λοχ- (cf. λέχος, 'bed').

8. **δυσμενέσιν**: cf. ἐποίησεν **68** 680 for metrical use of moveable -*n*. As Janko (1982: 67) notes, Ionian poets use this device freely: its scarcity in Tyrtaios points to his Laconian background. **ὁππότε**: an epicism, of Aeolic origin (< *yot-k^wo-). Att.-Ion. ὁπότε. Contrast κότε 1. **κεν**: an epicism (cf. **66** 110).

71. Tyrtaios of Sparta, frag. 11. 1–14 *IEG*. Quoted by Stobaios. Mid VII cent. BC. A call for steadfastness in the wars to subjugate Messenia. Metre: elegiac couplets. Also in Campbell (1982: 9). ▶▶ Dover (1964: 190–5), Murray (1993: 159–80).

> ἀλλ᾽, Ἡρακλῆος γὰρ ἀνικήτου γένος ἐστέ,
> θαρσεῖτ᾽· οὔπω Ζεὺς αὐχένα λοξὸν ἔχει·
> μηδ᾽ ἀνδρῶν πληθὺν δειμαίνετε, μηδὲ φοβεῖσθε,
> ἰθὺς δ᾽ ἐς προμάχους ἀσπίδ᾽ ἀνὴρ ἐχέτω,
> 5 ἐχθρὴν μὲν ψυχὴν θέμενος, θανάτου δὲ μελαίνας

κῆρας <ὁμῶς> αὐγαῖς ἠελίοιο φίλας.
ἴστε γὰρ ὡς Ἄρεος πολυδακρύου ἔργ᾽ ἀΐδηλα,
    εὖ δ᾽ ὀργὴν ἐδάητ᾽ ἀργαλέου πολέμου,
καὶ μετὰ φευγόντων τε διωκόντων τ᾽ ἐγέ<νε>σθε
10   ὦ νέοι, ἀμφοτέρων δ᾽ ἐς κόρον ἠλάσατε.
οἳ μὲν γὰρ τολμῶσι παρ᾽ ἀλλήλοισι μένοντες
    ἔς τ᾽ αὐτοσχεδίην καὶ προμάχους ἰέναι,
παυρότεροι θνῄσκουσι, σαοῦσι δὲ λαὸν ὀπίσσω·
    τρεσσάντων δ᾽ ἀνδρῶν πᾶσ᾽ ἀπόλωλ᾽ ἀρετή.

Come, take courage: for you are the race of Herakles the undefeated. Zeus has not turned his back on us yet. Nor should you fear massed ranks of men, nor take to flight; but let each man drive his shield straight towards the front fighters, (5) considering his own life hateful, and the black fates of death as dear as the rays of the sun. You are familiar with the destructive action of Ares, bringer of tears, and you have learned well the temper of toilsome war. (10) You have fled with the pursued and chased with the pursuers, young men, and had your fill of both. Those who have the courage to stand by each other and engage hand-to-hand in the front ranks—fewer among them perish, and they protect the soldiers behind them. But there is no good in men who run away.

1. **Ἡρακλῆος**: < *-κλεϜεσ-ος.
2. **λοξόν**: aslant, at an angle: a head-movement apparently implying disfavour. Perhaps a proverbial expression.
3. **φοβεῖσθε**: concrete sense (be put to flight), as in Hom.
6. **ἠελίοιο**: the uncontracted stem ἠελι- is necessary in dactylic metre. The epic (Aeolic) gen. ending is used freely by Tyrt. (very rare in Archil.).
8. **ἐδάητ(ε)**: aor. stem ἐδάην, 'I know, I have learned', to which a factitive pres. διδάσκω was formed.
10. **ἠλάσατε**: intrans., 'push up against'. Has a colloquial flavour (not apparently a feature of epic language).
12. **αὐτοσχεδίην**: for the root *segʰ- of σχεδόν, 'near' cf. σχήσω 69 15; αὐτο- reinforces the notion of 'close at hand'.
13. **σαοῦσι**: σαόω is a denom. vb. to σά(Ϝ)ος (Hom. aor. σαῶσαι). Att. σώιζω is back-formed to the contracted aor. σῶσαι.   **ὀπίσσω**: built to ὀπί (cf. *o-po-qo* 2a): the alternation ὀπίσσω ~ ὀπίσω derives

from *opi-ty-ō (suffix *-ti-* as in ὅσος, and cf. Lat. *tot* < *toti, etc.). Final -ω may be an old 'directive' (cf. **67** 159 ὧδε).
14. **τρεσσάντων**: a specifically Laconian term (see e.g. Hdt. 7. 231) for a deserter in battle (ptcpl. of τρέω): here with the epic licence -σσ- (on the analogy of dental-stem verbs). **ἀρετή**: in a famous excerpt (12 *IEG*) Tyrtaios discusses competing definitions of ἀρετή, and argues that bravery in battle is the true criterion.

72. Semonides of Amorgos, *On Women* 71–91 (7 *IEG*). Quoted by Stobaios. Late VII or late VI cent. BC. Part of a poem which classifies women in zoomorphic categories (mostly negative). Metre: iambic trimeters. Also in Campbell (1982: 13). ▶️ Lloyd-Jones (1975), Hubbard (1994).

> τὴν δ᾽ ἐκ πιθήκου· τοῦτο δὴ διακριδὸν
> Ζεὺς ἀνδράσιν μέγιστον ὤπασεν κακόν.
> αἴσχιστα μὲν πρόσωπα· τοιαύτη γυνὴ
> εἶσιν δι᾽ ἄστεος πᾶσιν ἀνθρώποις γέλως.
> 75 ἐπ᾽ αὐχένα βραχεῖα· κινεῖται μόγις·
> ἄπυγος, αὐτόκωλος. ἆ τάλας ἀνὴρ
> ὅστις κακὸν τοιοῦτον ἀγκαλίζεται.
> δήνεα δὲ πάντα καὶ τρόπους ἐπίσταται
> ὥσπερ πίθηκος· οὐδέ οἱ γέλως μέλει·
> 80 οὐδ᾽ ἄν τιν᾽ εὖ ἔρξειεν, ἀλλὰ τοῦτ᾽ ὁρᾶι
> καὶ τοῦτο πᾶσαν ἡμέρην βουλεύεται,
> ὅκως τί χὦς μέγιστον ἔρξειεν κακόν.
> τὴν δ᾽ ἐκ μελίσσης· τήν τις εὐτυχεῖ λαβών·
> κείνηι γὰρ οἴηι μῶμος οὐ προσιζάνει,
> 85 θάλλει δ᾽ ὑπ᾽ αὐτῆς κἀπαέξεται βίος,
> φίλη δὲ σὺν φιλέοντι γηράσκει πόσει,
> τεκοῦσα καλὸν κὠνομάκλυτον γένος.
> κἀριπρεπὴς μὲν ἐν γυναιξὶ γίγνεται
> πάσηισι, θείη δ᾽ ἀμφιδέδρομεν χάρις.
> 90 οὐδ᾽ ἐν γυναιξὶν ἥδεται καθημένη,
> ὅκου λέγουσιν ἀφροδισίους λόγους.

And another woman (Zeus created) from a monkey: this is by far the greatest evil Zeus has bestowed on men. Her face is repulsive: such a woman, as she makes her way through the town, is an object of everybody's mockery. (75) She is short in the neck, and moves with difficulty; she has no buttocks—she is all legs. Ah, wretched is the man who embraces such a mischief. She knows all manner of tricks and cunning ways, just like a monkey; nor does mockery worry her. (80) She will do no one a good turn, but looks to this, and considers this all day long: how to do the worst harm she can. And another woman (Zeus created) from a bee: the man who gets her is lucky. Upon her alone blame does not alight, (85) and under her the household flourishes and increases, and she grows old with her husband in mutual affection, and gives birth to a fine and famous brood. She is pre-eminent among all women, and a divine grace surrounds her. (90) Nor does she take pleasure in sitting with the women where they talk about sex.

71. **διακριδόν**: advb. formed to διακρίνω, 'distinguish'. Found in Hom. and Hdt.

72. **ὤπασεν**: epic verb.

74. **ἄστεος**: uncontracted gen. sing. < *ἄστεϝ-ος.   **ἀνθρώποις**: one of only two instances of dat. plur. -οις in Semon. Its rarity in Ionian iambic has tempted scholars to emend the text.

76. **αὐτόκωλος**: αὐτό- attached to a noun stem often means 'possessing the properties [of the noun itself] to an extreme degree'. In other cases it may imply reflexive action (esp. with a verbal stem: e.g. αὐτοδαής, 'self-taught'), autonomy, or a personal (perhaps possessive) relationship.

77. **ἀγκαλίζεται**: denom. formed to ἀγκάλη, 'curve of the arms' (cf. **69** 30).

78. **δήνεα**: with synizesis of εα (§23.2). An epic word, plural only.

79. **οὐδέ οἱ**: hiatus owing to the original presence of *ϝ-. Digamma is almost always observed in this pronoun in Greek poetry, even when ignored in all other words.

80. **ἔρξειεν**: see on ῥέζουσιν **68** 685.   **τοῦτ'**: one MS has τοῦθ' (cf. ὡς **66** 93).

82. **ὅκως**: E. Ionic (cf. **70** 1 κότε): §31.7.   **χὡς**: i.e. κ', an epic modal particle of Aeolic origin (all MSS): §36.7. West in *IEG* prints κὡς, which doubtless reflects Semonides' phonology more accurately (cf. τοῦτ' above).   **ἔρξειεν**: the opt. is influenced by the opt. in 80 (in spite of the primary tense of the main vb.).

84. **προσιζάνει**: ἰζάνω < *si-sd-an-, a reduplicated pres. formed to *sed- (cf. ἕζετο **67** 136). Intrans. 'sit, perch on' (usu. compounded) is found in epic through classical Att.

85. **κἀπαέξεται**: ἐπ-αέξεται (in crasis with καί). The epic form ἀ(F)έξω reflects *H₂weg-. Att.-Ion. αὔξω (*H₂ ewg-) is built on a different form of the root (cf. Lat. *augeō*).

86. **φιλέοντι**: with εο in synizesis (the MSS give φιλεῦντι): §30.7.

87. **κᾱλόν**: cf. καλή **69** 4.

88. **κάριπρεπής**: < ἀρι- (intensive particle, in crasis with καί) + πρεπής ('distinguished, outstanding', from πρέπω). A Homeric word.

89. **πάσῃσι**: §32.14 for the dat. plur.

73. Hipponax of Ephesos. Late VI cent. BC. H. Degani, *Hipponax* (Teubner, 1983). Appeals to Hermes, parodying traditional prayer form. His characteristic metre is the choliambic ('limping iambic') trimeter, in which the penultimate syllable is long. Also in Campbell (1982: 8). ▶▶ Degani (1984).

(a) Degani fr. 1–2 (3–3a *IEG*).

ἔβωσε Μαίης παῖδα, Κυλλήνης πάλμυν

. . .

«Ἑρμῆ κυνάγχα, μηιονιστὶ Κανδαῦλα,
φωρῶν ἑταῖρε, δεῦρό μοι σκαπερδεῦσαι.»

He shouted out, calling on the son of Maia, the Lord of Kyllene . . . 'Hermes dog-strangler—Kandaulas in Lydian—companion of thieves, come here and help me out!'

1. **ἔβωσε**: Ion. contraction of ἔ-βοα-σε. The sense 'call on, shout for' is post-Hom. (cf. Hdt. 8. 92, βώσας τὸν Θεμιστοκλέα ἐπεκερτόμησε . . .). Not a normal word for calling on a god, so may imply a difficult or undignified situation.   **πάλμυν**: a Lydian word which the Greeks seemed to have been familiar with (attested in a fragment of Aesch., and as the name of a Phrygian ally of the Trojans at *Il.* 13. 792). See Gusmani (1964), s.v. *qaλmλu-*.

2. **κυνάγχα**: voc. of κυν-άγχης. The 'dog-strangler' was the god who kept the dogs quiet while the thief was at work.   **μηιονιστί**:

Maionia is the Hom. term for Lydia. An advb. formed to μηιονίς (a fem. derivative in -ιδ- denoting either a female member or the territory of a particular group): cf. Hom. μεγαλωστί, Hdt. ὀνομαστί, etc. Thus Ἀττικιστί in V cent. Attic, perhaps an import from Ionic (cf. on **87** 92). **Κανδαύλα**: Kandaules is a Lydian king at Hdt. 1. 7, though Hdt. says the Greeks call him Myrsilos (an old Anatolian name *Mursilis* adopted by several Hittite kings). The first element of *Kandaules* has traditionally been connected with Gk. κυν-, Lat. *can*-, 'dog' (so Oettinger 1995, who analyses the second element as IE *teuH₂*-, be strong'); however, as an onomastic element *kan*- is better interpreted as the preverb seen in Lat. *com*- (so Schürr 2000): thus 'all-powerful' rather than 'having power over dogs'. This would make the regnal title easier to understand; but in a bilingual context the word-play still works, as Hippon. may have been deliberately punning on a Lydian word **kan*- (or similar) meaning 'dog' (I owe this suggestion to Craig Melchert).

3. **σκαπερδεῦσαι**: glossed συμμαχῆσαι in the Byzantine source of this line (John Tzetzes). Greek sources derive it from a noun σκαπέρδα, a game similar to a tug-of-war (see Oettinger 1995: 45 for a derivation from the Lydian verb 'to steal').

(b) **Degani fr. 42 (32 *IEG*).**

> Ἑρμῆ, φίλ᾽ Ἑρμῆ, Μαιαδεῦ, Κυλλήνιε,
> ἐπεύχομαί τοι, κάρτα γὰρ κακῶς ῥιγῶ
> καὶ βαμβαλύζω . . .
> δὸς χλαῖναν Ἱππώνακτι καὶ κυπασσίσκον
> 5 καὶ σαμβαλίσκα κἀσκερίσκα καὶ χρυσοῦ
> στατῆρας ἑξήκοντα τοὐτέρου τοίχου.

Hermes, dear Hermes, son of Maia, Kyllenian, I beg you—because I'm really freezing and my teeth are chattering . . . give a cloak to Hipponax, and a tunic and slippers and little furry boots—and sixty gold staters from the other side of the wall.

1. **φίλ᾽ Ἑρμῆ**: also at Ar. *Clouds* 1478, where a scholiast says: 'This is what thieves used to say to Hermes when they had been caught and were being punished, begging him to come and help them.' **Μαιαδεῦ**: the form of this matronymic is strange: apparently a comic version of the expected Μαιάδης. The combination of suffixes -δ-

(patronymic, but also diminutive) and -ευς is relatively rare (Chantraine 1933: 363): mostly of small animals (ἀλωπεκιδεύς Ar. *Peace* 1067) and often in comedy.

2. **κάρτα**: Ionic advb. (Att. μάλα, σφόδρα).

3. **βαμβαλύζω**: onomatopoeic.

4–5. **κυπασσίσκον** etc.: these terms are diminutives, of κύπασσις, σάμβαλον (σάνδαλον), and ἀσκέρα. All look like borrowings from a non-Greek source.

6. **τούτέρου τοίχου**: the general sense at any rate is clear, given the earlier appeal to Hermes as φωρῶν ἑταῖρε.

AEOLIC MONODY

74. Sappho of Lesbos. Late VII–early VI cent. BC. Text: Voigt (1971). Also in Page (1955), Campbell (1982), Hutchinson (2001). The two poems are in Sapphic stanzas. ▶▶ Hamm (1957), West (1970*a*), Hooker (1977), Bowie (1981).

(a) Fr. 1 (Voigt): quoted by Dionysius of Halicarnassus (with fragmentary witness from papyrus P. Oxy. 2288, published 1951).

> ποικιλόθρον᾽ ἀθανάτ᾽ Ἀφρόδιτα,
> παῖ Δίος δολόπλοκε, λίσσομαί σε,
> μή μ᾽ ἄσαισι μηδ᾽ ὀνίαισι δάμνα,
> 4 πότνια, θῦμον·
> ἀλλὰ τυίδ᾽ ἔλθ᾽, αἴ ποτα κἀτέρωτα
> τὰς ἔμας αὔδας ἀίοισα πήλοι
> ἔκλυες, πάτρος δὲ δόμον λίποισα
> 8 χρύσιον ἦλθες
> ἄρμ᾽ ὑπασδεύξαισα· κάλοι δέ σ᾽ ἆγον
> ὦκεες στροῦθοι περὶ γᾶς μελαίνας
> πύκνα δίννεντες πτέρ᾽ ἀπ᾽ ὠράνω_αἴθε-
> 12 ρος διὰ μέσσω·
> αἶψα δ᾽ ἐξίκοντο· σὺ δ᾽, ὦ μάκαιρα,
> μειδιαίσαισ᾽ ἀθανάτωι προσώπωι
> ἤρε᾽ ὄττι δηὖτε πέπονθα κὤττι
> 16 δηὖτε κάλημμι,
> κὤττι μοι μάλιστα θέλω γένεσθαι
> μαινόλαι θύμωι· τίνα δηὖτε πείθω

ἄψ] σ᾽ ἀγην ἐς Ϝὰν φιλότατα; τίς σ᾽, ὦ
20   Ψάπφ᾽, ἀδικήει;
καὶ γὰρ αἰ φεύγει, ταχέως διώξει,
αἰ δὲ δῶρα μὴ δέκετ᾽, ἀλλὰ δώσει,
αἰ δὲ μὴ φίλει, ταχέως φιλήσει
24   κωὐκ ἐθέλοισα.
ἔλθε μοι καὶ νῦν, χαλέπαν δὲ λῦσον
ἐκ μερίμναν, ὄσσα δέ μοι τέλεσσαι
θῦμος ἰμέρρει, τέλεσον, σὺ δ᾽ αὔτα
28   σύμμαχος ἔσσο.

19. Ϝὰν Edmonds: σὰν MSS and Voigt   20. ἀδικήει: ἀδίκησι
Voigt

Immortal Aphrodite on your richly wrought throne, daughter of
Zeus, weaver of wiles: I pray you, lady, do not crush my heart with
distress or with anguish; (5) but come hither, if ever at another
time you heard my voice from afar and gave ear to it, and came (to
me), leaving your father's golden house, yoking your chariot; and
beautiful (10) swift sparrows drew you over the dark earth, rapidly
beating their wings, from the sky through the mid-air; quickly
they arrived. And you, blessed one, with a smile on your immortal
face, (15) asked what was wrong with me now, and why I was
calling, and what exactly I desired for myself in the madness of my
heart: 'Who am I to persuade now to take you back to her
friendship? (20) Who is doing you wrong, Sappho? Indeed, if she
flees, she will soon pursue; if she refuses gifts, she will yet give
them; if she does not love, soon she will love even against her will.'
(25) Come to me now also, and release (me) from harsh anxieties;
and what my heart yearns to fulfil, fulfil (it), and be yourself my
helper in the battle.

1. **ποικιλόθρον᾽**: the traditional interpretation (here translated)
takes the second element as θρόνος. Another possibility is θρόνα
(neut. plur.), meaning 'flowers embroidered onto fabric' (cf. *Il.* 22.
441, θρόνα ποικίλ᾽ ἔπασσε): the adj. would refer to richly embroidered
robes.   **ἀθανάτ᾽**: the first syllable lengthened on an epic model.
Ἀφρόδιτᾰ: ancient grammarians, referring to this passage, cite a
short voc. ending (peculiar to Lesbian) in *a*-stem proper nouns.

3. **ὀνίαισι**: Lesb. *a*-stem dat. plur. (§32.14): the plur. perhaps under

epic influence (cf. ἀτασθαλίῃσιν **66** 104). The etymology of ἀνία/ὀνία is unclear: for Lesb. ὀν corresponding to Att.-Ion. ἀν(ά) §28.9. **δάμνᾱ**: imper., nasal infix stem (< *dm-n-eH₂).

5. **τυῖδ(ε)**: cf. hόπυι **38** 14 (Sappho also uses δεῦρυ in invocation to Aphrodite, fr. 2.1). **ποτα κἀτέρωτα**: -τα marks temporal adverbs in Lesb., vs. Att. -τε and WGk. -κα (§40.7). ἐτέρωτα (crasis with καί) is built on *ἐτέρω (for final -ω cf. ὀπίσσω **71** 13).

6. **ἀίοισα**: ptcpl., §34.11 (poetic verb, probably an old aor. stem: Hom. ἀίω, etc. has been recharacterized with present endings). **πήλοι**: the Hom. form πήλου points to orig. **kʷel-*.

8. **χρύσιον**: the adj. may go with ἄρμα. For adjs. in -ιος/-εος cf. on λιθίας **11** 21. Hom. χρύσε(ι)ον shows the suffix *-*eyos*, which contracted to -οῦς in Att.

9. **ὐπασδεύξαισα**: ὐπα- in Sapph. and Alk. (epigraphically in NW Gk.) perhaps on the analogy of κατα- (but cf. ὐπόδικον at **17** 5). Lesb. literary texts generally have original word-internal *Z* spelled out *ΣΔ*. This is most likely a later editorial decision made for the sake of orthographic clarity, since *Z* was also used in Lesb. for *dj* (or its reflex) < δι- (as in ζά for διά). Using -*ΣΔ*- was thus a useful reminder of the original phonological value of the cluster (which in the koiné had become [z]). It does not, therefore, imply that VI cent. Lesbian *Z* had a different value from contemporary Attic. For -αισα cf. ἀίοισα 6.

10. **ὤκεες**: < *ὤκεϝες. The word is epic and poetic. **περί**: ὑπέρ, 'over' may have been alien to Lesb. (Hodot 1990: 149): cf. οὐπέρ **15** 4 for the functional overlap. **γᾶς μελαίνᾱς**: re-shaping of a phrase found in Hom. epic (γαῖα μέλαινα, *Il.* 2. 699).

11. **δίννεντες**: an athem. pres. ptcpl. (§24.1). Hyper-Aeolic spelling, on the model of e.g. κρίννω (< **krin-y-*). The first syllable is long, so δίνεντες should be read. A poetic form (< **dinw-*): evidence suggests that post-consonantal *w dropped without compensatory lengthening in Lesb. (for the phrase cf. *Od.* 2. 151, ἐπιδινηθέντε τιναξάσθην πτερὰ πυκνά). For the ending, MSS give -ῆντες (would be the result of an analogical undoing of Osthoff's Law §23.3), -εῦντες (by confusion with Hom. δινεύω). **ὠράνω**: initial long syllable is guaranteed, but ὀρράνω would be expected in Lesb. (Blümel 1982: 102). ὀρρ- might have been replaced by ὠρ- by later copyists (esp. if written *OP*- originally). Cf. Hooker (1977: 84–6), and ὀράνω **75** (a)1.

12. **διά**: the only instance in Lesb. poetry where the word is scanned with two syllables (elsewhere the final -α is elided, or the word is written ζά, for which cf. on ὐπασδεύξαισα 9). **μέσσω**: the expected treatment in Lesb. of palatalized *t^h (Sappho also uses μέσος when metrically convenient, however): §23.8.

14. **μειδιαίσαισ(α)**: aor. ptcpl. Final -αισα < *-antya (§34.11), but αι in μειδιαι- is unmotivated and is probably a hyper-Aeolic spelling of μειδιᾱ- (cf. Palmer 1980: 115).

15. **ἦρε(ο)**: 2 sing. imperf. to *ἔρομαι (pres. indic. Att. ἐρέω, Ion. εἴρομαι). **ὄττι**: cf. **17** 16. **δηὖτε**: δὴ αὖτε. **κὦττι**: καὶ ὄττι.

16. **κάλημμι**: Att. καλέω (§24.1). The double -μμ- may be a hyper-Aeolic spelling (on the analogy of ἔμμι < *es-mi, etc.): but it is odd that it occurs only after η. No example of the 1 sing. active of a vowel-stem verb is attested epigraphically: it seems to have been recharacterized with an 'athematic' ending -μι (to make the first person morphology clearer): the rest of the paradigm may have had regular thematic endings, however. See also ἀδικήει 20.

18. **μαινόλαι**: dat. of μαινόλᾱς, 'maddened', a masc. adj. formed to pres. stem μαίν- (for the suffix *-ol-, relatively rare in Gk., cf. Lat. *crēdulus* formed to *crēdō*). The adjectival nature of what looks like a noun derives from the original participial function of the suffix (productive in other IE languages). Cf. fem. μαινόλις **69** 20.

19. **[ἄψ] σ' ἄγην ἐς Fάν**: a difficult line to reconstruct. I print Fάν for the sake of convenience (cf. fr. 164, τὸν Fὸν παῖδα κάλει, quoted by Apollonios Dyskolos in *On Pronouns*). Evidence indicates that *w- had dropped from Lesb. by Sappho's time, but it was part of the poetic tradition she inherited. See Parca (1982) and Hutchinson ad loc. for a discussion of the possibilities.

20. **Ψάπφ(οι)**: voc. (for the morphology cf. λεχώι **51** 16). Sappho spells her name (here and fr. 94.5) with Ψ-, other Greek writers with Σ- (incl. Alkaios fr. 384, where it is metrically guaranteed). It has been suggested that she used a variety of 'sampi' (cf. **20** A22) which was similar in shape to, and later mistaken for, *psi* (but see Liberman 1988). **ἀδικήει**: sources are confused (only αδικη is clear). Sappho elsewhere has ποθήω (with η presumably imported from the aor. and fut.). Some editors print athem. ἀδίκησι for the sake of consistency with κάλημμι (§24.1). But: (a) the analogical interference between athematic, thematic and vowel-stem inflection in Lesb.

makes such predictions hazardous; (b) the epigraphic data suggest that the form consistent with κάλημμι would be ἀδίκει; and (c) Sappho's complex literary language is in any case more than a reflection of the vernacular. See also φίλει 23.

22. **δέκετ(αι)**: for δεκ- cf. on ἡυποδεκόμενος **44** 3.

23. **φίλει**: all *e*-stem verbs in Sappho (apart from ἀδικήει 20) have this ending. Either borrowed from C-stem thematic verbs, or (Hodot 1990: 195) formed analogously to the 3 plur. φίλεισι < *φίλεντι.

24. **κωὖκ**: καὶ οὐκ.   **ἐθέλοισα**: but θέλω 17 (the normal form in Sappho and Alkaios). In E. Ionic θέλω is found in inscriptions and the Iambic poets, while epic has ἐθέλω. This phrase is reminiscent of *Od.* 2. 50, οὐκ ἐθελούσηι (Penelope).

25. **χαλέπᾱν**: gen. plur. (§30.2).

26. **ὄσσα**: cf. **66** 115, and μέσσω 12 above.   **τέλεσσαι**: reflects the analogical restoration of -σσ- in *s*-stems (aor. and fut.) which must have been under way at this period (Morpurgo Davies 1976). τέλεσον 27 is the older form (showing simplification of inherited *ss*): see on ὀππάτεσσι (b)11. Inscriptions of the IV cent. and later show -σσ- in *s*-stem verbs, and confusion -σ-/-σσ- in other stems.

27. **ἰμέρρει**: from *ἱμέρ-y- (§23.7).

28. **ἔσσο**: 2 sing. imper. of 'be', as in epic. Built on 3 sg. ἔστω with a 2 sing. ending added (the initial vowel of ἴσθι is anomalous).

(b) Fr. 31 (Voigt), quoted by 'Longinus' in *On the Sublime.*

> φαίνεταί μοι κῆνος ἴσος θέοισιν
> ἔμμεν᾽ ὤνηρ, ὄττις ἐνάντιός τοι
> ἰσδάνει καὶ πλάσιον ἆδυ φωνεί-
> 4 σας ὑπακούει
>
> καὶ γελαίσας ἰμέροεν, τό μ᾽ ἦ μὰν
> καρδίαν ἐν στήθεσιν ἐπτόαισεν·
> ὡς γὰρ <ἔς> σ᾽ ἴδω βρόχε᾽ ὤς με φώναι-
> 8 σ᾽ οὐδὲν ἔτ᾽ εἴκει,
>
> ἀλλὰ κὰμ μὲν γλῶσσα ἔαγε, λέπτον
> δ᾽ αὔτικα χρῶι πῦρ ὑπαδεδρόμακεν,
> ὀππάτεσσι δ᾽ οὐδὲν ὄρημμ᾽, ἐπιρρόμ-
> 12 βεισι δ᾽ ἄκουαι,
> κὰδ δέ μ᾽ ἴδρως κακχέεται, τρόμος δὲ

παῖσαν ἄγρει, χλωροτέρα δὲ ποίας
ἔμμι, τεθνάκην δ' ὀλίγω 'πιδεύης
16   φαίνομ' ἔμ' αὔτ[αι.
ἀλλὰ πὰν τόλματον, ἐπεὶ . . .

7–8. φώναισ': φώνησ' Voigt   11–12. ἐπιρρόμβεισι: ἐπιβρόμεισι
Voigt   13. κὰδ δέ: †ἔκαδε† Voigt; MSS †εκαδε† μ' ἴδρως ψῦχρος
κακχέεται (Longinus cod. P); ἀ δέ μ' ἴδρως κακὸς χέεται (*Anecdota
Oxoniensia*)

That man seems to me to be the equal of the gods, the one who
sits facing you and listens close by to your sweet voice and lovely
laughter, which sets my heart fluttering in my breast; for when
I look at you even for a moment—then I can no longer say a
word: but my tongue is fractured and at once a subtle flame runs
beneath my skin, I see nothing at all with my eyes, and my ears
buzz: sweat pours down me and I start to tremble, I am paler
than grass and to myself I seem close to death. But everything is
endurable, since . . .

2. **ἔμμεν(αι)**: athematic infin. (§36.3). Apart from ἔμμεναι, the
ending -μεναι is attested epigraphically only in δόμεναι, θέμεναι (i.e.
monosyllabic root aorists: cf. τίθην, δίδων): it is thus more restricted
in historical Lesb. than in the athem. infin. ascribed (by ancient
and modern commentators) to literary 'Aeolic' (e.g. in the epic
Kunstsprache).   **ὤνηρ**: ὁ ἄνηρ. The def. article, extremely rare in
Lesb. poetry, is here accounted for by the demonstr. adj. (Lobel 1927:
§22).   **ὄττις**: cj. (ὄστις MSS): other fragments of Sappho and
Alkaios give the stem ὀττ- (generalized from the neuter) throughout
the paradigm; in epigraphic texts both elements are inflected
(Blümel 1982: 269).
3. **ἰσδάνει**: cj. (ἰζάνει MSS). See on ὑπασδεύξαισα (a)9.
φωνείσᾱς: pres. ptcpl. (gen. sing., fem.) of an *e*-stem verb, restored
(ἀδύφων· σαῖς and φωνούσας MSS). The cj. reflects athem. *φωνεντ-
ya- (§24.1, but see on φώναισ' 7): §34.11.
5. **ἱμέροεν**: for the form (§13) cf. *pe-ne-we-ta* 1 (a).   **τό μ(οι)**:
relative (referring to the sound of the voice and the laughter): §32.13.
6. **στήθεσιν**: from inherited *στήθεσ-σι by simplification of -ss-.
In Sappho and Alkaios the *s*-stem dat. plur. is always -εσι (for -εσσι
in other C-stems, and the epic doublet -εσσι/-εσι, see §36.4 and

ὀππάτεσσι 11). **ἐπτόαισεν**: aor. of a vowel-stem verb, apparently an *a*-stem here (cf. μειδιαίσαισ᾽ (a)14), though generally in Gk. an *e*-stem. MSS give ἐπτόασεν: the hyper-Aeolic reading ἐπτόαισεν is found at Sapph. 22.14 (papyrus). For the instantaneous aorist cf. διελέξατο **66** 122.

7. **ἴδω**: subj., without modal particle. **ἐς**: added by modern editors *metri causa*. **βρόχε(α)**: neut. plur. (acc.), adverbial. Syllabic *$\mathring{r}$ gives *or*/*ro* in Lesb., Thess., and Boe. (§34.1): IE *$m\mathring{r}g^{h}u$-(cf. Lat. *brevis* < *$mreg^{h}u$-*i*-). **φώναισ(αι)**: aor. infin. A hyper-Aeolic spelling (φωνας MSS), for which cf. ἐπτόαισεν 6. (inscriptions, some 200 years later, give an aor. infin. in -ησαι to *e*-stem verbs). Forssman (1966: 80 f.) has argued that φώνασ᾽ is the right reading here, given the presence of φώνασε (an *a*-stem) in Pindar. In this case ἀδύφων· σαῖς 3 could be read (ἆδυ) φωναίσας.

8. **εἴκει**: impersonal, in the sense of Att. παρείκει, 'is open, is possible'.

9. **κάμ**: i.e. κατ (§23.4), preverb to ἔαγε (for tmesis see §24.6). The alternative reading ἀλλακαν was preferred by Page (ἀλλ᾽ ἄκāν, 'but in silence'), but the compd. κατάγνυμι is acceptable (cf. Radt 1970). **μέν**: cf. 76 50. **ἔαγε**: 3 sing. perf. (intransitive). The hiatus with γλῶσσα (which led Page and others to print ἔαγε with daggers) is also acceptable: arising from original presence of *w* in *ϝέϝāγε, it is a poetic feature and may have onomatopoeic effect. See Ford and Kopff (1976).

10. **ὑπαδεδρόμāκεν**: for the preverb cf. ὑπασδεύξαισα (a)9.

11. **ὀππάτεσσι**: Lesb. ὄππα < *ὀπ-μα (in other dialects the assimilation works the other way, giving ὄμμα). For the dat. plur. -εσσι see §36.4 and στήθεσιν 6. **ὄρημμ(ι)**: the stem ὄρη- seems to have been characteristic of E. Aeolic, and perhaps E. Ionic too (the Att. paradigm is built on an *a*-stem ὄρα-). Traces of athem. inflection in -η- can be seen in epic (e.g. ὄρηαι 2 sing., *Od.* 14. 343). MSS have ὄρηι μή. For -ημ(μ)ι cf. κάλημμι (a)16. **ἐπιρρόμβεισι**: athem. -εισι < *-εντι (§§24.1, 34.11).

12. **ἄκουαι**: contrast Att. ἀκοή < ἀκοϝή < *akowsā. The development of a diphthong from V*ww*V < V*ws*V is characteristic of E. Aeolic (hence perhaps epic ἀκουή). Here and at fr. 104 αὔως (< *ἀϝϝως < *awsōs) the diphthong is guaranteed by the metre.

13. **κάδ**: i.e. κατ (§23.4). **μ᾽**: μοι, enclitic with genitive

function (following κάδ), as occasionally in Hom.   **κακχέεται**:
i.e. κατ- (§§24.5, 23.4).

14. **παῖσαν**: < *πανσα- < *pant-ya- (cj., πᾶσαν MSS): §34.11.
ἄγρει: cf. on καταγρέθηι **17** 13. For the ending see φίλει (a)23.
15. **ἔμμι**: < *es-mi (§34.2).   **τεθνάκην**: perf. infin. (Att. τεθν-
άναι), formed by adding the pres. thematic infin. ending to the perf.
stem in -k-.   **ὀλίγω**: gen. sing. (neut.), governed by (ἐ)πιδεύης,
'lacking little'. For Lesb. and epic ἐπιδεύης (Att. ἐπιδεής) from
*-dews-ēs cf. on ἄκουαι 12.
17. **τόλματον**: not 'must be endured' (which would be τολμάτεον:
Chantraine 1933: 308): cf. ἐπαινετός, 'praisable', πιστός, 'trustable',
etc. The suffix -tos is not integrated into the Gk. verbal system (as in
Lat. *amātus*), but is important in adj. and noun formation.

75. Alkaios of Lesbos. Late VII–early VI cent. BC. Text: Voigt
(1971). Also in Page (1955), Campbell (1982). Drinking
songs. ▶ Hamm (1957), Hooker (1977), Bowie (1981).

(a) Fr. 338 Voigt (quoted by Athenaeus): Alcaic stanzas.

> ὔει μὲν ὀ Ζεῦς, ἐκ δ᾽ ὀράνω μέγας
> 2 χείμων, πεπάγαισιν δ᾽ ὐδάτων ῥόαι
> <   2 lines missing   >
> κάββαλλε τὸν χείμων᾽, ἐπὶ μὲν τίθεις
> 6 πῦρ, ἐν δὲ κέρναις οἶνον ἀφειδέως
> μέλιχρον· αὐτὰρ ἀμφὶ κόρσαι
> 8 μόλθακον ἀμφι<τίθει> γνόφαλλον . . .

Zeus is raining, out of the sky there's a great storm descending,
and the streams have frozen [. . .] To hell with the storm! Build up
a fire, mix the honey-sweet wine unstintingly, and put a soft pillow
about your temples . . .

1. **μέν**: cf. **76** 50.   **ὀ Ζεῦς**: very rare use of the article. Names
(unless accompanied by an adj.) are generally without the article
in Sappho and Alkaios (cf. on ὤνηρ **74** (b)2).   **ὀράνω**: single ρ is
surprising, given Att. οὐρανός/WGk. ὠρανός (perhaps < *Ϝορσανός):
§34.2. Most plausibly explained as a metrical simplification of -ρρ-
(paralled by δισχελίοις Alk. 69.2). Cf. on ὠράνω **74** (a)11.
2. **πεπάγαισιν**: 3 plur. ending < *-ανσι < *-anti (§34.11). The

earlier ending was -ᾱσι < *-n̥ti, but this was recharacterized with the addition of -n-.

5. **κάββαλλε**: imper., < κάτ- (§§24.5, 23.4). **τόν**: what Lobel (1927: §18) calls 'anaphoric' use of the article, referring to an entity (topic) already mentioned. **ἐπὶ . . . τίθεις**: athem. ptcpl. τίθεις < *τίθεντς, as in Attic: but the diphthong in Lesb. is real, while in Att. the digraph represents [ẹ:], §23.1 (for tmesis §24.6). 6. **κέρναις**: athem. pres. ptcpl. of κέρνᾱμι (Att. κεράννυμι): a them. ptcpl. is apparently attested in κέρνᾱν 17 13 (see note). MSS have κίρναις, which reflects the Hom. vocalism (for the development of -ι- from orig. zero-grade cf. Palmer 1980: 240): Lesb. has a tendency to open ι > ε next to ρ (as in Thess., Boe.). 7. **μέλιχρον**: adj. referring to the sweetness of honey (i.e. a -ρο- adj. built to μέλι with intrusive -χ- as in Hom. πενιχρός), or less likely the colour (χρώς). **αὐτάρ**: an epic word of Achaean ancestry (not elsewhere in Lesb., but attested in Cypriot). **κόρσαι**: with -ρσ- as in E. Ion. (Att. κόρρη). The sporadic preservation (in all dialects) of -ρσ-, -λσ- is difficult to account for (cf. ὀράνω 1): presumably due to morphological and analogical forces working against the phonology. 8. **μόλθακον, γνόφαλλον**: o-vocalism from syllabic resonants (§34.1). The expected Att.-Ion. γνάφαλλον is attested in koiné documents: the ε in literary Att. κνέφαλλον is odd (for initial κν- cf. κνάπτω, 'comb wool').

(b) Fr. 346 Voigt (quoted by Athenaeus): greater Asclepiad.

πώνωμεν· τί τὰ λύχν' ὀμμένομεν; δάκτυλος ἀμέρα·
2 κὰδ δ' ἄερρε κυλίχναις μεγάλαις, ἄιτα, ποικίλαις·
οἶνον γὰρ Σεμέλας καὶ Δίος υἶος λαθικάδεα
4 ἀνθρώποισιν ἔδωκ'. ἔγχεε κέρναις ἔνα καὶ δύο
πλήαις κὰκ κεφάλας, <ἀ> δ' ἀτέρα τὰν ἀτέραν κύλιξ
6 ὠθήτω

Let's start drinking—why should we wait for the lamps? Only a finger's breadth of the day is left. Take down the large cups, friend, the decorated ones. The son of Semele and Zeus gave wine to humans so we can forget our cares. Pour it in, mixing one part water to two of wine, and fill them to the top: and let one cup nudge the next.

1. **πώνωμεν**: edd. (πίνωμεν MSS). The stem of this verb alternates πῑ-/πω-/πο in Gk. (and other IE languages), perhaps reflecting orig. $*peH_3$ *-i-*. Aeolic dialects seem to have generalized πω- in the present (for Boeotian cf. Euboulos fr. 11 *PCG*). **τὰ λύχν(α)**: Lobel (1927: §18), noting that 'respectable people did not start carousing before dark', rightly sees an extension of the anaphoric use of the article in Lesb. in this phrase: the reference is proverbial. **ὀμμένομεν**: cj. (ἀμμ- MSS): §§24.5, 23.4. For Lesb. ὀν see §28.9.

2. **κὰδ . . . ἄερρε**: tmesis (§24.6); assimilation of κατ (§23.4). ἄερρε edd. (ἄειρε MSS): ἀέρρω (Ion. ἀείρω) < *ἀ(ϝ)έργω, §34.2. **ἄϊτα**: voc., a rare word meaning 'friend' (esp. 'boyfriend', ἐρώμενος) ascribed to Thess. at Theokr. 12. 14 (García Ramón 1999: 527–8). The first syllable must be the result of metrical lengthening (cf. ἀθανάτ' **74** (a)1).

3. **λᾱθικάδεα**: Hom. adj., acc. sing. (for the formation cf. ἑλκεσιπέπλους **66** 105). An *s*-stem acc. sing. -ην is found in some inscriptions (IV cent. and later) and in a papyrus of Alkaios ([π]ηλεφάνην, very fragmentary context): the morphology may also be epic here.

4. **κέρναις**: edd. (MSS κιρναις, κέρνα εἶς): cf. κέρναις (a)6.

5. **πλήαις**: edd. (πλε-, πλει- MSS). Adj., fem. plur. with κυλίχναις. A stem πλε- is found epigraphically (cf. **17** 9). πλῆος, if genuine, would be from *plē-yos (with loss of -y-): some support provided by a statement in an ancient grammarian that 'Aeolians turn ει into η as in πλείων πλήων', and by]πληον[in a papyrus scrap of Sappho (fr. 67 b4). **κάκ**: κάτ(α), with assimilation to following velar. The Gk. says 'down to the brim' rather than 'up to' (i.e. semantic focus on *pouring* rather than *filling*).

(c) Fr. 347 Voigt (put together from multiple quotations): greater Asclepiad.

τέγγε πλεύμονας οἴνωι, τὸ γὰρ ἄστρον περιτέλλεται,
2 ἀ δ' ὤρα χαλέπα, πάντα δὲ δίψαισ' ὐπὰ καύματος,
ἄχει δ' ἐκ πετάλων ἄδεα τέττιξ <πτερύγων δ' ὔπα>
4 <   line(s) missing   >
ἄνθει δὲ σκόλυμος, νῦν δὲ γύναικες μιαρώταται,
6 λέπτοι δ' ἄνδρες, ἐπεὶ <δὴ> κεφάλαν καὶ γόνα Σείριος
ἄσδει . . .

Soak your lungs with wine, because the dog-star is up. The season is harsh, everything is parched from the heat, the cicada whistles sweetly from the leaves [from under its wings] . . . The golden thistle is blooming: now the women are at their worst, but the men are feeble, since Sirius scorches their heads and knees.

The poem is a lyric adaptation of Hesiod, *Works and Days* 582–8.

1. **πλεύμονας**: in later Gk. πλεύμων was transformed into πνεύμων under the influence of πνέω, πνεῦμα (some MSS offer πν- here). The sing. πλεύμονα is also attested in MSS, in which case orig. *w- in (F)οἴνωι prevents hiatus (the *lectio difficilior* and perhaps preferable). **περιτέλλεται**: not necessarily an Ionism, as the root is *tel- rather than *kʷel- (for which see on τένται 51 17).

2. **δίψαισ(ι)**: either 3 sing. (athem.) of an *a*-stem vb. with hyper-Aeolic -αι-, or possibly 3 plur. < *-ανσι < *-anti (§34.11). **ὑπά**: edd. (ὑπό MSS): cf. ὑπασδεύξαισα 74 (a)9.

3. After τέττιξ earlier editors (including Page 1955: 303f.) inserted a fragment transmitted anonymously by Demetrius and generally assigned to Sappho (Voigt fr. 101a): see Liberman (1992) for reasons not to do this. <πτερύγων δ' ὔπα> is conjectured on the basis of the Hesiodic text.

5. **μιαρώταται**: interpreters have taken this to imply 'lustful, libidinous' (Hesiod has μάχλος).

6. **γόνα**: edd. (γόνατα MSS): from *γόνFα (cf. Hom. δούρα < δόρFα): for loss of F without compensatory gemination or lengthening in Lesb. cf. on δίννεντες 74 (a)11. The oblique stem in -ατ- started in the *n*-stems (where it is attested already in Myc.): it was extended to other neut. stems, more widely in Att. than elsewhere.

7. **ἄσδει**: edd. (ἄζει MSS): see on ὑπασδεύξαισα 74 (a)9.

DORIC CHORUS AND LYRIC MONODY

76. Alkman of Sparta, *Partheneion* 36–77 (fr. 3 Calame). From a papyrus (1 cent. AD) published in 1863. Late VII cent. BC. Metre: 14 line stanzas (mixed trochaic, dactylic, and Aeolic metre). A song written for a chorus of young women, apparently for a specific occasion. There are many difficulties in the interpretation: see Griffiths (1972), Calame (1977) with earlier bibliography. *PMG* 1. Also in Campbell (1982), Hutchinson (2001). ▶ Page (1951), Hooker (1977: 61–9), Cassio (1993), Cassio (in press).

ἔστι τις σιῶν τίσις·
ὁ δ᾿ ὄλβιος ὅστις εὔφρων
ἀμέραν [δ]ιαπλέκει
ἄκλαυτος· ἐγὼν δ᾿ ἀείδω
40 Ἀγιδ[ῶ]ς τὸ φῶς ὁρῶσ᾿
ὥτ᾿ ἄλιον ὅνπερ ἇμιν
Ἀγιδὼ μαρτύρεται
φαίνην· ἐμὲ δ᾿ οὔτ᾿ ἐπαινῆν
οὔτε [μ]ωμήσθαι νιν ἁ κλεννὰ χοραγὸς
45 οὐδ᾿ ἁμῶς ἐῆι· δοκεῖ γὰρ ἦμεν αὔτα
ἐκπρεπὴς τὼς ὥπερ αἴ τις
ἐν βοτοῖς στάσειεν ἵππον
παγὸν ἀεθλοφόρον καναχάποδα
τῶν ὑποπετριδίων ὀνείρων.
50 ἦ οὐχ ὁρῆις; ὁ μὲν κέλης
Ἐνητικός· ἁ δὲ χαίτα
τᾶς ἐμᾶς ἀνεψιᾶς
Ἁγησιχόρας ἐπανθεῖ
χρυσὸς [ὣ]τ᾿ ἀκήρατος·
55 τό τ᾿ ἀργύριον πρόσωπον,
διαφάδαν τί τοι λέγω;
Ἁγησιχόρα μὲν αὔτα·
ἁ δὲ δευτέρα πεδ᾿ Ἀγιδὼ τὸ Ϝεῖδος
ἵππος Ἰβηνῶι Κολαξαῖος δραμήται·
60 ταὶ πεληάδες γὰρ ἇμιν
Ὀρθρίαι φᾶρος φεροίσαις
νύκτα δι᾿ ἀμβροσίαν ἅτε Σήριον
ἄστρον ἀϜηρομέναι μάχονται.
οὔτε γάρ τι πορφύρας
65 τόσσος κόρος ὥστ᾿ ἀμύναι,
οὔτε ποικίλος δράκων
παγχρύσιος, οὐδὲ μίτρα
Λυδία, νεανίδων

ἰανογ[λ]εφάρων ἄγαλμα
70 οὐδὲ ταὶ Ναννῶς κόμαι
ἀλλ' οὐδ' Ἀρέτα σιειδής,
οὐδὲ Συλακίς τε καὶ Κλεησισήρα,
οὐδ' ἐς Αἰνησιμβρ[ό]τας ἐνθοῖσα φασεῖς·
Ἀσταφίς [τ]έ μοι γένοιτο
75 καὶ ποτιγλέποι Φίλυλλα
Δαμαρέτα τ' ἐρατά [τ]ε Ϝιανθεμίς·
ἀλλ' Ἀγησιχόρα με τείρει.

There is such a thing as the vengeance of the gods: that man is fortunate, who in goodness of heart weaves out his days without tears. As for me, I sing of the radiance of Agido—seeing her like the sun, which indeed Agido summons to shine upon us: but the illustrious choir-leader utterly forbids me to praise or disparage her—for she herself appears pre-eminent, as if one were to set among grazing herds a powerful stallion, a prize-winner with ringing hooves, the stuff of dreams. (50) Do you not see? The courser is Venetic: but the hair of my cousin Hagesichora blooms like pure gold, and her face of silver—why do I tell you openly? This is Hagesichora! But she who is second after Agido in beauty shall run as a Kolaxaian horse against an Ibenian; these Peleiades, you see, rising up like Sirius they contend with us as we bring a robe (?) to the Dawn goddess through the immortal night. (64) All our purple finery is not enough to beat them off, nor our golden bracelets, intricate and serpentine. Neither the Lydian headband, the delight of dark-eyed girls, nor even the locks of Nanno, nor Areta lovely as a goddess, nor Thylakis, nor Kleësithera: nor will you go to Ainesimbrota's house and say, 'May Astaphis be mine, and may Philylla look in my direction, and Damareta, and lovely Ianthemis'. No, it is Hagesichora who causes me heartache.

36. σιῶν: i.e. θεῶν, with raising of ε (§23.2). For the use of σ to designate the fricative [θ] < [tʰ] see §39.7 (and *hιππανσίδας* 34 1). Epigraphic evidence suggests that the spelling was adopted some time after Alkman: this therefore represents interference by later editors.

38. **ἀμέραν**: unaspirated (as attested at *IG* V 1. 213. 43 [**33**]). The h- in Attic (see **30** 13) is analogical rather than original, perhaps on ἕως, ἥλιος, or ἑσπέρα (cf. ἄλιον 41 for the converse). 39. **ἐγών**: §36.5. In archaic poetry the first person pronoun often signals a transition (esp. with δέ). **ἀείδω**: i.e. ἀ(ϝ)είδω, an epic form, but probably Lac. too in view of ἀϝηρομέναι 63 (Att. ἄιδω by contraction). 40. **Ἀγιδ[ῶ]ς**: gen. < *-όγος (for the morphology cf. on λεχώι **51** 16). The song appears to mark some important stage in the life of Agido: ritual passage to womanhood and marriage have been suggested. **φῶς**: contracted < φάϝος (the conditions under which intervocalic -ϝ- dropped in Lac. are not completely clear): cf. §39.1. 41. **ὦτ(ε)**: ὥ (instr. of the relative *yo-) plus τε, corresponding to Att.-Ion. ὥς (cf. ὥπερ 46). **ἄλιον**: lack of aspiration in certain WGk. dialects is unexpected: perhaps analogical on ἀμέρα. Here printed with smooth breathing because of preceding -τ'. **ἄμιν**: original short ι in WGk. 43. **φαίνην, ἐπαινῆν**: edd. (-εν pap.): -ην in φαίνην is metrically guaranteed, and seems certain in ἐπαινῆν (*brevis in longo* would be odd). No infin. in -εν in Alkm. is required by metre. 44. **[μ]ωμήσθαι**: edd. ([.]ωμεσθαι pap.), from stem μωμα-. **νιν**: WGk. enclitic pronoun (cf. on **45** 12) frequent in choral dialect. Occasional cases of μιν may be due to scribal confusion. **κλεννά**: from *κλεϝεσ-νός (cf. κλεινοί **61** 6). Elsewhere κλεεννός in choral lyric (from the Aeolic poetic tradition: Cassio 2005). This form may be the result of haplology (Lillo 1995), or perhaps analogous on the lyric alternation φαεινός/φαεννός. Less likely a mistaken transliteration by a later editor of ΚΛΕΝΑ (i.e. κληνά). The choir-leader has a 'speaking name' (*Hagesichora* 53), and may be a divine rather than a mortal figure. 45. **ἐῆι**: see §38.4 for the contraction. **ἤμεν**: athem. infin. < *es-men (§40.3). 46. **τώς**: demonstr. advb. picked up by ὥπερ (cf. ὥτ' 41). 48. Cf. the Hom. expression ἵππους πηγοὺς ἀθλοφόρους, *Il.* 9. 123–4. **καναχάποδα**: for the compd. adj. (two substantives: first element καναχά, 'noise') cf. ῥοδοδάκτυλος, 'with rosy fingers' (Schindler 1986).

49. **ὑποπετριδίων**: meaning is disputed. The second element may be connected with πτερά, 'wing' (dreams are often winged in Gk. literature) rather than πέτρα, 'rock'.

50. **ὁρῆις**: for the contraction cf. ἐῆι 45. **μέν**: shortened form of μήν (Dor. Aeol. μάν). The vowel shows it to be an Ionicism, which spread rapidly across the Greek poetic lexicon. **κέλης**: the epigraphic form in the V cent. was κέλεξ (see on **33** 13): κέλης may have been a competing variant, perhaps more suited to choral poetry; or it may have entered the scribal tradition from the koiné.

54. **[ὤ]τ(ε)**: see on 41.

56. **τοι**: dat. of τύ (§32.5).

58. **πεδ(ά)**: see on **17** 20. **Ἀγιδώ**: acc. < *-όγα **Ϝεῖδος**: pap. has τοειδος (hiatus guaranteed).

60. **ταί**: §40.5. **πεληάδες**: edd., πελειάδες pap. The change is hardly necessary: it is based on the view (difficult to evaluate) of ancient grammarians that as a rule ει > η before a vowel in 'Doric' (see Page 1951: 138). The word could mean either 'doves' or the Pleiad constellation, which would be rising at dawn. Most likely the latter, given the references to the night in 63.

61. **Ὀρθρίαι**: here capitalized as the dat. of a Spartan dawn-goddess, 'the Early One'. Could also be nom. plur., referring to the πεληάδες. **φᾶρος**: the pap. has a circumflex, but the scholion ad loc. quotes φάρος, 'plough', with the gloss ἄροτρον. The reading φάϝος, 'torch' has also been suggested (but cf. φῶς 40). **φεροίσαις**: ptcpl. with -οισα (cf. §34.11). A familiar feature of Lesb. phonology (ἄϊοισα **74** (a)6), but there is no epigraphic support for it in Lac. The theory that it was added to the text of Alkm. by Alexandrian editors because they knew it from the nearby Doric dialect of Cyrene has been disproven (Cassio 1993). It is almost certain that that Alkm. (and other composers of choral lyric) drew on an Aeolic-influenced literary tradition (Cassio 2005). The theory that it was a VII cent. variant in Lac. phonology, marginalized by the epigraphic period, is implausible owing to the extremely restricted distribution (e.g. acc. plur. τοίς, ταίς is not found: §34.11). Found also in Stesichoros, Ibykos, Pindar, and Theokritos.

62. **νύκτα δι' ἀμβροσίαν**: cf. Hom. ἀμβροσίην διὰ νύκτα, *Il.* 2. 57.

63. **ἀϝηρομέναι**: ἀνειρομέναι pap. Epigraphic texts from Sparta

spell [w] with both Ϝ and β: υ may be due to a copyist unfamiliar with Ϝ. The sequence αυ-, though unmetrical, would for an early editor have an Aeolic/epic pedigree: cf. on ἄκουαι **74** (b)12 and κανάξαις **68** 666 (for the real Lesb. form see ἄερρε **75** (b)2). For the 'Doric' accent cf. on παίδας **79** 211.

65. **τόσσος**: not necessarily an epicism: most WGk. dialects had -σσ- here (Crete is an exception: ὁπόττοι **52** 40). **ὦστ(ε)**: consecutive. García Ramón (1985: 90–3) argues that ὦτ(ε) would best represent Alkm.'s autograph (cf. 41 above), ὦστ(ε) reflecting the interference of a later editor.

67. **παγχρύσιος**: cf. χρύσιον **74**(a) 8.

69. **ἰανογ[λ]εφάρων**: compd. of ἴον, 'violet' (formally a cross between ἰογλέφαρος and κυανογλέφαρος: cf. **78** 1): Ϝ- restored in Ϝιανθεμίς **76**. For γλεφ- (elsewhere only in Pindar) cf. ποτιγλέποι **75**: the alternation points to an initial labiovelar.

70. **Ναννῶς**: gen. (cf. Ἀγιδῶς 40).

71. **σιειδής**: from θεο-ειδής (with syncope of -ο-, as in σιείκελοι < θεοείκελοι in the Lac. song at Ar. *Lys.* 1252). Cf. σιῶν 36.

72. **Συλακίς**: i.e. Θυλακίς 'poppy'. **Κλεησισήρα**: i.e. Κλεησιθήρα, from κλέ(Ϝ)ος and θήρα, 'hunting'.

73. **Αἰνησιμβρ[ό]τας**: gen. (understand 'house') of a 'speaking name': she is a wise woman who supplies love charms. **ἐνθοῖσα**: see on ὑπένθηι **51** 17. For the ending -οῖσα cf. φεροίσαις 61. **φασεῖς**: the circumflex (in the pap.) reflects the fut. infix -σε- characteristic of WGk. (§40.2).

76. **Ϝιανθεμίς**: edd. (note hiatus after τε), ἰανθεμίς pap. Composed of Ϝι-, 'violet' and ἀνθεμ-, an onomastic stem derived from ἄνθος (cf. Leumann 1950: 249–51).

77. **τείρει**: pap. Not inappropriate in the erotic context of the preceding lines: but if Hagesichora is a divine figure, edd. may be right to read τηρεῖ, 'watches over, protects'. τείρει has a spurious diphthong (§23.1), so in either case Alkm. would have written *ΤΕΡΕΙ*.

77. Stesichoros (south Italy or Sicily), fr. 222b (*P. Lille* 76A). Text: Bremer (1987). From a papyrus (III cent. BC, mummy cartonnage) published in 1977. Jocasta addresses Teiresias and

her sons. Early VII cent. BC. Metre: dactylic/dactylo-epitrite. ▶
Nöthiger (1971), Haslam (1978), Bremer (1987), Hutchinson
(2001).

ἐπ᾽ ἄλγεσι μὴ χαλεπὰς ποίει μερίμνας
μηδέ μοι ἐξοπίσω
πρόφαινε ἐλπίδας βαρείας.

οὔτε γὰρ αἰὲν ὁμῶς
205 θεοὶ θέσαν ἀθάνατοι κατ᾽ αἶαν ἱρὰν
νεῖκος ἔμπεδον βροτοῖσιν
οὐδέ γα μὰν φιλότατ᾽, ἐπὶ δ᾽ ἀμέρᾳ<ι ἐ>ν νόον ἀνδρῶν
θεοὶ τιθεῖσι.
μαντοσύνας δὲ τεὰς ἄναξ ἑκάεργος Ἀπόλλων
210 μὴ πάσας τελέσσαι.

αἰ δέ με παίδας ἰδέσθαι ὑπ᾽ ἀλλάλοισι δαμέντας
μόρσιμόν ἐστιν, ἐπεκλώσαν δὲ Μοίρᾳ[ι,
αὐτίκα μοι θανάτου τέλος στυγερο[ῖο] γέν[οιτο,
πρίν ποκα ταῦτ᾽ ἐσιδεῖν
215 ἄλγεσ<σ>ι πολύστονα δακρυόεντα[– –
παίδας ἐνὶ μμεγάροις
θανόντας ἢ πόλιν ἀλοίσαν.

ἀλλ᾽ ἄγε παίδες ἐμοῖς μύθοις φίλα[– ∪∪ – –
τᾶιδε γὰρ ὑμὶν ἐγὼν τέλος προφα[ίνω,
220 τὸμ μὲν ἔχοντα δόμους ναίειν π.[∪∪ – ∪∪ – –
τὸν δ᾽ ἀπίμεν κτεάνη
καὶ χρυσὸν ἔχοντα φίλου σύμπαντα [πατρός,
κλαροπαληδὸν ὃς ἄν
πρᾶτος λάχηι ἕκατι Μοιρᾶν.

225 τοῦτο γὰρ ἂν δοκέω
λυτήριον ὔμμι κακοῦ γένοιτο πότμο[υ
μάντιος φραδαῖσι θείου . . .

. . . to my grief add not gnawing anxiety, nor for my future make
woeful predictions. (204) For the deathless gods do not impose
unending strife for mortals on the holy earth, nor indeed
friendship: but daily the gods put a new disposition into men. May
lord Apollo, the worker from afar, not bring to fulfilment all these

your prophecies. (211) But if it is ordained for me to see my sons slain by each other, and the Fates have spun it thus—well, right away let hateful death bring about my end, before ever I should see such things, painful, laden with groans and tears [...] my sons killed within the palace, or the city captured. (218) But come, my sons, [listen] to my words [...] for thus do I predict for you the end: one of you shall have the house and dwell in it [...] the other shall leave, with the goods and the gold of his dear [father], all of it, whoever by lot shall take the first place, by the agency of the Fates. (225) For this, I think, shall prove the solution for you of this evil doom, which comes from the warnings of the divine seer.

201. **χαλεπὰς ... μερίμνας**: the quantity of the *a*-stem acc. plur. is generally unverifiable in Stes. The two cases which can be verified are short: he may have used whichever was convenient (cf. τροπάς **68** 663).

203. **ἐλπίδας**: orig. initial ϝ- accounts for the hiatus. Stes. follows epic in his use of this feature (may be observed or not, as convenient).

204. **αἰέν**: alternates with αἰεί in Hom. For Stes. a useful literary variant (so also in Alkm., Bacch., and Theokr.).

205. **θέσαν**: omission of the augment is a feature of epic language (cf. πιθόμην **66** 103). **αἶαν**: epic variant of γαῖα, probably by a process analogous to εἶβε **67** 153 (Haslam 1976). **ἱράν**: form attested in Lesb., but probably here an epicism.

206. **βροτοῖσιν**: see on κυανέοισιν **78** 1.

207. **γα**: expected WGk. form. **ἐ<ν> ... τιθεῖσι**: tmesis (§24.6), assuming the supplement is correct (and there are many Hom. parallels).

208. **τιθεῖσι**: < *τίθε-ντι. The pap. has no accents: editors follow the Hom. tradition in accenting this word, which reflects a late Ionic development (assimilation of 3 plur. athematic verbs to vowel-stems such as φιλοῦσι) rather than the phonology of Stes.'s poetry. Cf. §32.12.

209. **τεάς**: a WGk. form, but both τεός and σός (< *two-) are found in epic. **ἄναξ**: initial ϝ- is observed (lengthens the previous syllable): cf. ἐλπίδας 203.

210. **τελέσσαι**: aor. opt., 3 sing.

211. **παίδας**: edd. justify the accent (which is one mora forward of Att.-Ion. παῖδας) by ref. to papyrus frags. of Alkm., Ib., and Stes. which show sporadic 'progessive' accentuation of a type ascribed to Doric by ancient grammarians. See Probert (2003: 160–2).   **ὑπ' ἀλλάλοισι**: use of the dat. after ὑπό is a feature of epic syntax, where it lays stress on the implication 'at the hands of, under' (Chantraine 1953: 140 f.).   **ἰδέσθαι**: initial digamma not observed (cf. ἐλπίδας 203).

214. **ποκα**: edd. (τοκα pap.): §40.7.   **ἐσ-ιδεῖν**: initial digamma (ἰδεῖν) not observed.

215. **δακρυόεντα̣**: pap. This makes slightly odd scansion, and Ruijgh (in Bremer ad loc.) suggests δακρύεντα (i.e. the original form *δακρύεις < δακρυ+Ϝεντ-ς, without a linking vowel: cf. §13 and *pe-ne-we-ta* 1a).

216. **ἐνὶ μμεγάροις**: the scribe has written a double μ to indicate the previous syllable is heavy. An epic licence, by which a short vowel could count as long before μ-, ν-, λ-, ρ-(starting-point was words with initial sR-, such as μοῖρα < *σμοῖρα).

217. **ἀλοίσαν**: see on φεροίσαις **76** 61.

219. **ἐγών**: epic and WGk. form (§36.5).

220. **μέν**: cf. **76** 50.

221. **ἀπίμεν**: a WGk. form, but also in epic.   **κτεάνη**: poetic form. Since the ending is contracted (from -εα, neut. plur.), the uncontracted εα of the stem is unexpected (κτήνη elsewhere attested).

223. **κλαροπαληδόν**: advb. formed to an unattested verb; cf. διακριδόν **72** 71.

224. **πρᾶτος**: §38.2.   **ἔκατι**: see Leumann (1950: 251 f.) for the formation of this Hom. advb. (related to ἑκών, 'willing').

225. **δοκέω**: not found in epic in this sense: perhaps an intrusion of the vernacular.

226. **ὔμμι**: epicism (an Aeolic form): §34.2.

78. Ibykos of Rhegion, fr. 287 *PMG* (quoted by Proklos in his commentary on Plato's *Parmenides* 137). Later VI cent. BC
Metre: mostly dactylic. ▶▶ Nöthiger (1971)

> Ἔρος αὖτέ με κυανέοισιν ὑπὸ
> βλεφάροις τακέρ' ὄμμασι δερκόμενος
> κηλήμασι παντοδαποῖς ἐς ἄπει-

ρα δίκτυα Κύπριδος ἐσβάλλει·
5 ἦ μὰν τρομέω νιν ἐπερχόμενον,
   ὥστε φερέζυγος ἵππος ἀεθλοφόρος ποτὶ γήραι
   ἀέκων σὺν ὄχεσφι θοοῖς ἐς ἄμιλλαν ἔβα.

Once again Love looks at me meltingly from under dark eyelids
and with all types of beguilement hurls me into the endless nets of
Kypris. (5) Oh, I tremble at his coming, as a yoked prize-winning
horse, near to old age, goes unwillingly with his swift chariot into
the fray.

1. **κυανέοισιν**: Ib. more often has the short dat. (native to his and
most WGk. dialects): use of the long form (with -ν if convenient) is a
licence taken over from epic (§32.14).

2. **τακέρ(α)**: adj. built on the zero-grade stem *tH_2-k- (cf.
τήκω < *teH_2-k-). **ὄμμασι**: cf. ὀππάτεσσι **74** (b)11.

3. **ἐς**: edd. (for the metre), εἰς MSS. ἐς was generalized in both Ion.
and many WGk. dialects (§32.10): it is the normal form in choral
dialect.

4. **ἐσβάλλει**: edd., βάλλει MSS.

5. **νιν**: WGk. enclitic pronoun (cf. **76** 44). Supplied by edd. from
scholia which quote the phrase in the form τρομέων ἵν' (it has
dropped from the main text).

6. **ὥστε**: cf. on **76** 65.   **ἀεθλοφόρος**: Hom. adj. (so at **76** 48).
ποτί: both WGk. and Hom. (§40.8): cf. ποτί **66** 101.

7. **σὺν ὄχεσφι**: Hom. phrase (for the dat. ending see §11.4 and ἧφι
66 107).   **ἐς**: edd., εἰς MSS.   **ἔβα**: a 'gnomic' aor. (see on **68**
676 ὤρινε).

79. Pindar (Boeotia), *Olympian* 1 (lines 36–85). Part of a song
celebrating the victory of Hieron of Syracuse in the chariot-race
at the Olympic Games of 476 BC. Text: B. Snell–H. Maehler
(Teubner 1987). Metre: Aeolic (triadic). ▶▶ Forssman (1966),
Gerber (1982), Verdenius (1988), Instone (1996).

   υἱὲ Ταντάλου, σὲ δ' ἀντία προτέρων φθέγξομαι,
   ὁπότ' ἐκάλεσε πατὴρ τὸν εὐνομώτατον
   ἐς ἔρανον φίλαν τε Σίπυλον,
   ἀμοιβαῖα θεοῖσι δεῖπνα παρέχων,
40 τότ' Ἀγλαοτρίαιναν ἁρπάσαι,

δαμέντα φρένας ἱμέρωι, χρυσέαισί τ᾽ ἀν᾽ ἵπποις
ὕπατον εὐρυτίμου ποτὶ δῶμα Διὸς μεταβᾶσαι·
ἔνθα δευτέρωι χρόνωι
ἦλθε καὶ Γανυμήδης
45 Ζηνὶ τωΰτ᾽ ἐπὶ χρέος.

ὡς δ᾽ ἄφαντος ἔπελες, οὐδὲ ματρὶ πολλὰ μαιόμενοι φῶτες
ἄγαγον,
ἔννεπε κρυφᾶι τις αὐτίκα φθονερῶν γειτόνων,
ὕδατος ὅτι τε πυρὶ ζέοισαν εἰς ἀκμάν
μαχαίραι τάμον κατὰ μέλη,
50 τραπέζαισί τ᾽ ἀμφὶ δεύτατα κρεῶν
σέθεν διεδάσαντο καὶ φάγον.

ἐμοὶ δ᾽ ἄπορα γαστρίμαργον μακάρων τιν᾽ εἰπεῖν· ἀφίσταμαι·
ἀκέρδεια λέλογχεν θαμινὰ κακαγόρους.
εἰ δὲ δή τιν᾽ ἄνδρα θνατὸν Ὀλύμπου σκοποί
55 ἐτίμασαν, ἦν Τάνταλος οὗτος· ἀλλὰ γὰρ καταπέψαι
μέγαν ὄλβον οὐκ ἐδυνάσθη, κόρωι δ᾽ ἕλεν
ἄταν ὑπέροπλον, ἅν τοι πατὴρ ὕπερ
57b κρέμασε καρτερὸν αὐτῶι λίθον,
τὸν αἰεὶ μενοινῶν κεφαλᾶς βαλεῖν εὐφροσύνας ἀλᾶται.

ἔχει δ᾽ ἀπάλαμον βίον τοῦτον ἐμπεδόμοχθον
60 μετὰ τριῶν τέταρτον πόνον, ἀθανάτους ὅτι κλέψαις
ἁλίκεσσι συμπόταις
νέκταρ ἀμβροσίαν τε
δῶκεν, οἷσιν ἄφθιτον
θέν νιν. εἰ δὲ θεὸν ἀνήρ τις ἔλπεταί <τι> λαθέμεν ἔρδων,
ἁμαρτάνει.
65 τοὔνεκα προῆκαν υἱὸν ἀθάνατοί <οἱ> πάλιν
μετὰ τὸ ταχύποτμον αὖτις ἀνέρων ἔθνος.
πρὸς εὐάνθεμον δ᾽ ὅτε φυὰν
λάχναι νιν μέλαν γένειον ἔρεφον,
ἑτοῖμον ἀνεφρόντισεν γάμον
70 Πισάτα παρὰ πατρὸς εὔδοξον Ἱπποδάμειαν
σχεθέμεν. ἐγγὺς ἐλθὼν πολιᾶς ἁλὸς οἶος ἐν ὄρφναι
ἄπυεν βαρύκτυπον
Εὐτρίαιναν· ὁ δ᾽ αὐτῶι

πὰρ ποδὶ σχεδὸν φάνη.
75 τῶι μὲν εἶπε· «φίλια δῶρα Κυπρίας ἄγ᾽ εἴ τι, Ποσείδαον, ἐς χάριν
τέλλεται, πέδασον ἔγχος Οἰνομάου χάλκεον,
ἐμὲ δ ἐπὶ ταχυτάτων πόρευσον ἁρμάτων
ἐς Ἇλιν, κράτει δὲ πέλασον.
ἐπεὶ τρεῖς τε καὶ δέκ᾽ ἄνδρας ὀλέσαις
80 μναστῆρας ἀναβάλλεται γάμον

θυγατρός. ὁ μέγας δὲ κίνδυνος ἄναλκιν οὐ φῶτα λαμβάνει.
θανεῖν δ᾽ οἷσιν ἀνάγκα, τά κέ τις ἀνώνυμον
γῆρας ἐν σκότωι καθήμενος ἕψοι μάταν,
ἁπάντων καλῶν ἄμμορος; ἀλλ᾽ ἐμοὶ μὲν οὗτος ἄεθλος
85 ὑποκείσεται· τὺ δὲ πρᾶξιν φίλαν δίδοι.»

As for you, son of Tantalos, I shall utter an account different from
that of my predecessors. When your father invited (the gods) to
that well-ordered feast in their beloved Sipylos, reciprocating their
hospitality at banquets, (40) then the Lord of the gleaming trident,
his heart overcome with desire, seized you and brought you in his
golden chariot to the house of far-honoured Zeus on high: there,
on a second occasion, Ganymedes also came, (45) on the self-same
service for Zeus. When you were lost to view, and in spite of much
searching people were not able to take you back to your mother,
right away a jealous neighbour spread a tale in secret that they (the
gods) had cut you limb from limb with a knife into water boiling
furiously at the fire; (50) and at table, for the last course, had
divided out your flesh and eaten it. But for me it is impossible
to call any of the blessed ones a glutton. I stand back from that.
Profitless, most often, is the lot that falls to slanderers. Indeed, if
any mortal man was honoured by the guardians of Olympos, (55)
that man was Tantalos: but he could not digest his great good
fortune, and through insolence he met with ruin unsurpassed
which the Father hung over him, a mighty rock: striving
constantly to cast this from his head he wanders far from
happiness. He has this helpless life of perpetual toil, a fourth
trouble (60) among three others, a wearisome burden, because
from the immortals he stole the nectar and ambrosia with which
they had made him imperishable, and gave them to his drinking
companions. If any man hopes to escape god's notice in anything

he does, he is in error. (65) So the immortals thrust forth again his son to join once more the short-lived race of men. When his youthful beauty was at its bloom and down covered his darkening jaw, his thought turned to a marriage which was at hand: to receive renowned Hippodameia (70) from her father in Pisa. Coming close to the grey sea, alone in the darkness, he cried to the deep-roaring Lord of the noble trident: who appeared close by his feet. (75) He said to him, 'If the friendly gifts of the Cyprian (goddess) count at all in one's favour, Poseidon, check the bronze spear of Oinomaos and convey me in the swiftest chariot to Elis, and bring me to victory. (80) For in putting off his daughter's marriage he has slain thirteen suitors. Great danger does not call for a coward. Since we must die, why sit in the shadows and in vain nourish old age without renown, with no share in all that is fine? But for me this contest (85) shall be my goal: do you grant a welcome outcome.'

36. *Ταντάλου*: lengthened vowels in Pindar (§23.1) are represented in the vulgate by the spurious diphthongs of epic rather than the open *ω/η* of Doric (and Boeotian). This must represent a performance tradition: P. himself would have used *O* and *E*.   *σέ*: an epic (i.e. Ionic and literary Aeolic) form of the pronoun (§32.5): cf. *τε* 48 below.   *φθέγξομαι*: the 'Doric' future is not used (§40.2).

37. *τόν*: with demonstrative force (because the meal was famous, and P.'s version is to be different): cf. *τὰ λύχνα*, Alkaios 75 (b)1. *ὁπότ(ε) . . .τότ(ε)*: epic forms (§40.7). The text of P. has only *ὅτε*, *πότε*, but WGk. *τόκα* is occasionally found for *τότε*.

38. *ἐς*: the normal form in choral dialect (§32.10 and cf. 78 3 Ibykos). Boe. *ἐν* with the acc. is occasionally found in P. (perhaps a northern Doric form).

39. *θεοῖσι*: epic form (§32.13).

40. *Ἀγλαοτρίαιναν*: appellative built on *τρίαινα*, 'trident' (*τρι-*, 'three' plus fem. ending -*αινα*).   *ἁρπάσαι*: §40.4 (P. also uses forms in -*ξ*-).

41. *χρυσέαισι*: adj. of material in *-eyos (cf. Lat. *aureus*, and *πορφυρέην* 67 154): contrast *χρύσιον* 74 (a)8.   *ἀν'*: *ἀνά* with the dat. is found only in epic and lyric poetry.   *ἵπποις*: cf. the Hom. use of *ἵπποι*, 'chariot'.

42. **ποτί**: both WGk. and Homeric (cf. §28.7). Also Boe. **μεταβᾶσαι**: the sigmatic aor. could produce a factitive stem (cf. ἔστησα vs. ἔστην, etc.).

45. **Ζηνί**: analogical form built on the old acc. *Zῆν* < *dyēm (Skt. *dyām*). The usual form *Δι(F)ί* is formed on the orig. (zero-grade) stem *ΔιF*- (cf. on **8** 21 *ΔιFείθεμις*).

46. **ἔπελες**: equivalent to ἦσθα (cf. ἔπλετο **66** 116, πέλεται **68** 665). **μαιόμενοι**: vb. associated with epic and Lesb. lyric (cf. μαστροῖς **49** 1).

47. **ἔννεπε**: epic form.

48. **τε**: Instone ad loc. suggests this may be the acc. of *τύ* (§32.5) rather than the connective particle (in which case σέ 36 would be the result of scribal normalization): a scholion ad loc. glosses σε. So also Wackernagel (1892: 362).   **ζέοισαν**: from *ζε-οντ-ya. On these forms, reminiscent of literary (i.e. eastern) Aeolic (§34.11), see on φεροίσαις **76** 61.   **εἰς**: an epic licence (see ἐς 38).

49. **τάμον**: absence of augment is a licence inherited from epic (cf. πιθόμην **66** 103): §14.2.

50. **κρεῶν**: partitive gen. as the grammatical object.

51. **σέθεν**: epic form (cf. **67** 160).

52. **ἀφίσταμαι**: the unusual absence of connective particle (asyndeton) in this and the next phrase is rhetorical (expressing strong antipathy).

53. **ἀκέρδειά** : abstract formed to ἀκερδής (cf. on ἀτελέην **27** 7). **λέλογχεν**: moveable -ν (an epic feature, §32.7) is here used to lengthen a syllable.

54. **εἰ**: epic form (§40.6).

55. **ἦν**: cf. ἦς **45** 21 and §32.2.

57. **ἄν τοι**: editors, τάν οἱ MSS (cf. §32.12, and τόν 58).

59–60. **ἀπάλαμον** ... **ἀθανάτους**: metrical lengthening of the α privative (cf. **68** 668).

60. **μετὰ τριῶν**: cf. τριτο- **51** 23.   **κλέψαις**: aor. ptcpl. (cf. ζέοισαν 48).

61. **ἀλίκεσσι**: Aeolic -εσσι attached to an *o*-stem (§36.4): an epic licence.

64. **θέν νιν**: emendation of the unmetrical θέσαν αὐτόν of the MSS (a typical gloss that has replaced the original words). For WGk. (ἕ-)θέν cf. §32.1.   **νιν**: WGk. enclitic 3 sing. personal pron. (acc.):

45 12. **λαθέμεν**: WGk. (and Boe.) aor. infin. (§40.3). **ἔρδων**: for (*F*)ἔρδω < *Fέρζω see on ῥέζουσιν **68** 685.

65. **<οἱ>**: moved by edd. from after τοὔνεκα. 3 sing. pron., dat. (as at **45** 13) indicating Tantalus' involvement. Hiatus before (*F*)οι.

66. **αὖτις**: epic and Ion. form (Att. αὖθις may be analogical on advbs. in -θι). **ἀνέρων**: the stem without the secondary glide -δ- is taken from epic.

67. **πρός**: WGk. and Boe. ποτί (§40.8).

70. **Πισάτᾱ**: gen. (§24.3) of Πισάτᾱς, '(man) of Pisa'.

71. **σχεθέμεν**: aor. infin. (cf. δωσέμεν **66** 117) built to ἔσχεθον, with zero-grade of *segʰ- (cf. σχήσω **69** 15) and a factitive extension -θ-.

74. **πάρ**: apocope (§24.5): contrast παρά 70.

75. **μέν**: cf. **76** 50. Here emphatic. **Ποσείδαον**: voc. of the Att.-Ion. form (cf. on Ποhοίδαια **33** 12, and **39**).

76. **τέλλεται**: cf. περιτέλλεται **75** (c)1.

78. **Ἆλιν**: §38.5. An interesting intrusion of the local dialect of Elis into literary language.

79. **ὀλέσαις**: aor. ptcpl. (cf. ζέοισαν 48).

80. **ἀναβάλλεται**: absence of apocope, a literary feature (§24.5).

82. **τά**: an interrog. pron. derived from the neut. plur. *kʷi̯a (cf. Lat. *quia*). A very rare instance of a Boe. dialect form in Pindar (Leumann 1950: 48 f.): the Megarian in Ar. *Acharn.* has the WGk. form σά (the phonological equivalent in Att. is the indef. pron. ἄττα, a false segmentation of ὁποῖά ττα: §24.8). It is hard to see why P. should have used this form, which invites speculation on what stage of the text our vulgate reflects: was the Athenian version influenced by a performance tradition in neighbouring Boeotia? **κέ**: Aeolic (epic) particle: §36.7.

84. **κᾰλῶν**: so Att., Lesb., and most mainland WGk. dialects (Boe. κάλFος). Hom. epic has κᾱλ-, but there are a few instances of κᾰλ- in Hesiod (greatly outnumbered by κᾱλ-). Alkm. and the Doric literary tradition appear to use both as convenient. **ἄμμορος**: a Hom., evidently Aeolic, form (-μμ- < *-σμ-, cf. ἐνὶ μμεγάροις **77** 216).

85. **τύ**: WGk. form (although σύ is commoner in our text of Pindar): §32.5. **δίδοι**: 2 sing. imperat. (see **12** 2 for the form, and also the shape of the phrase).

THE CLASSICAL WORLD: 480–320 BC

80. Aeschylos (Athens), *Agamemnon* 239–63 (first play of the *Oresteia* trilogy, 458 BC). The end of the parodos (entry song) and the entry of Klytaimestra for the first scene. Text: D. Page (Oxford 1972). Metre: (239–56) lyric: iambic and cretic, (257–63) iambic trimeters. ▶▶ Denniston and Page (1957).

The chorus describe the sacrifice of Iphigeneia by her father Agamemnon, who was told by the prophet Kalkhas that this would produce a sailing wind for Troy. Their ode ends and they greet Klytaimestra.

κρόκου βαφὰς δ' ἐς πέδον χέουσα
240 ἔβαλλ' ἕκαστον θυτήρων ἀπ' ὄμματος βέλει φιλοίκτωι,
πρέπουσά θ' ὡς ἐν γραφαῖς, προσεννέπειν
θέλουσ', ἐπεὶ πολλάκις
πατρὸς κατ' ἀνδρῶνας εὐτραπέζους
245 ἔμελψεν, ἁγνᾶι δ' ἀταύρωτος αὐδᾶι πατρὸς
φίλου τριτόσπονδον εὔποτμον παιῶνα φίλως ἐτίμα.

τὰ δ' ἔνθεν οὔτ' εἶδον οὔτ' ἐννέπω·
τέχναι δὲ Κάλχαντος οὐκ ἄκραντοι.
250 Δίκα δὲ τοῖς μὲν παθοῦσιν μαθεῖν ἐπιρρέπει· τὸ μέλλον δ'
ἐπεὶ γένοιτ' ἂν κλύοις· πρὸ χαιρέτω·
ἴσον δὲ τῶι προστένειν·
τορὸν γὰρ ἥξει σύνορθρον αὐγαῖς.
255 πέλοιτο δ' οὖν τἀπὶ τούτοισιν εὖ πρᾶξις, ὡς
θέλει τόδ' ἄγχιστον Ἀπίας γαίας μονόφρουρον ἕρκος.

ἥκω σεβίζων σόν, Κλυταιμήστρα, κράτος·
δίκη γάρ ἐστι φωτὸς ἀρχηγοῦ τίειν
260 γυναῖκ', ἐρημωθέντος ἄρσενος θρόνου.
σὺ δ' εἴ τι κεδνὸν εἴτε μὴ πεπυσμένη
εὐαγγέλοισιν ἐλπίσιν θυηπολεῖς,
κλύοιμ' ἂν εὔφρων· οὐδὲ σιγώσηι φθόνος.

Trailing her saffron garment towards the ground she cast (240) a pitiful look from her eyes at each of the participants at the sacrifice: she stood out, like the subject of a picture, longing to

address them—since often she had sung at the banquets of her
father, hospitality for his male companions, and virginal with pure
voice had lovingly honoured that paean which accompanies the
third libation for her dear father. As for the rest, I neither saw it
nor do I talk of it. The skill of Kalkhas was not without fulfilment. (250) Justice comes down heavily on one side and brings
learning through suffering. The future you will know when it
comes. Rejoice in advance of it—it is the same to mourn in
advance. For when it comes it will be clear as the rays of the dawn.
Well, as for what follows let it turn out for the best, in accordance
with the wishes of this present guardian, sole defence of the Apian
land.

I have come out of reverence for your authority, Klytaimestra. For
it is right to honour the wife (260) of the man in command,
when the throne is empty of the male. Whether or not you have
learned something new as you sacrifice with hope of good news,
I would gladly hear. But there shall be no resentment if you are
silent.

239. **κρόκου βαφάς**: the use of abstract nouns for concrete (in
general rarer in Greek than in English) is characteristic of high tragic
language, and parodied in comedy.   **ἐς**: the normal form in choral
dialect, and also Ionic (§32.10 and cf. **78** 3 Ibykos). Tragedy uses both
as convenient.

240. **θυτήρων**: agent noun (confined to tragedy) built to θύω.
Agents in -τηρ were archaisms in Att.-Ion. (see Palmer 1980: 254),
where -της (orig. confined to compound nouns such as κυνηγέτης)
had become the standard form.   **ὄμματος**: poetic word (**78** 2):
Att. ὀφθαλμός.   **φιλοίκτωι**: hapax. The freedom with which tragic
language forms compounds was also parodied in comedy.

241. **προσεννέπειν**: a verb confined to Pindar and tragedy (cf.
79 47).

242. **θέλουσ(α)**: poetic and Ionic form (Att. uses ἐθέλω): cf. on
74 (a)24.

245. **ἔμελψεν**: epic and lyric verb.   **ἀγνᾶι**: with the ā characteristic of WGk. (in fact, all dialects apart from Att.-Ion.): the
principal marker of literary Doric in the lyric sections of Att. drama.
ἀταύρωτος: a harsh metaphor (picked up in a comic context at Ar.

Lys. 217): the adj. may be denominative, or based on a denom. vb. ταυρόω (Palmer 1980: 257).

250. **ἐπιρρέπει**: of scales, to sink in one direction; then 'allot' (trans.). The -ρρ- points to initial *wr-.

251. **κλύοις**: an epic and poetic verb. The syntax (with ἄν and a force close to the future) is not unusual.

255. **πέλοιτο**: for the sense εἴη cf. ἔπελες **79** 46 with refs. **τούτοισιν**: both tragedy and comedy use the long and short forms of the dat. plur. as convenient.

256. **τόδ' ἄγχιστον**: a ref. either to the chorus, or to Klytaimestra as she enters. The adj. is poetic and Ionic. **Ἀπίας**: the Peloponnese, or Argos specifically (Ἀπία from a mythical king Ἆπις: ā); here influenced by the Hom. ἐξ ἀπίης γαίας with a different adj. ἄπιος (built to ἀπό, with short initial α).

257. The chorus turn now to iambics, the usual conversational metre of Att. drama, as the singing ends and the scene with Klytaimestra begins. 'Doric' features of the language disappear, and the diction becomes slightly less exalted. Nevertheless, much of the vocab. is epic and poetic (σεβίζων, φωτός, τίειν, etc.).

260. **ἄρσενος**: epic and Ion. (§31.5). Like -ττ-, Att. -ρρ- was avoided in high poetry. So also Thuc.

81. Aristophanes (Athens), *Women at the Thesmophoria* 846–65 (City Dionysia, 411 BC). Text: C. Austin and D. Olson (Oxford 2004). Metre: iambic trimeters. ▶ Sommerstein (1994), C. Austin and D. Olson (2004).

The poet Euripides has persuaded a male relative to dress up as a woman and spy on the Thesmophoria (a women's festival). He has been caught, and is waiting for Euripides to rescue him from his suspicious guard Kritylla.

REL. ἰλλὸς γεγένημαι προσδοκῶν· ὁ δ' οὐδέπω.
τί δῆτ' ἂν εἴη τοὐμποδών; οὐκ ἔσθ' ὅπως
οὐ τὸν Παλαμήδη ψυχρὸν ὄντ' αἰσχύνεται.
τῶι δῆτ' ἂν αὐτὸν προσαγαγοίμην δράματι;
ἐγῶιδα· τὴν καινὴν Ἑλένην μιμήσομαι.   850
πάντως <δ'> ὑπάρχει μοι γυναικεία στολή.
KRIT. τί αὖ σὺ κυρκυνᾶις; τί κοικύλλεις ἔχων;

πικρὰν Ἑλένην ὄψει τάχ᾽, εἰ μὴ κοσμίως
ἕξεις, ἕως ἂν τῶν πρυτάνεών τις φανῆι.

REL. Νείλου μὲν αἵδε καλλιπάρθενοι ῥοαί,   855
ὃς ἀντὶ δίας ψακάδος Αἰγύπτου πέδον
λευκῆς νοτίζει μελανοσυρμαῖον λεών.

KRIT. πανοῦργος εἶ, νὴ τὴν Ἑκάτην τὴν φωσφόρον.

REL. ἐμοὶ δὲ γῆ μὲν πατρὶς οὐκ ἀνώνυμος,
Σπάρτη, πατὴρ δὲ Τυνδάρεως.

KRIT.   σοί γ᾽ ὤλεθρε 860
πατὴρ ἐκεῖνός ἐστι; Φρυνώνδας μὲν οὖν.

REL. Ἑλένη δ᾽ ἐκλήθην.

KRIT.   αὖθις αὖ γίγνει γύνη,
πρὶν τῆς ἑτέρας δοῦναι γυναικίσεως δίκην;

REL. ψυχαὶ δὲ πολλαὶ δι᾽ ἔμ᾽ ἐπὶ Σκαμανδρίοις
ῥοαῖσιν ἔθανον.

KRIT.   ὤφελες δὲ καὶ σύ γε. 865

RELATIVE. I've gone cross-eyed with looking out for him, but he's not appeared yet. So what could be keeping him? It must be that he's ashamed of the *Palamedes* because it's such a frigid drama. What play can I use to bring him here? (850) I know: I'll act out that new *Helen*. At any rate I've got lots of women's clothing.—KRITYLLA. What are you up to now? Why are you squinting about? I'll give you Helen in a minute if you don't behave yourself till one of the magistrates gets here.—(855) REL. These are the fair and virginal streams of the Nile which, instead of heavenly rain, waters the white plain of Egypt and its black, laxative-swallowing people.—KRIT. You're a criminal, by Hekate bringer of light.—REL. My fatherland is not without renown: (860) Sparta, and my father is Tyndareos.—KRIT. He's your father, you pest? Phrynondas, more like.—REL. I am called Helen.—KRIT. You're becoming a woman again, before you've paid the penalty for your earlier female impersonation?—REL. Many were the souls that perished for my sake by the streams of Scamander.—KRIT. A pity you weren't one of them.

847. **δῆτ(α)**: a particle alien to epic and lyric poetry, but common in comedy, and also found in tragic dialogue.

848. **Παλαμήδη**: the name of a play (produced in 415).

849. **τῶι**: Ion. *τέωι*, the older form of dat. *τίνι* (see *τέο* 70 1).

850. **καινὴν Ἑλένην**: Eur. *Helen*, produced in the previous year (412).

852. **κυρκυνᾶις**: lit. *to mix*, hence *hatch* (a plot).   **κοικύλλεις**: 'goggle'. Formed (according to Hesychius) to *κῦλα* (n. pl.), the bags under the eyes. Verbs in -*ύλλω* are hardly found outside comedy (see Peppler 1921: 152–3). The line illustrates the lively and colloquial language that is characteristic of comedy. So also *ἔχων*, 'keep doing', common in Ar.

855. These tragic lines are identifiable by the normal 'high' poetic diction of tragedy, and a stricter metrical pattern. They are the two opening lines of *Helen* (857 tails off into para-tragedy).

857. **μελανοσυρμαῖον**: instant bathos is provided by the comic compound. The third line of *Helen* is *λευκῆς τακείσης χιόνος ὑγραίνει γύας*.   **λεών**: *λāός* outside Att.-Ion. (§30.2).

858. **πανοῦργος**: with -*οῦργος* taken from compds. such as *κακοῦργος < κακό(F)οργος* (cf. on *κανναβιōργόν* 31 8). These compds. are usually accented on the last syllable: proper names (*Λυκοῦργος*, etc.) and these two terms have a retracted accent (perhaps the influence of the vocative: cf. Att. *πόνηρος* for *πονηρός*).

861. **Φρυνώνδας**: not a specific person, but a proverbial name (which could be used as an insult) associated with *πονηρία*.

863. **γυναικίσεως**: abstract formed to *γυναικίζω* (cf. *γυναικίζουσι* 84 7).

865. **ἔθανον**: the uncompounded verb is found only in high poetry (and similarly with other verbs: e.g. *ἱκνέομαι* in poetry, *ἀφικνέομαι* in prose).

82. Euripides (Athens), *Orestes* 126–51 (408 BC). Text: M. L. West (Warminster 1987). Metre: iambic trimeters, lyric (parodos 139–51, predominantly dochmiac).

▶▶ West (1987), Willink (1986).

Elektra sits by the sleeping Orestes, who is being driven mad by the Furies after killing his mother: her sour comments on the departing Helen are interrupted by the entrance of the chorus.

EL.   ὦ φύσις, ἐν ἀνθρώποισιν ὡς μέγ᾽ εἶ κακόν—
        σωτήριόν τε τοῖς καλῶς κεκτημένοις.

εἴδετε, παρ᾽ ἄκρας ὡς ἀπέθρισεν τρίχας,
σώιζουσα κάλλος; ἔστι δ᾽ ἡ πάλαι γυνή.
θεοί σε μισήσειαν, ὥς μ᾽ ἀπώλεσας   130
καὶ τόνδε πᾶσάν θ᾽ Ἑλλάδ᾽. ὢ τάλαιν᾽ ἐγώ·
αἵδ᾽ αὖ πάρεισι τοῖς ἐμοῖς θρηνήμασιν
φίλαι ξυνωιδοί· τάχα μεταστήσουσ᾽ ὕπνου
τόνδ᾽ ἡσυχάζοντ᾽, ὄμμα δ᾽ ἐκτήξουσ᾽ ἐμόν
δακρύοις, ἀδελφὸν ὅταν ὁρῶ μεμηνότα.   135
           ὦ φίλταται γυναῖκες, ἡσύχωι ποδί
χωρεῖτε, μὴ ψοφεῖτε, μηδ᾽ ἔστω κτύπος.
φιλία γὰρ ἡ σὴ πρευμενὴς μέν, ἀλλ᾽ ἐμοί
τόνδ᾽ ἐξεγεῖραι συμφορὰ γενήσεται.
CHO.   σῖγα σῖγα, λεπτὸν ἴχνος ἀρβύλας   140
           τίθετε, μὴ κτυπεῖτ᾽.
EL.   ἀποπρὸ βᾶτ᾽ ἐκεῖσ᾽, ἀποπρό μοι κοίτας.
CHO.   ἰδού, πείθομαι.
EL.   ἃ ἅ, σύριγγος ὅπως πνοὰ   145
           λέπτου δόνακος, ὦ φίλα, φώνει μοι.
CHO.   ἴδ᾽, ἀτρεμαῖον ὡς ὑπόροφον φέρω
           βοάν.
EL.   ναί, οὕτως.
κάταγε κάταγε, πρόσιθ᾽ ἀτρέμας, ἀτρέμας ἴθι·
λόγον ἀπόδος ἐφ᾽ ὅτι χρέος ἐμόλετέ ποτε·   150
χρόνια γὰρ πεσὼν ὅδ᾽ εὐνάζεται.

ELEKTRA. Oh nature, what a great evil you are to human beings—
and a saviour to those who have done well. Did you see how she
just cut off the ends of her hair, preserving her good looks? She's
the same woman she always was. (130) May the gods hate you, as
you have destroyed me and this man here and the whole of Greece.
Woe is me, here are my friends again, who join with me in songs
of lament. They're likely to rouse this sleeper from his rest—then
they'll cause my eyes to melt into tears, when I see my brother out
of his mind. Dearest women, come forward with a soft step—do
not clatter—do not let there be a noise: your friendship is well
meaning, but to wake him up will be a disaster for me.—CHORUS.
Hush! Hush! Let your boots tread softly (140); do not make a
noise.—EL. Move away over there, away from the sleeper.—CHO.

See, I'm doing as you say.—EL. Ah! Like the breath of a pipe made of soft reeds, my love—make your voice like that for me.—CHO. See, how I keep my noise still indoors.—EL. Yes, like that. Draw in, draw in, approach quietly. Tell me the business on which you have come. (150) For at long last he is settled and sleeps.

126. **ἀνθρώποισιν**: see τούτοισιν **80** 255.

129. **εἴδετε**: apparently addressed to the audience, a liberty with dramatic illusion reminiscent of comedy. Her chatty style nevertheless contains poetic forms such as ἀπέθρισεν (Archilochos), a syncopated form of ἀποθερίζω (formed to θέρος 'summer', i.e. 'to mow').

132. **θρηνήμασιν**: poetic noun (plur. only).

140. Lyric dialogue marks the entry of the chorus: hence Doric βᾶτ᾽, κοίτας, πνοά, etc. **ἀρβύλας**: a foreign import into Gk., and characteristic of Ionic (i.e. 'poetic' in Att.). MSS have ἀρβύλης. 140–2 are quoted by Dionysios of Halikarnassos (*De comp. verb.* 11) to illustrate his statement that in sung poetry the music overrides the pitch accent on the words: 'the phrase σῖγα σῖγα λεπτὸν are sung to one note, although each of the three words has both low and high pitch . . .'

150. **χρέος**: 'debt' in normal Attic, 'matter, affair' in poetry. **ἐμόλετε**: ἔμολον is found in Hom. and in Doric (not in Attic prose apart from Xenophon).

83. Herodotos 1. 37–8 (*c.*425 BC). Text: K. Hude (Oxford 1927). ▶▶ Sicking and Stork (1997: 158–64).

Kroisos, king of Lydia, explains to his son why he must not join the boar-hunt.

(37) ἀποχρεωμένων δὲ τούτοισι τῶν Μυσῶν ἐπεσέρχεται ὁ τοῦ Κροίσου παῖς ἀκηκοὼς τῶν ἐδέοντο οἱ Μυσοί. οὐ φαμένου δὲ τοῦ Κροίσου τόν γε παῖδά σφι συμπέμψειν λέγει πρὸς αὐτὸν ὁ νεηνίης τάδε· (.2) «ὦ πάτερ, τὰ κάλλιστα πρότερόν κοτε καὶ γενναιότατα ἡμῖν ἦν ἔς τε πολέμους καὶ ἐς ἄγρας φοιτέοντας εὐδοκιμέειν· νῦν δὲ ἀμφοτέρων με τούτων ἀποκλῄσας ἔχεις, οὔτε τινὰ δειλίην μοι παριδὼν οὔτε ἀθυμίην. νῦν τε τέοισί με χρὴ ὄμμασι ἔς τε ἀγορὴν καὶ ἐξ ἀγορῆς φοιτέοντα φαίνεσθαι; (.3) κοῖος μέν τις

τοῖσι πολιήτῃσι δόξω εἶναι, κοῖος δέ τις τῆι νεογάμωι γυναικί;
κοίωι δὲ ἐκείνη δόξει ἀνδρὶ συνοικέειν; ἐμὲ ὦν σὺ ἢ μέθες ἰέναι
ἐπὶ τὴν θήρην, ἢ λόγωι ἀνάπεισον ὅκως μοι ἀμείνω ἐστὶ ταῦτα
οὕτω ποιεόμενα.» (38) ἀμείβεται Κροῖσος τοισίδε· «ὦ παῖ, οὔτε
δειλίην οὔτε ἄλλο οὐδὲν ἄχαρι παριδών τοι ποιέω ταῦτα, ἀλλά
μοι ὄψις ὀνείρου ἐν τῶι ὕπνωι ἐπιστᾶσα ἔφη σε ὀλιγοχρόνιον
ἔσεσθαι, ὑπὸ γὰρ αἰχμῆς σιδηρέης ἀπολέεσθαι. (.2) πρὸς ὦν τὴν
ὄψιν ταύτην τόν τε γάμον τοι τοῦτον ἔσπευσα καὶ ἐπὶ τὰ παραλαμ-
βανόμενα οὐκ ἀποπέμπω, φυλακὴν ἔχων, εἴ κως δυναίμην ἐπὶ τῆς
ἐμῆς σε ζόης διακλέψαι. εἷς γάρ μοι μοῦνος τυγχάνεις ἐὼν παῖς·
τὸν γὰρ δὴ ἕτερον διεφθαρμένον [τὴν ἀκοήν] οὐκ εἶναί μοι
λογίζομαι.»

The Mysians were satisfied with these (words of Kroisos), and
there entered Kroisos' son, who had heard what the Mysians
requested. On Kroisos' refusal to send his son along with them, the
young man said to him: (.2) 'Father, it used at one time to be the
finest and noblest thing for us to win renown by going to wars and
on hunting expeditions; but now you have debarred me from
both, even though you have discerned in me no trace of cowardice
or lack of spirit. Now with what face must I show myself as I make
my way to and from the market-place? (.3) What kind of man shall
I seem to the citizens, and what kind of man to the wife I have just
married? What kind of husband will she think she lives with? So
then, either let me go to the hunt or give me a convincing reason
why this action of yours is best for me.' (38) Kroisos answered
with the following words: 'My son, I am doing this not because I
have found in you cowardice or any other disgraceful trait; no, a
vision appeared to me in a dream as I slept, and standing by me it
said you would not live long, for you would be killed by an iron
spear. (.2) Because of this vision I have hurried on your marriage,
and I refuse to send you to take part in these activities, keeping
guard in the hope that I may be able to keep you safe while I am
alive. For you are my only real son: for the other is afflicted [in his
hearing], and I do not count him.'

(37)

1. (**ἀπο-)χρεωμένων**: ptcpl. (pass.) < -χρηόμενος (§30.2): epic
(with synizesis of εω), Ion. and WGk. The verb grew out of χρή

(subst.), 'need, use'. Ion. forms in χρα- were formed analogically to the aor. (τιμήσασθαι : τιμᾶσθαι :: χρήσασθαι : x→ χρᾶσθαι) and passed into the koiné.   **τούτοισι**: §32.14   **ἐπ-εσέρχεται**: for ἐς see §32.10. The technical term for dramatic entrance. The 'historical' pres. tense is not found in Homer. It is a feature of classical historiography and the orators (and speeches in tragedy), traditionally interpreted as a stylistic device (vividness, etc.); modern work in discourse analysis, however, has emphasized its role in the structuring of the narrative (Sicking and Stork (1997) argue that in the present context it functions as a marker of a separate narrative unit—one which interrupts the progression of time in the main story).   **φαμένου**: ptcpl. of φημί, used along with φάς in epic and Ionic prose: both are alien to Att., which uses φάσκων.   **σφι**: 3 plur. pron. (not reflexive), dat. atonic: Homeric and poetic, but also found in WGk. epigraphic texts. Cf. on σφεις 7 10.   **νεηνίης**: §30.1.

2. **κοτε**: §31.7.   **ἦν**: §32.2.   **φοιτέοντας**: lit. Ionic (but not epic) has φοιτέω instead of expected φοιτάω. There are sporadic instances of the shift of αο/αω to εο/εω in vowel-stem verbs in Ion. and WGk. The variation is morphological rather than phonological, and seems to represent the beginnings of a general tendency in Gk. to assimilate the two patterns (in Ion. this would be helped by the identity of aor. and fut. forms). See Méndez Dosuna (1985: 223–5), Horrocks (1997: 242–6).   **εὐδοκιμέειν**: an epicism: the Hom. form of the e-stem infin.   **ἀποκληΐσας ἔχεις**: periphrastic perf. formed with ἔχω and the aor. ptcpl. Common in Hdt. and tragedy: not Homeric (see West 1978 on *Works and Days* 42). It is rare in Hellenistic Gk. and subsequently disappeared.   **τέοισι**: dat. plur. τίς (see τέο 70 1).

3. **πολιήτῃσι**: §32.14.   **ὦν**: see on 69 2.   **ἀμείνω**: cf. on πλέω 68 690 and §12.   **ποιεόμενα**: cf. ἐλεόθερος 21 8 (§30.7).

(38)

1. **οὔτε δειλίην οὔτε . . .**: Hdt.'s phrasing as well his diction sometimes has a Homeric ring (cf. *Il.* 1. 93).   **ἐπιστᾶσα**: psilosis (§31.6): rough breathings are written in the text (§23.10), but voiceless stops before aspirated vowels are not changed to θ, φ, χ (in contrast to the Hom. vulgate: νύχθ᾽ 66 102).   **σιδηρέης**: uncontracted, as in Hom. (cf. χρυσέαισι 79 41).   **ὑπό**: of an inanimate force is not uncommon in Greek. Not personification: rather

emphasizes the cause of the event (note that this is pivotal in the narration of the argument, and the subsequent tragedy). **ἀπολέεσθαι:** fut. mid. infin. Cf. Hom. ὀλέεσθαι: but the presence of ὀλεῖται at Hom. *Il.* 2. 325, where ὀλέεται would not scan, shows that Hdt.'s uncontracted form is purely graphic (§48.3).
2. **πρός:** 'with regard to, in accordance with'. Not Homeric, but found occasionally in historiography and tragedy. **μοῦνος:** < *μόνϝος (cf. on Πουλυδάμας **66** 100): §30.6. **ἐών:** §32.11. **τὴν ἀκοήν:** cf. on **74** (b)12.

84. Hippokratic corpus: *Airs, Waters, Places* 22. 1–7 (last quarter of the V cent. BC). Text: J. Jouanna (Paris 1996). ▸▸ Van der Eijk (1997).

ἔτι δὲ πρὸς τούτοισιν εὐνουχίαι γίνονται πλεῖστοι ἐν Σκύθηισι καὶ γυναικεῖα ἐργάζονται διαλέγονταί τε ὁμοίως καὶ αἱ γυναῖκες· καλεῦνταί τε οἱ τοιοῦτοι Ἀναριεῖς. (2) οἱ μὲν οὖν ἐπιχώριοι τὴν αἰτίην προστιθέασι θεῶι καὶ σέβονταί τε τούτους τοὺς ἀνθρώπους καὶ προσκυνέουσι δεδοικότες περὶ γ᾽ ἑωυτῶν ἕκαστοι. (3) ἐμοὶ δὲ καὶ αὐτῶι δοκεῖ ταῦτα τὰ πάθεα θεῖα εἶναι καὶ τἆλλα πάντα καὶ οὐδὲν ἕτερον ἑτέρου θειότερον οὐδὲ ἀνθρωπινώτερον, ἀλλὰ πάντα ὁμοῖα καὶ πάντα θεῖα· ἕκαστον δὲ ἔχει φύσιν τῶν τοιούτων καὶ οὐδὲν ἄνευ φύσιος γίνεται. (4) καὶ τοῦτο τὸ πάθος ὥς μοι δοκεῖ γίνεσθαι, φράσω· ὑπὸ τῆς ἱππασίης αὐτοὺς κέδματα λαμβάνει ἅτε ἀεὶ κρεμαμένων ἀπὸ τῶν ἵππων τοῖσι ποσίν· ἔπειτα ἀποχωλοῦνται καὶ ἑλκοῦνται τὰ ἰσχία οἳ ἂν σφόδρα νοσήσωσιν. (5) ἰῶνται δὲ σφᾶς αὐτοὺς τρόπωι τοιῶιδε. ὁκόταν ἄρχηται ἡ νοῦσος, ὄπισθεν τοῦ ὠτὸς ἑκατέρου φλέβα τάμνουσιν· ὁκόταν δὲ ἀπορρυῆι τὸ αἷμα, ὕπνος ὑπολαμβάνει ὑπὸ ἀσθενείης, καὶ καθεύδουσιν· ἔπειτα ἀνεγείρονται, οἱ μέν τινες ὑγιεῖς ἐόντες, οἱ δ οὔ. (6) ἐμοὶ μὲν οὖν δοκεῖ ἐν ταύτηι τῆι ἰήσει διαφθείρεσθαι ὁ γόνος. εἰσὶ γὰρ παρὰ τὰ ὦτα φλέβες, ἃς ἤν τις ἐπιτάμηι, ἄγονοι γίνονται οἱ ἐπιτμηθέντες· ταύτας τοίνυν μοι δοκέουσι τὰς φλέβας ἐπιτάμνειν. (7) οἱ δὲ μετὰ ταῦτα, ἐπειδὰν ἀφίκωνται παρὰ γυναῖκας καὶ μὴ οἷοί τ᾽ ἔωσι χρῆσθαί σφισι, τὸ πρῶτον οὐκ ἐνθυμεῦνται, ἀλλ ἡσυχίην ἔχουσιν. ὁκόταν δὲ δὶς καὶ τρὶς <καὶ> πλεονάκις αὐτοῖσι πειρωμένοισι μηδὲν ἀλλοιότερον ἀποβαίνηι, νομίσαντές τι ἡμαρτηκέναι τῶι θεῶι ὃν ἀπαιτιῶνται, ἐνδύονται στολὴν γυναικείην καταγνόντες ἑωυτῶν

ἀνανδρείην γυναικίζουσί τε καὶ ἐργάζονται μετὰ τῶν γυναικῶν ἃ καὶ
ἐκεῖναι.

Furthermore, many men among the Scythians become like
eunuchs: they do women's work, and speak like women. Such
people are called *Anarieis.* (2) Now the inhabitants ascribe
responsibility for the condition to a god, and they revere and
worship these men, all fearing for themselves. (3) My opinion
also is that these diseases are divine, but so are all the rest, and
none is more divine or more human than any other; they are all
alike, and all are divine. But each of these conditions has its own
natural cause, and none arises without a natural cause. (4) As for
this condition, I shall explain how, in my view, it comes about: as
a result of their equestrian lifestyle their joints become inflamed,
because their feet are constantly suspended from the horses;
those who are badly afflicted next become lame, and develop
sores in the pelvic area. (5) They attempt to treat themselves in
the following manner: at the onset of the illness they cut the vein
behind each ear; when the blood has ceased to flow they are
overcome by weakness, and fall asleep. When they wake up, some
are restored to health, and some are not. (6) It is, in my opinion,
by this treatment that their sexual functioning is destroyed: for
next to the ears are veins, the severing of which causes
impotence. It is these veins, it seems to me, that they sever. (7)
Afterwards, when they go to their wives and are unable to have
sex with them, they think nothing of it on the first occasion, and
let it rest. But when their second, third, and further attempts
have exactly the same result, they think they have committed
some offence against god, and they hold him to be the cause: so
they put on women's clothes, condemning themselves for
unmanliness, and they behave like women, joining with the
women in their tasks.

1. **τούτοισιν**: §§32.14, 32.7.   **εὐνουχίαι**: 'one who is like a
eunuch.' For the suffix -ίας meaning 'with a characteristic trait of'
see Chantraine (1933: 93). εὐνοῦχος, from εὐνή + ἔχω (see on
Πολιάχōι **33** 3), is first attested in Hipponax and probably translates
a term that the Greeks learned from the Persians in Asia Minor.
γίνονται: cf. γίνηται **7** 2.   **καλεῦνται**: §30.7.   **Ἀναριεῖς**: edd.,

ἀνδριεῖς MSS. Emendation is on the basis of Ἐνάρεες in Hdt. 1. 105, who gives a different account of the same phenomenon. Scythian was an Iranian dialect: a derivation from *a-* (privative) and *nar-* ('man', cf. Gk. ἀνήρ) would fit semantically.

    2. **προστιθέασι**: the usual Ion. form is τιθεῖσι (§32.12). **δεδοικότες**: perf. formed to δείδω, itself an old perf. (< *δε-δϝοι-α). **ἑωυτῶν**: see on ἑωυτῶι 21 7.

    3. **ἕκαστον δὲ ἔχει φύσιν κτλ**.: the polar structure and repetition are reminiscent of early Ionic exposition (e.g. Anaxagoras, fr. 12, on νοῦς).

    4. **ἱππασίης**: abstract in -σία formed to ἱππάζομαι (Homer, Hdt.). The formation was particularly productive in Ionic, and subsequently in the koiné.   **κρεμαμένων**: because there were no stirrups.   **ἰσχία**: perhaps the groin. In general the pelvis, which supports the body in sitting position (the *ischia* may also be the sitting bones, as in modern usage).

    5. **ὁκόταν**: §31.7.   **νοῦσος**: the lengthened vowel could be explained by supposing orig. *νόσϝος (Willi 2006); or the form may be a Homerism (cf. on Πουλυδάμας **66** 100). But cf. νοσήσωσιν 4.   **τάμνουσιν**: Att. τέμνω takes its vowel from aor. ἔτεμον (see on διατάμνοντος 35 12).   **ἐόντες**: §32.11.

    6. **ἤν**: edd., ἐάν MSS (cf. **19** 9).

    7. **γυναικίζουσι**: cf. **81** 863 γυναικίσεως.

85. Thucydides, 3. 36–7. The debate over Mytilene.
Late V cent. BC. Text: H. Stuart Jones (Oxford 1900).
▶▶ Denniston (1952: 1–22), Dover (1997).

The Athenian assembly has voted to punish the people of Mytilene for revolt by putting the entire male population to death, and enslaving the women and children. The next day they have second thoughts and convene another assembly.

(36.6) καταστάσης δ' εὐθὺς ἐκκλησίας ἄλλαι τε γνῶμαι ἀφ' ἑκάστων ἐλέγοντο καὶ Κλέων ὁ Κλεαινέτου, ὅσπερ καὶ τὴν προτέραν ἐνενικήκει ὥστε ἀποκτεῖναι, ὤν καὶ ἐς τὰ ἄλλα βιαιότατος τῶν πολιτῶν τῶι τε δήμωι παρὰ πολὺ ἐν τῶι τότε πιθανώτατος, παρελθὼν αὖθις ἔλεγε τοιάδε. (37) «Πολλάκις μὲν ἤδη ἔγωγε καὶ ἄλλοτε ἔγνων δημοκρατίαν ὅτι ἀδύνατόν ἐστιν ἑτέρων ἄρχειν, μάλιστα δ' ἐν τῆι νῦν ὑμετέραι περὶ Μυτιληναίων μεταμελείαι. (.2) διὰ γὰρ τὸ καθ' ἡμέραν ἀδεὲς καὶ ἀνεπιβούλευτον πρὸς ἀλλήλους καὶ ἐς τοὺς ξυμμάχους τὸ αὐτὸ ἔχετε, καὶ ὅτι ἂν ἢ λόγωι πεισθέντες ὑπ' αὐτῶν ἁμάρτητε ἢ οἴκτωι ἐνδῶτε, οὐκ ἐπικινδύνως ἡγεῖσθε ἐς ὑμᾶς καὶ οὐκ ἐς τὴν τῶν ξυμμάχων χάριν μαλακίζεσθαι, οὐ σκοποῦντες ὅτι τυραννίδα ἔχετε τὴν ἀρχὴν καὶ πρὸς ἐπιβουλεύοντας αὐτοὺς καὶ ἄκοντας ἀρχομένους, οἳ οὐκ ἐξ ὧν ἂν χαρίζησθε βλαπτόμενοι αὐτοὶ ἀκροῶνται ὑμῶν, ἀλλ' ἐξ ὧν ἂν ἰσχύι μᾶλλον ἢ τῆι ἐκείνων εὐνοίαι περιγένησθε. (.3) πάντων δὲ δεινότατον εἰ βέβαιον ἡμῖν μηδὲν καθεστήξει ὧν ἂν δόξηι πέρι, μηδὲ γνωσόμεθα ὅτι χείροσι νόμοις ἀκινήτοις χρωμένη πόλις κρείσσων ἐστὶν ἢ καλῶς ἔχουσιν ἀκύροις, ἀμαθία τε μετὰ σωφροσύνης ὠφελιμώτερον ἢ δεξιότης μετὰ ἀκολασίας, οἵ τε φαυλότεροι τῶν ἀνθρώπων πρὸς τοὺς ξυνετωτέρους ὡς ἐπὶ τὸ πλέον ἄμεινον οἰκοῦσι τὰς πόλεις.»

(36.6) The assembly was convened immediately, and various opinions were expressed by the different speakers: in particular by Kleon son of Kleainetos, who had on the previous occasion won the resolution to put (the people of Mytilene) to death. He was in general the most violent of the politicians, and by far the most influential with the people at that time. Coming forward again he spoke as follows: (37) 'On many occasions in the past I have thought that a democracy is incapable of ruling over others, and now especially in your present change of heart concerning the people of Mytilene. (.2) Because of the absence of fear and plotting in your daily relations with each other you feel the same way towards your allies, and when you are persuaded by their rhetoric to make a wrong decision, or give in through pity, you do not stop to think that softness brings danger to yourselves, not gratitude from your allies. You forget that your authority is despotic, and exercised over people who are themselves plotting, since they are ruled against their will; and who obey you, not because you grant them favours which harm yourselves, but because of your strength—it is this which gives you superiority over them, not your acquisition of their goodwill. (.3) But the worst thing of all will be if none of the decisions that we take is allowed to stand, and we fail to realize that a city which uses inferior laws which are immoveable is stronger than one which has fine laws which are never enforced; that ignorance combined with caution is more useful than irresponsible cleverness; and that on the whole it is ordinary people, rather than intellectuals, who run cities more effectively.'

(36)

6. **ἄλλαι τε**: for the expression of emphasis cf. **59** 4 on τά τ᾽ . . . καί. **ἐνενικήκει**: the plup. is rare in Gk., since relative anteriority was generally expressed with the aorist. The plup. simply denotes a state (i.e. the perfect) in the past, and is thus likely to be correlated with the imperf.   **ἐς**: the Ionic form (§32.10).

(37)

1. **δημοκρατίαν ὅτι**: a mixed complement structure. The regular classical acc. and ptcpl. construction has been replaced by acc. plus ὅτι (leaving acc. ἀδύνατον in a syntactically loose position). Perhaps an attempt to capture the anacolutha of live rhetoric.

2. **τὸ . . . ἀδεές**: Thuc. forms abstract substantives with article and neuter adj., and often qualifies them (as here), which is rare (Dover 1997: 34).   **ἀνεπιβούλευτον**: this illustrates both Thuc.'s fondness for adjs. in -τος (cf. on τόλματον **74** (b)17), and his willingness to form prepositional compounds (this was later to become a feature of koiné Greek).   **ξυμμάχους**: Thuc. uses ξυν-, the older Attic form, not συν- with Hdt. (cf. χσυλλήφσομαι **30** 7). Both are found in Homer and Attic drama.   **μεταμελείαι**: the first of a number of abstract nouns in the passage. This is characteristic of Thuc., who uses abstracts more frequently than most prose authors.   **ἢ λόγωι . . . ἢ οἴκτωι**: antithesis is a basic structuring principle in Thuc., but he often varies the construction in the antithesis to avoid Gorgianic symmetry.

3. **καθεστήξει**: intrans. fut. formed to the perf. ἕστηκα. **κρείσσων**: formed to *κρετ-, the *e*-grade of the stem seen in κράτος, etc. Thuc. uses the -σσ- of Ionic and other dialects rather than Att. -ττ- (§23.8): but the lengthened vowel ει is an Att. innovation (perhaps imported from ἀμείνων, ὀλείζων).   **πρός**: 'with regard to, compared to' (cf. **83** 38.2).

86. Xenophon (Athens), *Anabasis* 7. 6. 41–4 (early IV cent. BC). Text: E. C. Marchant (Oxford 1904). ▶▶ Gautier (1911).

Xenophon and the Greek army are in Thrace, near Byzantium. The local Thracian king Seuthes has failed to produce the pay he promised, and Xenophon has to deal with the rebellious soldiers.

(41) Πολυκράτης δὲ Ἀθηναῖος εἶπεν ἐνετὸς ὑπὸ Ξενοφῶντος· «ὁρῶ γε μὴν, ἔφη, ὦ ἄνδρες, καὶ Ἡρακλείδην ἐνταῦθα παρόντα, ὃς παραλαβὼν τὰ χρήματα ἃ ἡμεῖς ἐπονήσαμεν, ταῦτα ἀποδόμενος οὔτε Σεύθηι ἀπέδωκεν οὔτε ἡμῖν τὰ γιγνόμενα, ἀλλ᾽ αὐτὸς κλέψας πέπαται. ἢν οὖν σωφρονῶμεν, ἑξόμεθα αὐτοῦ· οὐ γὰρ δὴ οὗτός γε, ἔφη, Θρᾶιξ ἐστιν, ἀλλ᾽ Ἕλλην ὢν Ἕλληνας ἀδικεῖ.» (42) ταῦτα ἀκούσας ὁ Ἡρακλείδης μάλα ἐξεπλάγη· καὶ προσελθὼν τῶι Σεύθηι λέγει· «ἡμεῖς ἢν σωφρονῶμεν, ἄπιμεν ἐντεῦθεν ἐκ τῆς τούτων ἐπικρατείας.» καὶ ἀναβάντες ἐπὶ τοὺς ἵππους ὤιχοντο ἀπελαύνοντες εἰς τὸ ἑαυτῶν στρατόπεδον. (43) καὶ ἐντεῦθεν Σεύθης πέμπει Ἀβροζέλμην τὸν ἑαυτοῦ ἑρμηνέα πρὸς Ξενοφῶντα καὶ κελεύει αὐτὸν καταμεῖναι παρ᾽ ἑαυτῶι ἔχοντα χιλίους ὁπλίτας, καὶ ὑπισχνεῖται αὐτῶι ἀποδώσειν τά τε χωρία τὰ ἐπὶ θαλάττηι καὶ τὰ ἄλλα ἃ ὑπέσχετο. καὶ ἐν ἀπορρήτωι ποιησάμενος λέγει ὅτι ἀκήκοε Πολυνίκου ὡς εἰ ὑποχείριος ἔσται Λακεδαιμονίοις, σαφῶς ἀποθανοῖτο ὑπὸ Θίβρωνος. (44) ἐπέστελλον δὲ ταῦτα καὶ ἄλλοι πολλοὶ τῶι Ξενοφῶντι ὡς διαβεβλημένος εἴη καὶ φυλάττεσθαι δέοι. ὁ δὲ ἀκούων ταῦτα δύο ἱερεῖα λαβὼν ἐθύετο τῶι Διὶ τῶι βασιλεῖ πότερά οἱ λῶιον καὶ ἄμεινον εἴη μένειν παρὰ Σεύθηι ἐφ᾽ οἷς Σεύθης λέγει ἢ ἀπιέναι σὺν τῶι στρατεύματι. ἀναιρεῖ αὐτῶι ἀπιέναι.

Inspired by Xenophon, Polykrates the Athenian said: 'I see, gentlemen, that Herakleides too is present here—the man who received the property we worked hard for. He sold it, and failed to make over the proceeds to Seuthes or to us, but is secretly keeping it for himself. So if we have any sense, we shall seize him; for this man is no Thracian but a Greek, and being a Greek he is doing wrong to other Greeks' (42). Herakleides was panic-stricken on hearing these words, and approaching Seuthes he said, 'If we have any sense we shall leave here, out of the power of these people.' They got on their horses and were off, riding back to their own camp. (43) And after that Seuthes sent Abrozelmes his interpreter to Xenophon, urging him to stay behind with him, together with a thousand hoplites. Seuthes undertook to assign him the positions on the coast and to make good his other promises. He also said—treating it as a great secret—that he had heard from Polynikos that if Xenophon should fall into the hands of the Lacedaemonians he would undoubtedly be done to death by Thibron. (44) This was the report which many others, too, sent to Xenophon, saying he had been misrepresented and that he must be on his guard. When he heard these messages, Xenophon took two victims and, making sacrifice to Zeus the king, he enquired whether it was better for him to stay with Seuthes on the conditions which Seuthes proposed or to depart with his army. The god recommended him to depart.

41. **ἐνετός**: adj. derived from ἐνίημι, 'injected', hence 'instigated'. Found elsewhere only in Hellenistic Gk. **γε μήν**: this collocation occurs more frequently in Xen. than in the rest of Gk lit. put together (Denniston 1954: 347). The sense is progressive. **παραλαβών**: the prefix παρα- has the connotation of underhand or crooked behaviour. **ἐπονήσαμεν**: the vb. is rare in class. Gk., and unparalleled with χρήματα as object. **πέπαται**: πάομαι (Att. κτάομαι) is a word associated with WGk. (cf. on ἐπαμώχη 35 14). It is a good indication of the mixed character of Xen.'s language that he can use ἐπέπᾱτο and ἐκτῶντο in the same sentence (*Anab.* 1. 9. 19). **ἤν**: Ionic contraction of ἐάν (as opposed to Att. ἄν).

42. **ἐπικρατείας**: elsewhere mostly in Hellenistic Gk.

43. **θαλάττηι**: Xen. uses the Att. form rather than -σσ- with Hdt. and Thuc.

44. **ἐθύετο**: by a Xenophontic usage, mid. θύομαι subsumes both the meaning of 'sacrifice' and that of 'ask the god (to whom sacrifice is made)'. **λῶιον**: an adj. found in epic, Ionic, and high poetry, and in WGk inscriptions. It occurs in Att. prose only in Plato and only in this phrase (i.e. with ἄμεινον). **σύν**: very rare in Att. comedy and prose (Thuc. and the orators mostly use μετά). Its frequency in Xen. is remarkable, and is continued in the koiné. **ἀναιρεῖ**: the verb regularly used of the response of a god by means of an oracle.

HELLENISTIC POETRY

87. Theokritos (Syracuse), *Idyll* 15. 78–99. Early III cent. BC.
Text: Dover (1971). Metre: dactylic hexameter. ▶▶ Gow (1950),
Dover (1971).

*The scene is set in Alexandria around 272 BC. Two Alexandrian
housewives, Gorgo and Praxinoa, have gone to look at the Adonis
festival at the royal palace and are admiring the display. A stranger
accosts them.*

GOR. Πραξινόα, πόταγ' ὧδε· τὰ ποικίλα πρᾶτον ἄθρησον,
      λεπτὰ καὶ ὡς χαρίεντα· θεῶν περονάματα φασεῖς.
PRA. πότνι' Ἀθαναία, ποῖαί σφ' ἐπόνασαν ἔριθοι,   80
      ποῖοι ζωογράφοι τἀκριβέα γράμματ' ἔγραψαν.
      ὡς ἔτυμ' ἐστάκαντι καὶ ὡς ἔτυμ' ἐνδινεῦντι,
      ἔμψυχ', οὐκ ἐνυφαντά. σοφόν τι χρῆμ' ἄνθρωπος.
      αὐτὸς δ' ὡς θαητὸς ἐπ' ἀργυρέας κατάκειται
      κλισμῷ, πρᾶτον ἴουλον ἀπὸ κροτάφων καταβάλλων,   85
      ὁ τριφίλητος Ἄδωνις, ὁ κἠν Ἀχέροντι φιληθείς.
STR. παύσασθ', ὦ δύστανοι, ἀνάνυτα κωτίλλοισαι,
      τρυγόνες· ἐκκναισεῦντι πλατειάσδοισαι ἅπαντα.
PRA. μᾶ, πόθεν ὥνθρωπος; τί δὲ τὶν εἰ κωτίλαι εἰμές;
      πασάμενος ἐπίτασσε· Συρακοσίαις ἐπιτάσσεις.   90
      ὡς εἰδῇς καὶ τοῦτο, Κορίνθιαι εἰμὲς ἄνωθεν,
      ὡς καὶ ὁ Βελλεροφῶν. Πελοποννασιστὶ λαλεῦμες,
      Δωρίσδειν δ' ἔξεστι, δοκῶ, τοῖς Δωριέεσσι.
      μὴ φύῃ, Μελιτῶδες, ὃς ἁμῶν καρτερὸς εἴη,
      πλὰν ἑνός. οὐκ ἀλέγω. μή μοι κενέαν ἀπομάξῃς.   95
GOR. σίγη, Πραξινόα· μέλλει τὸν Ἄδωνιν ἀείδειν
      ἁ τᾶς Ἀργείας θυγάτηρ, πολύιδρις ἀοιδός,
      ἅτις καὶ πέρυσιν τὸν ἰάλεμον ἀρίστευσε.
      φθεγξεῖταί τι, σάφ' οἶδα, καλόν· διαχρέμπτεται ἤδη.

GORGO. Praxinoa, come over here. Look first at the embroideries,
how delicate they are, and how elegant—you'll say they're the
raiment of gods.—(80) PRAXINOA. Lady Athena, what weavers
worked them, what artists drew those lifelike pictures! How
realistic their stance, and how realistic their movement—they're
living, not woven! A skilful creature is man. And he himself, how

marvellous he is, lying on his silver (85) couch, as the first down grows on his temples: the thrice-loved Adonis, beloved even in the world below!—STRANGER. Do stop your endless chattering, you wretched turtle-doves! They'll be the death of me, with their broad vowels.—PR. Heavens, where is the man from? What is it to you, if we do chatter? (90) Get yourself (a slave) and give orders (to him): you are giving orders to Syracusan women. And, I'd have you know, we are Corinthians by descent, just like Bellerophon. We speak in the Peloponnesian manner: I suppose that Dorians are allowed to speak Doric? Let there be nobody with authority over me, Melitodes, (95) except one. I care nothing for you. You needn't smooth off the corn in an empty jar for me.—GO. Hush, Praxinoa: the Argive woman's daughter is about to sing the *Adonis*, the expert singer who did the best in the lament last year. She's going to sing something beautiful, I know: she's just clearing her throat.

78. πόταγ(ε): §40.8. The intrans. sense of the vb. is absent from classical Att. (found in Xen. and koiné Gk.).   ὧδε: 'hither' is a feature of Doric literature (and Homer: **67** 159): confined to tragedy in Attic.   πρᾶτον: §38.2.

79. χαρίεντα: for the form (§13) cf. *pe-ne-we-ta* **1** (a).

80. σφε: acc. plur. form, enclitic: epic and poetic (Att. σφᾶς < σφε- ας, cf. §32.5b).   ἐπόνασαν: for the sporadic interchange of *a*- and *e*-stem vbs. see on φοιτέοντας **83** 12.

82. ἐστάκαντι: for the ending see §31.3.   ἐνδινεῦντι: ἐνδινέω, 'move around' (§23.2b) has a colloquial feel. Neither verb nor simplex is used in Attic prose or comedy.

83. χρῆμ(α): a colloquial idiom. For σοφόν τι cf. ἄφατόν τι **88** 57.

84. αὐτός: i.e. Adonis.   ἀργυρέας: cf. on χρύσιον **74** (a)8.

85. κλισμῶ: this noun is masc. elsewhere.

86. τριφίλητος: for the intensive force of 'three' cf. on τριτο- **51** 23 (and **79** 60).

87. δύστανοι: the stranger also speaks in Doric. A playful ranking of literary convention over realism?

88. πλατειάσδοισαι: the WGk. ᾱ is 'broader' or 'flatter' than koiné η (originally [ε:], moving towards [i:]). For the ptcpl. see on Alkm. φεροίσαις (**76** 61). MSS of Theokr. usually give -σδ- for intervocalic -ζ- (cf. on ὑπασδεύξαισα **74** (a)9).

89. **τίν**: dat. (cf. on τέο **70** 1).

90. **πασάμενος**: for WGk. πάομαι (Att. κτάομαι) cf. on ἐπᾱμώχη **35** 14.

91. **Κορίνθιαι**: Syracuse was founded by Corinth.

92. **Πελοποννασιστί**: the advb. Ἀττικιστί is found as early as the V cent., formed to a verb Ἀττικίζειν; so also later Δωριστί, the likely model for the present form (cf. μηιονιστί **73**(*a*)2).   **λαλεῦμες**: 'chatter' in Attic, but the standard word for 'talk' in the koiné (§23.2*b*).

93. **Δωριέεσσι**: an Aeolic ending (§36.4) in a paradoxical position (cf. on 87).

94. **φύη**: opt. of second aor. φῦναι (ἔφυν), intrans. From *bhū̆-iē-t (the -*i*- of the opt. suffix has dropped).

95. **οὐκ ἀλέγω**: Hom. phrase.   **μή μοι . . .**: i.e. 'don't waste your breath'. χοίνικα 'measure' is presumably to be supplied with κενέαν.

96. **σίγη**: §38.4.

98. **ἀρίστευσε**: metrical lengthening of the first syllable (epic licence).

88. Kallimachos (Cyrene and Alexandria), *Hymn* 6. 53–77. Early III cent. BC. Text: Hopkinson (1984). Metre: dactylic hexameter. ▶️ Schmitt (1970), Hopkinson (1984).

Demeter (disguised as a priestess) warns the young Erysichthon not to cut down trees in her sacred grove and gets a rude response.

«χάζευ, ἔφα, μή τοι πέλεκυν μέγαν ἐν χροῒ πάξω.
ταῦτα δ' ἐμὸν θησεῖ στεγανὸν δόμον, ὧι ἔνι δαῖτας
55 αἰὲν ἐμοῖς ἑτάροισιν ἄδαν θυμαρέας ἀξῶ.»
εἶπεν ὁ παῖς, Νέμεσις δὲ κακὰν ἐγράψατο φωνάν.
Δαμάτηρ δ' ἄφατόν τι κοτέσσατο, γείνατο δ' αὖ θεύς·
ἴθματα μὲν χέρσω, κεφαλὰ δέ οἱ ἄψατ' Ὀλύμπω.
οἱ μὲν ἄρ' ἡμιθνῆτες, ἐπεὶ τὰν πότνιαν εἶδον,
60 ἐξαπίνας ἀπόρουσαν ἐνὶ δρυσὶ χαλκὸν ἀφέντες.
ἁ δ' ἄλλως μὲν ἔασεν, ἀναγκαίαι γὰρ ἕποντο
δεσποτικὰν ὑπὸ χεῖρα, βαρὺν δ' ἀπαμείψατ' ἄνακτα·
«ναὶ ναί, τεύχεο δῶμα, κύον κύον, ὧι ἔνι δαῖτας
ποιησεῖς· θαμιναὶ γὰρ ἐς ὕστερον εἰλαπίναι τοι.»

65 ἃ μὲν τόσσ᾽ εἰποῖσ᾽ Ἐρυσίχθονι τεῦχε πονηρά.
αὐτίκα οἱ χαλεπόν τε καὶ ἄγριον ἔμβαλε λιμόν
αἴθωνα κρατερόν, μεγάλαι δ᾽ ἐστρεύγετο νούσωι.
σχέτλιος, ὅσσα πάσαιτο τόσων ἔχεν ἵμερος αὖτις.
εἴκατι δαῖτα πένοντο, δυώδεκα δ᾽ οἶνον ἄφυσσον.

71 καὶ γὰρ τᾶι Δάματρι συνωργίσθη Διόνυσος·
70 τόσσα Διώνυσον γὰρ ἃ καὶ Δάματρα χαλέπτει.
οὔτε νιν εἰς ἐράνως οὔτε ξυνδείπνια πέμπον
αἰδόμενοι γονέες, προχάνα δ᾽ εὑρίσκετο πᾶσα.
ἦνθον Ἰτωνιάδος νιν Ἀθαναίας ἐπ᾽ ἄεθλα

75 Ὁρμενίδαι καλέοντες· ἀπ᾽ ὧν ἀρνήσατο μάτηρ·
«οὐκ ἔνδοι, χθιζὸς γὰρ ἐπὶ Κραννῶνα βέβακε
τέλθος ἀπαιτησῶν ἑκατὸν βόας.»

'Beat it,' he said, 'or I'll plant my big axe in your skin. These will roof my house, where I shall have splendid banquets constantly (55) for my friends.' The youth spoke, and Nemesis wrote down his evil words. But Demeter was unspeakably enraged, and became again a goddess. Her feet were planted on earth, and her head reached the heavens. The others, half-dead when they saw the goddess, (60) darted off immediately, leaving their axes in the trees. She let them go, because they were just followers, acting under the hand of necessity; but to their unpleasant lord she replied, 'Yes, yes, build a house, you dog, where you shall have banquets! For your dinners will be frequent in the future.' (65) With these words she devised evil for Erysichthon. Immediately she cast upon him a terrible, wild hunger, burning and mighty: he was tormented by a great disease. Miserable creature, as much as he ate, he wanted the same again. Twenty servants worked on his meal, twelve drew wine for him (70) (for Dionysos becomes indignant along with Demeter, and what provokes Demeter provokes Dionysos too). His embarrassed parents would not send him to pot-luck suppers or dinner-parties, but every kind of excuse was made up. The Ormenidae called (75) to invite him along to the games of Itonian Athena, but his mother declined the invitation: 'He's not at home, because yesterday he went off to Krannon to recover a debt of a hundred cows.'

53. **χάζευ**: mid. imper. (§23.2*b*). For the verb cf. on *ὑποχάδδην* **34** 5; in the same position at *Il.* 17.13 (*χάζεο, λεῖπε δὲ νεκρόν* . . .).

54. **ὧι ἔνι δαῖτας**: Homeric diction is freely employed throughout the hymn.

55. **ἄδαν**: Hopkinson (*ἄδην* MSS).   **ἀξῶ**: §40.2 (but most MSS have *ἄξω*).

57. **κοτέσσατο**: both lack of augment and lexeme are Homeric. **γείνατο**: a factitive in **-sa-* formed to (*ἐ*)*γένετο* (cf. *μεταβᾶσαι* **79** 42). Transitive (naturally) in Homer: perhaps *γείνετο* should be read here (see Hopkinson ad loc.).   **θεύς**: contraction (or synizesis) of disyllables is rare (§23.2*b*).

58. **ἴθματα**: root -*i*- of *εἶμι*, 'go' plus a suffix -*θμο*- (cf. *τεθμός* **56** 1).

61. **ἄλλως**: modern edd. (*ἄλλους* MSS).

63. **τεύχεο**: cf. on *χάζευ* 53.

65. **τόσσ(α)**: cf. *ὅσσα* **66** 115.   **εἰποῖσ'**: cf. on *φεροίσαις* **76** 61.

67. **νούσωι**: cf. *νοῦσος* **84** 5.

68. **πάσαιτο** : an epic and Ionic verb.   **αὖτις**: lit. Doric and epic (cf. **66** 79).

69. **εἴκατι**: §32.9.   **δυώδεκα**: the normal form in most dialects outside Att.-Ion.

72. **νιν**: cf. **45** 12.

74. **ἦνθον**: an assimilation of λ to ν attested sporadically in WGk. (incl. Cyrene, cf. *τένται* **51** 18) and Arc.

75. **ἀπ' ὧν ἀρνήσατο**: tmesis with *οὖν* is found in Hdt. and the Hippokratic corpus (with an aor. of repeated action, as here). It may have been a feature of Ionic (and perhaps Doric): cf. Denniston (1954: 430).

76. **ἔνδοι**: form found in a handful of WGk. dialects, incl. Cyrene (cf. **51** 18).

77. **τέλθος**: not found outside Kallimachos (Chantraine 1933: 365).   **βόας**: both this (Hom., koiné) and *βοῦς* (Att.) are analogically reformed (cf. **38** 16): orig. is perhaps *βῶς* (Theokr.) < **gʷōms*.

POST-CLASSICAL PROSE: THE KOINÉ

89. Septuagint: Genesis 18: 1–8: the divine visitation to Abraham. Greek translation from Hebrew, III–II cent. BC. Text: J. W. Williams (ed.), *Septuaginta*: vol. 1, *Genesis* (Göttingen 1974). Standard English translations of the Pentateuch are based on the Masoretic Hebrew text. ▶▶ Janse (1998), Fernández Marcos (2000), Janse (2002).

(1) ὤφθη δὲ αὐτῶι ὁ Θεὸς πρὸς τῆι δρυὶ τῆι Μαμβρή, καθημένου αὐτοῦ ἐπὶ τῆς θύρας τῆς σκηνῆς αὐτοῦ μεσημβρίας. (2) ἀναβλέψας δὲ τοῖς ὀφθαλμοῖς αὐτοῦ εἶδεν, καὶ ἰδοὺ τρεῖς ἄνδρες εἰστήκεισαν ἐπάνω αὐτοῦ· καὶ ἰδὼν προσέδραμεν εἰς συνάντησιν αὐτοῖς ἀπὸ τῆς θύρας τῆς σκηνῆς αὐτοῦ καὶ προσεκύνησεν ἐπὶ τὴν γῆν, (3) καὶ εἶπεν Κύριε, εἰ ἄρα εὖρον χάριν ἐναντίον σου, μὴ παρέλθηις τὸν παῖδά σου· (4) λημφθήτω δὴ ὕδωρ, καὶ νιψάτωσαν τοὺς πόδας ὑμῶν, καὶ καταψύξατε ὑπὸ τὸ δένδρον· (5) καὶ λήμψομαι ἄρτον, καὶ φάγεσθε, καὶ μετὰ τοῦτο παρελεύσεσθε εἰς τὴν ὁδὸν ὑμῶν, οὗ εἵνεκεν ἐξεκλίνατε πρὸς τὸν παῖδα ὑμῶν. καὶ εἶπαν Οὕτως ποίησον, καθὰ εἴρηκας. (6) καὶ ἔσπευσεν Ἀβραὰμ ἐπὶ τὴν σκηνὴν πρὸς Σάρραν καὶ εἶπεν αὐτῆι Σπεῦσον καὶ φύρασον τρία μέτρα σεμιδάλεως καὶ ποίησον ἐγκρυφίας. (7) καὶ εἰς τὰς βόας ἔδραμεν Ἀβραάμ, καὶ ἔλαβεν μοσχάριον ἁπαλὸν καὶ καλὸν καὶ ἔδωκεν τῶι παιδί, καὶ ἐτάχυνεν τοῦ ποιῆσαι αὐτό. (8) ἔλαβεν δὲ βούτυρον καὶ γάλα καὶ τὸ μοσχάριον, ὃ ἐποίησεν, καὶ παρέθηκεν αὐτοῖς, καὶ ἐφάγοσαν· αὐτὸς δὲ παρειστήκει αὐτοῖς ὑπὸ τὸ δένδρον.

(1) And God appeared to him by the oak of Mambre, as he was sitting by the door of his tent at noon. (2) Looking up he saw with his eyes, and lo three men stood before him; and seeing them he ran to meet them from the door of his tent and bowed down to the ground. (3) And he said, 'Lord, if I have found favour before you, do not pass by your servant. (4) Let water be brought, and let them wash your feet, and refresh yourselves under the tree. (5) And I will bring bread, and you shall eat; and afterwards you shall go on your way, because you turned aside for your servant.' And they said, 'So do as you have said.' (6) And Abraam hurried to Sarra in the tent and said to her, 'Hasten and knead three measures of fine flour and make loaves.' (7) And Abraam ran to the cattle and took

a tender and fine calf and gave it to his servant, and he made haste to prepare it. (8) And he took butter and milk and the calf which he had prepared, and set them before the men, and they ate; he himself stood by them under the tree.

1. **ὁ Θεός**: rendering of the ineffable name *yhwh*, replaced in Hebr. reading by 'ădônâi, 'my lord', and usually translated ὁ κύριος in the LXX. (The Engl. 1611 translation is usually LORD; *Jehovah* represents the consonants *yhwh* with the vowels of 'ădônâi, which is what most Hebr. manuscripts give.) **καθημένου αὐτοῦ**: an example of the koiné tendency to use gen. absolute even where the person is mentioned in another case (here dat. αὐτῶι).

2. **τοῖς ὀφθαλμοῖς αὐτοῦ**: αὐτοῦ is a literal rendering of the Hebr.; in the usual Greek idiom it would be omitted. **καὶ ἰδού**: the constant use of this expression in LXX and NT to mark a new stage in the narrative reflects Hebr. *wə-hinnêh* 'and behold'. **εἱστήκεισαν**: koiné form. Class. 3 plur. pluperf. εἱστήκεσαν has been remodelled under the influence of 3 sing. εἱστήκει. **ἐπάνω**: extension of the class. meaning 'above, over' to give the sense 'before'. **εἰς συνάντησιν αὐτοῖς**: Gk. reformation of Hebr. *li-qərât-âm*, 'for their meeting'. This kind of locution is frequent in the LXX, but the phraseology is found also in class. Gk. (Ar. *Clouds* 269, ἔλθετε δῆτ', ὦ πολυτίμητοι Νεφέλαι, τῶιδ' εἰς ἐπίδειξιν, 'Come, most honoured Clouds, to display yourselves to this man').

3. **χάριν**: translation of Hebr. *ḥên* 'grace, favour'. It is the word used in the NT for the key NT concept 'unmerited favour of God': hence Lat. *grātia* (Engl. *grace*). **παῖδα**: 'slave' (Hebr. 'ebed) rather than 'child'.

4. **λημφθήτω**: 3 sing. aor. pass. imper. of λαμβάνω (class. ληφθήτω); in the koiné the -μ- of the pres. spread to the aor. (and to the fut., so λήμψομαι 5). **νιψάτωσαν**: 3 plur. aor. imper. of νίπτω (back-formed from the aor. ἔνιψα < *-nigʷsa), which in the koiné is used in preference to class. νίζω (*nigʷyō): §55.4. **καταψύξατε**: a meaning which would have been expressed in the class. language by the mid. voice; in the koiné there is a tendency to replace the mid. by the act. (as here) or the pass. (§55.2). Cf. on **61** 4.

5. **φάγεσθε**: koiné fut. of ἐσθίω, formed from aor. ἔφαγον (perh. on the model of ἔπιον : πίομαι). **παρελεύσεσθε**: the Ion. fut. prevailed

in the koiné, being morphologically easier than Att. εἶμι.   **οὗ
εἵνεκεν**: conj. 'because' (cf. οὕνεκα), a literary form not reflecting
the spoken language. The long vowel of εἵνεκεν also reflects literary
precedents (found in Hdt. and deriving from epic: see on *e-ne-ka* **4**).
Except in this phrase, the translators of the LXX preferred ἕνεκεν (or
Att. ἕνεκα).   **εἶπαν**: 3 plur., §55.3.   **καθά**: i.e. καθ' ἅ, Hellenistic
form (Att. ὡς, ὥσπερ); καθάπερ (or κατάπερ) is found in class. Att.
and Ion. writers (cf. Denniston 1954: 490).   **σεμιδάλεως**:
σεμίδαλις is a Semitic loan-word (via Anatolian according to
Szemerényi 1974: 156), found in Greek as early as the V cent. Cf. Lat.
simila (It. *semola*).   **ἐγκρυφίας**: apparently because they were
baked buried in hot ashes (ἐγκρύπτω).

7. **βόας**: Homeric and koiné (see on **88** 77).   **μοσχάριον**: dimin.
of μόσχος (§56.4*c*).   **ἐτάχυνεν τοῦ ποιῆσαι**: ταχύνω 'hasten'
(trans.) is here constructed with gen. of the articular infin., a development in the literary koiné of the class. (esp. Thucydidean) use of
τοῦ + infin. to express purpose.   **ποιῆσαι**: a rendering of Hebr.
'ăśōt, 'make, do'; the specific sense required here 'dress, prepare
(meat)' has to be inferred from the fact that the Hebr. verb is often
used in this sense.

8. **ἐφάγοσαν**: 3 plur. aor. (class. ἔφαγον): §55.3.

90. Polybius (Megalopolis, Arcadia), *Histories* 2. 15. 2–9 Mid
II cent. BC. Text: P. Pédech (Paris 1970). ▶▶ Walbank (1957),
Foucault (1972).

Polybius describes the fertility of the Po valley.

(2) ἐλύμου γε μὴν καὶ κέγχρου τελέως ὑπερβάλλουσα δαψίλεια
γίνεται παρ' αὐτοῖς. τὸ δὲ τῶν βαλάνων πλῆθος τὸ γινόμενον ἐκ τῶν
κατὰ διάστημα δρυμῶν ἐν τοῖς πεδίοις ἐκ τούτων ἄν τις μάλιστα
τεκμήραιτο· (3) πλείστων γὰρ ὑϊκῶν ἱερείων κοπτομένων ἐν Ἰταλίαι
διά τε τὰς εἰς τοὺς ἰδίους βίους καὶ τὰς εἰς τὰ στρατόπεδα
παραθέσεις, τὴν ὁλοσχερεστάτην χορηγίαν ἐκ τούτων συμβαίνει
τῶν πεδίων αὐτοῖς ὑπάρχειν. (4) περὶ δὲ τῆς κατὰ μέρος εὐωνίας
καὶ δαψιλείας τῶν πρὸς τὴν τροφὴν ἀνηκόντων οὕτως ἄν τις
ἀκριβέστατα κατανοήσειε. (5) ποιοῦνται γὰρ τὰς καταλύσεις οἱ
διοδεύοντες τὴν χώραν ἐν τοῖς πανδοκείοις, οὐ συμφωνοῦντες περὶ
τῶν κατὰ μέρος ἐπιτηδείων, ἀλλ' ἐρωτῶντες πόσου τὸν ἄνδρα

δέχεται. (6) ὡς μὲν οὖν ἐπὶ τὸ πολὺ παρίενται τοὺς καταλύτας οἱ πανδοκεῖς, ὡς ἱκανὰ πάντ᾽ ἔχειν τὰ πρὸς τὴν χρείαν, ἡμιασσαρίου· τοῦτο δ᾽ ἔστι τέταρτον μέρος ὀβολοῦ· σπανίως δὲ τοῦθ᾽ ὑπερβαίνουσι. τό γε μὴν πλῆθος τῶν ἀνδρῶν, (7) καὶ τὸ μέγεθος καὶ κάλλος τῶν σωμάτων, ἔτι δὲ τὴν ἐν τοῖς πολέμοις τόλμαν, ἐξ αὐτῶν τῶν πράξεων σαφῶς καταμαθεῖν. (8) τῶν δ᾽ Ἄλπεων ἑκατέρας τῆς πλευρᾶς, τῆς ἐπὶ τὸν Ῥοδανὸν ποταμὸν καὶ τῆς ἐπὶ τὰ προειρημένα πεδία νευούσης, τοὺς βουνώδεις καὶ γεώδεις τόπους κατοικοῦσι, τοὺς μὲν ἐπὶ τὸν Ῥοδανὸν καὶ τὰς ἄρκτους ἐστραμμένους Γαλάται Τρανσαλπῖνοι προσαγορευόμενοι, τοὺς δ᾽ ἐπὶ τὰ πεδία Ταυρίσκοι καὶ Ἄγωνες καὶ πλείω γένη βαρβάρων ἕτερα. (9) Τρανσαλπῖνοί γε μὴν οὐ διὰ τὴν τοῦ γένους, ἀλλὰ διὰ τὴν τοῦ τόπου διαφορὰν προσαγορεύονται, τὸ γὰρ τρὰνς ἐξηρμηνευόμενον ἐστὶ πέραν.

A great abundance of rye and millet grows in the region. The quantity of acorns produced in the woodland which is scattered across the plain can be best appreciated by the following: (3) huge numbers of pigs are slaughtered in Italy both for private consumption and for the feeding of the army: it is from this plain that they get almost their entire supply. (4) The general cheapness and abundance of everything pertaining to food production can be most clearly understood as follows: (5) when travellers in the region make a stop in the inns, they do not strike a deal for each individual meal: instead they ask the inclusive price for board per person. (6) For the most part innkeepers take in travellers and provide all they need for half an *as* (i.e. about a quarter-obol). It is rare for the price to be higher than that. The numbers of the local population, (7) their size and fine appearance, and their courage in war, will emerge clearly from the events themselves. (8) On either side of the Alps (one side slopes down to the Rhone, the other to the above-mentioned plain) the mountainous regions which have sufficient soil are inhabited, on the northern side towards the Rhone by Gauls called 'Transalpine', and on the side sloping down to the plain by the Tauriskoi and the Agones and several other barbarian tribes. (9) The term Transalpine does not refer to a feature of the people, but of their location: for *trans* means 'on the other side'.

2. **γε μήν**: see on **86** 41 (Xen.).   **δαψίλεια**: formed to δαψιλής, 'abundant' (for the root cf. Lat. *daps*). An Ionic word which entered the koiné.   **γινόμενον**: cf. γίνηται **7** 2. Standard in the koiné. **δρυμῶν**: a poetic word in Attic, though not in all dialects (cf. **35** 19). It may have been current in P.'s own dialect, or perhaps in Ionic (§56.2). 3. **ὑïκῶν**: adjs. in -ικός seem to have taken off in Ionicizing sophistic and scientific language of the late V cent. (Chantraine 1933: 387): their use is parodied by Aristophanes (*Knights* 1375–81). They are extremely common from the IV cent. Cf. §55.6.   **ἱερείων**: from 'sacrificial animal' to 'animal raised/killed for food' (koiné). **ὁλοσχερεστάτην**: cf. ὁλοσχερέα **24** 7.   **χορηγίαν**: orig. 'requirement to pay for a chorus' (a form of tax on wealthy citizens); then 'wealth, abundance' and (in the koiné) 'supplies' in general.

5. **διοδεύοντες**: not attested before the koiné.

6. **ἡμιασσαρίου**: Lat. *semissis*, half an *as*.

8. **βουνώδεις, γεώδεις**: adjs. in -ώδης are particularly associated with the Ion. prose tradition and are frequent in P. (Foucault 1972: 24). See on καματώδεος **68** 664. βουνός is a WGk. word (attributed to Cyrene at Hdt. 4.199) which entered the koiné (and Mod. Gk.).

9. **τρὰνς ἐξηρμηνευόμενον**: engagement with Latin was the fate of the Greek language for the next several centuries.

91. New Testament. Text: E. Nestle–K. Aland, *Novum Testamentum Graece* (27ᵗʰ edn., Stuttgart 1994). ▶▶ Voelz (1984), Wilcox (1984), Janse (1998), (2002).

(*a*) **First letter of St Paul to the Korinthians (1 Cor. 13). Mid I cent. AD. Trans.: King James (Authorized) Version, 1611.**

(1) ἐὰν ταῖς γλώσσαις τῶν ἀνθρώπων λαλῶ καὶ τῶν ἀγγέλων, ἀγάπην δὲ μὴ ἔχω, γέγονα χαλκὸς ἠχῶν ἢ κύμβαλον ἀλαλάζον. (2) καὶ ἐὰν ἔχω προφητείαν καὶ εἰδῶ τὰ μυστήρια πάντα καὶ πᾶσαν τὴν γνῶσιν καὶ ἐὰν ἔχω πᾶσαν τὴν πίστιν ὥστε ὄρη μεθιστάναι, ἀγάπην δὲ μὴ ἔχω, οὐθέν εἰμι. (3) κἂν ψωμίσω πάντα τὰ ὑπάρχοντά μου καὶ ἐὰν παραδῶ τὸ σῶμά μου ἵνα καυχήσωμαι, ἀγάπην δὲ μὴ ἔχω, οὐδὲν ὠφελοῦμαι.

(4) ἡ ἀγάπη μακροθυμεῖ, χρηστεύεται ἡ ἀγάπη, οὐ ζηλοῖ, ἡ ἀγάπη οὐ περπερεύεται, (5) οὐ φυσιοῦται, οὐκ ἀσχημονεῖ, οὐ ζητεῖ

91	*Literary Texts*	267

τὰ ἑαυτῆς, οὐ παροξύνεται, οὐ λογίζεται τὸ κακόν, (6) οὐ χαίρει ἐπὶ
τῆι ἀδικίαι, συγχαίρει δὲ τῆι ἀληθείαι· (7) πάντα στέγει, πάντα
πιστεύει, πάντα ἐλπίζει, πάντα ὑπομένει.

(8) ἡ ἀγάπη οὐδέποτε πίπτει· εἴτε δὲ προφητεῖαι,
καταργηθήσονται· εἴτε γλῶσσαι, παύσονται· εἴτε γνῶσις,
καταργηθήσεται. (9) ἐκ μέρους γὰρ γινώσκομεν καὶ ἐκ μέρους
προφητεύομεν· (10) ὅταν δὲ ἔλθηι τὸ τέλειον, τὸ ἐκ μέρους
καταργηθήσεται. (11) ὅτε ἤμην νήπιος, ἐλάλουν ὡς νήπιος, ἐφρόνουν
ὡς νήπιος, ἐλογιζόμην ὡς νήπιος· ὅτε γέγονα ἀνήρ, κατήργηκα τὰ
τοῦ νηπίου. (12) βλέπομεν γὰρ ἄρτι δι᾽ ἐσόπτρου ἐν αἰνίγματι, τότε
δὲ πρόσωπον πρὸς πρόσωπον. ἀρτι γινώσκω ἐκ μέρους, τότε δὲ
ἐπιγνώσομαι καθὼς ἐπεγνώσθην. (13) νυνὶ δὲ μένει πίστις, ἐλπίς,
ἀγάπη, τὰ τρία ταῦτα· μείζων δὲ τούτων ἡ ἀγάπη.

(1) Though I speak with the tongues of men and of angels, and have not charity, I am become as sounding brass, or a tinkling cymbal. (2) And though I have the gift of prophecy, and understand all mysteries, and all knowledge; and though I have all faith, so that I could remove mountains, and have not charity, I am nothing. (3) And though I bestow all my goods to feed the poor, and though I give my body *to be burned*, and have not charity, it profiteth me nothing. (4) Charity suffereth long, and is kind; charity envieth not; charity vaunteth not itself, is not puffed up, (5) Doth not behave itself unseemly, seeketh not her own, is not easily provoked, thinketh no evil; (6) Rejoiceth not in iniquity, but rejoiceth in the truth; (7) Beareth all things, believeth all things, hopeth all things, endureth all things. (8) Charity never faileth: but whether there be prophecies, they shall fail; whether there be tongues, they shall cease; whether there be knowledge, it shall vanish away. (9) For we know in part, and we prophesy in part. (10) But when that which is perfect is come, then that which is in part shall be done away. (11) When I was a child, I spake as a child, I understood as a child, I thought as a child: but when I became a man, I put away childish things. (12) For now we see through a glass, darkly; but then face to face: now I know in part; but then shall I know even as also I am known. (13) And now abideth faith, hope, charity, these three; but the greatest of these is charity.

1. **λαλῶ**: 'chatter' in class. Attic, the normal word for 'talk' in later

Gk.　**ἀγάπην**: a LXX term, not particularly common in class.
Gk. Plato's dialogue on love (*Symposion*) uses ἔρως, sexual love; the general term is φιλία.

2. καὶ ἐάν κτλ.: for balance and chiasmus as 'well-known features of Semitic poetic style' see Voelz (1984: 959).　**εἰδῶ**: see βλέπομεν 12.　**οὐθέν**: see **45** 13.

3. ψωμίσω: in class. Gk., to feed with small morsels, with delicacies (Ar. *Knights* 715). The semantic development mirrors ψωμός 'morsel', dimin. ψωμίον > Mod. Gk. ψωμί, 'bread'.　**καυχήσωμαι**: 'that I may glory'; the alternative reading καυθήσομαι (fut. indic.) is translated by the 1611 version.

4. χρηστεύεται: a vb. built to χρηστός (§56.4*b*), attested elsewhere only in the LXX.

7. στέγει: earlier 'roof over, enclose' (cf. στέγανς **53** 32).

11. ἤμην: §55.1.　**γεγόνα, κατήργηκα**: §55.5.

12. βλέπομεν: 'look, look at' in Ar. (distinct from ὁράω), became in post-class. Gk. the standard vb. for 'see' (with aor. εἶδα): cf. §55.1.

(*b*) Gospel of Mark (6: 21–7). Mid–late I cent. AD. Trans.: Revised Standard Version (New York, 1946).

Salome's mother gets revenge on John the Baptist

(21) καὶ γενομένης ἡμέρας εὐκαίρου ὅτε Ἡρῴδης τοῖς γενεσίοις αὐτοῦ δεῖπνον ἐποίησεν τοῖς μεγιστᾶσιν αὐτοῦ καὶ τοῖς χιλιάρχοις καὶ τοῖς πρώτοις τῆς Γαλιλαίας, (22) καὶ εἰσελθούσης τῆς θυγατρὸς αὐτοῦ Ἡρωιδιάδος καὶ ὀρχησαμένης ἤρεσεν τῶι Ἡρώιδηι καὶ τοῖς συνανακειμένοις. εἶπεν ὁ βασιλεὺς τῶι κορασίωι· αἴτησόν με ὃ ἐὰν θέληις, καὶ δώσω σοι· (23) καὶ ὤμοσεν αὐτῆι ὅ τι ἐάν με αἰτήσηις δώσω σοι ἕως ἡμίσους τῆς βασιλείας μου. (24) καὶ ἐξελθοῦσα εἶπεν τῆι μητρὶ αὐτῆς· τί αἰτήσωμαι; ἡ δὲ εἶπεν· τὴν κεφαλὴν Ἰωάννου τοῦ βαπτίζοντος. (25) καὶ εἰσελθοῦσα εὐθὺς μετὰ σπουδῆς πρὸς τὸν βασιλέα ἠιτήσατο λέγουσα· θέλω ἵνα ἐξαυτῆς δῶις μοι ἐπὶ πίνακι τὴν κεφαλὴν Ἰωάννου τοῦ βαπτιστοῦ. (26) καὶ περίλυπος γενόμενος ὁ βασιλεὺς διὰ τοὺς ὅρκους καὶ τοὺς ἀνακειμένους οὐκ ἠθέλησεν ἀθετῆσαι αὐτήν. (27) καὶ εὐθὺς ἀποστείλας ὁ βασιλεὺς σπεκουλάτορα ἐπέταξεν ἐνέγκαι τὴν κεφαλὴν αὐτοῦ.

(21) But an opportunity came when Herod on his birthday gave a

banquet for his courtiers and officers and the leading men of Galilee. (22) For when Herodias' daughter came in and danced, she pleased Herod and his guests; and the king said to the girl, 'Ask me for whatever you wish, and I will grant it.' (23) And he vowed to her, 'Whatever you ask me, I will give you, even half of my kingdom.' (24) And she went out, and said to her mother, 'What shall I ask?' And she said, 'The head of John the baptizer.' (25) And she came in immediately with haste to the king, and asked, saying, 'I want you to give me at once the head of John the Baptist on a platter.' (26) And the king was exceedingly sorry; but because of his oaths and his guests he did not want to break his word to her. (27) And immediately the king sent a soldier of the guard and gave orders to bring his head.

21. **καί**: the most common connective in the NT; Mark's style is especially paratactic. Often invoked as Aramaic (or LXX) influence (cf. καὶ ἰδού **94** 2), but it seems also to reflect contemporary vernacular Gk. (Trenkner 1960).   **γενεσίοις**: usu. γενέθλια in class. Gk.   **μεγιστᾶσιν**: first attested in Menander, common in the LXX. Morphologically unusual: perh. a borrowing from Persian *mahistān* (Schwyzer 1939: 521).

22. **αὐτοῦ**: an alternative reading (translated by the RSV) is αὐτῆς τῆς.   **Ἡρωιδιάδος**: Herod (Antipas) had married his brother's wife Herodias (John declared this illegal).   **ἤρεσεν**: for the subject in the gen. absol. cf. **94** 1.   **συνανακειμένοις**: post-class. (§56.4*a*).   **κορασίωι**: dimin. (§56.4*c*).   **ὃ ἐάν**: the standard indef. pron. in Mark and Matthew (not in Luke, rare in John) corresponding to class. ὅ τι ἄν (see following).

23. **ὃ τι ἐάν**: indef. (class. ὅ τι ἄν): potential ἄν (ἄ) had become confused (§53.1) with ἄν (ᾱ) < ἐάν (§32.8).   **ἕως**: prep. with gen. (not a class. usage).

25. **θέλω ἵνα**: ἵνα with (or as a marker of) the subj. was spreading at the expense of the infin. in the spoken language. The ancestor of the Mod. Gk. subj. marker νά (Trypanis 1960).

26. **ἀθετῆσαι**: post-class. vb.

27. **σπεκουλάτορα**: Lat. *speculator*, 'scout'. The words was borrowed into Aramaic with the meaning 'Roman military official, executioner' (it is not, therefore, a direct borrowing from

Latin, but represents the influence of the writer's competence in Aramaic).

92. Lucian (Lukianos) of Samosata, Syria. *Rhetorum praeceptor* (The Professor of Public Speaking), 16–17. II cent. AD. Text: M. D. Macleod (Oxford 1974). ▶ Swain (1996: 45–9, 298–329).

Lucian's fraudulent professor gives some tips on how to impress one's audience

ἔπειτα πεντεκαίδεκα ἢ οὐ πλείω γε τῶν εἴκοσιν Ἀττικὰ ὀνόματα ἐκλέξας ποθὲν ἀκριβῶς ἐκμελετήσας, πρόχειρα ἐπ᾽ ἄκρας τῆς γλώττης ἔχε—τὸ ἄττα καὶ κᾆτα καὶ μῶν καὶ ἀμηγέπηι καὶ λῷστε καὶ τὰ τοιαῦτα—καὶ ἐν ἅπαντι λόγωι καθάπερ τι ἥδυσμα ἐπίπαττε αὐτῶν. μελέτω δὲ μηδὲν τῶν ἄλλων, εἰ ἀνόμοια τούτοις καὶ ἀσύμφυλα καὶ ἀπωιδά. ἡ πορφύρα μόνον ἔστω καλὴ καὶ εὐανθής, κἂν σισύρα τῶν παχειῶν (17) τὸ ἱμάτιον ἦι. μετὰ δὲ ἀπόρρητα καὶ ξένα ῥήματα καὶ σπανιάκις ὑπὸ τῶν πάλαι εἰρημένα, καὶ ταῦτα συμφορήσας ἀποτόξευε προχειριζόμενος εἰς τοὺς προσομιλοῦντας. οὕτω γάρ σε ὁ λεὼς ὁ πολὺς ἀποβλέψονται καὶ θαυμαστὸν ὑπολήψονται καὶ τὴν παιδείαν ὑπὲρ αὐτούς, εἰ 'ἀποστλεγγίσασθαι' μὲν τὸ ἀποξύσασθαι λέγοις, τὸ δὲ ἡλίωι θέρεσθαι 'εἱληθερεῖσθαι', τὸν ἀρραβῶνα δὲ 'προνόμιον', τὸν ὄρθρον δὲ 'ἀκροκνεφές'. ἐνίοτε δὲ καὶ αὐτὸς ποίει καινὰ καὶ ἀλλόκοτα ὀνόματα καὶ νομοθέτει τὸν μὲν ἑρμηνεῦσαι δεινὸν 'εὔλεξιν' καλεῖν, τὸν συνετὸν 'σοφόνουν', τὸν ὀρχηστὴν δὲ 'χειρίσοφον'. ἂν σολοικίσηις δὲ ἢ βαρβαρίσηις, ἓν ἔστω φάρμακον ἡ ἀναισχυντία, καὶ πρόχειρον εὐθὺς ὄνομα οὔτε ὄντος τινὸς οὔτε γενομένου ποτέ, ἢ ποιητοῦ ἢ συγγραφέως, ὃς οὕτω λέγειν ἐδοκίμαζε σοφὸς ἀνὴρ καὶ τὴν φωνὴν εἰς τὸ ἀκρότατον ἀπηκριβωμένος.

Next you must scrape together from somewhere or other fifteen or at most twenty Attic phrases, practise them carefully, and keep them ready at the tip of your tongue—*atta* and *kâita* and *môn* and *hamêgepê* and *lôiste*, and so on—and whenever you speak, sprinkle a couple of them on like a seasoning. Don't worry about the context—whether they sound out of place, discordant, or jarring: let your purple cloak be fine and flowery, even if your tunic (17) is the coarsest goats' hair. Next search out obscure and strange words, rarely used by the ancients: store them up and be ready to fire them off at a moment's notice at your interlocutors. This will make the common mob stare at you and take you for a wonder, so much more cultured than themselves; if (for example) you say 'ablute' instead of 'wash', 'apricate' instead of 'warm in the sun', an 'earnest' instead of a 'surety', or 'gloaming' instead of 'twilight'. And occasionally you yourself should make up some new, outlandish words: decree that a man who gives clear explanations be called 'eulectic', a clever man 'sophonoustic', or a pantomime artist 'cheirosophic'. If you commit a solecism or a barbarism then shamelessness should be your one remedy, with an instant reference to the name of someone who neither exists nor ever existed, a writer of poetry or prose: a wise man who approved your phrase, and whose mastery of language was unrivalled.

16. **γλώττης**: the Att. form. So also λεώς 17.   **ἄττα κτλ**: a very similar list of Atticizing 'condiments' is given by Luc. at *Lexiphanes* 21. On ἄττα see **79** 82.

17. **ἀποστλεγγίσασθαι**: 'scrape oneself down' (in Ar.). **ἀρραβῶνα**: A semitic borrowing attested in the class. period (προνόμιον in this sense not attested elsewhere).   **ὄρθρον**: morning twilight.   **σολοικίσῃς**: from Soloi in Asia Minor, it came to mean a mistake in syntax (Salmeri 2004), as opposed to *barbarismos*, a mistake in the use of a word (in the meaning, or the morphology: esp. of vernacular usage).

93. Galen (Pergamon), *De differentia pulsuum* ii. 5, 584–6. II cent. AD. Text: C. G. Kühn (Leipzig 1833, VIII, 59, repr. Hildesheim 1986). ▶▶ Hankinson (1994), Swain (1996: 56–63, 357–79), Barnes (1997).

Galen insists that he is not a rigid Atticist, but that the use of standard Greek is essential for clarity in medical writing.

ἡμεῖς μὲν γὰρ, ὥσπερ νόμισμα καθ᾽ ἑκάστην τῶν πόλεων ἴσμεν σύμβολον ὠνῆς καὶ πράσεως, ὃ τοὺς παραχαράττοντας οἱ νομοθέται κολάζουσιν, οὕτω καὶ διαλέκτων χαρακτῆρας ἴσμεν πολλούς, οὓς φυλάττειν ἀξιοῦμεν ἕκαστον τῶν ἑλομένων ὁντιναοῦν ἐξ αὐτῶν. ἡμεῖς μὲν οὖν συνῃρήμεθα τὴν κοινὴν καλουμένην διάλεκτον, εἴτε μία τῶν Ἀτθίδων (585) ἐστὶ, πολλὰς γὰρ εἴληφε μεταπτώσεις ἢ τῶν Ἀθηναίων διάλεκτος, εἴτε καὶ ἄλλη τις ὅλως. δείκνυμι γὰρ ἑτέρωθι τὴν ἡμετέραν περὶ τούτου γνώμην. καὶ ταύτην τὴν διάλεκτον πειρώμεθα διαφυλάττειν, καὶ μηδὲν εἰς αὐτὴν παρανομεῖν, μηδὲ κίβδηλον ἐπεισάγειν φωνῆς νόμισμα, μηδὲ παραχαράττειν. σὺ δέ, εἰ μὲν ἐπιθυμεῖς κατ᾽ αὐτὴν ἡμῖν διαλέγεσθαι, πρότερον ἐκμαθεῖν αὐτὴν πειράθητι, εἰ δ᾽ ἄλληι τινὶ χρᾷς, καὶ τοῦτο μήνυσον. εἰ μὲν γὰρ τῶν Ἑλληνίδων ἐστὶ μία, πάντως που καὶ ταύτην γνωρίζομεν· καὶ γὰρ καὶ τὰ τῶν Ἰώνων καὶ τὰ τῶν Αἰολέων καὶ τὰ τῶν Δωριέων ἀνελεξάμεθα γράμματα· εἰ δ᾽ οὐδεμία τούτων, ἀλλά τις τῶν βαρβάρων, καὶ τοῦτ᾽ εἰπέ, μόνον πειρῶ φυλάττειν αὐτὴν ἄχραντον, ἤ τις ἂν ἦι, καὶ μή μοι τρία μὲν ἐκ Κιλικίας φέρειν ὀνόματα, τέσσαρα δ᾽ ἐκ Συρίας, πέντε δ᾽ ἐκ Γαλατίας, ἓξ δ᾽ Ἀθήνηθεν. ἐγὼ γὰρ οὕτω πολλὰς ἐκμανθάνειν οὐ δύναμαι διαλέκτους, ἵν᾽ ἀνδράσιν εἰς τοσοῦτον πολυγλώττοις ἕπωμαι. δίγλωττος γάρ τις ἐλέγετο πάλαι, καὶ θαῦμα τοῦτο ἦν, ἄνθρωπος εἰς ἀκριβῶν διαλέκτους δύο· σὺ δὲ ἡμᾶς ἀξιοῖς πολλὰς ἐκμαθεῖν, δέον αὐτὸν ἐκμανθάνειν μίαν, οὕτω μὲν ἰδίαν, οὕτω δὲ (586) κοινὴν ἅπασιν, οὕτω δ᾽ εὔγλωττον, οὕτω δ᾽ ἀνθρωπικήν.

For just as we recognize that there is a currency for buying and selling in each of the cities, and that legislators punish those who debase it, so too we recognize many different types of language, and think it right for each person to maintain the integrity of whichever of them he has chosen. We for our part have chosen the so-called common dialect, whether indeed (585) it is a member of the Attic family (for the dialect of the Athenians shows marked differences), or whether it is completely separate. I have set out my views on this matter elsewhere. And it is this dialect that we try to maintain, and avoid breaking its rules: nor do we introduce spurious linguistic currency into it, or debase it. As for you, if you desire to converse in it with us, first try to master it; and if you use some other, tell us what it is. If it is one of the Greek dialects, I have no doubt that we shall be familiar with that as well. For we have read the literature of the Ionians, the Aeolians, and the Dorians. If it is not one of these, but one of the barbarian idioms, you can speak this too: but try to keep it pure, whatever it is, and do not give me three words from Cilicia, four from Syria, five from Galatia, and six from Athens, because I cannot master so many languages in order to follow men who are polyglot to this degree. In the past, indeed, one was called bilingual, and it was considered a marvel for one man to master two idioms: but you demand that we learn several, when in fact you yourself should just master one—and that your native tongue, a language (moreover) which is (586) shared by everyone, lends itself to good expression, and is universal in its qualities.

584. **ἴσμεν**: cf. §55.1.   **παραχαράττοντας**: the Att. form (§51.1): so also φυλάττειν, etc. (but τέσσαρα).

585. **ἑτέρωθι**: Galen wrote a number of works on language and on Atticism (see Barnes 1997: 6, 14).   **παρανομεῖν**: a little later (587) he maintains that he does not condemn barbarism or solecism (**92** 17) in Gk. (an anti-Atticist position), so long as he can understand what the speaker intends.   **χρᾶις**: cf. on ἀποχρεωμένων **83** 1.   **τῶν βαρβάρων**: sometimes in post-class. authors an expression like Λυδιστί seems to refer to the vernacular Gk. of the region in question (Neumann 1980: 178). Here it looks as if Galen is referring (sarcastically) to the non-Gk. languages (dialects respectively of late Luwian, Aramaic, and Celtic): i.e. 'speak whatever you like, but speak it properly'.   **τέσσαρα**: the standard koiné (hybrid) form.

Glossary of Linguistic Terms

Ablaut: vowel alternation within a word which has a semantic/grammatical significance: e.g. Gk. ἔλειπον (imperf.) vs. ἔλιπον (aor.). In an Indo-European context it denotes the various 'grades' of an IE root, stem, or suffix: (i) full grade with *e* or *o* (cf. Gk. φέρω, 'I carry', φόρος, 'burden'); (ii) zero grade (Gk. δίφρος, 'chariot'); and (iii) a 'lengthened' grade with *ē* or *ō* (Gk. φώρ, 'thief')

Affricate: an obstruent followed by a fricative: e.g. [tʃ] in Engl. *chat* is a combination of [t] and [ʃ] (the fricative which starts Engl. *shoe*)

Apical: consonant made with the tip of the tongue against the roof of the mouth, either behind the teeth (e.g. Fr. dental *t, d*) or at the alveolar ridge (Engl. alveolar *t, d*)

Apocope: the removal of the final element from a word (Gk. 'cutting off'); in Greek typically denotes the shortening of a preposition or preverb to one syllable (§24.5)

Assimilation: the influence of one sound on the articulation of a neighbouring sound, with the result that the two sounds become more similar (or identical): §23.4

Athematic: a category of both nouns and verbs in IE languages in which the endings are added directly to the stem, without the insertion of the so-called thematic vowel. In Greek this includes athematic verbs (the so-called -μι verbs like τίθημι), and consonant-stem (third declension) nouns. Greek *a*-stem nouns (the first declension) are in historical terms athematic, but the term athematic is generally reserved in classical linguistics for consonant stems. See *thematic*

Back vowel: a vowel articulated at the back of the mouth: as /ɔ:/ in *all*, /u:/ in *cool*

Close vowel: a vowel articulated with the tongue high in the mouth, close to the roof: as /i:/ in *keep*, /u:/ in *cool*. Sometimes referred to as a high vowel. Compare *Open vowel*

Denominative: a verb made from a noun: e.g. Gk. στεφανόω, 'I crown, wreath' from στέφανος

Dental: see *Apical*

Diektasis: the artificial unpacking (Gk. 'stretching out') of a long, contracted vowel into its supposed constituent elements (usually short + long), producing two vowels which are synchronically plausible but historically incorrect. Especially associated with epic poetry: cf. εἰσορόωσαν **67** 142

Dissimilation: a process whereby one of two similar or identical sounds (which need not be contiguous) changes its articulation to reduce the similarity: e.g. οἶσθα < *Ϝοιδ-θα. See also *Grassman's Law*

Fricative: a consonant involving friction (the result of constricting the airflow) rather than complete closure (for which see *obstruent*): as /θ/ in Engl. *thin* (contrast *tin*). The only fricative in classical Attic was /s/

Front vowel: a vowel articulated with the highest point of the tongue coming near the front of the mouth: as /i:/ in *beat*, /ɛ/ in *bet*

Grassmann's Law: sound-law for Greek proposed in 1863 by Hermann Grassmann (1809–77): §23.5

H₁, ***H₂***, ***H₃***: The so-called laryngeals, three phonemes (resonants) which were originally posited for IE by F. de Saussure to explain puzzling irregularities in vowel-length. They have apparently dropped from Greek, Latin, and Sanskrit, but when Hittite was deciphered in the early twentieth century it was found that in some circumstances they appear there as *h*. IE laryngeals can both colour and lengthen adjacent vowels in the daughter languages. See further Sihler §§165–7

Historical: a historical (or diachronic) linguistic approach studies the development of a language over time; whereas a synchronic approach studies its state at a particular point in time (concentrating on the structure rather than the history)

Haplology: the deletion of a sound or syllable from a sequence of two (or more) similar sounds. A form of *dissimilation* (q.v.)

Hypercorrection: a phenomenon whereby speakers who are aware of a difference between one language (or dialect) and another (often a prestige variety) overcompensate in an effort to reverse it; perhaps because the item is stigmatized for some reason, or because they are attempting to reproduce an idiom they are not perfectly at home in

Hypheresis: the dropping of a sound from a sequence (of unlike sounds) so that the length of the word is reduced by a syllable

Hypocoristic: a shortened form of a name; a pet-name or nickname

Labial: a sound made with the lips: often denotes bilabial stops such as *p*, *b*, etc.

Labiovelar: three phonemes reconstructed for IE , written *kʷ*, *gʷ*, *gʷʰ*. As the name suggests, they are velar consonants with lip-rounding (with *kʷ* as in Engl. *queen*). §10.6

Liquid: a consonant produced without complete closure (for which see *obstruent*), and without audible friction: in IE languages the term typically denotes [l], [r]. See also *Resonant*

Monophthongization: the process of turning a diphthong into a pure vowel, either by loss of one of the two elements, or by evolution into a different sound

Mora: the notional minimal element of length in a vowel. A long vowel and a diphthong contain two moras, a short vowel is one mora. In Greek the accent could theoretically fall on either the first or the second mora of a long vowel: πᾶν /páan/ 'all', Πάν /paán/ 'Pan'

Nasal: a consonant produced by passing air through the nasal cavity rather than the oral cavity: in Greek (and Engl.) such consonants are /m, n, ŋ/

Obstruent: a consonant produced by impeding the air-flow, either fully (a stop) or partially (a fricative)

Open vowel: a vowel articulated with the tongue low in the mouth: as /ɑ:/ in *father*. Sometimes referred to as a low vowel. Compare *Close vowel*

Osthoff's Law: sound-law for Greek proposed by Hermann Osthoff (1847–1909): §23.3

Resonant: a class of consonants which can be sounded continuously without audible friction, and may in some languages act as a vowel in certain positions in the word (typically, between two obstruents). In IE resonants (also known as sonorants) include liquids, nasals, [w], and [y]. Laryngeals are sometimes included in this category: although they may have been fricatives, they probably also acted as vowels in certain positions

Rhotacism: in Greek and Latin the change of (intervocalic or word-final) [s] to [r]

Substrate: an adj. used of a language (often a minority language, or one spoken by a socio-political underclass) which has supposedly influenced the development of a superimposed (majority or dominant) language

Synchronic: see under *Historical*

Syncope: the deletion of a medial (usually unaccented) vowel or syllable

Synizesis: a process whereby a vowel is realized as a glide before another vowel and loses most of its syllabicity (Gk. *synizēsis* 'collapse'); e.g. the second *i* in Engl. *million* [miljən]. Cf. Intro. §23.2

Thematic: a category of both nouns and verbs in IE languages in which the so-called thematic vowel (*e* or *o*) is inserted between the stem and the endings. In Greek this included verbs in -ω (the largest category of verbs in the historically attested language) and nouns of the second declension (λόγ-ο-ς, etc.)

Velar: a consonant produced by the back of the tongue against the velum or soft palate (and sometimes against the back part of the hard palate): as /k/ in *cat*, /g/ in *get*

References

ALLEN, W. S. (1958), 'Some problems of palatalization in Greek', *Lingua*, 7: 113–33.

ARENA, R. (1994), *Iscrizioni greche arcaiche di Sicilia e Magna Grecia*, iii. *Iscrizioni delle colonie euboiche* (Milan).

—— (1996), *Iscrizioni greche arcaiche di Sicilia e Magna Grecia*, iv. *Iscrizioni delle colonie achee* (Milan).

AUSTIN, C. and OLSON, S. D. (2004) (eds.), *Aristophanes Thesmophoriazusae* (Oxford).

BAKKER, E. J. (1999), 'Pointing to the past: verbal augment and temporal deixis in Homer', in John N. Kazazis and Antonios Rengakos (eds.), *Euphrosyne: Studies in Ancient Epic and Its Legacy, in Honor of Dimitris N. Maronitis* (Stuttgart), 50–65.

BALCER, J. M. (1978), *The Athenian Regulations for Chalkis*, Historia Einzelschr. 33 (Wiesbaden).

BALDI, P. (1983), *An Introduction to the Indo-European Languages* (Carbondale, Ill.).

BARNES, J. (1997), 'Logique et pharmacologie. A propos de quelques remarques d'ordre linguistique dans le *De simplicium medicamentorum temperamentis ac facultatibus* de Galien', in A. Debru (ed.), *Galen on Pharmacology* (Leiden), 3–33.

BEATTIE, A. J. (1975), 'Some notes on the Spensitheos decree', *Kadmos*, 14: 8–47.

BECK, H. (1999), 'Ostlokris und die "Tausend Opuntier". Neue Überlegungen zum Siedlergesetz für Naupaktos', *ZPE* 124: 53–62.

BENVENISTE, É. (1935), *Origines de la formation des noms en Indo-Européen* (Paris).

BERS, V. (1984), *Greek Poetic Syntax in the Classical Age* (New Haven, Conn.).

—— (1997), *Speech in Speech: Studies in Incorporated Oratio Recta in Attic Drama and Oratory* (Lanham, Md.).

BILE, M. (2006), 'Le grec du nord-ouest: état des lieux', in C. Brixhe and G. Vottéro (eds.), *Peuplements et genèses dialectales dans la Grèce antique* (Nancy), 71–98.

BJÖRCK, G. (1950), *Das Alpha impurum und die tragische Kunstsprache* (Uppsala).

Blümel, W. (1982), *Die aiolischen Dialekte* (Göttingen).

Boardman, J. (1980), *The Greeks Overseas*, 3rd edn. (London).

Bourguet, E. (1927), *Le Dialecte laconien* (Paris).

Bousquet, J. (1966), 'Le cippe des Labyades', *BCH* 90: 82–92.

—— (1988), 'La stèle des Kyténiens au Létôon de Xanthos', *REG* 101: 12–53.

Bowie, A. M. (1981), *The Poetic Dialect of Sappho and Alcaeus* (New York).

Bowie, E. (1990), 'Miles ludens? The problem of martial exhortation in early Greek elegy', in O. Murray (ed.), *Sympotica* (Oxford), 221–9.

Bremer, J. M. (1987), 'Stesichorus: the Lille papyrus', in id. *et al.* (eds.), *Some Recently Found Greek Poems, Mmemosyne* Suppl. 99 (Leiden), 128–74.

Brixhe, Cl. (1976), *Le Dialecte grec de Pamphylie: Documents et grammaire* (Paris).

—— (1987), *Essai sur le grec anatolien au début de notre ère*, 2nd edn. (Nancy).

—— (1991), 'La langue comme reflet de l'histoire ou les éléments non doriens du dialecte crétois', in id. (ed.), *Sur la Crète antique: histoire, écriture, langues* (Nancy), 43–77.

—— (2006), 'Situation, spécificités et contraintes de la dialectologie grecque: à propos de quelques questions soulevées par la Grèce centrale', in id. and G. Vottéro (eds.), *Peuplements et genèses dialectales dans la Grèce antique* (Nancy), 39–69.

—— and Hodot, R. (1993), 'A chacun sa koiné?' in Cl. Brixhe (ed.), *La Koiné grecque antique: Une langue introuvable?* (Nancy), 7–21.

Browning, R. (1969), *Medieval and Modern Greek* (London).

Brunel, J. (1984), 'Pour une interprétation de la "loi sacrée" de Cyrène, §5', *RPh* 58: 35–44.

Burkert, W. (1992), *The Orientalizing Revolution: Near Eastern Influence on Greek Culture in the Early Archaic Age* (Cambridge, Mass.)

Calame, C. (1977) *Les Choeurs de jeunes filles en Grèce archaique*, I. *Morphologie, fonction religieuse et sociale*; II. *Alcman* (Rome).

—— (1983), *Alcman. Introduction, texte critique, témoignages, traduction et commentaire* (Rome).

Campbell, D. A. (1982), *Greek Lyric Poetry*, 2nd edn. (London).

Carlier, P. (1984), *La Royauté en Grèce avant Alexandre* (Strasbourg).

Cassio, A. C. (1987), 'Sulla laminetta di Hipponion: Addendum', *ASNP* 17: 333–4.

—— (1993), 'Alcmane, il dialetto di Cirene e la filologia Alessandrina', *RFIC* 121: 24–36.

Cassio, A. C. (1994), ʻ*Κεῖνος, καλλιστέφανος*, e la circolazione dell'epica in area euboica', in B. D'Agostino and D. Ridgway (eds.), *Apoikia: I più antichi insediamenti greci in occidente. Scritti in onore di G. Buchner, Annali di Archeologia e Storia Antica*, NS 1 (Naples), 55–68.

—— (1996*a*), 'Da Elea a Hipponion e Leontinoi: lingua di Parmenide e testi epigrafici', *ZPE* 113: 14–20.

—— (1996*b*), 'La prose ionienne postclassique et la culture de l'Asie Mineure à l'époque hellénistique', in C. Brixhe (ed.), *La Koiné grecque antique*, ii: *La Concurrence* (Nancy), 147–70.

—— (1998), ʻ*γερωχία* e *ἀγερωχία*: comicità e dialetto nella *Lisistrata* di Aristofane', *SemRom* 1, 73–9.

—— (2000), 'Un epigramma votivo spartano per Atena Alea', *RFIC* 128: 129–34.

—— (2005), 'I dialetti eolici e la lingua della lirica corale', in F. Bertolini and F. Gasti (eds.), *Dialetti e lingue letterarie nella Grecia arcaica* (Pavia), 13–44.

—— (2006), 'Homer, Hesiod and the mainland dialects', J. H. Gray lectures, University of Cambridge (May 2006, unpublished).

—— (in press), 'Alcman's text, spoken Laconian, and Greek Study of Greek dialects', in *Die altgriechischen Dialekte, ihr Wesen und Werden*, IV. Internationales Kolloquium über Altgriechische Dialektologie, Berlin 2001.

Catling, H. W., and Cavanagh, H. (1977), 'Two inscribed bronzes from the Menelaion, Sparta', *Kadmos* 15: 145–57.

Chadwick, J. (1958), *The Decipherment of Linear B* (Cambridge).

—— (1969), ʻ*ταγά* and *ἀταγία*', *Studi . . . in onore di V. Pisani* (Brescia), 231–4.

—— (1973), 'The Berezan lead tablet', *PCPS* 199: 35–7.

—— (1976), *The Mycenaean World* (Cambridge).

—— (1987), *Linear B and Related Scripts* (London).

—— (1988), 'The Women of Pylos', in J.-P. Olivier and T. G. Palaima (eds.), *Texts, Tablets and Scribes: Studies E. Bennett, Minos* Supplement, 10 (Salamanca), 43–95.

—— (1992), 'The Thessalian accent', *Glotta* 70: 2–14.

—— (1996), *Lexicographica Graeca* (Oxford).

Chantraine, P. (1933), *La Formation des noms en grec ancien* (Paris).

—— (1953), *Grammaire Homérique*, ii: *Syntaxe* (Paris).

Choremis, A. (1992–8), ʻ*Μολύβδινο ἐνεπίγραφο ἔλασμα ἀπό τήν Κέρκυρα*', *Horos*, 10–12: 347–54.

Clarysse, W. (1993), 'Egyptian scribes writing Greek', *Chron. d'Égypte*, 68: 186–201.

COLDSTREAM, J. N. (2003), *Geometric Greece*, 2nd edn. (London).

COLLINGE, N. E. (1985), *The Laws of Indo-European* (Amsterdam).

COLVIN, S. C. (1999), *Dialect in Aristophanes: The Politics of Language in Ancient Greek Literature* (Oxford).

—— (2004), 'Social dialect in Attica', in J. H. W. Penney (ed.), *Indo-European Perspectives: Studies in Honour of Anna Morpurgo Davies* (Oxford), 95–108.

—— (2006), 'Autosegmental phonology and word-internal -*h*- in Mycenaean Greek', *Glotta*, 82.

CONSANI, C. C. (1989), 'Bilinguismo, diglossia e digrafia nella Grecia antica. Il lettere de Filippo V e i decreti di Larissa', *AION* 11: 137–59.

COWGILL, W. (1964), 'The supposed Cypriot optatives *duwanoi* and *dokoi*', *Language*, 40: 344–65.

—— (1965), 'Evidence for laryngeals in Greek', in W. Winter (ed.), *Evidence for Laryngeals: Papers of a Conference on Indo-European Linguistics* (Austin, Tex.), 93–162.

D'ANGOUR, A. (1999), 'Archinus, Eucleides, and the reform of the Athenian alphabet', *BICS* 43: 109–130.

DEGANI, H. (1984), *Studi su Ipponatte* (Bari).

DE JONG, I. (1987), *Narrators and Focalizers: The Presentation of the Story in the* Iliad (Amsterdam).

DENNISTON, J. D. (1952), *Greek Prose Style* (Oxford).

—— (1954), *The Greek Particles*, 2nd edn. (Oxford).

—— and PAGE, D. (1957) (eds.), *Aeschylus Agamemnon* (Oxford).

DE SIMONE, C. (1978), 'Nochmals zum Namen Ἑλένη', *Glotta*, 56: 40–2.

DICKINSON, O. (1986), 'Homer, the poet of the dark age', *G&R* 33: 20–37.

—— (1994), *The Aegean Bronze Age* (Cambridge).

DIVER, W. (1958), 'On the pre-history of Greek consonantism', *Word*, 14: 1–25.

DOBIAS-LALOU, C. (2000), *Le Dialecte des inscriptions grecques de Cyrène*, *Karthago*, 25 (Paris).

DOVER, K. J. (1964), 'The poetry of Archilochus', in *Archiloque*, Entretiens Hardt 10 (Geneva), 183–222; repr. in *Greek and the Greeks* (Oxford 1987), 97–121.

—— (1971), *Theocritus: Select Poems* (London: repr. Bristol 1992).

—— (1981), 'The language of classical Attic documentary inscriptions', *TPhS* 1–14; repr. *Greek and the Greeks* (Oxford 1987), 31–41.

—— (1987), 'Language and character in Aristophanes', in *Greek and the Greeks* (Oxford), 237–48.

—— (1997), *The Evolution of Greek Prose Style* (Oxford).

References

DREWS, R. (1988), *The Coming of the Greeks: Indo-European Conquests in the Aegean and the Near East* (Princeton).

DUBOIS, L. (1978), 'Le datif singulier en ι des thèmes en s- et en -εύς en arcadien', *Rev. Phil.* 52: 266–71.

—— (1985), 'Deux notes de dialectologie grecque', *Glotta* 63: 45–51.

—— (1986), *Recherches sur le dialecte arcadien*, I–III (Louvain).

—— (1995), *Inscriptions grecques dialectales de Grande Grèce*, i. *Colonies eubéennes. Colonies ioniennes. Emporia* (Geneva).

—— (1996), *Inscriptions grecques dialectales d'Obia du Pont* (Geneva).

—— (1999a), 'Glanes crétoises', in C. Dobias-Lalou (ed.), *Des dialectes grecs aux Lois de Gortyne* (Nancy), 59–64.

—— (1999b), 'La nouvelle loi sacrée de Sélinonte: bilan dialectologique', in A. C. Cassio (ed.), *Katà Diálekton: Atti del III Coll. Int. di Dialettologia Greca, 1996, AION* 19 (Naples), 331–46.

—— (2002), *Inscriptions grecques dialectales de Grande Grèce*, ii. *Colonies achéennes* (Geneva).

DUHOUX, Y. (1987), 'Les débuts de l'augment grec. Le facteur sociolinguistique', *Minos*, 20–2: 163–72.

DUNNETT, R. (1970), 'Thessalian κις', *Glotta*, 48: 88–91.

EBERT, J. (1996), 'Neue griechische historische Epigramme', in J. H. M. Strubbe *et al.* (eds.), *Energeia. Studies . . . presented to H. W. Pleket* (Amsterdam), 19–25.

EDELSTEIN, E. J. and L. (1945), *Asclepius: Collection and Interpretation of the Testimonies* (Baltimore).

EDWARDS, G. P. (1971), *The Language of Hesiod in its Traditional Context*, Phil. Soc. Publ. 22 (Oxford).

—— and R. B. (1974), 'Red letters and Phoenician writing', *Kadmos*, 13: 48–57.

EFFENTERRE, H. VAN (1973), 'Le contrat de travail du scribe Spensithios', *BCH* 97: 31–46.

EIJK, PHILIP J. VAN DER (1997), 'Towards a rhetoric of ancient scientific discourse: some formal characteristics of Greek medical and philosophical texts', in E. Bakker (ed.), *Grammar as Interpretation: Greek Literature in its Linguistic Contexts* (Leiden), 77–129.

ENGELMANN, H. (1985), 'Wege griechischer Geldpolitik', *ZPE* 60: 165–76.

ÉTIENNE, R. and ROESCH, P. (1978), 'Convention militaire entre les cavaliers d'Orchomène et ceux de Chéronée', *BCH* 102: 359–74.

EVANS, T. V. (2001), *Verbal Syntax in the Pentateuch: Natural Greek Usage and Hebrew Interference* (Oxford).

FARAONE, C. A. (1991), 'The agonistic context of Greek binding spells', in C. Faraone and D. Obbink (eds.), *Magika Hiera* (Oxford), 3–32.

FENIK, B. C. (1978), 'Stylization and variety: four monologues in the *Iliad*', in id. (ed.), *Homer, Tradition and Invention* (Leiden), 68–90.

FERNÁNDEZ MARCOS, N. (2000), *The Septuagint in Context*, tr. W. Watson (Leiden).

FORBES, KATHLEEN (1958*a*), 'The formation of the so-called Aeolic optative', *Glotta* 37: 165–79.

—— (1958*b*), 'The relations of the particle ἄν with κε(ν), κα, καν', *Glotta* 37: 179–82.

FORD, B. B. and KOPFF, E. C. (1976), 'Sappho fr. 31.9: a defense of the hiatus', *Glotta* 54: 52–6.

FORSSMAN, B. (1966), *Untersuchungen zur Sprache Pindars* (Wiesbaden).

FOUCAULT, J.-A. (1972), *Recherches sur la langue et le style de Polybe* (Paris).

FOWLER, R. (2004), 'The Homeric question', in R. Fowler (ed.), *The Cambridge Companion to Homer* (Cambridge), 220–32.

FRAENKEL, E. (1932), 'Zu griechischen Inschriften', *Glotta* 20: 84–93.

—— (1956), 'Zur griechischen Wortforschung', *Glotta* 35: 77–92.

GAGER, J. G. (1992), *Curse Tablets and Binding Spells from the Ancient World* (Oxford).

GARBRAH, K. A. (1978), *A Grammar of the Ionic Inscriptions from Erythrae: Phonology and Morphology* (Meisenheim/Glan).

GARCÍA RAMÓN, J.-L. (1975), *Les Origines postmycéniennes du groupe dialectal éolien. Étude linguistique, Minos* Suppl. 6 (Salamanca).

—— (1978), 'Zu den griechischen dialektalen Imperativenendungen -*nton, -sthon*', *ZVS* 92: 135–42.

—— (1985), '*hôte* und *hôste* bei Alkman und Pindar', *MSS* 46: 81–101.

—— (1987), 'Geografía intradialectal Tesalia: la fonética', *Verbum*, 10: 101–51.

—— (1993), 'Dos problemas de lingüística tesalia', in E. Crespo *et al.* (eds.), *Dialectologica Graeca: Actas del II Coloquio Internacional de Dialectología Griega* (Madrid), 125–46.

—— (1999), 'Cuestiones de léxico y onomástica tesalios', in A. C. Cassio (ed.), *Katà Diálekton: Atti del III Coll. Int. di Dialettologia Greca, 1996, AION* 19 (Naples), 521–52.

GARLAND, R. (1985), *The Greek Way of Death* (Ithaca, NY).

GARRETT, A. (1999), 'A new model of Indo-European subgrouping and dispersal', in S. Chang, L. Liaw, and J. Ruppenhofer (eds.), *Proc. of the Twenty-Fifth Annual Meeting of the Berkeley Linguistics Society* (Berkeley), 146–56.

—— (2006), 'Convergence in the formation of Indo-European subgroups: phylogeny and chronology', in P. Forster and C. Renfrew (eds.), *Phylogenetic Methods and the Prehistory of Languages* (Cambridge), 139–51.

GAUTHIER, P. (1971), 'Les ξένοι dans les textes athéniens de la seconde moitié du Vᵉ siècle av. J.-C.', *REG* 84: 44–79.

GAUTIER, L. (1911), *La Langue de Xénophon* (Geneva).

GERBER, D. E. (1982), *Pindar's Olympian One: A Commentary*, Phoenix Suppl. 15 (Toronto).

GOW, A. S. F. (1950), *Theocritus: Edited with Translation and Commentary* (Cambridge).

GRIFFIN, J. (1980), *Homer on Life and Death* (Oxford).

GRIFFITHS, A. (1972), 'Alcman's Partheneion, the morning after the night before', *QUCC* 14: 7–30.

—— (2006), 'Stories and story-telling in the *Histories*', in C. Dewald and J. Marincola (eds.), *The Cambridge Companion to Herodotus* (Cambridge), 130–44.

GUARDUCCI, M. (1965), 'Sulla tabella bronzea iscritta di Francavilla Marittima', *Rendiconti dell' Accademia dei Lincei*, 20: 392–5.

GUSMANI, R. (1964), *Lydisches Wörterbuch* (Heidelberg).

HAINSWORTH, J. B. (1957), 'The plural of abstract nouns in the Greek epic', *BICS* 4: 1–9.

HAJNAL, I. (1995), *Studien zum mykenischen Kasussystem* (Berlin and New York).

—— (2004), 'Die Tmesis bei Homer und auf den mykenischen Linear B-Tafel: ein chronologisches Paradox?', in J. H. W. Penney (ed.), *Indo-European Perspectives: Studies in Honour of Anna Morpurgo Davies* (Oxford), 146–78.

HAMM, E.-M. [Voigt] (1957), *Grammatik zu Sappho und Alkaios* (Berlin).

HANKINSON, R. J. (1994), 'Usage and abusage: Galen on Language', in S. Everson (ed.), *Language: Companions to Ancient Thought, 3* (Cambridge).

HANSEN, P. A. (1976), 'Pithecusan humour. The interpretation of "Nestor's Cup" reconsidered', *Glotta*, 54: 25–40.

HASLAM, M. W. (1976), 'Homeric words and Homeric metre: two doublets examined', *Glotta*, 54: 201–11.

—— (1978), 'The versification of the new Stesichorus', *GRBS* 19: 29–57.

HEISSERER, A. J. (1980), *Alexander the Great and the Greeks: The Epigraphic Evidence* (Norman, Okla.).

—— (1984), 'IG XII, 2, 1: The monetary pact between Mytilene and Phokaia', *ZPE* 55: 115–32.

HELLY, B. (1970), 'La convention des Basaidai', *BCH* 94: 161–89.

HERRMANN, P. (1981), 'Teos und Abdera im 5. Jahrhundert v. Chr. Ein neues Fragment der *Teiorum Dirae*', *Chiron*, 11: 1–30.

HODOT, R. (1990), *Le Dialecte éolien d'Asie: la langue des inscriptions, VIIe s. a.C.–IVe* (Paris).

—— (2006), 'Un point de vue sur le lesbien', in C. Brixhe and G. Vottéro (eds.), *Peuplements et genèses dialectales dans la Grèce antique* (Nancy), 155–79.

—— and HEISSERER, A. J. (1986), 'The Mytilenean decree on Concord', *ZPE* 63: 109–28.

HOOKER, J. T. (1977), *The Language and Text of the Lesbian Poets* (Innsbruck).

—— (1980), 'Thessalian *ΤΑΓΑ*', *ZPE* 40: 272–3.

—— (1987), 'Homeric φίλος', *Glotta*, 65: 44–65.

HOPKINSON, N. (1984), *Callimachus, Hymn to Demeter. Edited with Introduction and Commentary* (Cambridge).

HORNBLOWER, S. (2007), 'Victory language in Pindar, the historians and inscriptions', in D. N. Maronitis and M. Paizi-Apostolopoulou (eds.), *Contests and Rewards in the Homeric Epics*, Proc. of the 10th International Symposium on the Odyssey, 2004 (Athens).

HORROCKS, G. (1980), 'The antiquity of the Greek epic tradition: some new evidence', *PCPS* 206: 1–11.

—— (1987), 'The Ionian Epic tradition: was there an Aeolic phase in its development?', *Minos*, 20–2: 269–94.

—— (1997), *Greek: A History of the Language and Its Speakers* (London).

HUBBARD, T. K. (1994), 'Elemental psychology and the date of Semonides of Amorgos', *AJP* 115: 175–97.

HUMBERT, J. (1960), *Syntaxe grecque*, 3rd edn. (Paris).

HUTCHINSON, G. O. (2001), *Greek Lyric Poetry: A Commentary on Selected Larger Pieces* (Oxford).

INSTONE, S. (1996), *Pindar: Selected Odes, Edited with Introduction, Translation and Commentary* (Warminster).

JAMESON, M. H., JORDAN, D. R., and KOTANSKY, R. D. (1993), *A Lex Sacra from Selinous*, GrRomByz Monographs 11 (Durham, NC).

JANKO, R. (1982), *Homer, Hesiod and the Hymns* (Cambridge).

—— (1984), 'Forgetfulness in the golden tablets of Memory', *CQ* ns 34: 89–100.

—— (1994), 'The origins and evolution of the Epic diction', in id. (ed.), *The Iliad: A Commentary*, vol. iv (13–16) (Cambridge), 8–19.

—— (1998), 'The Homeric poems as oral dictated texts', *CQ* ns 48: 1–13.

JANSE, M. (1998), 'La koiné au contact des langues sémitiques, de la Septante au Nouveau Testament', in Cl. Brixhe (ed.), *La Koiné grecque antique*, iii: *Les Contacts* (Nancy), 99–111.

—— (2002), 'Aspects of bilingualism in the history of the Greek language', in J. N. Adams, M. Janse, and S. Swain (eds.), *Bilingualism in Ancient Society: Language Contact and the Written Word* (Oxford), 332–90.

JASANOFF, J. (2003), ' "Stative" *ē-* revisited', *Sprache*, 43: 127–70.

JEFFERY, L. H. (1990), *The Local Scripts of Archaic Greece*, 2nd edn. rev. A. W. Johnston (Oxford).

—— and MORPURGO DAVIES, A. (1970), 'POINIKASTAS and POINIKAZEN: BM 1969. 4–2. 1. A New Archaic Inscription from Crete', *Kadmos*, 9: 118–54.

JOBES, K. H., and SILVA, M. (2000), *Invitation to the Septuagint* (Grand Rapids, Mich.).

KEARNS, E. (1994), 'Cakes in Greek sacrifice regulations', in R. Hägg (ed.), *Ancient Greek Cult Practice from the Epigraphical Evidence* (Stockholm), 65–70.

KILLEN, J. T. (1979), 'The Knossos Ld (1) Tablets', in E. Risch and H. Mühlestein (eds.), *Colloquium Mycenaeum: Actes du sixième colloque international sur les textes mycéniens et égéens tenu à Chaumont sur Neuchâtel 1975* (Geneva), 151–82.

KOERNER, R. (1981), 'Vier frühe Verträge zwischen Gemeinwesen und Privatleuten auf griechischen Inschriften', *Klio*, 63: 179–206.

KOURINOU-PIKOULA, E. (1992–8), '*Μνᾶμα γεροντείας*', *Horos*, 10–12: 259–76.

KURYLOWICZ, J. (1972), 'L'origine de *N EFELKUSTIKON*', in *Mélanges P. Chantraine* (Paris), 75–81.

LEJEUNE, M. (1943), 'Sens et emplois des démonstratifs *ὅνε, ὅνι, ὅνυ*', *RPh* 17: 120–30.

—— (1954), 'Observations sur le cypriote', *BSL* 50: 68–78.

—— (1968), 'Chars et roues à Cnossos: structure d'un inventaire', *Minos*, 9: 9–61; repr. *Mémoires de philologie mycénienne*, III (Rome 1972), 285–330.

—— (1971), 'Le dédicace de *Νικάνδρη* et l'écriture archaique de Naxos', *RPh* 45: 209.

—— (1972), *Phonétique historique du mycénien et du grec ancien* (Paris).

—— (1973), 'Le dossier sarapeda du scribe 24 de Pylos', *Minos*, 14: 60–76; repr. *Mémoires de philologie mycénienne*, IV (Rome 1997), 67–85.

LEUMANN, M. (1950), *Homerische Wörter* (Basel).

LIBERMAN, G. (1988), 'Alcée 384 LP, Voigt', *RPh* 62: 291–8.

—— (1992), 'Lire Sappho dans Démétrios, *Sur le style*', *QUCC* 40: 45–8.

LIDONNICI, L. R. (1995), *The Epidaurian Miracle Inscriptions* (Atlanta, Ga.).

LILLO, A. (1987), 'The Arcadian genitive forms type *ἀμέραυ* from Tegea', *Glotta*, 65: 88–93.

—— (1988), 'The Dorian numeral τέτορες', *MSS* 49: 71–3.

—— (1995), 'El hapax *klenna* y la lengua poética de Alcmán', *Emerita*, 63: 21–45.

LINK, S. (1991), 'Das Siedlungsgesetz aus Westlokris', *ZPE* 87: 65–77.

LLOYD-JONES, H. (1975), *Females of the Species: Semonides on Women* (London).

LOBEL, E. (1927), 'The employment of the definite article in Lesbian', in id. (ed.), *Alkaiou Melê: The Fragments of the Lyrical Poems of Alcaeus* (Oxford), pp. lxxiv–xciv.

LÓPEZ EIRE, A. (1986), 'A propos de l'attique ὤν, οὖσα, ὄν', *Glotta*, 64: 213–16.

—— (1993), 'De l'attique à la koiné', in C. Brixhe (ed.), *La Koiné grecque antique*, i: *une langue introuvable?* (Nancy), 41–57.

—— (1999), 'Nouvelles données à propos de l'histoire de l'attique', in A. C. Cassio (ed.), *Katà Diálekton: Atti del III Coll. Int. di Dialettologia Greca, 1996, AION* 19 (Naples), 73–107.

LORD, A. (1960), *The Singer of Tales* (Cambridge, Mass.).

LURAGHI, N. (forthcoming), 'Local scripts from nature to culture', in P. Haarer (ed.), *Alphabetic Responses to Western Semitic Writing*, Conference, Oxford 2004.

LURIA, S. (1959), 'Burgfrieden in Sillyon', *Klio*, 37: 7–20.

McDEVITT, A. S. (1968), 'A Thessalian in Magna Graecia?', *Glotta*, 46: 254–6.

MACGILLIVRAY, J. A. (2000), *Minotaur: Sir Arthur Evans and the Archaeology of the Minoan Myth* (London).

MALLORY, J. P. (1989), *In Search of the Indo-Europeans* (London).

MASSON, E. (1967), *Recherches sur les plus anciens emprunts sémitiques en grec* (Paris).

MASSON, O. (1961), *Les Inscriptions chypriotes syllabiques* (Paris: réimpression augmentée 1983).

—— (1983), 'Remarques sur quelques passages de la tablette chypriote d'Idalion', *BSL* 78: 261–81.

MATTINGLY, H. (1961), 'Athens and Euboea', *JHS* 81: 124–32.

MAYSER, E. (1970), *Grammatik der griechischen Papyri aus der Ptolemäerzeit*. Bd. 1.1: *Einleitung und Lautlehre*, 2. Aufl. bearb. von Hans Schmoll (Berlin).

MEILLET, A. (1924) *The Comparative Method in Historical Linguistics*, English edition tr. G. B. Ford (Paris 1970).

—— (1929), *Aperçu d'une histoire de la langue grecque*, 3rd edn. (Paris).

MELENA, J. L. (1975), *Studies on Some Mycenaean inscriptions from Knossos Dealing with Textiles, Minos* Suppl. 5 (Salamanca).

Méndez Dosuna, J. (1982), 'Une autre question de dialectologie grecque: connaît-on beaucoup d'exemples assurés de nominatifs masculins en -ā?', *Glotta*, 60: 65–79.

—— (1985), *Los dialectos dorios del Noroeste* (Salamanca).

—— (1991), 'On <*Z*> for <*Δ*> in Greek dialectal inscriptions', *Sprache*, 35 (1991–3): 82–114.

—— (1993*a*), 'Metátesis de cantidad en jónico-ático y heracleota', *Emerita*, 61: 95–134.

—— (1993*b*), 'El cambio de <ε> en <ι> ante vocal en los dialectos griegos', in E. Crespo *et al.* (eds.), *Dialectologica Graeca: Actas del II Coloquio Internacional de Dialectología Griega* (Madrid), 237–59.

Merkelbach, R. (1975), 'Nochmals die Bleitafel von Berezan', *ZPE* 17: 161–2.

—— (1982), 'Zu dem neuen Text aus Teos', *ZPE* 46: 212–13.

—— and West, M. L. (1967), *Fragmenta Hesiodea* (Oxford).

Mitchell, T. F. (1980), 'Dimensions of style in a grammar of educated spoken Arabic', *ALing.* 11: 89–106.

Molinos Tejada, T. (1990), *Los Dorismos del Corpus Bucolicorum* (Amsterdam).

Morpurgo Davies, A. (1965), 'A note on Thessalian', *Glotta*, 43: 235–51.

—— (1966), 'An instrumental-ablative in Mycenaean?', in L. R. Palmer and J. Chadwick (eds.), *Proc. of the Cambridge Colloquium on Mycenaean Studies* (Cambridge), 191–202.

—— (1968), 'Thessalian patronymic adjectives', *Glotta*, 46: 85–106.

—— (1976), 'The -εσσι datives, Aeolic -*ss*-, and the Lesbian poets', in ead. and W. Meid (eds.), *Studies . . . offered to Leonard Palmer* (Innsbruck), 181–97.

—— (1978), 'Thessalian εὔντεσσι and the participle of the verb *to be*', in F. Bader *et al.* (eds.), *Étrennes de septentaine: Travaux de linguistique et de grammaire comparée offerts à M. Lejeune* (Paris), 157–66.

—— (1983), 'Mycenaean and Greek prepositions: *o-pi*, *e-pi*, etc.', in A. Heubeck and G. Neumann (eds.), *Res Mycenaeae: Akten des VII. Int. Myk. Coll. 1981* (Göttingen), 287–310.

—— (1985), 'Mycenaean and Greek language', in A. Morpurgo Davies and Y. Duhoux (eds.), *Linear B: A 1984 Survey* (Louvain), 75–126.

—— (1997), 'Particles in Greek epigraphical texts: the case of Arcadian', in A. Rijksbaron (ed.), *New Approaches to Greek Particles (Proceedings of a Colloquium . . . to honour C. J. Ruijgh)* (Amsterdam), 49–73.

—— (1998), *Nineteenth-Century Linguistics* (London).

Mukařovský, J. (1932), 'Standard language and poetic language', in

P. Garvin (ed. and tr.), *A Prague School Reader on Esthetics, Literary Structure, and Style* (Washington, DC 1964), 17–30.

MURRAY, O. (1993), *Early Greece*, 2nd edn. (Cambridge, Mass.).

NAGY, G. (1970), *Greek Dialects and the Transformation of an Indo-European Process* (Cambridge, Mass.).

—— (1990), *Pindar's Homer: The Lyric Possession of an Epic Past* (Baltimore).

—— (1995), 'An evolutionary model for the making of Homeric poetry: comparative perspectives', in J. Carter and S. Morris (eds.), *The Ages of Homer* (Austin, Tex.), 163–79.

NEUMANN, G. (1980), 'Kleinasien', in G. Neumann and J. Untermann (eds.), *Die Sprache im römischen Reich der Kaiserzeit* (Cologne and Bonn), 167–86.

NÖTHIGER, M. (1971), *Die Sprache des Stesichorus und des Ibycus* (Zurich).

OETTINGER, N. (1995), 'Anatolische Etymologien', *Hist. Sprachforschung*, 108: 39–49.

PAGE, D. L. (1951), *Alcman: The Partheneion* (Oxford).

—— (1955), *Sappho and Alcaeus* (Oxford).

PALMER, L. R. (1980), *The Greek Language* (London).

—— and BOARDMAN, J. (1963), *On the Knossos Tablets: Two Studies* (Oxford).

PARCA, M. (1982), 'Sappho 1.18–19', *ZPE* 46: 47–50.

PARKE, H. W. (1967), *The Oracles of Zeus* (Oxford).

PARKER, R. (1983), *Miasma: Pollution and Purification in Early Greek Religion* (Oxford).

PEPPLER, C. W. (1921), 'Comic terminations in Aristophanes: part V', *AJP* 42: 152–61.

POWELL, B. P. (1991), *Homer and the Origin of the Greek Alphabet* (Cambridge).

PROBERT, P. (2003), *A New Short Guide to the Accentuation of Ancient Greek* (Bristol).

—— (2006), *Ancient Greek Accentuation* (Oxford).

PUGLIESE CARRATELLI, G. (1974), 'Un sepolcro di Hipponion e un nuovo testo orfico', *Par. Passato*, 29: 108–26.

—— (2003), *Les Lamelles d'or orphiques*, French tr. A.-Ph. Segonds and C. Luna (Paris).

RADT, S. (1970), 'Sapphica', *Mnemosyne*, 23: 337–47.

RHODES, P. J. and OSBORNE, R. (2003), *Greek Historical Inscriptions 414–323 BC* (Oxford).

RIJKSBARON, A. (1994), *The Syntax and Semantics of the Verb in Classical Greek*, 2nd edn. (Amsterdam).

RISCH, E. (1974), *Wortbildung der homerischen Sprache*, 2nd edn. (Berlin).
—— (1975), 'Sprachliche Betrachtungen zum neuen Archilochos-Fragment', *Grazer Beiträge*, 4: 219–29.
—— (1987), 'Zum Nestorbecher aus Ischia', *ZPE* 70: 1–9.
RIX, H. (1976), *Historische Grammatik des Griechischen* (Darmstadt).
ROBERT, J. and L. (1983), *Amyzon, fouilles d'Amyzon en Carie*. I. *Exploration, histoire, monnaies et inscriptions* (Paris).
ROESCH, P. (1974), 'Sur le tarif des poissons d'Akraiphia', *ZPE* 14: 5–9.
ROSEN, R. M. (1990), 'Poetry and sailing in Hesiod's *Works and Days*', *ClAnt* 9: 99–113.
ROUGEMONT, G. (1973), 'Le hiéroménie des Pythia et les "trêves sacrées" d'Eleusis, de Delphes et d'Olympie', *BCH* 97: 75–106.
ROWLANDSON, J. (1998), *Women and Society in Greek and Roman Egypt: A Sourcebook* (Cambridge).
RUIJGH, C. J. (1966), 'Quelques remarques sur l'absence de καί et sur l'emploi des particules -qe and -de dans les textes mycéniens', in L. R. Palmer and J. Chadwick (eds.), *Proc. of the Cambridge Colloquium on Mycenaean Studies* (Cambridge), 203–10.
—— (1967), *Études sur la grammaire et le vocabulaire du grec mycénien* (Amsterdam).
—— (1968), 'Observations sur la "métathèse de quantité"', *Lingua*, 21: 382–99; repr. in *Scripta Minora* (Amsterdam 1991), i. 312–29.
—— (1970), *Rapport critique: P. Chantraine, Dictionnaire étymologique de la langue grecque. Tome I [Paris 1968]. Lingua*, 25: 302–21; repr. in *Scripta Minora*, i. 571–90.
—— (1971), *Autour de 'TE épique'; études sur la syntaxe grecque* (Amsterdam).
—— (1975), *Compte rendu: H. W. Hauri, Kontrahiertes und sigmatisches Futur [Göttingen 1975]. Kratylos*, 20: 82–91; repr. in *Scripta Minora*, i. 368–77.
—— (1976), *Chars et roues dans les tablettes mycéniennes* (Amsterdam).
—— (1979), 'Faits linguistiques et données externes relatifs aux chars et aux roues', *Colloquium Mycenaeum* (Neuchâtel), 207–20; repr. in *Scripta Minora*, i. 138–50.
—— (1981a), *Compte rendu: V. Lüttel, Κάς und καί. Dialektale und chronologische Probleme im Zusammenhang mit Dissimilation und Apokope [Göttingen 1981]. Kratylos*, 26: 115–20; repr. in *Scripta Minora*, i. 399–404.
—— (1981b), 'Interprétation hypothétique de la tablette Va 15 de Pylos', *ZAnt* 31: 47–62; repr. in *Scripta Minora* (Amsterdam 1996), ii. 3–18.

—— (1984), 'Le dorien de Théocrite: dialecte Cyrénien d'Alexandrie et d'Égypte', *Mnemosyne* 37: 56–88; repr. in *Scripta Minora*, ii. 405–37.

—— (1988), 'Sur le vocalisme du dialecte chypriote au premier millénaire av. J.-C.', in O. Masson and J. Karageorghis (eds.), *The History of the Greek Language in Cyprus* (Nicosia), 131–51; repr. in *Scripta Minora*, ii. 455–75.

—— (1989), *Compte rendu: J. Méndez Dosuna, Los dialectos dorios del Noroeste [Salamanca 1985]. Mnemosyne*, 42: 155–63; repr. in *Scripta Minora*, ii. 483–91.

—— (1990), 'La place des enclitiques dans l'ordre des mots chez Homère d'après la loi de Wackernagel', in H. Eichner and H. Rix (eds.), *Sprachwissenschaft und Philologie: Jacob Wackernagel und die Indogermanistik heute* (Wiesbaden), 213–33; repr. in *Scripta Minora*, ii. 627–47.

—— (1992), 'L'emploi mycénien de -*h*- intervocalique comme consonne de liaison entre deux morphèmes', *Mnemosyne*, 45: 433–72; repr. in *Scripta Minora*, ii. 159–98.

Ruipérez, M. S. (1966), 'Mycenaean *ijereja*: an interpretation', in L. Palmer and J. Chadwick (eds.), *Cambridge Colloquium on Mycenaean Studies* (Cambridge), 211–16.

Sacco, G. (2001), '*ΓΗΣ ΠΑΙΣ ΕΙΜΙ*. Sul v.10 della laminetta di Hipponion', *ZPE* 137: 27–33.

Salmeri, G. (2004), 'Hellenism on the periphery: the case of Cilicia and an etymology of *soloikismos*', in S. Colvin (ed.), *The Greco-Roman East*, *YCS* 31 (Cambridge), 181–206.

Schindler, J. (1986), 'Zu den homerischen ῥοδοδάκτυλος-Komposita', in A. Etter (ed.), *O-o-pe-ro-si. Festschrift Ernst Risch* (Berlin), 393–401.

Schmitt, R. (1970), *Die Nominalbildung in den Dichtungen des Kallimachos von Kyrene* (Wiesbaden).

Schürr, D. (2000), 'Lydisches III: Rund um lydisch "Hund"', *Kadmos*, 39: 165–76.

Schwyzer, E. (1928), 'Zu griechischen Inschriften, 8: Zu den Tafeln von Herakleia', *RhM* 77: 225–37; repr. in *Kleine Schriften* (Innsbruck 1983), 792–9.

—— (1939), *Griechische Grammatik*, i (Munich).

Sealey, R. (1994), *The Justice of the Greeks* (Ann Arbor, Mich.).

Sharples, R. W. (1983), '"But why has my spirit spoken with me thus?": Homeric decision-making', *G&R* ns 30: 1–7.

Sicking, C. M. J. and Stork, P. (1997), 'The grammar of the so-called historical present in ancient Greek', in E. Bakker (ed.), *Grammar as Interpretation: Greek Literature in its Linguistic Contexts* (Leiden), 131–68.

SICKLE, J. VAN (1976) (ed.), *The New Archilochus, Arethusa* (special issue), 9: 2.

—— (1989), 'Praise and blame for a "full commentary" on Archilochus, First Cologne Epode', *BICS* 36: 104–8.

SKUTSCH, O. (1987), 'Helen, her name and nature', *JHS* 107: 188–93.

SLINGS, S. R. (1986), '*ΕΙΛΗΦΑ*', *Glotta*, 64: 9–14.

—— (1987), 'Archilochus: first Cologne epode', in J. M. Bremer *et al.* (eds.), *Some Recently Found Greek Poems, Mnemosyne* Suppl. 99 (Leiden).

SOKOLOWSKI, F. (1962), *Lois sacrées des cités grecques. Supplément* (Paris).

—— (1969), *Lois sacrées des cités grecques* (Paris).

SOMMERSTEIN, A. (1994) (ed.), *Aristophanes: Thesmophoriazusae* (Warminster).

STERIADE, D. (1982), *Greek Prosodies and the Nature of Syllabification*, Diss. MIT; repr. Garland Press (New York 1993).

STOOP, M. W. and PUGLIESE CARRATELLI, G. (1966), 'Tabella con iscrizione arcaica', *Atti e memorie della Società Magna Grecia*, 6–7 (1965–6), 14–21.

STRUNK, K. (1961), 'Der böotische Imperativ δίδοι', *Glotta*, 39: 114–23.

—— (1986), 'Kypr. (ε)ὺ für ἐπί: eine vox nihili?', in A. Etter (ed.), *O-o-pe-ro-si. Festschrift Ernst Risch* (Berlin), 253–69.

SWAIN, S. (1996), *Hellenism and Empire: Language, Classicism, and Power in the Greek World, AD 50–250* (Oxford).

SZEMERÉNYI, O. (1956), 'The genitive singular of masculine -ā- stems in Greek', *Glotta*, 35: 195–208; repr. in *Scripta Minora*, iii (Innsbruck 1987), 1079–92.

—— (1960), *Studies in the Indo-European System of Numerals* (Heidelberg).

—— (1964), *Syncope in Greek and Indo-European* (Naples).

—— (1965), 'Etyma Graeca i', *Sprache*, 11: 1–24; repr. in *Scripta Minora*, iii. 1196–219.

—— (1967), 'The history of Attic οὖς and some of its compounds', *SMEA* 3: 47–88; repr. in *Scripta Minora*, iii. 1273–314.

—— (1968*a*), 'The Mycenaean and the historical Greek comparative and their Indo-European background', in A. Bartoněk (ed.), *Studia Mycenaea* (Brno), 25–36; repr. in *Scripta Minora*, iii. 1326–37.

—— (1968*b*), 'Mycenaean: a milestone between Indo-European and historical Greek', *Atti e memorie del primo congresso internazionale di Micenologia 1967. Incunabula Graeca*, 25 (Rome), 1: 715–25; repr. in *Scripta Minora*, iii. 1315–25.

—— (1974), 'The origins of the Greek lexicon: *ex oriente lux*', *JHS* 94: 144–57; repr. in *Scripta Minora*, iii. 1441–54.

—— (1979), 'The consonant alternation *pt/p* in early Greek', in E. Risch and H. Mühlestein (eds.), *Colloquium Mycenaeum* (Geneva), 323–40; repr. in *Scripta Minora*, iii. 1476–93.

Teodorsson, S.-T. (1974), *The Phonemic System of the Attic Dialect 400–340 BC* (Göteborg).

—— (1977), *The Phonology of Ptolemaic Koine* (Göteborg).

Thompson, D'Arcy W. (1947), *A Glossary of Greek Fishes* (Oxford).

Thompson, R. J. E. (1998), 'Instrumentals, datives, locatives and ablatives: the *-phi* case form in Mycenaean and Homer', *PCPS* 44: 219–50.

—— (2001), 'Prepositional use in Arcado-Cypriot and Mycenaean: a bronze age isogloss?', *Minos*, 35–6: 395–430.

Threatte, L. (1980), *The Grammar of Attic Inscriptions*, i: *Phonology* (Berlin).

—— (1996), *The Grammar of Attic Inscriptions*, ii: *Morphology* (Berlin).

Thumb, A. and Kieckers, E. (1932), *Handbuch der griechischen Dialekte*, i (Heidelberg).

—— and Scherer, A. (1959), *Handbuch der griechischen Dialekte*, ii (Heidelberg).

Thür, G. and Taeuber, H. (1994), *Prozessrechtliche Inschriften der griechischen Poleis: Arkadien* (Vienna).

Trapp, M. (2003), *Greek and Latin Letters: An Anthology, with Translation* (Cambridge).

Trenkner, S. (1960), *Le Style kai dans le récit Attique oral* (Assen).

Trypanis, C. A. (1960), 'Early medieval Greek ἵνα', *Glotta*, 38: 312–13.

Tucker, E. (1990), *The Creation of Morphological Regularity: Early Greek Verbs in -éō, -áō, -óō, -úō and -íō*, HS Ergänzungsheft, 35 (Göttingen).

Uguzzoni, A. and Ghinatti, F. (1968), *Le tavole greche di Eraclea* (Rome).

Vatin, C. (1963), 'Le bronze Pappadakis: étude d'une loi coloniale', *BCH* 87: 1–19.

—— (1971), 'Le Tarif des poissons d'Akraiphia', in F. Salviat and C. Vatin (eds), *Inscriptions de Grèce centrale* (Paris), 95–109.

Verdenius W. J. (1972), 'Callinus fr. i. A commentary', *Mnemosyne*, 25: 1–8.

—— (1988), *Commentaries on Pindar*, vol. 2 (Leiden).

Versteegh, K. (2002), 'Alive or dead? The status of the standard language', in J. N. Adams, M. Janse, and S. Swain (eds.), *Bilingualism in Ancient Society: Language Contact and the Written Word* (Oxford), 52–74.

Voelz, J. W. (1984), 'The language of the New Testament', *ANRW* 25/2: 893–977.

Voigt, E.-M. [Hamm] (1971), *Sappho et Alcaeus. Fragmenta edidit Eva-Maria Voigt* (Amsterdam).

294   *References*

Vollgraff, W. (1948), *Le Décret d'Argos relatif à un pacte entre Knossos et Tylissos, KNAW* 51:2 (Amsterdam).

Vottéro, G. (2006), 'Remarques sur les origines "éoliennes" du dialecte béotien', in id. and C. Brixhe (eds.), *Peuplements et genèses dialectales dans la Grèce antique* (Nancy), 99–54.

Wackernagel, J. (1892), 'Über ein Gesetz der indogermanischen Wortstellung', *IF* 1: 333–436; repr. in *Kleine Schriften*, i (Göttingen 1956), 1–103.

Wachter, R. (1999), 'Evidence for phrase structure analysis in some archaic Greek inscriptions', in A. C. Cassio (ed.), *Katà Diálekton: Atti del III Coll. Int. di Dialettologia Greca, 1996, AION* 19 (Naples), 365–82.

Walbank, F. W. (1957), *A Historical Commentary on Polybius*, vol. 1: *Commentary on Books 1–6* (Oxford).

Wallace, R. (1983), 'An illusory substratum influence in Pamphylian', *Glotta*, 61: 5–12.

Watkins, C. (1971), 'Hittite and I-E studies: the denominative statives in -ē-', *TPhS* 51–93.

—— (1976), 'Syntax and metrics in the Dipylon vase inscription', in A. Morpurgo Davies and W. Meid (eds.), *Studies . . . offered to Leonard R. Palmer* (Innsbruck), 431–41.

Weiss, M. (1994), 'Life everlasting: Latin *iûgis* "everflowing", Greek ὑγιής "healthy", Gothic *ajukdûþs* "eternity" and Avestan *yauuaêjî-* "living forever"', *MSS* 55: 131–56.

Welles, C. Bradford (1934), *Royal Correspondence in the Hellenistic Period* (New Haven, Conn.).

West, M. L. (1970a), 'Burning Sappho', *Maia*, 22: 307–30.

—— (1970b), 'On Lesbian accentuation', *Glotta*, 48: 194–8.

—— (1974), *Studies in Greek Elegy and Iambus* (Berlin and New York).

—— (1978) (ed.), *Hesiod: Works and Days* (Oxford).

—— (1987) (ed.), *Euripides: Orestes* (Warminster).

—— (1988), 'The rise of the Greek epic', *JHS* 108: 151–72.

Whitley, J. (2001), *The Archaeology of Ancient Greece* (Cambridge).

Wilcox, M. (1984), 'Semitisms in the New Testament', *ANRW* 25/2: 978–1029.

Williams, D. (1982), 'Aegina, Aphaia Tempel. IV. The inscription commemorating the construction of the first limestone temple and the other features of the sixth-century temenos', *Arch. Anzeiger*, 55–68.

Willetts, R. F. (1967), *The Law Code of Gortyn* (Berlin).

Willi, A. (2003a), *The Languages of Aristophanes* (Oxford).

—— (2003b), 'καί—mykenisch oder nachmykenisch?', *Glotta*, 79: 224–48.

—— (2006), 'Unholy diseases, or why Agamemnon and Tuthaliya should not have offended the gods', *OWPLPP* 11: 190–206.

WILLINK, C. W. (1986) (ed.), *Euripides: Orestes* (Oxford).

WILSON, J.-P. (1998), 'The illiterate trader?', *BICS* 42: 29–53.

WOODARD, R. D. (1997), *Greek Writing from Knossos to Homer* (Oxford).

WYATT, W. F. (1992), 'Homer's linguistic forebears', *JHS* 112: 167–73.

YAMAGATA, N. (1997), 'ἄναξ and βασιλεύς in Homer', *CQ* 47: 1–14.

.

General Index

Thessalian
  accent 95
Thucydides 61
tmesis 31
tragedy 57–8
Tyrtaios 53–4

verbs
  contract (athematic) 28–9
  aorist
    focus function 135
    gnomic 204, 235
    non-temporal/instantaneous
      193–4, 197, 222
    reanalysed as present 218
  future 29–30
    built to aor. stem 208, 263
    built to perf. stem 254
    suppletive 155
  perfect
    built to aor. stem 208
    periphrastic 249
    reanalysed as pres. 252
  present
    built to aor. stem 205, 211, 263
    built to perf. stem 199
    'historic' 249
    nasal infix 137, 218

  reduplicated 214
vernacular
  in epigraphic language 44
  in literary languages 49
  in koiné/Hellenistic Greek 63–6, 68,
    269, 271, 273
  in poetry 54–60, 62, 220, 234
  see also colloquial language
vowels 10–11, 23–4
  assimilation 34, 96, 103, 122, 135,
    140, 144, 155
  contraction (Attic-Ionic) 36, 39,
    (West Greek) 45
  hypheresis 39, 108, 139
  nasalized (Cypriot) 32,
    (Pamphylian) 48
  prothetic 39
  quantitative metathesis 36, 196
  semi-vowels 10
  syncopated 96, 101, 155, 247
  see also diphthongs, resonants

Wackernagel's law (particles) 194
West Greek 44–7
  see also Doric, North-west Greek
Xenophon 61–2
  ps.-Xenophon (*Ath. Pol.* 2. 7–8) 65
    (*Ath. Pol.* 2. 1) 128

Index of Latin words